Modes of Thought addresses a topic of broad interest to the cognitive sciences. Its central focus is on the apparent contrast between the widely assumed "psychological unity of mankind" and the facts of cognitive pluralism; the diverse ways in which people think; and the developmental, cultural, technological, and institutional factors that contribute to that diversity.

Whether described in terms of modes of thought, cognitive styles, or sensibilities, the diversity of patterns of rationality to be found between cultures, in different historical periods, between individuals at different stages of development, remains a central problem for a cultural psychology. *Modes of Thought* brings together anthropologists, historians, psychologists, and educational theorists who manage to recognize the universality in thinking and yet acknowledge the cultural, historical, and developmental contexts in which differences arise.

Modes of thought

Modes of thought

EXPLORATIONS IN CULTURE AND COGNITION

EDITED BY

David R. Olson
Ontario Institute for Studies in Education

Nancy Torrance
Ontario Institute for Studies in Education

CAMBRIDGE
UNIVERSITY PRESS

Published by the Press Syndicate of the University of Cambridge
The Pitt Building, Trumpington Street, Cambridge CB2 1RP
40 West 20th Street, New York, NY 10011–4211, USA
10 Stamford Road, Oakleigh, Melbourne 3166, Australia

First published 1996

Printed in the United States of America

Library of Congress Cataloging-in-Publication Data

Modes of thought : explorations in culture and cognition / edited by
David R. Olson, Nancy Torrance.
  p. cm.
Papers originally presented at a workshop held at the University of Toronto.
Includes index.
ISBN 0–521–49610–1. – ISBN 0–521–56644–4 (pbk.)
1. Cognition and culture – Congresses.   2. Cognitive styles –
Congresses.   3. Thought and thinking – Congresses.   I. Olson, David
R., 1935– . II. Torrance, Nancy.
BF311.M574   1996
153.4'2 – dc20
                                                                    95–46610
                                                                         CIP

A catalog record for this book is available from the British Library.

ISBN 0–521–49610–1 Hardback
ISBN 0–521–56644–4 Paperback

Contents

Contributors

SCOTT ATRAN, CNRS-CREA   École Polytechnique, 1 rue Descartes, 75005 Paris, France, and Institute for Social Research, University of Michigan, Ann Arbor, MI 48109

JEROME BRUNER   Faculty of Law, New York University, 6 Washington Place, New York, NY 10012

SUSAN CAREY   Department of Brain and Cognitive Sciences, Massachusetts Institute of Technology, Cambridge, MA 02139

YARON EZRAHI   The Hebrew University of Jerusalem and the Israel Democracy Institute; correspondence to: the Israel Democracy Institute, P.O.B. 4702, Jerusalem 91040, Israel

CAROL FLEISHER FELDMAN   Department of Psychology, New York University, 6 Washington Place, New York, NY 10012

IAN HACKING   Institute for the History and Philosophy of Science and Technology, University of Toronto, Toronto ON M5S 1A1, Canada

DAVID A. KALMAR   Department of Psychology, New York University, 6 Washington Place, New York, NY 10012

DEANNA KUHN   Department of Psychology, Teachers College, Columbia University, New York, NY 10027

GEOFFREY LLOYD   Darwin College, Cambridge CB3 9EU, England

KEITH OATLEY   Center for Applied Cognitive Science, Ontario Institute for Studies in Education, 252 Bloor Street West, Toronto ON M5S 1V6, Canada

DAVID R. OLSON   Center for Applied Cognitive Science, Ontario Institute for Studies in Education, 252 Bloor Street West, Toronto ON M5S 1V6, Canada

CAMERON SHELLEY   Philosophy Department, University of Waterloo, Waterloo ON N2L 3G1, Canada

BRIAN STOCK   School of Graduate Studies, University of Toronto, Toronto ON M5S 1A1, Canada

STANLEY J. TAMBIAH   Department of Anthropology, Harvard University, William James Hall, 33 Kirkland Street, Cambridge, MA 02138

PAUL THAGARD   Philosophy Department, University of Waterloo, Waterloo ON N2L 3G1, Canada

MYRON TUMAN   Department of English, University of Alabama, Box 870244, Tuscaloosa, AL 35487-0244

Preface

The chapters in this volume are a product of a workshop held in Toronto, September 27–28, 1993, which was planned to take advantage of the presence of Geoffrey Lloyd, Master of Darwin College, University of Cambridge, who delivered the paper published in this volume (Chapter 2) as the Stubbs Lecture at University College, University of Toronto, on the final day of the workshop. We are indebted to the Social Science and Humanities Research Council of Canada, the Metropolitan Toronto School Board, the Spencer Foundation, and University College and its principal, Lynd Forguson, for their support.

A four-hour radio documentary on this topic based on interviews with the participants was prepared by David Cayley for CBC Radio. Copies of the transcripts of these broadcasts are available from CBC RadioWorks, Box 500, Station A, Toronto, Ontario M5W 1E6, Canada.

1
Introduction

David R. Olson

Whether described as modes of thought, mentalities, sensibilities, or cognitive styles, the possibility of pluralism in cognition continues to be an appealing, indeed obvious, and yet puzzling notion. The obviousness is indicated by the fact that the abstract sciences are not required to convince us that children are different from adults, men from women, scientists from policymakers, the schooled from the unschooled, and East from West. The puzzle arises from difficulties in understanding how the ultimate "psychic unity of mankind" can give rise to such human and cultural diversity.

The traditional answer to this question has been formulated in terms of the evolution of rationality. The history of mankind is the history of the formulation and testing of increasingly abstract yet increasingly precise models of the world and our place in it as formulated in our abstract sciences. That development depends on the discovery and application of logical principles for formulating and evaluating arguments. Human development, correspondingly, is seen as a matter of the growth of logical thinking, as in the work of Piaget, and the effects of schooling may be seen as a matter of the growth of critical thinking and disciplined, logically organized knowledge. Failures to achieve these Utopian ideals, whether across cultures or across individuals, were seen as products of primitive or underdeveloped powers of rationality.

The past three decades have been witness to a loss of faith in simple progress of any kind, let alone intelligence and rationality. Indeed, they have witnessed the rise of several new and plausible explanations for human and cultural differences in cognition. Greene (1994, p. 425) has alerted us to the dangers of the idea of a "single exclusive way of knowing." Instead of simple progress in one dimension, cultural and cognitive differences may be characterized in terms of specialization designed to achieve particular goals. These specializations involve ways of experiencing, interpreting, and expressing our understanding of ourselves and the world. There may be as many modes of thought as there are specialized forms of discourse or genre. Talk and thought suited to one is not necessarily suited to some other. Science holds sway in dealing with the impersonal, objective world, politics with the social world, whereas fiction holds sway in the private, personal, or perspectival world. In allowing for such diversity, however, we create a new problem, that of deciding which modes of thought and discourse are privileged, that is, which mode or modes command our deepest respect, the right to state "the bottom line." Science has, until recently, played just that role.

Even within the mode of thought that we think of as sharing a scientific mode of discourse, there are different domain-specific knowledge systems that adopt quite different types of causal explanations (Carey, this volume). The physical sciences appeal to mechanical or causal explanations – a matter of forces acting on objects. The biological sciences appeal to teleological or functional explanations: the purpose of the heart is to circulate the blood and that of the frontal lobes is to execute plans. The psychological sciences explain by appeal to intentional states such as thinking and wanting. Thus thinking in each domain may rely upon domain-specific knowledge organized around domain-specific causal principles rather than on more general logical or discourse ones.

A third possibility is that modes of thought reflect certain social and cultural systems somewhat in the way that Durkheim claimed that all thought was, at base, social. Although such claims have remained rather opaque, they seem to imply that cultural practices can determine to some extent how claims are justified and how causes are attributed. The social norms will determine which explanations are called into play and which, when internalized, will become ways of thinking about events. Ezrahi (this volume) makes just such a case for the social and political basis of appeal to deductive as opposed to empirical justification. Although one can become more and more sophisticated in thinking in any of these ways, no one way is intrinsically superior to the others.

At the same time as we are increasingly sensitive to diversity in modes of thinking, our simple faith in the growth and development of rationality, especially as represented by the strict sciences, has begun to wane. There is the collapse of faith in the value and authority of scientific knowledge (Ezrahi, 1990). Scientific advance is not to be denied, yet it is equally clear that science alone can no longer be claimed "to serve as common ground for adjudicating knowledge-claims" (Rorty, 1979, p. 317). The possibility of multiple perspectives on ourselves and the world, what some think of as "multiple realities," requires that we recognize that our sciences have evolved in a particular cultural context and are addressed to particular goals. In addition, it requires a new respect for alternative modes of thought and the social and cultural contexts in which they have evolved.

The topic of cultural differences in modes of thought was addressed explicitly in the volume from which this volume takes its name published a quarter century ago and edited by anthropologists Robin Horton and Ruth Finnegan (1973). For the writers of that volume, a central question was how to reconcile traditional with modern conceptions of science, religion, and social organization. Comparisons were difficult if not impossible because the very notions science and religion are particular cultural products not universal activities shared by vastly different cultures. Gellner summarized much of the debate by arguing that Western science was a kind of specialization or bureaucratization in which the conceptual tools became more refined to serve more specific purposes, but in so doing, these specialized tools became less useful for anything else. In the West, scientific concepts have become remarkably successful for a narrow range of purposes, but they have lost, in the process, their usefulness for ordering or organizing our social interests and goals. The concepts developed in traditional cultures, Gellner pointed out, are much more all-purpose; concepts such as ''the wise man'' combine the virtues of truth and goodness, whereas in Western ones, the social roles of scientist and clergyman, like the conceptual roles of facts and values, are carefully distinguished. So, too, error and sin may be either conflated or distinguished depending on the cultures involved. The ways in which these social conditions relate to cognitive structures and epistemological assumptions have remained, to say the least, unclear.

While comparisons across historical or cultural boundaries make differences more obvious, differences in the ways people construe, represent, and interpret the world, themselves, and others are equally important within a culture. Scientific thinking, one kind of thinking well, has to find its place within these patterns of construal. This is, of course, not to disparage scientific thinking but to understand it and, through understanding, promote it in the contexts where it is appropriate. The schools provide the most important of those contexts. Indeed, belief in the possibility and value of systematic scientific thought coincides with history of education in the West. The cognitive and cultural significance of a scientific mode of thought warrants much of the educational effort in both developed and developing countries. Its significance is seen both in the traditional focus on teaching academic disciplines and in more recent concerns with fostering critical thinking.

From both epistemological and educational perspectives, then, scientific thinking has come to be seen as merely one mode of thought, a Modernist or paradigmatic mode, which may be contrasted with an alternative Postmodern or narrative mode of thought. The latter puts a new emphasis on the more local, domain-specific contextualized knowledge, which is interpretive in nature and socially or collaboratively constructed. While educational institutions from preschools to universities have argued for the superiority of the Modernist or paradigmatic mode and devoted their resources to its achievement, work in a variety of fields has begun to show the validity, or at least the productivity, of the Postmodern assumptions about knowledge and its formation. Knowledge, on this latter view, is largely a matter of inventing plausible and defensible stories. Scientific thinking and scientific discovery, far from being the product of private genius, occurs within a socially shared paradigm, often through collaborative activities. Critics of Postmodernism see it, in part, as a throwback to Premodern sensitivities, the mode of thought that preceded the rise of the scientific, paradigmatic tradition.

One way of threading a path through these alternatives is as stages in the discourse as one moves from hunch and intuition to fully fledged theory development. Latour and Woolgar (1979) demonstrated how discourse shifts from the personal narrative talk of the laboratory to the logical objective talk of the published paper. According to those authors, the scientists they studied at the Salk Institute appeared to attempt to transform their statements, which began as expressions of speculations, inferences, and conjecture, into statements that could stand as autonomous representations of nature. In the reading of such published papers, experts appear to reverse this scheme, attempting to recover

the unexpressed hunches and assumptions of the narrative underlying the published version (Geisler, 1994). Whatever the case, we have begun to recognize
the great diversity in both the content and forms of thought, and the time has
come to sort out the relations among them and the conditions necessary for
their development.

The discussion takes on a particular urgency in the theory and practice of
education, which tends to oscillate between social concerns with mastery of
a fixed curriculum and humane concerns with the mental lives of children,
the debate surrounding the child-centered movement. The child-centered
movement began with the assumption that children brought to school the
basic intuitions on which formal schooling and advanced education could be
built. But a clear line was drawn between the practical knowledge acquired
in nonschool contexts and the theoretical knowledge that was the focus of
the school, the latter being primarily concerned with "the world on paper"
(Laurillard, 1993; Olson, 1994). In some more current formulations of the
child-centered movement, children are assumed to possess the very cognitions
and cognitive processes that earlier child-centered educators thought could
be acquired only by systematic study. Children, by these Postmodern lights,
are assumed to be already competent theory formulators and inference makers
and to be equipped by nature with the very concepts educators have traditionally thought it their duty to impart. They are thought to be natural learn-
ers, meaning makers, and knowledge constructors. The role of the school,
the authorities, is to keep out of the way and allow children to get on with
their collaborative world making; the job of the school is to provide "materials and encouragement" as Gardner has ironically put it in another context
(1990, p. *x*). By minimizing the differences between the cognitions of preschool children and their more educated siblings, such Postmodernist
educational theorists come into direct conflict with the more traditional assumptions about the importance of acquiring the cultural stock of knowledge
and "learning to think" in advanced, indeed culturally mandated, forms.

Fortunately, these general and pervasive concerns take a more precise form
in the examination of alternative modes of thought that have begun to appear
in many fields of study including history, anthropology, psychology, as well
as education. These disciplinary perspectives serve as a means of organizing
the chapters in this volume. The challenge in each of these fields is to acknowledge the gains marked by increasingly specialized modes of thought
while at the same time acknowledging the possibility, indeed the necessity,
of pluralism in our thinking about thinking.

The history of thought

Geoffrey Lloyd (1990, this volume) examined in detail the conceptual
changes involved in the development in classical Greece of the scientific view
of the world, a view that persists, indeed predominates, to this day. He contrasts this scientific view with that in traditional societies and with that in
another highly literate society, ancient China. He finds that the Greeks were

unique in their search for demonstrative proofs, conclusions that could be justified by appeal to explicitly stated premises that could be treated as axiomatic, that is, as self-evident. This mode of thought yielded important results in such domains as mathematics and astronomy but was also applied even to topics such as medicine, which defy simple proof. On this view, scientific thinking in the West is a mode of thought with a particular and distinctive cultural history, although Lloyd is quick to point out that there are other kinds of scientific thinking besides those that happened to originate in Greece.

Stanley Tambiah (1990, this volume) examines the hegemony on rationality held since the seventeenth century by the Modernist or scientific mode of thought. More traditional forms of thought came to be seen as occult, magical, or "enchanted." Tambiah does not deny the importance or the cultural specificity of Western science, but he argues that science is premised on but one of the many cultural functions of language. Language is used not only to represent, the Saussurean mode, but also to participate, the Herder/Bakhtin mode. He shows how the reliance on these modes varies from culture to culture, period to period, and context to context, a variability that allows "multiple orientations to the world."

Brian Stock (1983, this volume) examines the historical evolution of the Western notion of the independent self in the writings of Augustine, Petrarch, and Descartes, contrasting that with the notion of the interdependent self more characteristic of Eastern traditions. He suggests that the Western notion of the self, which views behavior as a manifestation of inner intentional states and sees the self as cut off from both society and nature, is the precondition for the evolution of modern scientific thought. On this view, then, not only is scientific thought distinctive, it is premised on equally distinctive representations of the self.

Ian Hacking (1975, this volume) examined the shifts in meaning that common terms underwent in the formation of modern scientific cultures. In this volume he focuses on the changing conception of human nature that followed on the adoption into popular thought of statistical, normal distributions. Only in the midnineteenth century did the concept of "normal" people arise. We take for granted the validity of such a concept as a normal child without recognizing the cultural assumption of such a description. Hacking spells these out in some detail. Again, this constitutes a distinctive, historically developed mode of thought attendant with its uses and misuses.

Yaron Ezrahi (1990, this volume) examines the alternative means of thinking about and justifying the exercise of political power. He contrasts the "civic epistemology" of feudal societies, in which political authority was marked by the adorned, opaque, symbolic spectacle of monarchy, with that of democratic societies, in which the exercise of political power is based on the transparency of political forms and the right of every individual to see and know what is going on. He suggests that the privileging of either the deductive or the empirical mode of reasoning depends upon its use in achieving a balance between individual freedom and the social order. The current and increasing suspicion that processes are not as visible and comprehensible and open to everyone as they purport to be may be part of a more general loss of faith in the positivism of the seventeenth century and, hence, the appeal of Postmodernism.

The anthropology of thought

Although Jerome Bruner (1986, this volume) was among the first cognitive psychologists to distinguish narrative from paradigmatic modes of thought and to examine the development of these modes in the thinking of young children, in this volume he places these differences in a more general theory of the universal aspects of making meaning in any cultural context. He proposes that there are four basic frameworks that people use in making sense of themselves and their world. The *intersubjective* mode allows the recognition that intentional states are shared with others. The *agentive* mode allows the recognition of doings rather than happenings in themselves and others. The *deontic* mode captures the network of norms and obligations that make up the social world. The *epistemic* mode governs the knowledge and understanding produced by representing the world linguistically as facts, analogies, and theories. These modes are universal and provide the common basis on which cultural and cognitive diversity is built.

Carol Feldman (1991, this volume) identifies modes of thought with modes or genres of discourse, different forms of language for different cultural and cognitive purposes. Adopting von Wright's distinction between Aristotelian and Galilean modes of explanation, the former by appeal to intentional causation, the latter to mechanical causation, Feldman raises the question as to the most appropriate means for examining intentionality in life and literature where behavior is better seen as chosen rather than as caused. Feldman addresses this intentionality through literary *genres*, modes of discourse embodied in texts and cognized by readers, which serve as basic modes of thinking. Genres provide frameworks in which plots are interpreted even if genre selection is often not conscious. Feldman reports a series of studies that show that subtle clues may invite a reader to take a text as, say, autobiography rather than fiction and, hence, to employ quite different interpretive stances even if modern critics see them as closely related.

Keith Oatley (this volume) examines the nature of inference and emotion in narrative and paradigmatic contexts. The narrative mode results from the application of a set of mental models that underwrite planful action to the project of recognizing the plans and goals of others. This not only makes narrative comprehensible but it allows the evocation of emotion by identification with the experiences of others in fictional contexts. By contrast, reading in the paradigmatic tradition lacks the possibility of identification and the corresponding emotion. Both narrative and scientific or paradigmatic thinking involve the three types of inference that Peirce described as inductive, deductive, and abductive. What characterizes the patterns of inference making in writerly readings of literature and in participation in science is that these modes are essentially social and have been selected and passed on in particular cultural institutions, often through education. These require people to take different roles and to use the different forms of inference as parts of a coordinated whole.

David Olson (1994, this volume) makes an argument for the possibility of a literate mentality, a kind of mentality premised on attention to the form as opposed to the meaning-intentions expressed through the language. Literal meaning, he argues, is a by-product of such a formal orientation to language as is the possibility of strict deduction and logical proof. Such knowledge is essentially metalinguistic. But once acquired as a kind of discipline on the use and understanding of language, it is equally applicable to thinking about nature and the self. The result can be either a kind of pedantic strictness or a more analytic, disciplined mode of thought of broad applicability across more specialized cognitive domains.

Cameron Shelley and Paul Thagard (this volume) examine one mode of thought, mythological thinking, which is usually regarded as incompatible with scientific thought, and show how it, like science, is based on analogy. Analogy is a rational process that is based on mappings between the symbolic domain, the source, and the to-be-understood domain, the target. While analogy is at the base of strict induction – boy is to girl as man is to woman – in mythology the network of parallels is complex and polysemous. Shelley and Thagard examine psychoanalytic, structuralist, and functionist theories as well as their own theory of analogy as explanations of mythological thought. In so doing they show that thought, even the most mystical and occult, is based on a smaller set of perhaps universal mental operations.

The development and education of thought

Susan Carey (1985, this volume) argues that the knowledge that children acquire in the course of schooling is built upon a set of ontological preconceptions that children bring to their experience. Children are innately, and hence universally, predisposed, she suggests, to acquire such domain-specific knowledge as that of animals (including people), number, and mechanics. The predispositions come in the form of implicit causal frameworks or "theories" that even infants use to organize their experience, seeing physical events in terms of mechanical causes, behavioral ones in terms of intentions, and biological ones in terms of functions. Yet because these frameworks can change, genuine cultural and conceptual differences are possible, and many depend upon education for their development.

Scott Atran (1990, this volume) examines thinking across very different cultures in one specific domain, namely, biology. Biological classifications are remarkably universal as Atran shows in his comparison of Mayan folk taxonomies with American ones, a universality that leads Atran to hypothesize a cognitive living-domain module as part of the innate cognitive architecture of all human beings. Yet culture does have a role as he points out. As the number of known species increased – as they did during the age of discovery (and record keeping, one may add) – higher-order classifications such as "families" were introduced, which led to the reorganization or the abandonment of lower-order classes. Trees, for example, while ecologically "natural," were abandoned by Linnaeus as "philosophically lubricious." Science education, Atran discovered, had little effect on folk taxonomies; basic modes of thought, he suggests, are universal.

Deanna Kuhn (1991, this volume) suggests that scientific reasoning is far from universal. Her research attempts to specify the relation between every-day thinking and the more educated scientific thinking called for by the school. The conceptual hurdle is primarily epistemological, coming to see thinking as argument and argument as consisting of relations between theory and evidence. Even high school students tend to simply "pocket" evidence when it is compatible with their causal theories and ignore it otherwise. Only the most sophisticated thinkers competently distinguish claims from evidence and use the latter to assess the validity of the former. Science education can play a critical role, she suggests, in the development of this somewhat specialized mode of thought, a mode, once acquired, that may be applied to everyday thinking as well.

Myron Tuman (1992, this volume) examines the recent concern in educational contexts with collaborative thinking. The emphasis on "process" and on "networking," he points out, has replaced the traditional emphasis on teacher authority and on the personal acquisition of "objective" knowledge. He suggests, like Ezrahi, that the newer emphasis reflects a loss of confidence in the solutions of the past and in the scientific modes of thought that gave rise to them. But the appeal of critical Postmodern modes of thought that displace the authority of the society, including the teacher, carries important risks. Tuman adopts Gorz's notion that science, criticism, and art are creative arenas of human expression, "areas of cultural life governed by rules determined and enforced outside one's immediate social group." Tuman describes access to these realms of human experience as forms of literacy, for they present the possibility of escaping the limits of one's more immediate socially constructed world. Building on G. H. Mead's writings on the self, Tuman argues that education must allow for both the social formation of the individual consciousness, the "me," but also for the individual as an agent of change, the "I." Social constructionism, with its emphasis on consensus and cooperation, may put at risk some of our other cherished values, namely, personal autonomy and scientific thought. Tuman offers an important corrective to what may otherwise become a tyrannical fad.

PURPOSE OF THE VOLUME
This volume is designed to serve four broad purposes. The first is to advance our understanding of thought by bringing together the work of scholars who, in their own work, have found it useful to distinguish alternative modes of thought whether in historical, anthropological, psychological, or educational contexts. Bringing together these perspectives allows us to establish the importance of the concept of modes of thought, the defining features of these alternative modes, their utility for various purposes, and conditions under which such modes develop.

Second, the chapters in this volume address the universality of these modes of thought to allow us to see more clearly the stamp put upon cognition by the biases and predispositions of human beings as knowers and by the social organization of which they are a part. The chapters show that thought in all cultures and all stages of development does share some fundamental features: Bruner's list included intentionality, agency, deontic, and epistemic properties; others appealed to forms of inference, to domain-specific foundational theories, and to simulation and analogy as basic properties of all thought.

Third, the chapters in this volume indicate the openness of cognition to cultural specializations of a quite radical sort. These may take the form of domain-specific conceptual systems, of specialized genres of language, of a specialized epistemology, of a scientific mode of language and thought, of a culturally specific form of theoretical thinking, or even of a particular literate form of thinking, all of which have developed in particular cultural contexts to serve particular purposes. Perhaps even more important are the differences between the hierarchical societies with their bias toward deductive modes of thought and egalitarian societies with their bias toward empirical modes, whether these are played out in the larger society, as Ezrahi noted, or within the school, as Tuman has noted. While thinking is indeed universal, the form it takes is quite different, depending on external cultural factors as well as considerations that are internal to the conceptual system itself. While the human mind may be limited in the kinds of entities and relations it can detect and entertain, individuals and cultures have been extraordinarily inventive in developing systems and structures that simultaneously position the thinker within the social order and advance mastery of the physical and social world. In this view we are not so far from that expressed in the earlier volume on modes of thought: knowledge in any individual and in any society is both cognitive and social, it makes the world comprehensible and at the same time allows us to form agreements with our fellows. As the chapters in this volume indicate, culture is the product of this inventiveness.

A fourth purpose of this volume is more pragmatic and is concerned with the role that education plays in the development of specialized modes of thought. Educational reform in much of North America has put a new emphasis on the importance of the ability to think critically, the form of paradigmatic thinking produced by education in general and science education in particular. At the same time educational policy has shifted from an emphasis on the acquisition of formal, paradigmatic knowledge to an emphasis on cooperative, collaborative learning in a more narrative mode. How are these two seemingly contradictory goals – truth and consensus – to be reconciled, let alone achieved, in the school? The problem has some urgency for educators with responsibility for the design and evaluation of curricula that promote a broad range of modes of thought at the same time accommodating unprecedented cultural diversity. To see these goals clearly is the first step to making some progress toward achieving them.

Of course, there remain many open questions: Can particular modes of thought be used to explain cultural differences or vice versa? Which is the cart and which is the horse? Do modes of thought have a history in Western culture? How do modes of thought relate to modes of discourse? Are developmental psychologists to continue to explain development in terms of increasingly abstract formal systems, a view we attribute to Piaget, or is development to be seen as the elaboration of domain-specific forms of knowledge? Is development to be seen in terms of personal and private cognitive restructurings or rather in the development of increasingly elaborated and contextualized, cooperatively constructed mental models? Will cognitive models of the mind have to incorporate not one but perhaps several modes if they are to be at all adequate to representing the mind? And perhaps most important of all, how do we recognize excellence among all this diversity?

More practical questions include: Should psychologists and educators "listen" for such different conceptual orientations and modify their approaches accordingly? In contexts of teaching and learning, is the traditional focus on formal modes of thought to be allowed to maintain its ascendancy? As educational practice increasingly turns toward dialogue and cooperative learning with its emphasis on shared knowledge and cooperation, is something of the older emphasis on truth and logic lost? Is critical thinking, the matter of an individual's deciding what to believe, compatible with collaborative, cooperative, and consensual thinking? How is such thinking to be encouraged or developed? How is it to be evaluated?

The chapters in this volume are a product of a workshop that was planned to take advantage of the presence in Toronto of Geoffrey Lloyd, Master of Darwin College, University of Cambridge, who delivered the paper published in this volume as the Stubbs Lecture at University College, University of Toronto, on the final day of the workshop. We are indebted to the Social Science and Humanities Research Council of Canada, the Metropolitan Toronto School Board, the Spencer Foundation, and University College and its principal, Lynd Forguson, for their support.

References

Atran, S. (1990). *Cognitive foundations of natural history*. Cambridge: Cambridge Univ. Press.
Bruner, J. S. (1986). *Actual minds, possible worlds*. Cambridge, MA: Harvard Univ. Press.
Carey, S. (1985). *Conceptual change in childhood*. Cambridge, MA: MIT Press.
Ezrahi, Y. (1990). *The descent of Icarus: Science and the transformation of contemporary democracy*. Cambridge, MA: Harvard Univ. Press.
Feldman, C. F. (1991). Oral Metalanguage. In D. R. Olson & N. Torrance (Eds.), *Literacy and orality* (pp. 47–65). Cambridge: Cambridge Univ. Press.
Gardner, H. (1990). *Art education and human development*. Los Angeles, CA: The Getty Center for Education in the Arts.
Geisler, C. (1994). *Academic literacy and the nature of expertise*. Hillsdale, NJ: Erlbaum.
Greene, M. (1994). Epistemology and educational research: The influence of recent approaches to knowledge. *Review of research in education* (Vol. 20). Washington, DC: American Educational Research Association.
Hacking, I. (1975). *The emergence of probability: A philosophical study of early ideas about probability, induction and statistical inference*. Cambridge: Cambridge Univ. Press.

Horton, R., & Finnegan, R. (Eds.) (1973). *Modes of thought*. London: Faber.

Kuhn, D. (1991). *The skills of argument*. New York: Cambridge Univ. Press.

Latour, B., & Woolgar, S. (1979). *Laboratory life: The social construction of scientific facts*. London: Sage.

Laurillard, D. (1993). *Rethinking university teaching*. London: Routledge.

Lloyd, G. E. R. (1990). *Demystifying mentalities*. Cambridge: Cambridge Univ. Press.

Olson, D. R. (1994). *The world on paper*. Cambridge: Cambridge Univ. Press.

Rorty, R. (1979). *Philosophy and the mirror of nature*. Princeton, NJ: Princeton Univ. Press.

Stock, B. (1983). *The implications of literacy*. Princeton, NJ: Princeton Univ. Press.

Tambiah, S. J. (1990). *Magic, science and religion and the scope of rationality*. Cambridge: Cambridge Univ. Press.

Tuman, M. (1992). *Word perfect: Literacy in the computer age*. London, UK: Falmer Press.

PART I
The history of thought

2
Science in antiquity
THE GREEK AND CHINESE CASES AND THEIR
RELEVANCE TO THE PROBLEMS OF CULTURE
AND COGNITION

Geoffrey Lloyd

I am concerned with three interrelated questions that can be expressed, na-
ively, as follows. Did science develop differently in ancient Greece and in
ancient China? Secondly, if so, can we say why? Third, what can we learn
from such an investigation about more general issues to do with the relationships between culture and cognition? The analysis of the presuppositions
implicit in formulating the questions in that way will bring to light some
important methodological points, clarify some potential misconceptions, and
indicate some of the limitations of what I think we can hope to achieve in
this area. First, I should make clear what I mean by *science* in this context.
Obviously in antiquity we are not dealing with the highly institutionalized
phenomenon that we are used to, today, in universities and research laboratories. On the strictest reading of science, we have to concede that the term
is not applicable to anything before the present century. But that is, no doubt,
to be unduly restrictive, and I shall use the term conventionally as a place-
holder for a variety of specific inquiries we can identify in both China and
Greece. I shall concentrate on astronomy, mathematics, and medicine (though
that list is not exhaustive, of course: one could include geography, optics,
mechanics, and much else besides).

Those three rubrics themselves are, of course, also problematic (and not
just because the last two, mathematics and medicine, stretch beyond the
bounds of what some would count as science). But following a methodology
I have defended elsewhere,[1] I take it that our first task is to analyze what the
ancient investigators themselves thought they were trying to do, their conception of their subject matter, their aims and goals. Of course I do not mean
to say that we can ever put ourselves in their shoes. All history has, to be
sure, to be evaluative. And that in turn means that it is not merely a matter
of reporting what the ancients *said* they were doing, as if we have to take
their word for it; for we clearly can and must inspect what they actually did
and reflect (as the ancients themselves sometimes did) on the matches and
mismatches between what some claimed to do and what they did, between
theory and practice. But how *they* saw the subjects they were engaged in
must be our starting point.

So I take astronomy to encompass what they included in the study of the
heavens. That comprised not just calendar studies and the description of the
constellations and investigation of the movements of the sun, moon, and
planets, but also – in both Greece and China, though in different ways – the

study of celestial omens or other attempts to predict events on earth, in other words what we call *astrology*. Again by *medicine* I mean whatever theories and practices of healing we find. And similarly *mathematics* must be held to comprise the study of numbers and figures, however that was pursued, that is with whatever ambitions, including the ambition to master the universe by cracking its numerological codes.

But then a second preliminary methodological warning relates to the problem of generalizing about ancient Greek and Chinese science, so construed, and the unpacking of science into such components as astronomy, mathematics, and medicine, immediately suggests one important point. We should certainly not expect, and in fact we do not find, precisely the same features prominent in and across *all* those different fields in either ancient Greece or ancient China. We must allow that what is true of the methods, aims, and preoccupations of mathematics differs from those of astronomy, which differ in turn from those of medicine, and so on.

The first point here is that we must pay due attention to the *multiplicity* of both Greek and Chinese investigations in different *domains*. The second is that we must also do so, so far as different *periods* go.[2] Greek science before the Christianization of the Greco-Roman world spreads over some 800 years, from the fifth century B.C. to the third century A.D., some of them centuries of very considerable change, and Chinese science before the impact of Buddhism covers an equivalent period where again the point about change also holds.

A third point is that there is yet another type of multiplicity at work *within* each of the domains I have mentioned, again in both ancient cultures. We are dealing with more than just a *single* tradition in mathematics, astronomy, and medicine, in both Greece and China. The point is most easily made with reference to medicine.[3] In both societies we have first a literate tradition, though in neither case is that totally homogeneous. Just as that variety within the Hippocratic Corpus has for some time been accepted by Greek scholars, so, too, the diversity between the *Huangdi neijing* and the medical texts on the silk scrolls excavated at Mawangdui is recognized by Chinese ones and indeed the divergences *between* the various traditions of the *Inner Canon* (the *taisu* and the *suwen* and *lingshu*[4]). But then in both societies, in addition to healers represented among the literate elite there were others marginal to it, in China the *yong yi* and *su yi*, let alone the *wu* (shamans), in Greece the root cutters, drug sellers, midwives, and various practitioners of temple medicine. But the point can also be argued, if with less clearly demarcated groupings, for the various strands that went to make up astronomy and mathematics. It just will not do, we have to remind ourselves, to take Euclid's *Elements* and works like it to stand for the *whole* of Greek mathematics, ignoring the traditions of the study of problems of mensuration (for which we have evidence in Hero of Alexandria) or of protoalgebra (for which we can turn to Diophantus). And similarly for Chinese astronomy, *li fa* refers primarily to calendar studies, but *tian wen* covers cosmography and the study of the movements of the stars and the portents they betoken,[5] and again we should not underestimate the diversities between them, nor of the contributions to them made from within and from without the Astronomical Bureau. More on that later.

The moral of these preliminary caveats is that we must embark on our study with far more modest expectations than are generally entertained by those with comparativist ambitions. Can we make any headway at all? Given both the biases and the lacunae of our sources (Greek and Chinese) as well as the difficulty in their interpretation, it must be acknowledged that the most we can hope for is some very tentative and provisional suggestions (I shall not call them results), some of which are applicable only to a small part of the total field.

But in that spirit and with those provisos, I shall attempt some brief exploratory forays, first into mathematics; second, into astronomy; third, into medicine and the study of the body, to test whether there are important differences between China and Greece, and if so, why, and what we can learn from this for more general investigations into the relations between culture and cognition.

I tackle mathematics first for the simple reason that this is the broad area where expectations as to the uniformity of early investigations are likely to be at their strongest. Surely no one is going to deny that $2 + 2$ is 4 in both China and Greece. Surely the square on the hypotenuse of a right-angled triangle is equal to the sum of the squares on the other two sides, whether we call this Pythagoras' theorem, or *Gou Gu*. Indeed, indeed. Mathematical truths do not vary across cultures. But the status of those truths and what they are truths about, the nature of mathematical objects or its subject matter, *are* questions to which different answers have been given, and not just in modern times.[6]

While Greek and Chinese mathematicians secured what can be called identical results, that does not mean to say that their preoccupations and the questions they chose to focus on were always the same nor that their styles of reasoning were. In the matter of styles of reasoning, in particular, there is one very marked difference observable between parts of Greek and the whole of ancient Chinese mathematics, and this relates to the deployment of proof in the axiomatic–deductive mode. Please note, before I go any further, that I insist on the term *parts*, since it certainly cannot be said that the whole of extant Greek mathematics shares this particular feature. However, considerable sections of our Greek mathematical texts *do* present results in what we may call Euclidean form, where certain indemonstrable starting points, axioms (or common opinions), definitions, and hypotheses or postulates are first set out, and the mathematician proceeds to the strict deductive proof of a sequence of theorems. Euclid's own *Elements* are the best-known example, of course, but Archimedes, too, often proceeds similarly, setting out explicitly the postulates needed for his studies in, for example, *On the Sphere and Cylinder* and *On Conoids and Spheroids*. He does the same in his statics and hydrostatics, in *On the Equilibrium of Planes* and *On Floating Bodies*, and further afield still we find the astronomer Aristarchus proceeding in a similar fashion in his *On the Sizes and Distances of the Sun and Moon*.

The important feature of the method in question is that, to the requirement for strict deductive rigor, it adds the requirement for axioms. While deductive reasoning is widespread in mathematics of all types, not all such reasoning aims to base conclusions on a limited number of explicit indemonstrable starting points (howsoever classified).

One way of confirming that point is by reference to the extant remains of classical Chinese mathematics,[7] notably the two chief early classics (from the first century B.C. and first A.D.), the cosmographic and mathematical work known as the *Zhoubi suanjing*, and the more purely mathematical *Jiuzhang suanshu (Nine Chapters of the Mathematical Art)*, together with the early commentary tradition on the latter especially, starting with Liu Hui in the third century A.D. Now the mathematics that these works contain is, at points, at a high level of sophistication. Liu Hui, for instance, uses a method of circle division to arrive at an approximation of the circle–circumference ratio (i.e., what we call π) that is comparable in accuracy to that of Archimedes: we have evidence, too, of his sustained attacks on such questions as the volumes of the sphere and pyramid, and for his study of the volumes of curvilinear solids, we find him using a special case of Cavalieri's theorem.[8] Yet at no point in any of these Chinese texts is there any suggestion that reference to axioms or postulates of any kind is necessary or desirable. The notion of an axiom itself is, indeed, totally absent from classical Chinese mathematics, indeed from classical Chinese thought in its entirety.

This does not mean that there were no procedures for establishing and verifying results. On the contrary. The results themselves were often obtained by the application of what we should call algorithms: but as Karine Chemla, for one, has shown, the validation of those algorithms *is* sometimes carried out.[9] To give just one extremely simple example, in his discussion of the addition of fractions in the first chapter of the *Nine Chapters*, Liu Hui shows that the formula we might represent as $a/b + c/d = (ad+bc)/bd$ is truth preserving. This he does by first citing the steps of the original algorithm and naming the procedures it depends on: "every time denominators multiply a numerator which does not correspond to them, we call this homogenize (*qi*). Multiplying with one another the set of denominators, we call this equalize (*tong*)."[10] But it had been shown that $a/b = ad/bd$ (and $c/d = bc/bd$), that is, that the same fraction may or may not be expressed in its lowest terms. So he now remarks that once cross multiplication has occurred, the addition can be effected and "the procedures cannot have lost the original quantities."[11]

What Liu Hui has done is to rewrite the algorithm to *show* that it is truth preserving. That is as good a *proof* of the procedure as anyone could wish, surely, provided, that is, that we do not limit our notion of what will count as a proof to axiomatic–deductive demonstration in the Euclidean style – provided, that is, that we do not stipulate that for a proof to be a proof it has to be cast in that style. For what more should we expect of the proof of a procedure than an explanation of how and why it works, however that explanation itself proceeds?

So we encounter an apparently fundamental difference in this regard between parts of Greek and Chinese mathematics. The problem is not so much why axiomatic–deductive demonstration is absent from the Chinese traditions as why it was a preoccupation of some Greek ones. The problem is not the Chinese lack of axioms, since they evidently got along perfectly well without them. Perfectly well, we should remark, not just for practical purposes, when mathematics is applied to concrete problems, say of calculation or mensuration. Although Chinese mathematics has repeatedly been characterized as *purely practical* in orientation, that is a gross exaggeration, for there are plenty of theoretical concerns as well. One example to which I have already alluded is the studies of π, the circle–circumference ratio, in the commentaries on the *Nine Chapters*. For practical purposes a value of 3 or 3 1/7 is generally adequate enough. Indeed for these purposes Liu Hui himself adopts 157/50, that is, 3.14, as a good approximate value. Yet in their investigations of the procedures that could be brought to bear to yield closer and closer approximations, the commentators pursue the circle division method to the point where they were calculating the areas of an inscribed polygon of 192 and more sides.[12] Indeed in his studies of the volumes of various rectilinear solids, Liu Hui explicitly remarks that some of the shapes are "of no practical use"[13] but worth investigating, nevertheless, for by their means an attack may be launched on other problems.

Moreover it is not just from a Chinese, but also from some of our own modern perspectives that some of the original Euclidean procedures may seem strange. I am not saying that the drive for axiomatization as such seems so (though no doubt Euclid's conceptions of his indemonstrables differ rather from those of modern axiomatizations). Rather it is Euclid's determination to make all his definitions explicit, for use, indeed, in the subsequent proofs, that may seem odd. From a modern standpoint some of the terms he takes so much trouble defining might more appropriately be deemed to be primitives in the system, not in need of explicit definition, but themselves implicitly defined by the very mathematics derived on their basis.[14]

This example shows one thing pretty clearly. There was nothing preordained in the particular way in which one particular Greek mathematical tradition developed via the development of axiomatic–deductive modes of demonstration. Our problem is the more acute in that, once Euclid's *Elements* had shown the way, the model it represented was imitated in a wide variety of fields, in some at least of which one might have thought it was quite inappropriate. I have mentioned that Archimedes' statics and hydrostatics are cast in an axiomatic–deductive mold, and here there may be nothing very surprising about Archimedes' ambition to geometrize these studies as far as possible. The same is true also of Aristarchus' *On the Sizes and Distances*, where again, while the initial hypotheses are astronomical, the subsequent arguments are purely geometrical in character. But what are we to say of the ambition in the second-century A.D. physician Galen to deploy proofs *more geometrico* in medicine, not just deductive arguments, but arguments based on self-evident primary premises? Although valiant attempts have been made to justify the bid to produce axiomatic–deductive proofs in medicine,[15] it has to be said that the attempt to specify primary premises there that will meet the requirements of being both necessary and self-evident is chimerical. He appears to have thought that the principle that opposites are cures for opposites is one such: the trouble is that what will count as an opposite is opaque, and when it is clarified, the principle risks being merely vacuous or circular.

The problems may seem intractable enough, but an indirect approach may yield at least some tentative conjectures to help resolve them. One obvious feature that axiomatic–deductive demonstration possesses that other modes of reasoning lack is that it produces certainty. Everything depends on the status of the axioms. But where they can be claimed to be self-evident and the subsequent deductive reasoning is valid, then the conclusions reached have a claim to be not just true, but incontrovertible.

Now certainty and incontrovertibility are admirable qualities in the end results of reasoning, and so there may be no special need to look for any particular motivation for the ambition to secure them. Maybe. But that there is more to the historical question than that suggests emerges, I believe, if we consider some of the background to the development of the notion of strict demonstration in fourth-century B.C. Greece. The first clear statement in our extant texts of the need for demonstrations to be based on indemonstrables comes not in mathematics, but in philosophy, in Aristotle, who insists on the point with an argument: all demonstrations proceed from premises, and although intermediate premises may be the conclusions of prior demonstrations, the *primary* premises of all must themselves be indemonstrable to avoid an infinite regress, for what premises could they be demonstrated from?[16] Moreover, again so far as our extant texts go, it was Aristotle who first set out a taxonomy of the different *types* of indemonstrables, namely (on his view), definitions, axioms, and hypotheses. Even before Aristotle, Plato, too, clearly represents strict demonstration as the ideal, even though he does not set out a *theory* of what makes a demonstration a demonstration.

But it is not just the positive views on strict demonstration that Plato and Aristotle offer that are significant for our purposes, but also what it is contrasted with. Both take strict demonstration as the goal for the highest style of philosophizing – not that they have identical views on that. But both contrast that style with other inferior modes of reasoning. Thus Plato is particularly exercised to contrast philosophy with the merely plausible or persuasive, and he leaves us in no doubt that the type of thing he has in mind includes, especially, what he considers the irresponsible teachings of the likes of Protagoras and Gorgias and the kinds of arguments deployed in the law courts and political assemblies – sophistic and rhetoric, in short.[17] Similarly Aristotle, too, contrasts demonstrative arguments (where the premises must be necessary as well as true) first with dialectical ones (based on generally accepted opinions or on the admissions of interlocutors) and then with a whole sequence of other lower, not to say deviant, modes of reasoning. These include peirastic (examination arguments), eristic (where the aim is just victory in the argument itself), sophistic (which he thinks of as directed at enhancing reputation – showing off), as well as the three main branches of rhetoric: forensic, deliberative, and epideictic.[18]

In the background to this extraordinary proliferation of categories of argument and arguer we can detect the intense rivalry that existed in fourth-century B.C. Greece between competing claimants to intellectual leadership and prestige. Of course the extent to which Greek mathematics in general and Euclid in particular were influenced by the Aristotelian theory of demonstration set out in the *Posterior Analytics* is controversial and never likely to be fully resolved because of the lack of direct evidence for pre-Euclidean mathematics.[19] But if we see that our problem is a *general* one and ask not just why Greek mathematics developed the axiomatic–deductive method, but why Greek philosophy did so, too, then the negative reactions we see in both Plato and Aristotle to the models of reasoning provided by the legal and political domains may offer some clues. For both Plato and Aristotle, demonstration is the key factor in their justification for their claim that their high philosophizing is different from and superior to all other modes of reasoning. *They* are, at best, merely persuasive: but demonstration can and does yield certainty. If so, this may suggest that Greek intellectuals sought and claimed incontrovertibility chiefly in a bid to outdo their rivals and downgrade their merely plausible arguments.

Inevitably, this is all, very conjectural. Yet the hypothesis withstands one negative test rather well. If the demand for certainty in Greece owes something to an adverse reaction to the merely persuasive arguments used in the law courts and assemblies, we can test whether or not an equivalent stimulus existed in China by investigating their traditions of legal and political argument. Certainly the hypothesis would be seriously undermined if there were such a stimulus and yet no corresponding preoccupation with securing certainty.

The first fundamental point relates to Chinese attitudes toward the legal experience, whether in civil or criminal cases, and to litigiousness in general.[20] Civil law as such was, in any event, almost unheard of. More generally, so far from positively delighting in litigiousness, as many Greeks seem to have done, so far from developing a taste for adversarial argument in that context and becoming quite expert in its evaluation, the Chinese avoided any brush with the law as far as they possibly could. Any dispute that could not be resolved by arbitration was felt to be a breakdown of due order and as such reflected unfavorably on *both* parties, whoever was in the right.

There was thus no forensic oratory worth speaking of, since the contexts for its use were lacking. Yet there were plenty of other occasions for the development and practice of the techniques of persuasion.[21] In the *Shuo nan* chapter of *Hanfeizi*, we have evidence for self-conscious reflection on those techniques, and the *Zhanguoce* offers numerous examples of their practice. However both the theory and the practice show some contrasts with Greek deliberative oratory. First the primary contexts for its deployment differ. The circumstances that play the role of model in China relate primarily to the persuasion of the prince or ruler. Of course, individuals, including rulers, were sometimes the targets of Greek persuasion, too, but more often the audience was the citizen body in assembly.

Second and more important, it seems significant that in *Hanfeizi* the focus of attention is on the psychological aspects of persuasion rather than on the analysis of the styles of argument as such. Advice is offered on how to avoid offending the prince. Of course, such considerations are addressed also in Greek manuals of Rhetoric. Aristotle, for one, discusses the need to take into account the emotions and prejudices of the audience and advises on how to present yourself as a person who can be trusted. But what he also does is to give an analysis of the modes of argument available to the orator, the enthymeme and paradigm, the equivalent in rhetoric of the syllogism and induction. It is that extra step that brings to the fore the contrasts between the merely plausible and the certain – the topic we are chiefly interested in as the background to the development of the notion of axiomatic–deductive demonstration. The Chinese writers, too, certainly react negatively to some features of the techniques of persuasion but not so much to particular modes of argument as to cleverness in speaking in general. What is regularly opposed to the art of speaking in China is the living embodiment of the *Dao*, the person of the sage. The contrast with the Greeks speaks volumes. Although Greeks, too, were often suspicious of clever speakers, what happens in some writers at least is that what is opposed to rhetoric is true philosophy. What is opposed to persuasion is demonstration, but both those are a matter of *logos,* word, speech, account.

My first foray has focused on demonstration in mathematics and philosophy. For my second I turn to the rich materials for the study of the heavens. In China, as in Greece, this comprised a number of different inquiries: the regulation of the calendar, cosmography sometimes combined with the study of the movements of the planets, and then, third and often especially, the investigation and prediction of portents. There are certainly very considerable similarities in the objects studied and in some at least of the reasons for studying them. But a closer look reveals also considerable differences, especially in the latter.

Take, first, a point to do with the perceived relevance of the study of the heavens for the entire welfare of the country. In China the whole subject was of intense importance to the emperor, for he was personally responsible for keeping the natural order and the political order in tune.[22] The regulation of the calendar was not just a matter of practical concerns, for instance for agriculture, but a question with wide-ranging implications for the order of the state. This importance is reflected in the institutionalization of the subject. The Astronomical Bureau was set up already in Han times, and it lasted all the way down to the Qing, the last imperial dynasty. True, some important ideas originate with outsiders, though if the ideas proved acceptable, their originators often found themselves appointed to posts within the bureau; that even happened, eventually, to the Jesuit Schall.[23] But the existence of the bureau testified to the political significance of the subject.

Getting the calendar right was, to be sure, also an interest of Greek astronomers; but the reception of their work was quite haphazard. Meton and Euctemon already gave good approximations for the lengths of the solar year and lunar month in the 430s B.C. But instead of this leading to a general standardizing of the calendar, the various independent Greek city-states generally persisted in using their own conflicting lunisolar calendars, with different officials responsible not just for observation of the new moon to fix the start of a new month, but also for deciding on the timing of intercalary months. It took the Roman Julius Caesar to impose a more orderly calendar across the Greco-Roman world, but that wasn't until the mid-first century B.C.

But then so far as the styles of astronomical theory developed in China and Greece go, the most striking difference relates to the eventual Greek construction of geometrical models to represent the movements of the sun, moon, and planets, and why they should have pursued that goal is as big a puzzle as the ambition to give strict demonstrations in mathematics, until we see that in part at least it is the same puzzle. After all, for the purposes of predicting those movements, once their main periodicities are determined, numerical procedures may be perfectly adequate, though they will need adjusting as inaccuracies come to light. Moreover the accuracy of geometrical models can never exceed that of the quantitative parameters they incorporate.

However, the characteristic that geometrical models possess that numerical ones lack is their would-be demonstrative nature. The array of concentric spheres or of epicycles and eccentrics enabled their interrelations to be deduced and explained. The position of a planet could be derived from the geometrical structure of the model, though of course this still had to be interpreted with specific values for its various components, such as the speeds and angles of inclination of the spheres in the concentric model.

The conjecture would be that it was the possibility of such *geometrical demonstrations* that proved the principal attraction to the Greeks of the style of astronomical theory we find from Eudoxus to Ptolemy and beyond. Indeed that is not just pure conjecture, for Ptolemy himself confirms in the Proem of the *Syntaxis* that, in his view, that is precisely where the great strength of mathematical astronomy lies. It is superior, he says, both to "physics" (the study of nature) and to theology, but why? Physics deals with the unstable qualities of changing material objects, and theology is concerned with what is utterly obscure. Mathematics (including astronomy), by contrast, holds out the promise of firm and unshakable knowledge, since its proofs proceed by indisputable methods, namely, those of arithmetic and geometry.[24]

This major divergence in the *aims* of astronomical theory in China and in Greece has repercussions also on that other principal branch of heaven studies, the investigation of portents and the prediction of events on earth. The preferred mode of astrological prediction in Greece, from the Hellenistic period on, is genethlialogy, that is, the casting of horoscopes, geometrical and thus far deductive in character, though recognized by Ptolemy as far from demonstrative since the interpretation of the characters of the planets was based on opinions drawn from ancient tradition, even though he would have claimed that that tradition was generally reliable and had stood the test of time. Compared with the study of the movements of the heavenly bodies themselves, the attempt to derive predictions from them for events on earth is, in Ptolemy's view, secondary, uncertain, and conjectural, even though, as he also claims, its *potential* usefulness for all sorts of practical questions concerning the lives of individual human beings is far greater.[25]

In China, by contrast (where horoscopes are in any case a relatively late *import*[26]), the chief concern was not the fortunes of ordinary individuals, but overwhelmingly with that of a single individual, the ruler himself, and thus with the welfare of the empire as a whole. Portents, on this view, are expressions of the will of heaven communicated to the ruler to encourage or admonish him.[27]

Chinese astronomers certainly shared with Greek ones ambitions to extend the domain of what can confidently be predicted, to limit the sphere of the truly portentous in the sense of the totally unpredictable. In China this was a major stimulus to the concerted attack on the problems of predicting lunar and then eventually solar eclipses, where as Sivin has shown, one cycle after another was developed over the hundreds of years of the functioning of the Astronomical Bureau.[28] However, the goals and expectations in China and Greece were different in one crucial respect. The chief aim of the Chinese predictions was not to miss an eclipse.[29] But if they predicted one that did not occur, that could be, and was, put down to the great virtue of the emperor. Such was his virtue, the thought was, that an eclipse that would have occurred, but for it, did not. So the nonoccurrence of a predicted event did not count *against* the astronomer so much as *for* the emperor.

The order of the heavens was a major preoccupation in both China and Greece, and in both ancient civilizations a matter with grave consequences for morality. But that order was subject to exceptions, in China, that Greek geometrical models could not, in principle, admit. Why the Greeks spent so much time, from the fourth century B.C. on, on planetary models was not just because Plato was supposed to have told them to do so,[30] but rather because their *apparent irregularities* threatened the very notion of celestial order itself. They had to be geometrized to be understood, and once so geometrized, could then be cited as evidence not of irregularity in the heavens, but of regularity. The heavens thereby manifest, as Ptolemy puts it, sameness, good order, proportion, and freedom from arrogance, qualities which the study of astronomy inculcates in us.[31] But the Chinese read the sky both with far greater confidence that it is inherently orderly – that is how *tian* is understood – and at the same time with a far more open mind about its possible messages for earth, messages directed, in any event, in the first instance, to the emperor. That helps to explain why so much more attention is paid to comets and to supernovas, the latter of which often seemed to have been invisible to the Greeks. Chinese theories imposed far less rigid patterns on the order they expected, and they would no doubt have been amazed at the Greek ambition to *prove* celestial regularity.

Thus far my forays have been into mathematics and astronomy. Faced with the awesome variety of material concerning the diverse traditions of inquiry and practice in medicine in China and Greece, our task of assessing relevant similarities and differences there is even more daunting, and my comments must be even more selective. At first sight, the similarities, both in the use of certain diagnostic and investigative techniques and in some of the general circumstances surrounding medical practice in China and Greece, are impressive. In both the doctor engaged in the intent examination of the external appearance of the patient, the Hippocratic *facies* (as in *Prognosis*, Chapter 2) and the Chinese technique of diagnosis from the five colors, *se*.[32] In both, pulse lore is elaborated as a means of inferring internal states, especially pathological disturbances, in the body. In both, dissection was (eventually, and in China appreciably later than in Greece)[33] used to study anatomical structures. In both civilizations, again, there is rivalry not just between the learned and folk medical traditions, but also within the learned. Thus we have good direct evidence of this in China in the biography of Chunyu Yi in Sima Qian's *Shiji* (dating from the first century B.C.). This is an explicit apologia by a doctor who had been the subject of a denunciation, where Chunyu Yi offers an account of a series of case histories, where he records his diagnosis and treatments (comparable in some ways to the case histories in the Hippocratic *Epidemics* and in Galen).[34] But in the process he criticizes a number of other practitioners, some unnamed, others named, including a patient who was himself a doctor, named Sui, who had invoked the authority of the famous Bianque, but without any proper understanding of his teaching (so Chunyu Yi says).[35]

Yet when all that is said, the differences are also profound. First as to rivalry, Chunyu Yi shares much more with his opponents than is sometimes the case in Greek medicine. True, he claims his diagnoses (chiefly based on the pulse) are all successful, theirs not (understandable in a text that is a self-defense).[36] But he uses more or less the same therapies (moxa, stone therapy, drugs) as they. On the Greek side, the degree of disagreement, in medicine as elsewhere, *could* be much more radical.[37] Thus while some insisted on basing medicine on an understanding of hidden causes and underlying reality, others argued that that was irrelevant and/or unattainable and that medicine should focus solely on what produces cures. While most Greek doctors used the same battery of treatments, some, the so-called Methodists, rejected them and concentrated just on countering the lax with the restricted and vice versa.[38]

Dissection itself was controversial in Greece. While some thought it essential as the source of the anatomical knowledge the doctor needs, others, the Methodists again and the Empiricists, dismissed it as useless or irrelevant.[39] As for those who justified it, the explicit argument in Aristotle is that it revealed the causes of the structures in the body, especially the formal and final causes. One might suggest a parallelism with Greek astronomy, where planetary irregularities were turned into proofs of nature's regularity, thanks to geometrical models. So, too, in anatomy, while contemplating the insides of the body was (Aristotle concedes) revolting in itself, nevertheless this led to a greater understanding of the beauty and the craftsmanship of nature, a theme taken up and elaborated by Galen, notably in his "hymn" to nature, the teleological account of the purposes that every part of the body serves in his *On the Uses of Parts*.

Then a further factor at work in the Greek use of dissection emerges from other texts in Galen, which show that in some cases dissections were conducted not just for research, nor even for pedagogy (to train the next generation of doctors). Galen refers to competitive public dissections where animals, sometimes exotic ones, were cut up and rival experts attempted to predict the outcome. On one such occasion the animal was an elephant, and the audience placed bets on who would turn out to have described the structure of its heart correctly. It is clear that these performances were mainly for show:[40] this was a way of winning a reputation, if not notoriety, as also, in a less sensational way, were the public debates on such questions as the fundamental constituents of the human body we hear about already in the Hippocratic Corpus, debates often adjudicated by the lay audience, the bystanders themselves.[41] The very idea that there should be public confrontation between experts on basic questions of physics or anatomy is profoundly un-Chinese, as also is the notion that the winner in such a confrontation should be decided by the public itself.

It is not just points to do with form or style that are at stake in these differences, but also substantial issues to do with the contents of concepts and theories, indeed the way the human body itself was viewed. In the broadest terms, the body was the locus of *Qi*, vital breath, for the Chinese: that was what the doctor was interested in and looked *for* when he looked *at* the colors.[42] For the Greeks, or many of them at least, the body was a system of structures: that was what those who dissected were looking for when they opened the body up. Again the idea that the human body should be in tune with the cosmos runs through much Chinese medical thought and indeed cosmology. The five colors correspond to and resonate with the five phases (all manifestations of *Qi*), and this was part of the shared discourse of Chinese thinkers at least from Han times, when this whole system of correspondences was brought into canonical form. True, in Greece too the idea that the macrocosm and microcosm should tally is also sometimes expressed. But that bland general statement by itself conceals or does not reveal the enormous diversity that existed in Greece, (1) on the nature of the macrocosm itself, (2) on that of the microcosm, (3) on the political images used to describe both, and finally (4) on the actual political ideals that those images in turn reflect. For some Greeks the cosmos is a monarchy under the benevolent rule of an intelligent craftsmanlike force, but others represented it rather as an oligarchy or democracy of balanced powers or even, in the case of Heraclitus, as anarchy, since for him justice is strife and war rules.[43] These divergences in the way the cosmos was conceived reflect the equally radical disagreements on political ideals and are in turn reflected in divergent models of the human body, where balance sometimes depended on unified rule or control, sometimes on the equality of powers between opposing forces. The contrast with the classical Chinese, united behind the ideal of the benevolent rule of the emperor, is dramatic.

The evidence available for a study such as I have sketched out is enormously rich, and my three tentative forays have done no more than scratch the surface of the problem. But let me turn now briefly, in conclusion, as I promised, to the question of what might be learned here for more general issues to do with the problems of culture and cognition.

Those who investigate problems of cognitive development in children or young adults tend to adopt as their working assumption that there are basic uniformities in all humans. An infant aged one year or a child aged three or six will perform very similarly in experimental situations to others of the same age, whatever their background – findings that may no doubt be taken to corroborate that working assumption at least up to a point. Some historians and philosophers of science, whether or not taking their lead from cognitive scientists, argue similarly that basic human conceptions of space, time, causality, number, even natural kinds, are cross-culturally invariant.

Yet such a view is obviously under considerable strain from the apparent diversities in the *explicit* theories and concepts actually developed in cultures worldwide, including ancient cultures. Wherever ancient Greeks and Chinese may have started, as infants, they certainly seem to have ended with quite different sets of beliefs (and not just a single set on either side) about the stars, the human body, health and disease, indeed I would also add (though I would need a good deal of space to justify the point) about space, time, causality, number, and nature themselves.[44]

To that difficulty two types of retort are possible. The first would argue that whatever views may be expressed by the actors themselves, at a deeper level there are implicit cross-cultural universals that can be elicited by questioning, provided you ask the right questions (cf. Atran). That remains of course a pure conjecture where the members of ancient societies are concerned since we cannot question them. But the more important point is that if we are studying early attempts to *explain* the world, we have no option but to take the *explicit* theories and concepts actually used in all their diversity as the chief, indeed the sole direct, evidence. So there may be a sense in which at points (if not across the board) universalists and comparativists may be arguing past one another, in that the subject matter they are wrestling with is, in the one case, the postulated implicit assumptions, in the other, the explicit theories the actors themselves propose.

But then the second type of retort would have it that the kinds of theories I have been discussing do not count as real science at all. The argument would be that science, to be science, *has to be* universal, and if there are divergences in the theories in question, that just shows their inadequacies as science. But that equally *a priori* view is also deeply unsatisfactory. Inadequacies, even failures, cannot be taken to show that an inquiry is *not* science, for not even physics in the twentieth century is adequate through and through, is it? Rather it would be more plausible to argue that the history of science is a history of repeated failures, though that is not totally satisfactory either in that there are failures and failures, a difference between straight failures and failures that appear as temporary successes.

What our studies illustrate is that there is nothing inevitable about the way in which astronomy, mathematics, and medicine developed, and their international modern character should not mask their very divergent early manifestations (and not just in China and Greece). Of course in one sense the subject matter of both Greek and Chinese inquiries was the same in that both studied numbers and geometrical figures, the stars, the human body, and so on. But as we have seen, the differences in the theories and concepts they developed relate not just to presentation, but also to the questions they chose to focus on and, correspondingly, to the answers they chose to give to them.

However, if there are these differences, can we begin to say why? If we reject the immanentist and universalist stances I mentioned, can we not expect to be accused of cultural relativism and/or determinism? Well, in that I have been so accused, the danger obviously exists. But the hypotheses I wish to propose and the program of research they suggest are (I hope) more modulated, more tentative, and more modest in their pretensions than the use of such grand but vague labels as relativism and determinism allows to emerge.

First as to 'determinism.' The lines of attack that my forays suggest may be most promising relate the differences in the inquiries pursued to differences in the values of the societies in question, to their social and political institutions, and to the institutions within which the ancient investigators themselves worked.[45] But the question is how far such an approach can take us. I am very far from suggesting myself that the entire intellectual products of ancient Greek and Chinese science are constrained by such factors (general as their influence is). The very variety in those products that I have insisted on tends to defeat any simple single causal explanation. We have, in particular, to allow that in both ancient societies there were highly idiosyncratic individuals who stood outside the main groups and traditions – a Heraclitus or a Wang Chong – though, as we can see, always at the risk of being marginalized, misunderstood, and quickly forgotten.

Then as to 'relativism,' where disambiguation is always badly needed. Of course, in one sense my claim that astronomy, mathematics, and medicine developed very differently in China and in Greece is a claim that the different forms they took have to be related to the varying circumstances of their development. So far, then, a relativist. Yet not at all so in other more important respects, in that I have been assuming, all along, that comparison is possible, indeed that judgment and evaluation are inevitable, that is that the factors at work in the developments we are studying (and indeed in *our* study of them) do not solely consist of the influences that come from the values of society and the institutions of the investigators, but partly also from the subject matter of the investigations themselves, even if there is no such thing as an *unmediated* access to that subject matter – whether in science or in the history of science.

It is precisely here that the study of science in ancient civilizations may have some general lessons to offer. The stars that were there to be observed have not changed – not substantially at least. We can identify Vega whether as *Zhi nü* (Weaving Girl) or as Lyra (its Greek name) or as alpha Lyrae, even though in both the Chinese and Greek cases, constellations were also named by this star, and they, the constellations, certainly differ. Nor has the human body changed substantially, for all that some of the diseases that affect it may have. It is the conceptual framework within which those observations were conducted that has varied and continues to do so. To be sure, reality is always socially constructed in a sense; but that construction reflects the investigators' claims (varied ones, for sure) that it was indeed reality that they were investigating and that sometimes checks the investigations, even if sometimes a reality claim is just a persuasive device and no one can step completely outside the conceptual framework within which they operate.

What are the limits to which criticism of one's own conceptual framework is possible? If criticism is possible, does it not presuppose a wider framework? Yes, of course. However as to explicit criticisms and modifications of explicit parts of existing belief systems, we can see this happen before our very eyes when we study both Greece and China, even while the modes of expression of those criticisms vary. Similar processes were at work in later developments that led eventually to modern science, with its distinctive values and institutions. But the history of early investigations in ancient civilizations is the history of the acquisition of a potential for cognitive development, not just with respect to what was believed, but also with regard to the ways of getting to believe it. Where Greece and China are concerned, to go no further afield, that history shows both that the ways of acquiring that potential differed and indeed that the potential acquired did. Not that, in either case, the new potential corresponded closely to the expectations that might be generated by naive retrospection from the eventual emergence of modern science. There is much more to be learned about the specificities of those potentials and how they are acquired than I have been able to indicate, but I hope to have shown some of the ways in which in both ancient cultures the investigations undertaken were influenced by the particular values of the society in question and the particular institutions within which the investigators worked. On the one hand, there is the way of adversariality and argument, the dominant Greek way. On the other, there is the construction of the more pragmatic ideal of the sage, the living embodiment of wisdom, the more usual Chinese way. *Logos,* then, and the *Dao:* yet both the one and the other offered prospects, as I have suggested, for the transformation of cognitive capabilities.

Notes

1 See G. Lloyd, *The Revolutions of Wisdom* (*RW*), Univ. of California Press, Berkeley, 1987, pp. 1 f. and "Methodological issues in the comparison between East and West," in *Is It Possible to Compare East and West?*, H. Numata and S. Kawada (eds.), Pedilavium, Tokyo, 1994, pp. 23–36.
2 We are dealing, very roughly, with material that dates from the fifth century B.C. to the third century A.D., but of course neither the beginnings nor the ends of classical Chinese science and the Greek counterpart are at all well defined. However, we are concerned with the scientific activity that antedates the official Christianization of the Roman Empire in the one case and the impact of Buddhism in the other.
3 Cf. G. Lloyd, "The definition, status, and methods of the medical *techne* in the fifth and fourth centuries," in *Science and Philosophy in Classical Greece*, A. C.

30   GEOFFREY LLOYD

Bowen (ed.), Garland, New York, 1991, pp. 249–60, and "The transformations of ancient medicine" (*TAM*), *Bulletin of the History of Medicine* 66, 1992, pp. 114–32.

4 N. Sivin, *Traditional Medicine in Contemporary China*, Centre for Chinese Studies, Univ. of Michigan, Ann Arbor, 1987, offers the best general introduction to traditional Chinese medicine, cf also "Text and Experience in Classical Chinese Medicine," in *Knowledge and the scholarly medical traditions*, D. Bates (ed.) Cambridge Univ. Press, Cambridge 1995, pp. 177–204. On the composition of the *Huangdi neijing*, see especially Yamada Keiji, "The formation of the *Huang-ti nei-ching*," *Acta Asiatica* 36, 1979, pp. 67–89. There is a selection of texts in translation in the appendix to Paul U. Unschuld, *Medicine in China*, Univ. of California Press, Berkeley, 1985.

5 See most recently C. Cullen, *Astronomy and Mathematics in Ancient China: The Zhou Bi Suan Jing*, Cambridge Univ. Press, Cambridge, forthcoming, who renders *tian wen* 'celestial patterns' and *li fa* 'calendrical methods.'

6 There is, for instance, a radical dispute between Plato and Aristotle on the nature of mathematical objects and on what mathematical truths are truths about. See especially I. Mueller, "Aristotle on geometrical objects," *Archiv für Geschichte der Philosophie* 52, 1970, pp. 156–71 (reprinted in *Articles on Aristotle*, J. Barnes, M. Schofield, and R. Sorabji (eds.), London, 1979, Vol. 3, Duckworth, pp. 96–107); J. Lear, "Aristotle's philosophy of mathematics," *Philosophical Review* 91, 1982, pp. 161–92; and the articles collected in *Mathematics and Metaphysics in Aristotle*, A. Graeser (ed.), Paul Haupt Verlag, Bern, 1987.

7 A brief analysis is given in Li Yan and Du Shiran, *Chinese Mathematics: A Concise History*, Clarendon Press, Oxford, 1987.

8 See D. B. Wagner, "Liu Hui and Tsu Keng-Chih on the volume of a sphere," *Chinese Science* 3, 1978, pp. 59–79, at pp. 61 ff.

9 See, for example, K. Chemla, "Resonances entre démonstration et procédure: Remarques sur le commentaire de Liu Hui (IIIè siècle) aux *Neuf Chapitres sur les Procédures Mathématiques* (Iᵉʳ siècle)', *Extrême-Orient–Extrême-Occident* 14, 1992, pp. 91–129.

10 In the edition of Qian Baocong, *Suanjing shishu*, Zhonghua, Beijing, 1963, this is on p. 96.

11 Ibid.

12 Ibid. p. 105; cf. Li and Du (op. cit.), p. 68. The investigation continues with the study of an inscribed polygon of 3,072 sides, with a final result of 3.1416 (Qian, op. cit., p. 106). However, the question of which sections of the commentary, at this point, are the work of Liu Hui himself and which that of later commentators is disputed: see D. B. Wagner, "Doubts concerning the attribution of Liu Hui's commentary on the *Chiu-Chang Suan-Shu*," *Acta Orientalia* 39, 1978, pp. 199–212, at p. 206 f.

13 See D. B. Wagner, "An early Chinese derivation of the volume of a pyramid: Liu Hui, third century A.D.," *Historia Mathematica* 6, 1979, pp. 164–88, at p. 182.

14 Cf. I. Mueller, *Philosophy of Mathematics and Deductive Structure in Euclid's Elements*, MIT Press, Cambridge, Mass., 1981.

15 See J. Barnes, "Galen on logic and therapy," in *Galen's Method of Healing*, F. Kudlien and R. J. Durling (eds.), Brill, Leiden, 1991, pp. 50–102; R. J. Hankinson, "Galen on the foundations of science," in *Galeno: Obra, Pensamiento e Influencia*, J. A. Lorez Ferez (ed.), Universidad Nacional de Educacion a Distancia, Madrid, 1991, pp. 15–29. In the contrary sense, see my "Theories and practices of

demonstration in Galen," in *Festschrift G. Patzig: Rationality in Greek thought*, M. Frede and G. Striker (eds.), Oxford Univ. Press, Oxford, forthcoming.

16 Aristotle, *Posterior Analytics*, 1.1–3, for example, 72b18 ff.

17 The evidence is set out in G. Lloyd, *Magic, Reason and Experience* (*MRE*), Cambridge University Press, Cambridge, 1979, pp. 100–2.

18 Ibid., pp. 62 ff.

19 However, a concern with the distinction between demonstrative and merely likely arguments *in the field of mathematics* surfaces in two texts in Plato, *Phaedo* 92d and *Theaetetus* 162e, discussed in *MRE*, p. 116.

20 On Chinese law and legal procedures, see A. F. P. Hulsewé, "Ch'in and Han law," in *The Cambridge History of China*, D. Twitchett and M. A. N. Loewe (eds.), Cambridge Univ. Press, Cambridge, 1986, Vol. 1, ch. 9, pp. 520–45; cf. Hulsewé, *Remnants of Han Law*, Leiden, 1955, Vol. 1, and *Remnants of Ch'in Law*, Brill, Leiden, 1985.

21 See, for example, Jean Levi, "L'art de la persuasion à l'époque des Royaumes Combattants (Vᶜ–IIIᵉ siècles av. J. C.)," *Extrême-Orient–Extrême-Occident* 14, 1992, pp. 49–89; and cf. Lloyd, "The Agora Perspective," *Extrême-Orient–Extrême-Occident* 14, 1992, pp. 185–98, at pp. 187–90.

22 Cf. N. Sivin, who refers to "The Chinese theory of the natural order and the political order as resonating systems, with the ruler as a sort of vibrating dipole between them," in "Cosmos and computation in early Chinese mathematical astronomy," *T'oung Pao* 55, 1969, pp. 1–73, at p. 7.

23 On the history of the astronomical bureau, see, for example, Ho Pen Yoke, "The astronomical bureau in Ming China," *Journal of Asian History* 3, 1969, pp. 137–57; and Jonathan Porter, "Bureaucracy and science in early modern China: The imperial astronomical bureau in the Ch'ing period," *Journal of Oriental Studies* 18, 1980, pp. 61–76. On Schall's role in the calendar controversies of the seventeenth century, see Huang Yi-Long, "Court divination and Christianity in the K'ang-Hsi era," *Chinese Science* 10, 1991, pp. 1–20.

24 See Ptolemy, *Syntaxis* 1.1 Proem, Heiberg 1.6. 17–21: μόνον δὲ τὸ μαθηματικόν, εἴ τις ἐξεταστικῶς αὐτῷ προσέρχοιτο, βεβαίαν καὶ ἀμετάπιστον τοῖς μεταχειριζομένοις τὴν εἴδησιν παράσχοι ὡς ἂν τῆς ἀποδείξεως δι' ἀναμφισβητήτων ὁδῶν γιγνομένης, ἀριθμητικῆς τε καὶ γεωμετρίας.

25 Ptolemy devotes *Tetrabiblos* 1.3. 10.14–17.10 to showing in what ways astrology is useful, for example, both in regard to goods of the mind and those of the body, where, in both cases, foreknowledge is beneficial, as giving calm and as allowing one to discern what suits one's own temperament and idiosyncrasy. Even though astrology can do less, he says, with regard to the acquisition of wealth and fame, in book 4 he discusses what can be learned from it also in those respects.

26 See Shigeru Nakayama, "Characteristics of Chinese Astrology," *Isis* 57, 1966, pp. 442–54, at p. 442.

27 Ibid. and Kiyosi Yabuuti, "Chinese astronomy: Development and limiting factors," in *Chinese Science*, S. Nakayama and N. Sivin (eds.), MIT Press, Cambridge, Mass., 1973, pp. 91–103, at p. 91.

28 See Sivin, op. cit. (n. 22).

29 See Sivin, op. cit., p. 25, (n. 22).

30 Simplicius, at *In Cael.* 488.11 ff, quotes Sosigenes who may be drawing on the history of astronomy written by Aristotle's pupil Eudemus. But there is no evidence in the extant dialogues of Plato to confirm that he stimulated the develop-

ment of astronomical models based on the regular circular movements of concentric spheres.

31 Ptolemy, *Syntaxis* 1.1, Proem, He berg 1.7.17–24: πρός γε μὴν τὴν κατὰ τὰς πράξεις καὶ τὸ ἦθος καλοκαγαθίαν πάντων ἂν αὕτη μάλιστα διορατικοὺς κατασκευάσειεν ἀπὸ τῆς περὶ τὰ θεῖα θεωρουμένης ὁμοιότητος καὶ εὐταξίας καὶ συμμετρίας καὶ ἀτυφίας ἐραστὰς μὲν ποιοῦσα τοὺς παρακολουθοῦντας τοῦ θείου τούτου κάλλους, ἐνεθίζουσα δὲ καί ὥσπερ φυσιοῦσα πρὸς τὴν ὁμοίαν τῆς ψυχῆς κατάστασιν.

32 This theme is explored in S. Kuriyama, "Visual knowledge in classical Chinese medicine," in D. Bates (ed.), op. cit., pp. 205–34.

33 Kuriyama, op. cit., notes 52 and 53, cites *Lingshu*, ch. 12, and the Wang Mang biography in *Han Shu*, ch. 69b, as the two sole surviving references to dissection in the Han. Saburo Miyasita, "A link in the westward transmission of Chinese anatomy in the later middle ages," *Isis* 58, 1967, pp. 486–90, remarks that when the first human dissections were carried out under the Sung, they were done on criminals. Celsus also tells us that this was the case with the human subjects dissected and vivisected by Herophilus and Erasistratus at Alexandria, Proem to *De Medicina* 1 paras 23 ff. On the early history of dissection in Greece, see ch. 8 of G. Lloyd, *Methods and Problems in Greek Science* (*MP*), Cambridge Univ. Press, Cambridge, 1991.

34 The similarities and differences are the subject of a forthcoming study by E. Hsu and myself.

35 Case 22, in ch. 105 of the *Shi Ji*, 2810–11.

36 Thus even in the cases where the patients examined by Chunyu Yi die, he *predicts* this, sometimes to the day.

37 Hippocratic medicine is also remarkable for the explicit and aggressive claims made by the authors of some of the treatises, for the introduction of new medical theories and practices claimed, in some cases, to be of major importance. See, for example, *RW* ch. 2, on such texts as *On Regimen* I–III, *On Regimen in Acute Diseases*, and *On Airs Waters Places*.

38 On the methodological and epistemological disputes in Hellenistic medicine, see especially H. von Staden, *Herophilus: The Art of Medicine in Early Alexandria*, Cambridge Univ. Press, Cambridge, 1989; M. Frede, *Essays in Ancient Philosophy*, Univ. of Minnesota Press, Minneapolis, 1987, ch. 12–15; and on Methodism in particular, cf. G. Lloyd, *Science Folklore and Ideology*, Cambridge Univ. Press, Cambridge, 1983, Part III, ch. 6.

39 See *MP*, ch. 8, and *RW*, pp. 158–67.

40 See Paola Manuli and Mario Vegetti, *Cuore, sangue e cervello*, Il Saggiatore Milan, 1977; Mario Vegetti, *Il Coltello e lo Stilo*, Milan, 1979; *Tra Edipo e Euclide*, Il Saggiatore Milan, 1983; *TAM*, p. 122.

41 See *RW*, pp. 94 ff., on *On the Nature of Man*, ch. 1, and other Hippocratic texts.

42 As emphasized by Kuriyama, op. cit., p. 216

43 I have explored the rival political images used in Greek cosmology in G. Lloyd, *Polarity and Analogy*, Cambridge Univ. Press, Cambridge, 1966, Ch. 4.

44 For the notion of causation in ancient China, see the articles by N. Sivin and Francesca Bray, in D. Bates (ed.) op. cit., and in ancient Greece, see G. Lloyd, "Ancient Greek concepts of causation in comparativist perspective," in D. Sperber, D. Premack and A. J. Premack (eds.), Clarendon Press, Oxford, 1995, pp. 536–56, and on the Greek view of nature, see *MP*, ch. 18. Broader comparativist studies of notions of space have been undertaken by the Cognitive Anthropology Research Group of the Max Planck Institute for Psycholinguistics, for example,

SCIENCE IN ANTIQUITY   33

"Relativity in Spatial Conception and Description," by Stephen C. Levinson, Working Paper No. 1, 1991.
45 This is one of the central themes of the collaborative studies currently being undertaken by myself and Nathan Sivin, provisionally entitled *Tao and Logos*.

3
Relations of analogy and identity
TOWARD MULTIPLE ORIENTATIONS TO THE WORLD

Stanley J. Tambiah

All thinking is analogising, and 'tis the use of life to learn metonymy.
Ralph Waldo Emerson

3.1 The relation between words and things

In an influential essay entitled "Analogy versus Identity," included in a book
he edited with the title *Occult and Scientific Mentalities in the Renaissance*,[1]
Brian Vickers has argued that what distinguishes the Renaissance occult tradition from the emergent scientific tradition was their respective attitudes
toward the relation between words and things, *verba* and *res*; and more generally signs and their referents. The mistake of the occult tradition (the Renaissance Neoplatonism of Ficino and Pino) consisted in imputing a direct,
even causal, relationship between the word and its referent (what Ogden and
Richards called the "denotative fallacy"; Cassirer, "the hypostatization of
the word"; or in the terminology of Saussure, the confusing of the signifier
with the signified). The corrective to this linguistic confusion was the notion
that the linguistic sign is conventional and arbitrary.[2] (Apparently the debate
about words and things began with Plato's *Cratylus* where both views of
language's relation to reality, natural versus conventional, are argued back
and forth, with the final judgment being given in favor of the separation
between language and reality.) Vickers argues that the new philosophers and
scientists, like Galileo, Bacon, and Hobbes, argued for the conventional or
arbitrary relation between language and reality.[3]

The main thrust of Vickers's exposition is that the Renaissance Neoplatonist mystical and magical tradition believed in "natural language," that is,
an "innate union of signifier and signified," and the new scientists and ex-
perimentalists held that "the linguistic sign is conventional, its meaning given
by society." Magical, astrological, and alchemical thought and practices were
predicated on this root fallacy of natural language.

In sum the Vickers narrative is as follows: In the late sixteenth and seventeenth centuries, there were two incompatible views on the relationship
between language and reality. "In the scientific tradition, a clear distinction
is made between words and things and between literal and metaphorical language. The occult does not recognize this distinction: words are treated as if
they were equivalent to things and can be substituted for them. Manipulate
the one and you manipulate the other" (p. 95). Thus in the occult tradition

"analogical" relations[4] are transformed into "identity" relations; a conventional relation between word and thing is made into a direct or causal or natural relation.

In passing, it may be noted that Foucault in his *Order of Things*[5] had preceded Vickers in giving a similar but fuller and richer account of an allegedly momentous change of episteme in regard to how language relates to reality. Foucault attributes to the Port-Royal school of the seventeenth century the new conception of "representation" that replaced the sixteenth-century Renaissance notion of "similitude" or "resemblance" between sign and object. The new theory of the linguistic sign, framed as a binary opposition, held that the sign as a thing representing was *other* than the thing represented.[6] This is the semiological notion that came to maturity later with Saussure that the relation between signifier and signified is primarily arbitrary and conventional. In Foucault's exposition the fundamental configuration or episteme of sixteenth-century knowledge consisted of "the reciprocal cross-reference of signs and similitudes." The practices or operations based on this way of knowing based on relations of "resemblance," was what was labeled "magic." In Foucault's view too the sixteenth-century view that produced the operations of "magic" is replaced by the seventeenth-century episteme associated with Cartesian rationalism, mechanistic philosophy, and positivist science. In the new analogical view, language is an analysis and a linear ordering of thought according to the rules of general grammar, and proposition is to language what representation is to thought.

There are certain problems in Vickers's (and Foucault's) exposition of the epistemological shift.

1. Vickers tends to present the Renaissance discourse as a divergent debate between two sets of antagonists: the scientists and protoexperimentalists on the one side and the Neoplatonist practitioners of the occult arts on the other side. But Frances Yates and her associates have submitted that, viewed in terms of the context of that time (a historicist view), there was a copresence among the practitioners of magical, mystical, mathematical, and instrumental views and operations, such that a sorting of them into separate and exclusive "scientific" and "occult" groupings is unrealistic. The unambiguous separation is really a retrospective narrative of the alleged linear march of science. Similarly, Charles Webster has persuasively argued that much of the history of science literature developed in the present century has exaggerated "the extent of the epistemological shift occurring between the Ages of Paracelsus and Newton" and that there were "remarkable elements of continuity sufficient to indicate an important degree of contiguity between the world views of the early sixteenth and late seventeenth centuries."[7]

2. However, while at several points and as a main submission Vickers presents the two sides as mutually exclusive and tends to assert that those he labels as "scientists" are or were in fact "rational," he is too good a scholar not to admit (if only in passing) that many personages he places on the scientific side of the debate also held some unquestioned and unconfirmed beliefs in alchemy and in microcosm–macrocosm correspondences.

3. Be that as it may, it is critical to point out, since Vickers fails to

underscore what he reports in passing, that those exemplars of the scientific and empiricist–instrumental mode of thought, such as Francis Bacon and Daniel Sennert, who attacked Paracelsus for his occult thought, themselves took for *granted* as *natural, axiomatic*, and beyond *debate* certain aspects of the Christian doctrine and cosmology and certain dualities of thought, which were clearly problematic, even contradictory, to those precepts they professed as scientists.

For example, Bacon's allegedly "graver charges" against Paracelsus gives the show away as to why Paracelsus was repudiated: "By mixing the divine with the natural, the profane with the sacred . . . you have corrupted . . . both human and religious truth . . ." (cited by Vickers, p. 133). Bacon accused Paracelsus and his disciples of exalting "the power of the imagination to be much one with the power of miracle-working faith."

Again, Daniel Sennert, cited as an important proponent of scientific thought, attacked in 1619 practitioners of Paracelsus's "false Chymistry" with its "peculiar" religion for they "mix prophane [profane] and holy things together." Thus for Bacon and Sennert it was axiomatic that God could perform "miracles" and proclaim "revelations," that "religious truth" was of a different order from "human truth," and things "sacred" and "profane" were a natural division and cannot be mixed.

There are other dualities paraded by persons identified by Vickers as "scientists" and whose criticisms of Paracelsus's theorizing are presented by him as not problematic. I am therefore forced to ask a question Vickers does not ask: were not some of the assertions of the critics of Paracelsus, like Van Helmont and Erastus, equally guilty of "fanciful" and "unprovable" constructions such as the insistence on a strict separation that must be made between the "spiritual" and the "corporeal," and on the necessity to maintain "barriers between the natural, human and divine"? Libavius is quoted as insisting that there is a hierarchical world in "which nature, man, and God" have their own spheres and modes of operation. Paracelsus's heresy is supposed to stem from his advocacy of a unified cosmos of correspondences between the three domains. Vickers as exegetist, while pointing out that Paracelsians "confused the power of man and the powers of God," never pauses to ask whether their critics themselves could "rationally" justify this separation as natural and non-controversial categories of knowledge and truth.

In truth then when Paracelsus was accused of magical thought, what was meant was that he was committing heresy against Christian theological truths: that there is a "religious truth" propounded in the Bible that cannot be denied or infringed by humanly constructed knowledge and that the divine is to be kept separate from the natural and the human.

So the charges against *occultism*, aside from the criticism of unprovable and fanciful "correspondences" imputed in its cosmology and the false operations based on them, were also importantly charges of *heresy*. The heresy consisted in imagining a correspondence and an interaction of features and powers between the domains of the divine, astral bodies, nature, and human beings, each of which while possessing their special properties did also interact in specific ways (postulates that, for example, would be perfectly acceptable in Hindu and Confucianist cosmologies). In other words Paracelsus's non-dualistic vitalism was repugnant not so much because his critics had "proved" his theories to be empirically false, but because in their eyes he failed to separate and protect the Bible and biblical truths from human operations based on ideas of harmonies and correspondences between the celestial and terrestrial worlds that were capable of setting in motion active principles and spiritual agencies that inhered within the cosmological scheme. Vickers fails to point out that there was no way in which Bacon could have proved that either there was a "naturally" or axiomatically given dichotomy of profane and sacred worlds that ought not to be aligned and brought into correspondence.

Moreover it is relevant to note that Paracelsus himself insisted that his "natural magic" had its foundation in Christian faith and that it was "done by means, by the help and assistance of the Father of all Medicines, our Lord Jesus Christ, our only Saviour."[8] He drew examples from the Bible in support of his schemes postulating microcosm–macrocosm correspondences. Webster explains that Paracelsus and Newton did not subsist in intellectual worlds alien to one another, and that for both of them "the working out of the nature of humanity's relationship with the creator constituted their primary intellectual mission."[9] Relevant to my theme is Martin Bernal's observation that Newton himself had in his early work followed his Neoplatonist teachers in their respect for Egypt. (After all, although Copernicus's mathematics was derived from Islamic science, his heliocentricity seems to have come with the Egyptian notion of a divine sun in the new intellectual environment of Hermeticism in which he was formed.) But toward the end of the seventeenth century, the Egyptian menace to Christianity (which had earlier provoked Bruno's immolation) was seen as staging a comeback and posing a threat to radical enlightenment. Thus Newton spent the last decades of his life trying to diminish Egypt's importance. "Newton was concerned with a threat to his conception of physical order and its theological and political counterparts – a divinity with regular habits and the Whig constitutional monarchy. *The threat was of pantheism implying an animate universe without need for a regulator or even a creator*" [emphasis added].[10]

My intention in reviewing these debates and attitudes is not so much to defend or rehabilitate Paracelsus and others of the so-called Neoplatonist occult tradition or to describe in detail their cosmologies or to declare invalid the scientific attainments of Enlightenment rationalism, but to make the different point that insofar as the new "scientists" and "protoexperimentalists" charged and dismissed the "occultists" with false reasoning, they also may have thrown out as irrational and indefensible a whole other mode (or modes) of orientation to the world and of world making.

My objective is not to argue that the occult identity relations and practices based on them were "true" or "correct" – many of them were inefficacious – but to underscore the point that there are many social discourses and communication contexts among us at all times and places where the imputation of identity between signs and their referents is operative.

In certain contexts human actors do convert metaphorical or metonymical or contiguity relations to real or identity relations, and in doing so, they are not behaving irrationally, but showing a propensity that occurs in ritual practices, literary productions, and mass movements of various kinds based on religious, linguistic, ethnic, and class identities and interests. Moreover, the Saussurean notion of the "conventional" relation between verbal signifier and signified that applies at the level of lexemes and morphemes does not and cannot repudiate the "motivated" uses of language in human social communication and construction of meaning as, for example, spelled out by Bakhtin. As I shall explain later, both modalities co-exist and collaborate in generating speech and literary productions, which as genres embody authorial motivations, design features, and expected outcomes. The Saussurean and Bakhtinian contributions to the study of language are of quite different orders and together deliver an ampler understanding of forms of life.

3.2 The normalization of the occult orientation

I want to stick my neck out and ask provocatively whether the time is ripe to "normalize" some features of what was previously dismissed as irrational expressions of the magical and occult mentality and also subsequently dismissed as superstitious features of the "religious mentality" once positivist science asserted its hegemony.

Just as Roman Jakobson rescued Frazer's notions of "sympathetic" and "contagious" magic, which Frazer associated with magical thought, "the bastard sister of science," and made them general operations of the human mind, so it is timely for us to rescue many features of the analogy versus identity relations, which the Renaissance thinkers grappled with in their debate between "scientific" and "occult" mentalities ("true" science versus "false" science).

Western intellectual discourse, especially that mode associated with post-Enlightenment rationality, has tended to push us on an exclusionary path such that we have gotten into the habit of coining certain polarities or binary oppositions and valuing one term in the pair positively and the other negatively. Thus we speak of myth versus truth (myth is "fantasy," truth is "reality"), of analogy versus identity (analogy as a vehicle of scientific or rational propositional thought, identity as a postulate of occult thought).

What if we correct the asymmetry, and while according scientific discourse its full value, also accept that there are contexts in which iconic and indexical relations (to use Charles Peirce's concepts) or metaphorical and metonymical relations (to use Jakobson's) are converted into "identity relations" or "relations of participation"? "Participation" is a concept I have developed in my book *Magic, Science, Religion and the Scope of Rationality*[11] and is similar to the concept of "identity relations," which I use here following Vickers. Such identifications happen all the time among us, and if that is the case, we ought to be investigating how it is and why it is that human experience in certain communicative contexts seeks or acquires ordering in terms of these identifications, which have a powerful impact on many spheres of their life.

Semiotics as Peirce defined it or semiology as Saussure conceived it as the study of sign systems included both verbal and non-verbal signs. If the linguistic sign is a prominent type of the former, visual signs are an important category of the latter. In the following sections I propose to discuss two examples that portray identification and participation at work as culturally meaningful and socially consequential processes. The first example concerns a well-known visual sign, the Stars and Stripes, the national flag of the United States. The second is linguistic ethno-nationalism, a ubiquitous and critical phenomenon of our time. These examples may help us to approach the prospect of accepting multiple orientations to the world as meaningful (but not un-problematic) orderings of experience.

3.2.1 FLAG WAVING AND FLAG BURNING

A court in Georgia that upheld a conviction for flag burning in 1983 made this ruling, which perfectly encodes the problem that I am seeking to probe in this address:

> Symbols are useful because they make tangible and concrete that which is intangible or otherwise incapable of meaningful observation. The amalgam of institutions, people and ideas, both past and present which make up our nation certainly cannot be observed. Thus the flag facilitates a citizen's identification with his country. In that respect, it is a unifying factor which is useful in rallying the people's support for their country in time of peace and war.

An explosive issue that has cropped up periodically in the United States is whether the government at both the state and federal levels has the legitimate power to punish a politically motivated burning of the American flag, usually referred to as the Stars and Stripes, and even more fondly and proudly as Old Glory.

The last case – a cause célèbre – arose from an arrest outside the 1984 Republican National Convention in Dallas, when Gregory Lee Johnson participated in a flag-burning protest in front of City Hall. Johnson, a member of the Revolutionary Communist Youth Brigade, was convicted under a Texas statute that declares the U.S. flag to be a "venerated object that permits criminal prosecution of those who desecrate it."[12] Johnson was sentenced to a year in jail and fined $2,000, but the Texas Criminal Appeals Court reversed the decision on constitutional grounds. Undaunted, the district attorney for Dallas County, John Vance, urged the U.S. Supreme Court to reinstate the conviction and to "squarely address" and affirm the central issue that the state has the right to protect the Stars and Stripes as a symbol of national unity and to jail those who dared to "desecrate" it.

In late March of 1989, as the Supreme Court prepared to hear the case, there was much public apprehension and concern and many polemical assertions and exchanges for and against the so-called conservatives essentially asserting that the symbol of national unity should not be allowed to be desecrated and the so-called liberals and advocates of civil liberties arguing that burning (or for that matter waving) a flag is a form of expression of "symbolic speech'' and upholding the punishment would severely damage the rights guaranteed by the First Amendment. In the event the so-called Reagan-packed Rehnquist court[13] surprised many by holding by a bare 5–4 majority that burning or mutilating the flag is not a criminal act and the right to do it was protected by the Constitution. Justice William Brennan, possibly mindful of President Bush's outraged remark, ''The flag is too sacred to be abused. If it is not defended, it is defamed,'' wrote in his judgment, ''We do not consecrate the flag by punishing its desecrators, for in doing so we dilute the freedom that this cherished emblem represents. . . . Our decision is a reaffirmation of the principles of freedom and inclusiveness that the flag best reflects'' and are protected by the First Amendment.[14]

My concern with the flag burning issue is not the juridical one of whether flag burning should be punishable or not, but to direct our attention to the complexity and contextuality of the historical and political processes of meaning construction, meaning layering, and meaning condensation and of the relations of identity that surround the promiscuous and ambiguous use of the words ''symbol'' and ''symbolic'' by all participants, both protagonists and antagonists, when they claim that the Stars and Stripes is a ''symbol of nationhood and unity'' (as Justice Rehnquist once declared) or that ''it stands not only for the principles for which our country stands but also represents the actions that our nation has taken throughout its history in the service of freedom'' (as the Texas application to the Supreme Court asserted) or that burning a flag is a form of ''symbolic speech'' and thus guaranteed by the First Amendment (as in an earlier instance Chief Justices Earl Warren and Warren Burger held as champions of First Amendment values).

What is the semiotic relation between the flag, the Stars and Stripes, the individual citizens, and the United States of America as a country and nation-state? A minimalist, citing Saussure (one is tempted to say out of context), might say that a flag is an arbitrary sign, that if it stands for the country or nation or nation-state or whatever, that relation between the signifier and the signified is not intrinsic or natural, but purely conventional. But many, perhaps a majority, of Americans, both conservatives and liberals, feel and say that their flag is more than an arbitrary/conventional sign; it integrally shares in or embodies or is associated with the country's history, its political values, its patriotism, its wars and battles, that is, it bears an inseparable relation of identity with these conceptions, memories, values, and claims. That the stars on the flag ''iconically'' represent the number of states and the stripes, the original thirteen colonies may be an additional factor in their investing it with vitalism.

A very large number of Americans feel that flag burning is unpatriotic and is an act of desecration. The vast majority of the states have statutes allowing for legal sanctions against desecrating the flag, and it is likely that at the time of the Supreme Court's hearing of the Texas application in March 1989, given the chance for a referendum, the majority vote in the country would have been in favor of declaring flag burning a crime.

Indeed let us start with the country's highest elected politicians. Declaring that he was ''viscerally'' against the court's decision, and at a hurriedly arranged photo opportunity in front of the Iwo Jima memorial near Arlington National Cemetery (a World War II memorial to commemorate the largest number of U.S. soldiers killed in the Pacific Theatre in any single battle), President Bush expressed his outrage that I quoted before: "The flag is too sacred to be abused. If it is not defended, it is defamed." He then said he favored legislation by the Congress to remedy the Court's action in the form of a constitutional amendment.[15] Not to be outdone, lawmakers on Capitol Hill, members of both parties, waited their turn in an all-night session to fulminate against the Supreme Court decision. Indeed, the electoral rewards of "draping oneself in the American flag," as the expression goes, were capitalized on by Bush in the 1988 presidential election "by visiting a flag factory in New Jersey and attacking Michael Dukakis for once vetoing a bill that would have required teachers to lead their students in the Pledge of Allegiance each day."[16]

What is the nature of the American "fetishism" focused on Old Glory? While many countries engage in flag waving, in no country I have visited have I seen, as in the United States, so many private homes (let alone public buildings) in small towns and suburbs, belonging to both middle-class and blue-collar workers, sporting fluttering Stars and Stripes from white flag-poles.

In public life, the flag is proudly waved at all those community and national rites and ceremonies that Robert N. Bellah labeled as civil religion. But identification with the flag seems most intense and fevered when the public responds to appeals to show support for government policy, especially when the country goes to war. To give the most recent example, the popularity of the Gulf War in 1991 was affirmed by the vast numbers of the American public carrying and waving flags to the gratification of both the government and flag factories.

While no doubt the flag is associated with many collective memories, it is war and death, especially of presidents by assassination or soldiers in battle or policemen on duty, that call for the most poignant display of the flag draped over the coffins and later presented to the widows. War veterans' organizations are the staunchest defenders of the flag.

Now, when dissenters mutilate the flag, they do so not because they are semiotic minimalists, but because they understand all too well that their action is an effective protest against a governmental policy or state action that enjoys public support. They understand well the condensed layers of association people have transposed to the flag and the relation of identity people have with it. So when Gregory Johnson torched the flag in 1984 and his comrades chanted, "America, the red, white and blue, we spit on you," they were inviting arrest. In February 1989 a student of the School of the Art Institute of Chicago spread the Stars and Stripes on the floor as his exhibit, inviting viewers to walk on it. Predictably, picketing veterans' groups shut down the exhibition for several days.[17]

Let me conclude by remarking that while the United States provides us with a remarkable and conspicuous site for plumbing the processes of representation and exemplification focused on the national flag, the recent upheavals in Eastern Europe and the Baltic states also affords us with a dramatic opportunity to study the semantic and semiotic implications of political uses of national flags. Some months ago a television series called *Face to Face*, introduced by Hendrik Smith, showed massive rallies of swaying Latvian crowds – men, women, and children – waving the revived Latvian national flag as a triple gesture of their political resistance to Soviet imperialism, their emancipation and political independence from it, and their gaining their freedom.

3.2.2 LINGUISTIC ETHNO-NATIONALISM

In terms of current international relevance for the so-called ethnic conflicts raging in South Asia, Eastern Europe, and elsewhere, the phenomenon of linguistic ethno-nationalism is an urgent case to study. What are the relationships between a language, its native speakers, and the cultural capital and the social reality they construct?

Linguistic ethno-nationalism asserts a consubstantial identity between a collectivity of people and the language they speak and transmit. The people in question share a strong sense that their language and their oral and literary productions – poetry, myths, folklore, epics, and philosophical, religious, historical, even scientific text – are intimately, integrally, and essentially connected with them as owners, creators, and sharers of that legacy. Such potent exclusivist identity that overlooks and suppresses exchanges, borrowings, and interactions between languages and their speakers and the migrations of peoples becomes even more divisive and intense when the heritage of language is conflated with ethnicity and race, religion, territory, and homeland.

Linguistic ethno-nationalism, a strong motivator and advocate of claims of collective entitlements and preferential policies in nineteenth- and twentieth-century worldwide politics, has a weighty bearing on the double question of how people see language as relating to the world (to "reality") and also how it relates to its speakers, the relation between words and things and between words and human beings, questions that engrossed both Renaissance and Enlightenment thinkers and philosophers of Europe as well as the poets, grammarians, and religious reformers of many Eastern and Western countries. However, it also relates to many other issues regarding the interconnections between people, language, and the social and cultural worlds they construct and according to which they live and act that were not posed in earlier times and are critical to the expanded horizons of later times, especially in the epochs of nationalism and ethno-nationalism from the late eighteenth century to the present.

Herder's philosophy and Central and Eastern European developments. Johann Gottfried Herder, as the philosopher of Volksgeist, was probably Europe's most sympathetic nineteenth-century theorist of a historicist and romantic conception of ethno-nationalism, in which the identity relation between a people and their literary heritage played a constitutive role. He was "one of the leaders of the romantic revolt against classicism, rationalism, and faith in the omnipotence of scientific method – in short, the most for-

midable of the adversaries of the French *philosophes.*''[18] Herder opposed the
universalist stance, stemming from France in the eighteenth century, and its
belief in scientific rationalism and progress. Herder's conception of Volksgeist was in substance and spirit against the conception of the nation-state as
a universal project and held in abhorrence the centrality that it gave the state
as the organizer of life.

A recent commentator remarks that Herder's voluminous work, *Reflections
on the Philosophy of the History of Mankind* (printed in Riga in the years
1784–1791), ''was destined to become the romantic manifesto of ethnic or
Volk identity in Eastern and Central Europe, the bible of a nativist cultural
rebellion against Frenchified cosmopolitanism and a political assault against
the dynastic empires – Russian, Austrian, Prussian and Turkish – that had
emerged in the medieval world.''[19]

For Herder a people's language and its literature were integrally involved
in the shaping of that people's cultural consciousness. He held that human
groups are ''made one by common traditions and common memories, of
which the principal link and vehicle – the very incarnation – is language.''[20]
As Herder himself eloquently put it: ''Has a nation anything more precious
than the language of its fathers? In it dwell its entire world of tradition,
history, principles of existence; its whole heart and soul.''[21] This is necessarily so because humanity thinks in words and other symbols: thought, feelings, and attitudes are incorporated in symbolic forms, whether it be poetry,
worship, or ritual.

Thus Herder's advocacy of the historical and cultural distinction stems
from his view of ethno-nations that they develop and employ different linguistic genres and that nuances in linguistic use are pointers to different forms
of collective identity and experience.

Herder's Romantic vision, although in itself not political in orientation (he
was totally opposed to the aggressive nationalism of the nation-state), did in
fact powerfully influence certain nationalist movements in Germany and Eastern Europe.

It took only a certain twist for this notion of a distinctive people to be
transformed in the hands of National Socialism and its Fascist and Nazi
propagandists to a demonic philosophy of Aryan racial superiority and to
discrimination against allegedly dangerous and sinister minorities living
among majority populations and their expulsion from the fatherland or their
extermination in death camps. Though Hitler and his associates were the arch
exponents of this pathological philosophy of racial superiority and special
destiny, leading eventually to imperial expansion and subordination of ''inferior'' peoples, some of these same attitudes and conceptions of ethno-
nationalism have been operative among many of the ethnic nationalities of
Eastern Europe and the former USSR and are today breaking out in Yugo-
slavia, Czechoslovakia, Rumania (which are in the process of fragmenting),
and in many of the previous Soviet republics, among which the Armenian–
Azerbaijani hostilities are the most vicious.

I do not intend here to examine further the course of ethno-nationalism in
Europe, but turn to India to explore manifestations of attributing identity

relations between language and its speakers and its representations of the world.

3.3 The personification and politics of language in India

India is a striking example of identity relations, claimed between language and its speakers, being a major factor in the practice of ethno-nationalist politics.[22]

The Herderian molding of Volksgeist in which language acts as a carrier of multivalent values, interests, and messages is certainly not unique. Though Herder may have been a particularly eloquent philosopher of it, similar formulations by advocates of mother-tongue and sons-of-the-soil ethno-nationalism can be found in many parts of Asia. India, however, is a rich exemplification of the Tower of Babel parable. A unitary nation-making project has been fragmented by linguistic and other forms of regional divisiveness and pluralism.

The identity between language and its native speakers was passionately propounded by Gandhi and argued on behalf of the Indian National Congress as an anti-colonial and pro-self rule Swaraj cause. Gandhi wrote in *Young India* in 1938 as follows:

> Surely it is a self-demonstrated proposition that the youth of a nation cannot keep or establish a living contact with the masses unless their knowledge is received and assimilated through a medium understood by the people. . . . A language is an exact reflection of the character and growth of its speakers.

But the problem in India was that at the time of independence some 179 languages and 544 dialects were spoken throughout the country. The Eighth Schedule of the Constitution listed 14 officially recognized languages selected on the bases of number of speakers and their alleged degree of literary development. (Sanskrit, the classical language, now known only to a minority, was included for cultural and historical reasons.)

The Indian National Congress's propagation of indigenous mother tongues had a divisive effect once independence was won. The problem of "linguism," as it was called in India, consisted in the demand for states to be territorially demarcated on the basis of the dominant languages regionally in place. The deliberations of the Linguistic Provinces Commission of 1948 and of the subsequent States Reorganization of 1955 resulted in the states being largely drawn on a linguistic basis. But as may be expected, once the linguistic principle was accepted, there was bound to be tensions and dissatisfactions felt in multilingual states with sizable minorities speaking languages other than that of the majority. Moreover, one of the inevitable consequences of industrialization and economic development is the migration of peoples between states. These population movements, resulting in dramatic changes in demographic proportions, have additionally compounded ethnic conflict in India, especially in the northeast.

The Punjab region in India has been an arena where issues of language, religion, and ethnic identity have become explosively compounded and substantialized. In 1966 the Punjab state was partitioned to form a new state of Punjab (dominated by the Sikhs) and a Hindi-speaking state called Hariyana. The 1966 partition was to a significant degree induced by many Hindus in Punjab, whose mother tongue was Punjabi, declaring themselves for political reasons to be Hindi speakers. The most recent twist in the story is the demand by the Sikhs (led by the fundamentalists whose hero was Bhindranwale, who was killed together with his followers when the Golden Temple at Amritsar was invaded by Indian troops) for a separate state of Khalistan on the basis of both language and religious affiliation.

In twentieth-century India, with mounting rather than diminishing intensity, participatory democracy and mass electoral politics, staged and enacted at both federal and state levels, have triggered and fueled the spiraling interplay of two propensities of language.

One is the personification and romanticization of language as the spirit, image, and embodiment of the creative capacities, pristine purity, past memories, and future aspirations of a people. The people are substantialized as an ethnic collectivity ("race") naturalized in a territory (*bhumiputra*) that is their homeland and uniquely devoted to and nourished by their linguistic heritage.

The other propensity is the usefulness of this "organic unity" conflating language, "race," and territory as a political platform, from which to pursue highly self-conscious, instrumental, and pragmatic goals that are linked to the use of language as a vehicle for the conduct of many tasks of modern life.

Thus in recent decades all these complex issues surrounding language and its speakers have come into play in India (and elsewhere in Pakistan, Sri Lanka, Thailand, Malaysia, and so on).

1. Language as mother tongue and medium through which the culture and historical consciousness of a people is transmitted and experienced.
2. Language as a medium of administration and its political relevance for demarcating a territorial unit such as a state or a province within a federal or unitary polity.
3. Language as a medium for instruction and education and the implications of literacy and learning for employment, journalism, and print capitalism.
4. Language as a vehicle and agent for "democratization" of a country and for eliminating or reducing the privileges enjoyed during Western colonialism by an English-educated "collaborating" elite.
5. Language as the focus and ground of linguistic politics and self-conscious regionalism. (The South Indian Dravidian movement is an illustration of this theme and will be mentioned shortly.)
6. Linguistic revivalism as the high road to the flowering of regional and minority cultures and their links to popular religious devotional movements and political resistance.

With regard to this last point, it is worth noting that in India, there have over time risen several *bhakti*-type movements, anti-hierarchical and anti-

Brahmanical in spirit, and appealing to the lower social orders and employing the everyday spoken tongue. Let me cite some examples from South India, though other equally apt examples can be cited from other regions.

The Virasaiva religious movement in Mysore during the tenth through twelfth centuries was a *bhakti*-oriented "social upheaval by and for the poor, the low caste and the outcaste against the rich and the privileged; it was a rising of the unlettered against the literate pundit, flesh and blood against stone."[23] Virasaiva, meaning militant or heroic saivism or faith in Siva, was the faith of the Lingayats.

In the twentieth century, South India again has been the breeding ground of political movements such as the Justice Party founded in 1916 and the Self-Respect movement of the 1920s, which were the precursors of the DMK (Dravida Munnetra Kazhagam) and its breakaway groups. Anti-North, anti-Aryan, anti-Sanskrit, anti-Brahmin, these movements have glorified the Tamil language as the divine goddess (Tamilteyvam), as the mother (Tamiltay) who produced the milk imbibed by the Tamil people. This mother nurtured long ago the golden age of Tamil identity and Tamil culture, embodied in the Cankam classics, and shaped an egalitarian society that is the antithesis of the caste-bound, anti-feminist, Sanskritic culture over which the ritualist Brahmins preside.[24] It is claimed that the true original religion of the Tamils was Saiva Siddhanta, based on the Tirumurai books written in Tamil and the Agamas, accessible to the non-Brahmanical orders.

Thus the cry Tamilnad for the Tamilians is, on the one hand, a type of Herderian romantic historicist language-centered ethno-nationalism – as an enthusiast put it: "If we live, we live for Tamil; if we die, we will die for Tamil" – and on the other, a calculated explosive as well as pragmatic ideology that is fashioned to win elections, to exercise regional power in local as well as federal politics.

3.4 The non-arbitrary and motivated uses of language

The "arbitrariness" or "conventionality" of language, that is, the relation between linguistic signs or lexemes and their referents, being by and large arbitrary in the manner stated by Saussure is true only at one level of linguistic analysis. It is equally and more significantly true at the different level of utterance and inscription, at the level of texts, discourses, genres of speech, that their shape and patterning may have iconic and indexical relations to that which they represent or bring into being. The oratorical or authorial intentions and rules of generation of these larger productions, the conventions of their structuring, sequencing, and patterning, frequently show a distinct purposiveness and a "motivated" likeness to their objects of representation. It is in this way that different literary and oral genres and traditions are created and deployed.

There are various examples of iconic coding (in the sense Gregory Bateson gave it) whereby linguistic productions iconically create the contours of the phenomenon being discussed. I have discussed this issue elsewhere.[25] For instance, Gossen has shown how the "stacking" of parallel couplets and recursive recitation produce in Chamula ritual an iconic analogue of the cycles of creations of cosmic order in their spatial and temporal regularity and cumulative effect.[26] The effectiveness of these operations is that the cosmos or some portion of it is created at the ritual site, made to come alive, and constitutes the arena for further ritual action.

Again, Paul Friedrich has cited both Benveniste and Jakobson as arguing for the relative non-arbitrariness of language in the sense I have indicated. Friedrich suggests that Jakobson's involvement with the most individual of language phenomena – lyric poetry – may have something to do with the position he took. Jakobson concluded his 1965 essay on the "Quest for the Essence of Language" with the assertion that "the principle of iconicity, patent in the syntax and morphology invalidates the dogma of arbitrariness."[27]

Friedrich sums up the case for non-arbitrariness of language as follows:

> The creative use of language, and poetic creativity above all, to a significant degree involves iconic and indexical symbolism and the relations of phonetic and lexical structure with the real world and with the deeper systems of meaning in the semantic and cultural codes.[28]

One last, but by no means the least, theorist, Bakhtin, makes the case beyond doubt when he persuades us to move from the usual internal grammatical and syntactical analyses of language in terms of sentences to the larger in scale communicative contexts in which utterances create and constitute speech genres. The steps by which Bakhtin builds his exposition are as follows: the distinction between sentence and utterance; utterance implying an anticipated and recursive speaker–addressee dialectic, exchange, and response; utterances building up components of larger discourses (genres), the understanding of which must go beyond the traditional procedure of linguistic analysis in terms of grammar, syntax, and rules of sentence construction.[29]

The preliminary dismantling of the traditional approach allows Bakhtin to advance his positive characterization of how speech genres are constructed according to their principles, rules, and processes of generation guided by authorial intent; by speaker's motives and speech plans; by conventions regarding beginnings and endings of genres and of sequencing of responses; and by the degree of formalization required and creativity allowed in the production of the genre in question.

3.5 Toward multiple orientations to the world

In conclusion, in the light of what I have discussed before, I shall set down some seven propositions that prepare the ground for consideration of multiple orientations to the world.

1. There are motivated and purposive constructions and uses of linguistic productions whose understanding requires us to move to levels of analysis other than that pertaining to the Saussurean notion of arbitrariness of language. The motivated uses of language, which I discussed in the foregoing section, exemplify some of the dialectical and recursive processes and mech-

anisms by which speakers and writers of a language map and constitute their reality, which they in turn personify and objectify as their culture. This culture as reality and legacy then is viewed as giving the actors their identity, their existential meaning, their motivational orientations and sense of special destiny.

2. It is not my intention to criticize indiscriminately or deny the validity of the scientific mode of knowledge construction and practices stemming from it. I have in mind here the physical sciences. For me, the scientific community, with its rules of procedure, relevant evidence, inference and demonstration, that is to say, as an interpretive community, is involved in systematic "reality testing" and the construction of one order of knowledge. This mode of knowledge construction is no doubt a major achievement of humanity and, in its present form, of Western civilization. Although it is only one ordering of reality, it has developed its own internal self-reflexive critical basis to a point unknown in other disciplines and in principle admits membership in the scientific community on a universalistic basis.[30]

3. My project and strategy of attempting to normalize certain processes of association, previously denigrated or dismissed as only characteristic of occult and magical thought is linked to the proposal that we *all* participate in multiple orientations to the world, or in many "ways of world making" (to use Nelson Goodman's phrase).[31] These orderings are incommensurable with scientific rationality in the sense that they can neither be reduced to nor meaningfully judged against that yardstick.

4. Many orthodox and successful scientists participate within the framework of science only some of the time, when they enter and focus on the domain of scientific work. These same scientists participate in other modalities of experience and in other ways of world making and do so without the need to face objections of incompatibility, incoherence, or contradiction. The world of science is not a total institution in the sense Erving Goffman[32] defined it.

5. I have tried to suggest that the so-called occult or magical thought and action, which a powerful current of scientistic rationalism has tried to push out or exclude as not consistent with rational thought, is not so alien to us moderns. It may have its excesses, but it is also a regular feature of our associational thought and of our establishing meaningful relationships and our achieving certain effects and outcomes. An extended theory of semiotics, poetics and ritual action helps us to see better the logic of these associational operations and their powerful role in social life.

6. Not only the powerful arrowlike thrust of empiricist scientific experimental and causal thought but also, working in collusion, the anti-ritualistic stance of much Protestant theology may have forced into dark corners orders of experience and ways of world making as inferior, subordinate, even irrational. It has taken a lot of counter-cultural anthropological and historical probing and formulating to recognize these inferiorized modes of being, experiencing, and becoming in the world as normal and enriching as well as problematic and conflictual in ways similar to the manner in which scientific

thought and practice have had their positive beneficial and negative, their logical and lucid, as well as rhetorical and propagandist sides.

7. Our high valuation of technocratic knowledge and of the technocratic ordering in the world tends to sanctify science and scientific knowledge as the true knowledge, which therefore can legitimately intervene in the world and shape its course and affairs. As the discussions of Habermas relating to "knowledge and interests"[33] and of Foucault in terms of "knowledge/power" have sensitized us, the supremacy of science as knowledge allows its practitioners not only to make extra-scientific and rhetorical claims, but even more importantly to intervene in the world and shape its course and affairs. This virtually hegemonic claim makes it one of the most important "forces of production" in our modern world in the defining and shaping of corporate structures, regimes of bureaucracy, and consumerist imperatives. Some of the operational as well as moral evaluative claims scientists make are political and mercenary claims, claims that are as much rhetorical, persuasive, performative, and contestable as the alleged practices and uses of magic in the accounts of savage societies and the medieval world. (Versions and portions of alleged scientific knowledge can be and are invoked by different interest groups, and the scientific claim that wins is not infrequently that which has the backing of powerful interests and wins the political contest. Examples are investments in nuclear power as opposed to solar power, and the exploitation versus the preservation of natural forests.) There is no need to labor the point the reasons for and the implications of why the science of warfare has had an important and persuasive place in the hierarchy of production preferences and the generation of employment in the United States, the former USSR, and certain other countries.

Notes

1 Brian Vickers, ed. *Occult and Scientific Mentalities in the Renaissance* (Cambridge: Cambridge Univ. Press, 1984).
2 By arbitrary Saussure meant that the choice of the signifier by the speaker is "unmotivated" in that "it actually had no natural connection with the signified." Ferdinand Saussure, *Course in General Linguistics* (New York: McGraw Hill, 1966), p. 69.
3 Vickers cites Bacon as holding that "words are but the current tokens or marks of popular notions of things" (in *Advancement of Learning*); Hobbes as asserting that "Names are signs not of things, but of our cogitations" (in *Leviathan*); and Locke's "Essay Concerning Human Understanding" (1690) as including a refutation of natural language theories and recalling Hobbes, Bacon, and the long tradition back to Aristotle and Plato.
4 Vickers does not spell out the notion of "analogy." Standard dictionary glosses include the following features: a similarity of rates or proportions; resemblance in particulars between things otherwise unlike; agreement or resemblance in certain aspects as in form or function; similarity without identity. A more informative discussion of analogy and its use in two senses – the "scientific predictive" and the "conventional persuasive" – is to be found in my essay, "Form and Meaning

of Magical Acts,'' in Stanley J. Tambiah, *Culture, Thought and Social Action* (Cambridge: Harvard Univ. Press, 1985), Ch. 2. Though Vickers's understanding of analogy is unsophisticated, I shall follow his usage here since I am testing his ideas in this essay.

5 Michel Foucault, *The Order of Things, an Archaeology of Human Sciences* (New York: Pantheon Books, 1973), Ch. 4.

6 Foucault sees parallel epistemic shifts in other systems of knowledge constructed in the eighteenth and nineteenth centuries, for example, Linnaean classification in botany and zoology and Adam Smith's theory of money and value.

7 Charles Webster, *From Paracelsus to Newton: Magic and the Making of Modern Science* (Cambridge: Cambridge Univ. Press, 1982), pp. 1, 11.

8 Paracelsus, *The Archidoxes of Magic* (New York: Samuel Weiser, 1975), pp. 94–95. He firmly distinguished his ''natural magic'' from witchcraft, necromancy, sorcery, and other forms of ''demonic magic'' and roundly condemned them for using ''ceremonies, consecrations, conjurations, blessings and curses'' (ibid., pp. 82–83).

9 Webster, op. cit., p. 21. The point I wish to make here is that Paracelsus's cosmological writings and his ''natural magic'' did fit into a larger Christian theological framework from his point of view. ''God, who is the Creator of the Whole Work of Nature, hath as much power in Heaven, and also that he giveth power and virtue to those operations in Metals, Herbs, Roots, Stone and such like things'' (Paracelsus, op. cit., p. 92).

10 Martin Bernal, *Black Athena. The Afroasiatic Roots of Classical Civilization*, Vol. 1, *The Fabrication of Ancient Greece, 1785–1985* (New Brunswick, N.J.: Rutgers Univ. Press, 1987). Bernal also refers to Richard Bentley (a friend of Newton) as the popularizer of Newton's Whig scheme of science around 1693. He also makes this charge: ''Throughout the eighteenth and nineteenth centuries we find a *de facto* alliance of Hellenism and textual criticism with the defence of Christianity'' (p. 27).

11 Stanley J. Tambiah, *Magic, Science, Religion, and the Scope of Rationality* (Cambridge: Cambridge Univ. Press, 1990).

12 Quoted by Martin Garbus, ''The 'Crime' of Flag Burning,'' *The Nation* (March 20, 1989), pp. 369–370.

13 It is noteworthy that Justice William Rehnquist, now chief justice, wrote a dissent about 18 years ago when the Court refused to declare flag burning a crime, saying that ''the true nature in this case is not only one of preserving the physical integrity of the flag but also one of preserving the flag as an important symbol of nationhood and unity. . . . It is the character not the cloth of the flag that the states seek to protect.'' Cited by Garbus, op. cit.

14 Walter Isaacson, ''O'er the Land of the Free,'' *Time* (July 3, 1989), p. 14.

15 Such a momentous step, if implemented, would require the vote of two-thirds of both houses of Congress, ''a sledgehammer to kill a fly,'' as a commentator put it.

16 Isaacson, op. cit., p. 15.

17 It is interesting to note that Jasper Johns, Robert Rauschenberg, and sixteen other artists, some of whom had used the flag in their work, filed an *amicus curiae* brief in the Texas case, objecting to the criminal action against Johnson and asserting ''what is [offensive] to one man may be a work of art to another.''

18 Isaiah Berlin, *Vico and Herder. Two Studies in the History of Ideas* (London: Chatto and Windus, 1976), p. 145.

19 Frank E. Manuel, ''A Requiem for Karl Marx,'' *Daedalus, Journal of the Amer-*

ican Academy of Arts and Sciences, The Exit from Communism 121.2 (spring 1992), pp. 12–13.

20 Ibid., p. 165.

21 Cited By Berlin, op. cit., p. 165.

22 See Stanley J. Tambiah, "The Politics of Language in India and Ceylon," *Modern Asian Studies* 1.3 (1967), pp. 215–240.

23 See A. K. Ramanujan, *Speaking of Siva* (Baltimore, Md.:Penguin Books, 1972), p. 21. Basavanna, the Lingayat founding prophet, in his *vacanas* preached against the Hindu caste system and the mediating role of the Brahmans in religious worship. The *bhakti*-infused Jangama devotee, virtually a renouncer, moved from village to village "representing god the devoted, a god incarnate" (ibid., p. 21). These *vacana* lines express the sentiments: "Listen, O Lord of the meeting rivers,/ things standing shall fall,/but the moving ever shall stay."

24 I am indebted for references to the recent Tamil rhetoric and imagery to Sumathi Ramasamy's "Deconstructing Language: Periyar Ramasami Critique of Tamil Consciousness," paper read at the 44th annual meeting of the Association for Asian Studies, Washington, D.C., 1992. For information on twentieth-century South Indian politics, see Eugene F. Irschick, *Politics and Social Conflict in South India, The Non-Brahmin Movement and Tamil Separatism, 1916–1929* (Berkeley: Univ. of California Press, 1969); and Robert L. Hardgrave, Jr., *The Dravidian Movement* (Bombay: Popular Prakashan, 1965).

25 See Tambiah, "A Performative Approach to Ritual," in *Culture, Thought and Social Action*. See also Gregory Bateson, *Steps to an Ecology of Mind* (London: Intertext Books, 1972).

26 Gary Gossen, "To Speak with a Heated Heart: Chamula Canons of Style and Good Performance," *Explorations in the Ethnography of Speaking*, R. Bauman and J. Sherzer, eds. (London: Cambridge Univ. Press, 1974).

27 R. Jakobson, "Quest for the Essence of Language," *Diogenes* 51 (Fall), pp. 21–37. Cited by P. Friedrich. "The symbol and its relative non-arbitrariness." In *Linguistics and Anthropology*, ed: M. Dale Kinkade, Kenneth L. Hale, and Oswald Werner, eds. (Lisse: The Peter de Ridder Press).

28 Friedrich proposes and illustrates a "consubstantialist theory" from the point of view of the user of the language in this way: "The case for non-arbitrariness in syntax is even stronger. Syntactic constructions such as the clause are to varying degrees icons of the underlying sequence of ideas, the temporal sequence of described events corresponding to the order of lexical symbols. As a felicitous example, the explicit segments of a described path or of a complicated culinary recipe must in their linear syntactic sequence correspond to the referential sequence. And it is universally true that positions at the beginning and end of a clause (or a poetic line) usually have some feature of emphasis or force. Passive constructions somewhat emphasize the object of action and facilitate the (often artificial) non-mention of the actor, as in scientific prose" (ibid., pp. 235–36).

29 M. Bakhtin, *The Dialogue Imagination*,(ed: Michael Holquist, ed. (Austin's Univ. of Texas Press, 1983).

30 I therefore disagree with Richard Rorty in his Postmodernist text *Consequence of Pragmatism* (Minneapolis: Univ. of Minnesota Press, 1982) insofar as he is asserting a purely "pragmatist" view of science that holds that "truth" is a compliment paid to knowledge that pays off in practical terms. As Bernard Williams has remarked, if scientists accepted Rorty's pragmatist argument of seeing science as "one genre of literature," they would hardly think it worth their while to practice it. On the other hand, I am fully in accord with Rorty's advocacy of

multiple ways of relating to the world as meaningful and useful and reasonable. It has also been suggested that insofar as Rorty's relativist philosophy is innocent of discourses and implications of power, it eclectically celebrates the status quo.

31 Nelson Goodman, *Ways of World Making* (Indianapolis: Hackett, 1985).
32 Erving Goffman, *Asylums: Essays in the Social Situation of Mental Patients and Other Inmates* (New York: Doubleday, 1961).
33 Jurgen Habermas, *Toward a Rational Society*, Jeremy J. Shapiro, trans. (London: Heinemann, 1971).

4
Self, narrative, and memory
REFLECTIONS ON AUGUSTINE, PETRARCH,
AND DESCARTES

Brian Stock

Under the influence of Augustine's *Confessions*, the manner in which Western thinkers discussed the self underwent a transformation[1] that indirectly
reflected a shift from oral to written discourse within the literate, educated
society of the Middle Ages. For the authors whose works determined the
boundaries of thinking about the self, the person, or the individual in this
period, the relationship between the self and the words or images by which
it was configured became a topic of extensive discussion: concept and communication thus emerged as aspects of the same problem along with questions
of memory, narrative, and autobiographical writing. The figures who most
clearly marked the phases of change were Augustine (354–430), Petrarch
(1304–1374), and Descartes (1596–1650).

Augustine adhered to the commonsensical notion that self-understanding
is to a large degree linguistic. Put simply, he believed that we understand
ourselves best through the words by which we express our thoughts. When
we learn to speak, we take our first tentative steps toward self-expression and
self-understanding, as he did in *Confessions*, book 1.6–8. We do not understand ourselves through single words, of course, but through words spoken
in sequences of meaningful sounds that make up sentences, paragraphs, and
larger units of discourse. These sound sequences are what Augustine calls
narrative (*narratio*), that is, a series of verbal signs to which significance
(*significatio*) is attached. The limitations of self-knowledge are accordingly
those of language. Because words imperfectly express our thoughts and because our thoughts may in turn imperfectly configure interior or exterior
realities, our linguistic understanding of the self (or for that matter anything
else) may be incomplete.

When we hear a sequence of words that constitutes a narrative, how are
we able to understand what the words mean? In his well-known discussion
of time in *Confessions*, book 11, Augustine proposed that we accomplish this
feat through memory. The difference between the sensory impressions that
sound creates in the ears and the meanings that sequences of words convey
to the mind depends on our memory of the sensory impressions and our
consequent recognition of their significance. When I say, "I pick up the
book," the sound of the syllables, "I/pick/up" is still in my thoughts when
the sentence ends, making it possible for me to grasp the meaning, which is
not "I," "pick," "up," or "the book," but "I pick up the book." Augustine
argued that this short-term memory is involved in all understanding that re-

lates the parts of a spoken or written statement to the whole and by implication that memory is the basis of what is later called the "hermeneutic
circle." He also maintained that such recognition presupposes a type of linguistic understanding that does not arise from particular sentences, but operates intentionally within the mind. We remember, recognize, and intend all
at once.

Is the resulting narrative self a plausible self? In one sense, no. Augustine
did not mistrust all stories, as did Plato. He thought that the problems of
stories arose chiefly through the potentially different reactions of members
of the implied audience. Interpretations differ, and there is no way of telling
which is right. A person cannot even be certain that the construal of the
meaning of her or his life history is correct, as Augustine's attempt to make
sense out of his past illustrates. However, his negativism on this topic did
not lead him to adopt the view favored by Buddhist and postmodernist thinkers for different reasons, namely, that the self is an entirely imaginary construction. He was convinced that the self has a reality – indeed, his trinitarian
theology of "image and likeness" depends on this assumption. Further, he
realized that the words that we speak about ourselves are nothing but words
unless they inhere in a surer source of information. And, inasmuch as our
self-understanding begins and ends with our words, that source can only exist
outside the circle of language – in some metalinguistic and therefore metaphysical realm.

His view represents a pragmatic advance on earlier Hellenistic considerations of the self, at least in the sophistication with which he integrated the
routines by which human thinking concerning self-knowledge is channeled,
patterned, and reproduced. He proposed that to think about the self in any
sense is to engage in an ethical activity. We reflect on the self as if our
notions about ourselves existed on a Platonic ladder of potentially better and
worse types of narratives. We automatically evaluate our story against a version in which we can improve ourselves (or conversely, against one which
represents an inferior alternative). In other words, we recognize the existence
of an ethically oriented master-narrative, even if it is not always in our
thoughts when we weigh the value of individual acts. Augustine believed that
the source of this superior narrative is ultimately divine and that the evidence
for its existence is found in the Bible; there, the deity does not speak in a
language understandable to all humans but through the linguistically accessible
medium of scripture, in which the means of betterment is revealed to the
knowledgeable, that is, the educated reader. As a consequence, self-understanding is an interpretive activity that has much in common with other types
of literary exegesis; and selves, to the degree that they are so interpreted, are
divisible into genres like types of writing.[2] Although the self may be unde-
finable through language, it can nonetheless be made the subject of inquiry
like a text that has to be read, understood, interpreted, and reperformed.

Augustine's method for getting at self-knowledge, which I have sketched
very briefly, reflected a shift from oral to written cultural debate within ancient education. The concern for relations between the self, being, and the
spoken word in earlier works of philosophy, for instance in Plato, derived in

part from the fact that the writings of philosophers were intended to be read aloud rather than silently as they would be nowadays. Even when a text was supposed to be read and studied silently, an attempt was made to create the illusion that the reader was participating in an oral event; an example is the edition of Plotinus's *Enneads*, prepared and published by his student Porphyry. In such works, the written text was a means of communication rather than a repository of facts: it was a reference point in the transition from one type of oral discourse to another.[3] Augustine, following ancient exemplars, remained formally committed to rhetorical and philosophical notions of orality; however, in the *Confessions*, he created a type of discourse concerning the self in which attention was focused on the reader rather than the speaker as the literary model for selfhood. His narrative theory of the self results from this oral yet readerly dialogue. As a result, his self is not the matterless stuff of abstract discussion but is bound up with personality, character, and autobiography.

Augustine stands at the beginning of a lengthy medieval tradition that reaches a turning point in the autobiographical writings of Petrarch. In contrast to Augustine, Petrarch appeared to believe that the most plausible sort of self is one that is constructed from the literary remains of other selves. His chief source of inspiration was the *Confessions* of Augustine, which he discovered, studied, revised, and incorporated into his various accounts of his spiritual adventures. A poet of distinction, Petrarch discreetly avoided discussing one of Augustine's blind spots – his disapproval of classical poetry, which he thought unfit for a Christian. The austere elder Augustine would certainly have disapproved of Petrarch's youthful outpouring of carnal emotion on behalf of a spiritualized Laura, and Francis, who represents Petrarch in the *Secretum*, is sensitive to that potential dissatisfaction. However, had Petrarch been as subtle a reader of Augustine as he was an admirer of his literary achievement, he would have perceived the irony of the bishop of Hippo's diatribe against poetry and rhetoric, since Augustine drew on the works of ancient literature that he knew in telling his life history, possibly to the point of creating the famous conversion scene in Milan in 386 out of a tissue of purely literary events.

Petrarch's best-known autobiographical statement is found in the letter in which he describes his "ascent of Mt. Ventoux" (*Fam.* 4.1). Generations of readers were convinced that this marked the turning point between medieval and Renaissance views of the self until it was shown that Petrarch redated the letter in which the account appears in order to make his age correspond to that of Augustine when the latter converted to the religious life. Petrarch revised his letter collection until he was satisfied that its literary echoes were just right. It is here, rather than in his slavish imitation of ancient dialogues, that one finds his true conversation with his inner self: a conversation that cannot be a spoken dialogue because its product, being printed, is destined for a reading audience. It was the presentation of himself as a reflection of his ancient learning that Petrarch chiefly wanted to leave to posterity. In the *Secretum*, a dialogue takes place with Augustine in which the bishop of Hippo expresses many of the philosophical views in which he himself would like to believe. There is no original philosophy – nothing for instance to compare with Augustine's wrestling with the problems of memory and time in the *Confessions* – just a literary representation of philosophical positions. Moreover, the contrast is not only between the speakers' views but more significantly between two time zones, an idealized past and a menaced present, both of which are configured in a manner that detaches them from specific times and places. If Augustine is ambivalent about book learning, Petrarch's self-image seems unable to exist without this bookishness. He may be distinctively "modern" in his notion of authorship, but he is beyond modernity in his inability to conceive the self outside the boundaries of its literary associations.

Petrarch wrote in the dawn of the age of the printed book. His notion of the self and his literary achievement are inconceivable outside his vision of book culture. He carried a manuscript copy of Augustine's *Confessions* with him wherever he went: his incessant search for the medieval manuscript sources of ancient literature had as its goal a modern library, which was envisaged as a gateway to learning for all who could read. Augustine believed that the self was real but not fully accessible through language: Petrarch seemed to respond with the view that the self could be fully accessible through books but by implication never ontologically real. The literary conquest of the self is suggested both by his prose works and more eloquently by his poetry, where the self hovers between emotionally charged opposites – heat and cold, love and hatred, community and estrangement. The solid ontology of the self that is the bedrock of Augustine's faith is at times overwhelmed by the sheer force of Petrarch's personal feelings, as if the God in which he believed had condemned him to the consequences of his amatory and literary ambitions. If he represents a nascent age of printing, books, and readers, the age would appear to mock him, and he responds to the challenge with less irony than one might expect. Nonetheless, in his studied insecurity concerning literary configurations of selfhood, he is more than halfway to the scepticism of Montaigne.

Another important change in the mode of conceiving the self between Augustine and Petrarch concerns their respective attitudes toward memory. Augustine formally rejected Plato's theory of reminiscence; however, he subtly adapted its essentials to his notion of linguistic and cognitive recognition. In this approach, the external aids to recall, including the tools that make up the ancient arts of memory, are chiefly useful as signposts for inner knowledge that is present in the mind but unrecognized by the subject. By contrast, in Petrarch, artificial memory, as represented by the manuscript book, becomes a source of information in itself, neither presupposing nor acting in concert with any mental operation that does not originate in the sensory perception of the words on the page. For this reason, in Petrarch but not in Augustine, a person can effectively become his or her own book. Augustine believed that narrative provides the individual in search of self-knowledge with clues concerning the self before sin entered the world with time and after it will presumably disappear. The present is a Pauline reference point for the distant past and the future. In Petrarch, this eschatological thinking is stage scenery: the real drama is in the here and now, like the act of reading itself. As a consequence, the presentation of self in the *Secretum* is somewhat theatrical. Far from transcending the scholasticism that he disdained, Petrarch was its last flowering – the transformation of modes of being in the soul into fluctuating literary representations.

I conclude with a word about Descartes, who was the antithesis of a writer like Petrarch, inasmuch as he was sure of what he knew and did not know concerning the self. In his search for the self's reality within the logical proof of the "cogito," he is acknowledged to be an extension of Augustine, whose illustration of the existence of self-consciousness was never utilized by Petrarch. He wrote Part One of the *Discours de la méthode*, well aware of Augustine's description of his childhood temptations through education in the *Confessions*. His disdain of the study of letters echoed Augustine's rebuttal of classical grammatical and rhetorical education, in which the bishop of Hippo asserted that the student learned of words rather than things. Descartes pretended as did Augustine that he early believed that "by means of books a clear and certain knowledge could be obtained of all that was useful in life."[4] But, whereas Augustine sought his certainty in faith, Descartes looked for it in mathematical principles. He constructed a narrative in thought whose denouement was a non-narrative paradigm. His firm distinction between mind and body would appear to deny the possibility of a narrative self. But that is evidently not what he intended; otherwise he would not have written the *Discours* in French in order to appeal to a vernacular audience of persons untutored in the Latin science and philosophy on which his arguments rested. His favorite metaphor – the tree of knowledge whose roots are in metaphysics and whose branches comprise physical sciences – inheres in a theological narrative about self, understanding, and knowledge of the world. He differed chiefly from his predecessors in seeking a type of internality that depends on the operations of the mind alone. In that search, the Western self moved from its earlier metaphysical interdependencies to a tentative position of philosophical autonomy and, in the wake of that transformation, to new and troubling perplexities that remain a part of the discussion of the self to this day.

Notes

1 This chapter summarizes research that is more extensively documented in two of my publications, "The Self and Literary Experience in Late Antiquity and the Middle Ages," *New Literary History* 1994, 25: 839–852; and *Augustine the Reader: Meditation, Self-Knowledge, and the Ethics of Interpretation*, Cambridge, Mass.: Harvard Univ. Press (1996).
2 For a comparable view argued from contemporary psychology, see Jerome Bruner and Susan Weisser, "The Invention of Self: Autobiography and Its Forms," in *Orality and Literacy*, David R. Olson and Nancy Torrance, eds., Cambridge: Cambridge Univ. Press, 1991, pp. 129–148.
3 On this aspect of later ancient thought, see above all Pierre Hadot, *La citadelle intérieure: Introduction aux Pensées de Marc Aurèle*, Paris: Presses Universitaires de France, 1992, pp. 51–68; and, on the important relations between Hadot, Michel

Foucault, and other contemporary discussions of the question, see Arnold I. Davidson, ''Ethics as Ascetics: Foucault, the History of Ethics, and Ancient Thought,'' in *Foucault and the Writing of History*, Jan Goldstein, ed., Oxford: Blackwell, 1994, pp. 63–80.

4 René Descartes, *Discours de la méthode*, ler partie, Etienne Gilson, ed., 5th ed., Paris: J. Vrin, 1976, p. 4. Brian Stock, trans.

5
Normal people

Ian Hacking

During the nineteenth century, the idea of normal people displaced the Enlightenment ideal of Human Nature. The transition is pervasive and infects all of the ways in which we undertake the human sciences, social studies, medicine, and ecology. No field is more suffused with the idea of normalcy than educational theory and practice. Normality does not name a mode of thought. It is a meta-concept that structures a great many modes of thinking. It is one of the most understudied phenomena of the industrial and information-theoretic worlds in which we lived and live. It can be thought of in many contexts, including the political. Here is William Connolly in his recent *Politics and Ambiguity*. He emphasizes norms and normalization more than I shall in what follows. This is because of his analysis of democracy, whose "social ontology," he holds, is "a trunk with two main branches. The trunk is formed by the principle of a subject realizing its essence in a larger world" (Connolly, 1987, p. 9). One branch is individualist, the other is collectivist. Connolly holds that recourse to what counts as normal is an essential way of enabling the two counterpoised branches to interact. In the course of his argument, he points to the extraordinary efflorescence of normality during the past century or so:

> If, as I have suggested, contemporary democratic theory tends to obscure normalizing tendencies built into modern democratic practice, where are the disciplines which foster and maintain these norms? They are located below the threshold of practices incorporated into the logic of democratic legitimation. . . . The proliferation of dualities of normality (normal/abnormal, healthy/sick, rational/irrational, responsible/irresponsible, stable/unstable) correlates with the enlargement of life into which bureaucratically enforced norms have penetrated. The growth of the latter has been dramatic. By comparison, for instance, to a hundred years ago, a much larger proportion of the American population today is either employed in institutions whose primary purpose is to observe, control, confine, reform, cure, or regulate other people (e.g., the police, the military, intelligence agencies, polling centers, reform schools, therapeutic centers, halfway houses, prisons, welfare agencies, nursing homes, judicial institutions) or is the object of these operations (e.g., illegal aliens, prisoners, tax evaders, dissidents, welfare recipients, delinquents, the mentally disturbed, the retarded, nursing home clients, divorcees).
> (Connolly, 1987, p. 8)

Connolly, a political scientist, is properly preoccupied by relatively manifest features of our society, even if normalizing tendencies are obscured by present theories about democracy. Hence he emphasizes institutions whose mandate is to enforce norms. I see that as only one aspect of the way in which the idea of being normal acts upon us and influences our interactions with others. I intend to guide you, both in time and subject matter, behind the scene that Connolly so forcefully describes.

Kinds of people

There are many different if interlocking reasons for thinking about *normal*, the idea. I should first explain my own. I do not expect every reader to agree with me, but I would like to make plain the way that I organize this chapter.

I am interested in kinds of people and their behavior, especially those kinds that are, or have become, objects of knowledge, of scientific inquiry. For short I give the name *human kinds* to these objects of scientific investigation and speculation. I intend an obvious parallel to the philosopher's expression *natural kinds*.

There are a great many alleged differences between the natural and the human sciences. I don't believe in them or at any rate, most of the alleged differences are far from my present concern. I don't, for example, believe in exactly two different methodologies, one for the natural sciences, one for the human sciences. I don't believe that one requires positivist inferences while the other demands *Verstehen*. But I do think that many human kinds do importantly differ, in one respect, from natural kinds. I hold a very general thesis about human kinds, which I won't defend or elaborate here. I think that human kinds have what I call a *looping effect*. In our scientific attempts to know about people and their behavior – sometimes for the sheer sake of knowledge and understanding, but usually in order to help them, to change them, to cure them, to make them behave better, to socialize them – we constantly create new classifications. But the classifications and our knowledge interact with the people classified, who often change or modify their behavior simply in the light of being classified and known about. Also the devising of new classes means that new descriptions of behavior become available. If intentional action is action "under a description," new classifications of behavior change the space of our possibilities: there are new things to do, new ways to be, new kinds of intentional acts to perform. As people quite literally do new things or modify old behaviors, the very knowledge that came into being with the new classifications has to be adjusted, corrected, changed, demanding new knowledge, new classes, and so it goes. Thereby arises what I call the looping effect of human kinds (Hacking, 1995).

This is the only theoretical difference between the natural sciences and the positive human sciences that I shall attend to here. Is there such a looping effect? I state this doctrine not to defend it here, but to place my discussion of normalcy within this perspective. The idea of normalcy is one of the primary enforcers of the looping effect of human kinds.

A metaconcept

The idea of normalcy is at one remove from most of the topics discussed in this volume, although it almost deserves the title of a mode of thought in its own right. Thinking about what's normal or not and worrying about being abnormal, is an endemic feature of both our popular and our scientific culture. The route is from scientific to popular rather than the other way about. Wanting to fit in, to behave pretty much like other people, aside from a few personal choices, must be a characteristic feature of most people in most societies. Perhaps that is a tautology; that's part of what's involved in being a society. But the way of describing the general run of practices and conditions as normal is inherited from more scientific, esoteric talk and practice. I am here concerned with the knowledge end of normalcy, with normality as a mode not so much of thought as of knowledge. It is a way of conceptualizing people and their behaviors. What I call human kinds are kinds about which we try to have knowledge, objects of at least proto-sciences, and it is in connection with such kinds that the idea of the normal exerts its greatest power.

We should begin, however, with a logical fact. Normalcy is what I call a metaconcept, or a second-order concept. These labels will be more familiar to logicians than educators or sociologists. The point is that nothing is normal, full stop. The adjective "normal" has a clear meaning only in conjunction with a noun phrase: a normal five-year-old. In this respect it resembles many English adjectives. One is the word "real." When one speaks of a real X, the criteria for being X are what matter: a real constable, a real Constable. There is no direct sense (argued J. L. Austin, and I agree) in which something can simply be *real* (Austin, 1962, pp. 62–77).

There are lots of words like that. As the logician Gottlob Frege taught well over a century ago, there is no such thing as simply being two. How many are on the stage? (We are watching Bartok's opera, *Bluebeard's Castle.*) Two singers, five people, one opera. Numbers, in Frege's formulation, are concepts that apply to concepts. Existence, as Kant taught over two centuries ago, is not a predicate, although it can sensibly be used as a predicate of predicates. In similar fashion there is no such thing as simply being normal. Your temperature is normal. It's normal to have trouble remembering proper names at your age. A normal five-year-old can (so said Gesell in 1926) draw a triangle from a copy, interpret humor, discriminate weights, and lace shoes.

When I call "normal" a second-order concept, I do not mean that it is more general than some others but that it does not apply directly to individual things or living beings at all. A first-order concept, such as "five-year-old child" applies (or does not apply) to individuals without further ado. So do more general concepts such as "child," "person," or "mammal." But "normal" does not apply until we append a first-order concept, such as "child."

A creature of the nineteenth century

The first modern colloquial meaning of "normal" listed in my dictionary (*Collins*) is "usual, regular, common, typical." *The Oxford English Dictionary* reports that this usage became current only after 1840 and cites a translation from a French biological work in 1828 as the first occurrence in English. The French Revolution did give us the *écoles normales*, set up in 1794. They were to establish the standard for well-regulated education of revolutionary citizens. They were to set the norms for teaching, what should be done, and what should be required. That is the second sense of "normal" given by my dictionary, "constituting a standard." In fact the first given sense, that of being usual or typical, emerged in French only later. A French historical dictionary gives Balzac's *Eugénie Grandet* of 1833, where the context is "the normal state," in this case, the normal state of a nose. Later, in *Cousine Bette*, laziness is called the normal state of artists. Balzac notoriously liked to mock medical jargon, and "normal," in its sense of usual or typical, comes from medicine, and there, the historical dictionaries notwithstanding, we must go for the origins of the modern meaning of "normal."

The classic history of normalcy is Georges Canguilhem's *The Normal and the Pathological*, which began as a *thèse* for the French doctorate of medicine in 1943 (Canguilhem, 1978). That book is no mere narrative. It is an account of how the idea of normalcy entered medicine at a particular conjuncture, as part of the pair normal/pathological. It played an essential role in a struggle between the physiologists and the pathologists in their attempt to settle who would have primary rights over the human body. Canguilhem was well aware that there are many routes to the idea of the normal. On the standard or "norm" side of normal, the new industrial world needed norms of manufacturing, if only so that the parts of machines would fit together. The great armies of the Napoleonic era needed standards. But above all, the battle between physiology and pathology determined the empirical side of normality, namely, as what is usual, to be expected – or healthy.

To oversimplify, the debate went like this. Is disease to be defined as deviation from good health, which is "normal"? Or is the normal to be defined as absence of pathological symptoms and organs? Needless to say, the debate required for its very existence a view of disease as localized in organs and tissues. It required pathological anatomy, in which the defects in parts of cadavers could be recognized by essentially visual criteria – one could see what was wrong with the organ. These criteria were independent of the symptoms of the sick person when still alive. Thus two sets of criteria, physiological and living, and pathological but dead, vied with each other as the very nature of disease.

Canguilhem located the emergence of the normal/pathological above all in the work of the French physician F. J. V. Broussais (1772–1838). In 1816 this young military doctor was a radical critic of what he called the received theories of medicine. He was hated by the establishment. By 1831 he was the professor of general pathology in the medical faculty of Paris. One of his core theses was truly innovative in its day. He held that there is a continuum between the normal and the pathological and that each must be understood to understand the other. How did normality pass beyond the range of medicine? Auguste Comte, near the beginning of his *Système de politique positive*, wrote that "until Broussais, the pathological state obeyed laws completely different from those governing the normal state, so that observation of one could decide nothing for the other. . . . I do not hesitate to state that Broussais's principle [that there is a continuum between the normal and the pathological] must be extended in" the direction of the collective organism, "and I have often applied it there to confirm or perfect sociological laws" (Comte, 1851, Vol. 1, pp. 651–652). William Connolly listed several "dualities of normality (normal/abnormal, healthy/sick, rational/irrational, responsible/irresponsible, stable/unstable)." His list is excellent except that it omits the root duality, normal/pathological.

Comte lifted the medical concept of the *normal state*, or condition of an organ of the body, and made it available for describing society. Indeed, by what seems almost a monstrous pun, he turned this term devised for discussing the body into one that could apply to the normal, that is, healthy, *state* (body politic). Today we are more familiar with Durkheim's writing on normal and pathological societies than with Comte's interminable analyses. Durkheim's lineage is direct, simple and on the surface for all to read. It goes back to Comte, and from there back to Broussais. No depth analysis is needed here. My account of the matter is deeply in debt to Canguilhem's analysis (Hacking, 1990, ch. 17).

Displacing human nature

I began by saying that the Enlightenment idea (and ideal) of Human Nature was displaced during the nineteenth century by the idea of normal people. I mean that with complete seriousness: it is a very strong claim that I do not expect everyone to believe on the spot. I shall not repeat my argument here, but it is a background assumption of this chapter. Not that I rely on it for what I shall say; rather I am driven by it. It makes what I say germane to the philosophy and practice of education. Let me explain why.

What we might call Human-Nature-Thinking is assuredly one highbrow mode of thought, shared by all the memorable figures of the Enlightenment. It was at the core of their moral philosophy. It underlay their vision of rationality. Now one of the themes of the editors' organization of this volume is a contrast between modern and postmodern, with rationality, abstraction, theorizing, and unification of knowledge being a feature of the modern. I do not myself much use those words, "modern" and "postmodern," so popular at present and clearly so helpful to many other thinkers. But here goes. I do think that the modern is all too often described by supposedly postmodern thinkers in a disastrously "modern" and totalizing way, as if our postmoderns were so oedipally transfixed that they regress to modernism when thinking about modernism. The earlier era of human nature and the utterly different present era of normal people are both presented, by our thoroughly modern postmodernists, as part of what they call the modern. It is true that the organizing concepts of human nature and of normal people are both hegemonic. Each provides a way of thinking that is applied to human beings – their actions and their societies – in every possible aspect. Each provides a completely unifying theme and even methodology. Each in short is what is currently called modern. They are nevertheless completely different ways of thinking, and we smudge and blend them at our peril.

I do not say that we have simply lost the concept of human nature. I do not say that *normal people* have *replaced* human nature in our frame of thinking. I say that one conception has *displaced* another. In a vast range of reflections about people and societies we ask after what is normal for a person, in some respect or another, rather than thinking about the nature of being human. How many research grants at our host institution, the Ontario Institute for the Study of Education, make reference to normality and abnormality in people or their behavior? How many are about a contrast between normal and somehow abnormal children, be they gifted or hindered? Lots, I am told. How many grants investigate human nature? How many, in their grant proposals, state that they are about to investigate the nature of children?

One might well say, for example, that the research of Susan Carey and others into the cognitive development of children is into the nature of the developing child, an aspect of human nature. As a matter of fact we don't put it that way. We talk about normal development, the maturation of normal children, the normal range of abilities, the normal range of ages at which various conceptual organizations can be elicited from children.

From a distance one can quite properly see cognitive science as an investigation of human nature or, as Noam Chomsky has so often put it, of the human mind. There is no doubt that the cognitive revolution marked a return to human nature, one made most explicit by Chomsky in his homage to the Enlightenment, *Cartesian Linguistics*. Certainly the nature/normal polarity is quite different from that described by David Olson, who contrasts the modern with Jerome Bruner's notion of narrative thinking. There is nothing narrative about normality. Insofar as postmodern movements oppose unification and encourage diversity, they are also opposed to normalization and, at least from within ivory towers, opposed to many of the institutions mentioned by William Connolly in my opening quotation. But I believe that both cognitivists and postmodernists would be unwise to underestimate the way in which the idea of the normal permeates our lives. I believe it to be inescapable. It may also be integral to what makes a democratic society possible, for that regretfully is Connolly's theme.

It may also be part of what makes an avowedly egalitarian society possible. That takes us closer to the day-to-day working of innumerable non-controlling bits of administration and bureaucracy. The broad range of the middle classes in our societies all collaborate in using normality as a guide in life. It is part of our ethos that we don't want dictators, yet we can't possibly manage all the information that involves public decisions, zoning, garbage collecting, schooling, safety, health. Normality and deviations furnish not only the oil that smooths our debates; it is also the machinery that maintains us in discussion. Some of my remarks will sound as if I'm trying to undermine the normal; the situation is more complex and, as Richard Rorty puts it, ironic. Normality, to switch metaphors, is one of the threads woven into the fabric of daily life in a communicative age. We can't escape it without ripping apart the cloth in which we so dearly need to wrap ourselves.

Fact and value

It may seem strange to date usage of the word "normal" (meaning common, usual, or typical) back only to the 1820s. Yet every historical dictionary in every language confirms that. Of course there has always been Latin *norm-* and the Greek *ortho-*. *Norma* was Latin for a T square. These Greek and Latin roots automatically span the conventional distinction between fact and value. T squares make a right angle: at ninety degrees (descriptive) and right (evaluative). A line normal, or orthogonal, to another is a perpendicular, descriptive, but it is also called right because it is right. The orthodox are, from the point of view of the relevant doxa, right, but we also describe people as orthodox. Orthodontists put the teeth of children right, improve them. They force the teeth to be like those of normal children – a purely descriptive dental structure but, of course, the way children's mouths ought to be. The middle classes spend a fortune on braces, and their children endure years of a kind of oral clitorodectomy or circumcision, all in honor of the great god Normal.

My dictionary's second sense of "normal," as constituting a standard, seems to precede its first sense, of usual or typical. Canguilhem's medical history shows how the first sense became paramount. When "normal" came to mean healthy and to contrast with pathological, it came to be more descriptive – the general run of healthy people. But, of course, what it was describing was desirable. Who would not want a normal heart, kidneys, liver, spleen, lungs, as opposed to diseased ones, subject for pathology? As the word was transferred to sociology and politics, normal conditions were the good ones. Warring states normalized relations. Durkheim, who explicitly considered some societies – including the one in which he found himself – to be pathological, strongly wanted a return to what he conceived of as normalcy.

Thus one can use the word "normal" descriptively to say how things are. But one can also use it to say how things ought to be, to say what is healthy and desirable. The magic of the word is that one can often do both things with a single utterance. The norm may be what is usual, but our most powerful ethical constraints are also called norms. (Incidentally, "norm" in this sense is an even more recent usage than "normal.")

The normal curve

Perhaps the most powerful, but not the only, scientific meaning of "normal" has been fixed for over a century by that most influential of metasciences, the theory of statistical inference. During the 1880s Francis Galton, inventor of regression and correlation, began to call the curve of errors "the Normal curve'' – with a capital *N* because he thought the bell-shaped curve represented the way that many measurable biological characteristics were normally distributed in populations.

It is instructive to trace a brief history of this curve; for more detail, see, for example, Gigerenzer et al. (1989). The curve begins with tossing a fair coin many times. If we toss it 100 times and note only the number of heads, we may get any of the 101 results 0, 1, . . . , 100. The central results, such as 49 or 53, will occur more often in repetitions of this experiment, and a graph of this distribution will be a hump, with almost nothing at the tails (0, 1, 2, or 98, 99, 100). As early as 1708 Abraham de Moivre proved that as we make the number of tosses increase without bound, the limit of this binomial distribution is a smooth curve, which we now describe as shaped like a bell. The next step was the curve of errors, studied around 1800 by Laplace and Gauss. It was a model of the distribution of errors of measurement around a true unknown value, such as the position of a heavenly body. By 1850, at the hands of the astronomer Quetelet, it had become the distribution of many biological quantities, the mean was no longer a true value, regardless of measurement, but an average characteristic of a population. Finally, because the curve was found approximately in so many distributions, psychological tests – most famously IQ tests – were designed so that the distribution of results would follow the curve of errors. In the 1880s Francis Galton began to call the curve of error ''Normal'' – with a capital *N*. His protégé Karl Pearson confirmed this nomenclature in the 1890s. The influence of the biometric and eugenic work of Galton and Pearson was so great that the name stuck in English – but only in English. In other languages we have the probability curve, the Gaussian curve, the curve of errors. But if the curve was the normal or usual distribution, then it could be used to calibrate constructed or theoretical quantities. Thus the distribution of intelligence was ''normalized'' so that the distribution of answers to test questions was distributed along a curve of errors. This was not an empirical discovery, as was the fact that many biometric quantities are so distributed. Instead, tests were designed to have this normal distribution of results.

Thus the progress of the bell curve is as follows: (1) coin tossing; (2) a curve of errors modeled by a Gaussian distribution whose mean is a true unknown quantity, given in nature; (3) a biometric distribution whose mean is an average and that may be a stable property of a population; (4) an artificial distribution of measurements designed so as to take the shape of the curve of errors, because that is believed to be ''normal'' for biological measurements.

Mediocre and normal

There is another tension on the value side of normality. In its medical roots, the normal contrasts with the pathological. The normal is healthy, the good, the desired. That was put in place in the 1820s. Later in the century, normality picked up the statistical connotations that I have just described. Quetelet set things up when, in the 1840s, he gave us the average man. Any characteristic of a human being that could be measured could be averaged, and we could plot the dispersion or deviation around the mean. Thus *l'homme moyen* came into being, cloaked in a Gaussian curve of error. Quetelet began with a distribution of chests of soldiers from Scottish Highland regiments, but he ploughed on and in no time was measuring intellectual and moral qualities as best he could. Crime, suicide, madness, and the like were his meat, but he did not stop at the seamy side of life; he had distributions for poetic talent too. The Aristotelian Golden mean would be replaced by the physiognomy of the average man, which would be the canon of beauty henceforward. After that it would become a mental standard, a moral standard, a spiritual standard.

Deviations weren't thought about sufficiently before Francis Galton, who in the 1870s worked out the theory of regression and correlation. We tranquilly speak of regression toward the mean. That comfortable elitist Galton was more blunt. He who invented the idea called it regression toward mediocrity. The curve in terms of which one did the computations came to be called "the normal curve" – Galton's term, but made official by his protégé Karl Pearson. Notice that in this usage the normal is not necessarily desirable. For we get the normal as mediocre rather than the normal as healthy. Hence arises a fundamental tension. I have found it useful to represent the tension in terms of two figureheads, Galton and Durkheim (Hacking, 1990, pp. 168–169). Durkheim worked within the normal/pathological medical tradition transmitted to his generation by Comte and a host of others. Galton worked within the statistical tradition transmitted to him by Quetelet, but where Quetelet saw the average, the mean, as a canon of beauty – thus still in the medical tradition – Galton transformed it to something else. We still work unwittingly with both notions and glide effortlessly from one to the other without consciously noticing it or, at any rate, without noting it.

Yet our language reflects our apperceptions, our dim awarenesses. Allow me to put on my hat as a philosopher in the tradition of linguistic analysis. Consider phrases of the form "a normal N," where N is a noun: a normal child. We use this form of words – and I mean exactly this form of words, not some paraphrase – only for nouns for kinds of things or beings for which we think there may be health or pathology, or so it appears. A normal bridge? A normal pie? If we overhear talk of a normal lake, we at once think of one that is not polluted or turned acid by rain, that is, a healthy, nonpathological lake.

We don't use the expression "a normal N" in a bell-shaped, Galtonian way, where the normal may be mediocre. We use it in a Broussaisian, medical way. A normal eight-year-old contrasts with a child who is retarded or disturbed but not (at first hearing) with a gifted eight-year-old. But, to return to my historicist mode, it is not to be thought that the concept "eight-year-old *child*" automatically takes the metaconcept "normal." On the contrary, the eight-year-old must be thought of as a being whose development can be healthy or pathological, and that requires an entire infrastructure of medical, pedagogic, and psychological thinking.

Normal and typical

There's one last tension that I must mention in this anatomy of normality. The dictionary said that "normal" means common, usual, typical. But when we turn to the social, human, medical, educational, and even cognitive sciences, there's a very big divide between the typical and what is normal as determined by statistical analysis. The battles have been fought out over and over again. For social scientists we have the contrast between Durkheim and Weber. Weber believed in ideal types. Durkheim, although no Galtonian, used a century of French suicide statistics as the basis of what seems to be his most oft-cited book. In medicine in the 1850s Claude Bernard inveighed against statistics. Since he was investigating urine at the time, he rudely said that if you want the urine of the average man, collect it at the pissoir of the gâre de Lyon. No, insisted this greatest of biomedical investigators, we want an individual and to know about that man and his urine as specimens of the type. In social economics Ferdinand Le Play provided the most extraordinary household budgets of the European worker, from the Urals to Sheffield, from Lapland to North Africa. The first stage in his inquiry was to spend a very long time in a community, talking to many people, especially leadership people, to determine the typical mining family of the region, the typical laundress and her family, the typical cabinetmaker and his family.

American studies of child development provide a cameo illustration of the struggles between the normal as typical and the normal as statistical. I take for granted here the idea that children do develop physically, mentally, and morally in a lawlike way. That is itself by no means a universally human conception, but one that, as the West knows it, was established as common knowledge only during the nineteenth century. Even within that framework, the normal child was something new. Perhaps the first author to publish that very phrase was the founder of American psychology and teacher of the first generation American graduate students in the subject, G. Stanley Hall. In 1879 he had already written descriptively, using the phrase "normal people." He was writing about the normal child by 1891. By 1894 his students would routinely say, for example, "Ten boys, normal, were tested." I am indebted to James Wong's *The Very Idea of the Normal Child* (1993) for this and the following information.

Hall's conception was not statistical. Its roots were in the journals, transcribed by parents, about their children's growing up. Charles Darwin was a trendsetter. In 1877 he published notes on the intellectual and physical development of an infant: his son. Specially formatted diaries for noting the developmental events of childhood were in print from 1882 as *The Mother's Record*. In 1883 Hall published his findings about the knowledge of children entering school (a study patterned after much earlier German work). Does the child know the number 3? The number 4? Its elbow? Has it ever seen a beehive? A willow? He made his results known as *The Contents of Children's Minds*. The consequences for child-centered education were immense. Here I emphasize only that Hall aimed at describing the typical child entering school. His model was in some ways Galtonian, but it was not statistical.

How was it Galtonian? Galton had made composite photographs of military officers, criminals, Jews, using multiple exposures to produce what he held to be characteristic physiognomy of each class. Hall designed questionnaires whose results could be combined to give the characteristic mental profile of a child at a certain age. The project went mad, for Hall won the ear of Elias Russell, principal of Worcester Normal School, who set his student teachers to the task, producing 14,000 profiles that no one could do anything with. Hall designed a questionnaire for children's anger. He demanded of the teacher-reporters that they be "photographically objective, exact, minute and copious in detail" and then asked for "any notes, however incomplete, upon any aspect of the subject." The next generation of students didn't care for this. "Empirical philistinism," said Hugo Münsterberg at Harvard. In 1890 Catell gave the first American mental tests; in the next decade a statistical methodology was to emerge that has ever since characterized American empirical psychology. Hall's search for an account of the typical child was usurped by the rule that only statistical data would count. As British statistical techniques crossed the Atlantic, the normal, as statistical rather than typical, became dominant.

This is not to say that the typical disappeared. Piaget's developmental studies are the most famous of those that relied on a few favored children. There is still a very interesting tension in that field. This is to be expected. If one is investigating fundamental cognitive laws of the human mind, statistics should not matter. In an enquiry into human nature, rather than normal people (in this case, children), statistics should be irrelevant; it is the type that counts. Yet at the same time there might be a distribution of rates of development of children sorted along some lines or other, social, educational, familial, geographical, ethnic, racial, birth order, rural/urban, who knows what. What are the relevant types? Our colleges teach the solution: use statistics!

Human kinds

Now I briefly return to my starting point, human kinds. By human kinds I mean kinds of people and their behavior, about which we hope to have knowledge and we think fit the needs for scientific enquiry. A few of these kinds are denoted by old words, such as "child." More are denoted by amalgams and extensions: There have been five-year-olds forever, but "five-year-old" is a neologism. Most human kinds are denoted by new words or words with new meanings: "autistic" for children (devised by Leo Kanner, publishing in 1943), "gifted," "moron" (invented by H. H. Goddard, one of the early testers of intelligence). Even "genius" in its present sense is a new word. The endless array of terms remodeled, retooled, or simply invented for the scientific study of human beings is unlike the comparable array propagated in the natural sciences. For we apply these terms to people and their behavior. Sometimes those who are described take the names upon themselves; others, such as the autistic child, are too weak with respect to the namers to use the names themselves. But the lives of the named are arranged to fit the categories into which they are fitted. Those who accept the names see themselves anew and have new descriptions under which they may act. A new human kind leaves little in place. Where microphysics has its principle of indeterminacy, according to which measurement affects the measured, the human sciences have the phenomenon of looping, whereby classifying affects members of the class, who change or mold themselves accordingly. Or, resentfully, the classified may elevate their class, escaping from their classifiers (gay pride, black power). Or they may change themselves so as no longer to fit the criteria. In any event the very features of the class into which they were classified change, and so the classifiers must go back to work, reclassifying, redefining, recharacterizing.

The metaconcept of normalcy gives an extra spin within the looping. For we not only have a class, but also a distribution of a characteristic within a class, centering on the normal. Broussaisian medical-normal is good, healthy. We want to make members of the class normal and invent all sorts of normalizing techniques. Members of the class who hear what's normal want to be healthy and normal and do their best to conform, thereby changing, to say the least, the statistical distribution. But then there is Galtonian mediocre-normal. The ambitious don't want to be that, and so they change and hence change distributions. Such a phenomenon is played out annually across the United States with the Standard Achievement Tests, the Graduate Record Examinations, and the like. These are cunningly designed to be completely neutral for American white middle-class students, whatever their background. But all those white middle-class children who are fairly mediocre but have ambitions or are prodded by family, teachers, or peers go to SAT courses or work through an SAT book "guaranteed to increase your score by at least 30 points." Few human kinds are as regimented as those devised by educators or better known to those who are sorted, namely, the students. Hence nowhere else is there so much self-conscious looping in valiant attempts to work the system of classification to advantage. This is merely an extreme, a mockery of the normal, but in almost every case, I venture, in which a human kind becomes susceptible to the metaconcept of normalcy, there is an increase in the interaction between the classification and the people or behaviors that are classed. There are two different styles of interaction depending upon whether the medical or the mediocre type of normalcy is in play. Since, on occasion, both may be in play at once in connection with the same classification, there may be a wrenching tension, and hence the two types of normalcy interfere analogously to the way in which different optical wavelengths can interfere to produce diffraction patterns.

I do not regard this as the end of the story, but it is a good point at which to close this discussion. This volume derives from a workshop held under the auspices of the Ontario Institute for the Study of Education. Many well-informed educators, education researchers, and administrators have nagging worries about the idea of normal children, abilities, development. By enlarging the panorama, I hope they may be better able to grasp and formulate those worries. For it is part of the ideology of normality that it is neutral, objective, a way of assessing what *is*. And so it is. But simultaneously two other things are true of normalcy. First, it is a powerful instrument for saying what *ought* to be, for such is the magic of "normal" that it spans *is/ought*. Second, unlike the descriptors of the natural sciences, it leaves nothing in its place; by saying what *is*, it at once sets going changes in the status quo. To exaggerate: As soon as you've said what's normal, it isn't.

References

Austin, J. L. (1962). *Sense and Sensibilia*, reconstructed from the manuscript notes by G. J. Warnock. Oxford: Oxford Univ. Press.

Canguilhem, Georges (1978). *The Normal and the Pathological*, C. R. Fawcett, trans. Dordrecht and Boston: Reidel.

Comte, August (1851). *Système du politique positive*. Paris: Algave.

Connolly, William E. (1987). *Politics and Ambiguity*, Madison: Univ. of Wisconsin Press.

Gigerenzer, Gerd, et al. (1989). *The Empire of Chance: How Probability Changed Science and Everyday Life*. Cambridge: Cambridge Univ. Press.

Hacking, Ian (1990). *The Taming of Chance*. Cambridge: Cambridge Univ. Press.
   (1995). "The Looping Effects of Human Kinds," in *Causal Cognition: A Multidisciplinary Approach*, D. Sperber et al., eds. Oxford: Oxford Univ. Press, pp. 351–383.

Wong, James (1993). The Very Idea of the Normal Child, Ph.D. thesis, University of Toronto.

6

Modes of reasoning and the politics of authority in the modern state

Yaron Ezrahi

6.1 Holism, individualism, and modern modes of reasoning

In the dedication of *The Prince* to Lorenzo di Medici of Florence, Niccolo Machiavelli expresses the hope that the distinguished reader of his book will not deem it "presumptuous on the part of a man of humble and obscure condition to attempt to discuss and direct the government of princes, for, in the same way that landscape painters station themselves in the valleys in order to draw mountains or high ground, and ascend an eminence in order to get a good view of the plains, so it is necessary to be a prince to know thoroughly the nature of the people, and one of the populace to know the nature of princes."[1] Within a universe organized according to the principle of hierarchy, Machiavelli implies, there is first the view of society from the top, the view opened to the monarch at the peak of the pyramid; then there is the view from the bottom, where the subjects raise their eyes to see the monarch and the aristocracy above them. The former is the view of a single person who can see the whole people from the highest point of the social ladder. The latter consists of the views of a multitude of individual subjects looking at their king from their lower station. Both the monarch and the populace are looking at each other from opposite sides of the same pyramid.

Machiavelli does not mention – and in fact discards – the traditional notion of a God's-eye view, the divine gaze that sees simultaneously both the king and his subjects from above. A view that encompasses the entire socio-political order, including the ruler and the ruled, presupposes a superhuman perspective stationed outside the temporal and spatial frames of the mortal gaze. Machiavelli's works, insofar as he focuses upon the interactions between the prince and his subjects, implicitly claim to approximate or inherit the divine perspective that encompasses the entire political order from a point outside it. Machiavelli is, of course, thus laying down the foundations of the eventual claims of a science of politics to constitute a superior knowledge of public affairs because, beyond the actions of the principle actors, it also

I am indebted to Don Handelman and the late Lea Shamgar-Handelman whose works as well as our ongoing conversations made invaluable contributions to my thinking on the subject of this chapter. I am grateful also to Mordechai Kremnitzer for useful critical comments on sections of this chapter.

encompasses their interactions and effects. *The ability to have an outsidelike view of the whole is disengaged here from the social position of the individual observer and grafted onto his method of thinking and reasoning.*

Here Machiavelli anticipates the detached scientific outlook on phenomena as a secular equivalent of a God's-eye synoptic view of the world, as a product of a method available, at least in part, to any "man of humble and obscure condition."[2] Machiavelli's concern that his book should not be regarded as presumptuous is, therefore, understandable. The thought that individual thinkers such as Machiavelli or Galileo can imitate the divine powers of comprehensive viewing by adopting what gradually came to be regarded as scientific methods of thinking and reasoning was seen by many as arrogant. The impression of arrogance was, however, tempered by the gradual development of a conception of scientific knowledge as the product of cooperation among many individuals, a view that, on the whole, competed successfully with the alternative notion of scientific knowledge as the product of a few geniuses with divinelike powers of reasoning.

Science, therefore, increasingly came to be regarded as both a more democratic and more valid way of knowing because of the reliance on methods that could be used to discipline and augment individual thinking as well as "externalized" as techniques of conveying or demonstrating claims of knowledge to others. As such, the rise of scientific modes of thinking was associated with the empowerment of the individual as a challenger of hierarchical forms of both knowledge and authority. As Louis Dumont argues persuasively, the most important single characteristic of modern ideology is the rise of the category of the individual as an entity prior to and constituent of the socio-political whole.[3]

Within modern, increasingly secular societies, the spreading values of individualism and the complementary value of egalitarianism supported the evolution of a conception of science as a mode of thinking and persuading which is compatible with the assault on traditional hierarchies and the construction of novel, modern forms of authority. In the works of early modern thinkers such as Hobbes and Descartes, for example, the ontologization of the individual is inseparable from scientific modes of thinking and reasoning, which allow individuals to become sufficiently detached from the world to be able to criticize the commonly shared ideas of things and reconstruct the world on a new basis. Scientific methods of reasoning based on mathematics, geometry, or careful observations thus became trusted as the means by which the whole, the idea as well as the institutions of the socio-political order, can be saved without conceding or denying the individualistic egalitarian presuppositions of new conceptions of knowledge and political authority. As the foundations of the modern socio-political order, individualism and egalitarianism had, therefore, redefined the parameters of the very relations between thinking, knowing, or viewing on the one hand and political authority on the other.

Perhaps the most fundamental problem faced by modern political and social thought following the discrediting of pre-given natural or divinely created hierarchies was how a conception of the whole could be developed and sustained despite the corrosive and fragmenting affects of individualism and egalitarianism. Put another way, the question was how hierarchy, authority, and legitimacy could be grounded in individualistic–egalitarian axioms.[4] The dimensions of the change posed by this question are apparent if one juxtaposes modern modes of thought, which have supposedly allowed equal individuals to reach agreement or "reason alike" without relying on hierarchical authority, with traditional modes of thought that presupposed the primacy of order and hierarchy over the individuals conceived as its parts. I would like to suggest that the powers of modern styles of thought, such as probabilistic, empirical reasoning or even deductive reasoning, which proceeds from testimonies about sense experience, derived much of their attraction for thinkers such as Hobbes and Locke from their perceived utility as techniques of thought by means of which individuals could discover and agree on their appropriate relations to the socio-political order as a whole. Deliberately simplifying the point for the purposes of our discussion, I would like to suggest that by comparison with traditional conceptions of order, according to which the whole is primary and the particular individuals are its derivative parts, modern conceptions of order imply the primacy of the individual and define the whole, the collective order, as derivative. Thus, while in traditional styles of social or political thought, the parts are deduced from knowledge of the pre-given whole, in modern socio-political thought, the movement, as is paradigmatically illustrated in social contract theories, is from the independent individuals to the whole. *While traditional deductive and teleological modes of reasoning characteristically upheld the building of the order from top to bottom, modern modes like empirical probabilistic reasoning derived some of their special power from their apparent relevance as modes of thought and reasoning, which can uphold the process of building the political order from the bottom up, from the parts to the whole.* Furthermore, attempts to anchor knowledge claims in what a multiplicity of discrete individuals can experience, or in universalistic forms of reasoning they can master, had profound political significance when examined against the constraints imposed on the political order by forms of experiencing and reasoning, which seemed available only to a few privileged individuals.

Once the central issue posed by modern political theory as to how the polity or the state could be built from the bottom up, from a multitude of discrete individuals to a socio-political whole, the question of what were "natural," feasible, or valid modes of thought; of reasoning; or of social consent became inseparable from the question of how and what kind of political order and authority could be established. If in traditional hierarchical systems the presumed givenness of the whole has tended to stress the issue of how the parts hang together, in non-hierarchical systems, the questions of moving from discrete elements to a whole raised the much more acute problem of how an order, how a whole, is at all possible. In some respects, one can suggest, therefore, that within socio-cultural contexts where hierarchical systems are conceived uncritically as unconditional givens, modes of thought or reasoning tended to relate to authority in terms of their latent functions as justifying or legitimating relations of subordination. By comparison, in the context of individualistic–egalitarian systems, modes of thought or reasoning have often become engaged in the prior dilemma of how, from a starting point of the non-order inherent in the condition of egalitarian individualism, a social order can be composed or constructed at all.

By implication, the question about the available and desirable modes of thought is much more socially or politically loaded where the central issue is how the actions of discrete individuals can be coordinated to generate a stable order. Where the socio-political order is conceived as primordial or natural, the role of thought is much more confined to legitimating the pre-established relations among the parts or between the parts and the whole.

Our schematic correlation of modes of thought or reasoning with structures of authority must, however, be qualified. Any account of socio-historical experience is bound to suggest a much more complex mix of often competing and contradictory uses of the same modes of thoughts and reasoning. As we shall see, for instance, in the case of Hobbes, in some contexts modes of reasoning that proceed from parts to a whole can, in fact, serve substantially holistic and only formally individualistic and egalitarian conceptions of order. What is important to our discussion is to contrast two modes of reasoning. The first implicitly constructs the individual as a thinking agent and also empowers that individual to think and act in a non-conformist way, to be a builder of novel structures and institutions. The second merely serves to le-gitimate the adjustment of individual conduct to pre-determined norms as the expression of voluntary individual choices. We are also concerned here with how different styles of reasoning are perceived as influencing socially wider patterns of behavior. Such political aspects of reasoning suggest why argu-ments about the valid modes of thinking or reasoning are very often, explic-itly or implicitly, arguments about who can or ought to participate in the socio-political process or in the economic, moral, or cultural spheres of action and what kinds of relations between participants are possible and desirable. The modern ideological move from corporate and hierarchical images of or-der to egalitarian individualism was largely accompanied by the valorization of modes of reasoning that appeared to be compatible with the idea of in-dividuals as autonomous thinking agents as well as with the idea of the same individuals as thinking and acting agents who can reach agreements and so-cially coordinate their actions.

6.2 Modes of reasoning and the constitution of the modern order

Most influential attempts to explore and systematize modes of reasoning that can uphold a social order based on voluntary individualism were made by early modern thinkers such as Descartes, Hobbes, and Locke. Descartes took a most crucial step in the construction of the modern individual by dignifying the self as a thinking agency. He did this by the double move of *skepticism*, which separates the individual from the given world which his critical mind decomposes, and constructionist, methodical *rationalism* by which the indi-vidual reconstructs the world on a new basis. The Cartesian move to link thinking and the ontological privileging of the individual as a distinct being defines the modern parameters of the relations between thought and authority. Descartes anchors the individual in a mode of thought that is at once individual, even reflexively individualistic, and social, both self-referential and socially communicable, a mode of thought by which the world is not found but rather constructed by procedural reason that each individual can discover within his/her own mind. While Descartes considers using skeptical thought in order to decompose the world before he resorts to rational thought to reconstruct it, the shift from the use of reason to negate and decompose to using reason to affirm and compose is not unproblematic. Some of Descartes's critics thought that by following the skeptical course of thinking, Descartes was never able to convincingly shift to the other mode.[5]

What distinguishes the Cartesian move as modern is largely the coupling of the contemplative and constructive functions of reason. While for Augustine the self moves through introspection to a spiritual ascent in the course of which the individual as an imperfect fragment (of creation) seeks to find his/her place within the perfect, divine whole, for Descartes the thinking subject is not teleologically bound to a given cosmic order. The thinking subject is self-constituted as a master of "procedural reason"[6] that each individual can, in principle, use in order to mentally construct and understand the world as a mechanism. To understand the world as a machine is, of course, also to open the way for instrumental-controlling reason.[7] It is as if Descartes provides a method for the individual construction of the order of which he/she is both a creator and a part. The methodical employment of one's own reason provides each individual with a tool to detach from and then re-engage in the world. Reason validates procedures through which discrete individuals can make safe inferences that in turn, pattern their actions and interactions. The "methodical doubt," the Cartesian act of detachment and negation, allows the individual, as it were, to step outside the world and view it from a semi-divine external perspective. In Descartes, thinking divinizes individualism. Individual existence and, therefore, also the authority of the individual are founded here on the act of reflexive thinking. Just as the observer has to distance him/herself in order to have a better view of the object, reason allows the thinking subject to step back from the familiar conventions in order to have an "objective" conception of the world. Descartes empowers the individual to discover within his/her own mind the procedure of thinking through which both the integrity of individuals and their interactions can be secured.

Despite the profound differences in their respective theories of knowledge and politics, Hobbes, like Locke, believed that all reasoning starts with sense experience and moves by means of the correct use of words to more elaborate acts of inferring, proving, and demonstrating. Particularly pertinent to our discussion is Hobbes's pre-occupation with the sources of errors in human reasoning and with the problem of controversies. While he holds that controversies depend for their settlement upon the intervention of authoritative third-party arbitrators, he still tries to contain the potential areas and dangers of conflicts of opinion by establishing the "right" methods of reasoning. "All men, by nature," observes Hobbes, "reason well when there are good principles, for who is so stupid, as both to mistake in geometry and also to persist in it when another detects his error in him."[8] Hobbes combines here the capacity of all individuals "to reason alike," their capacity "to reason well," and, finally, their capacity to be persuaded or pressured by others to correct their own errors of reasoning. Reasoning well is a process that is upheld and reinforced by other people and is, therefore, partly a social process. Hobbes relies on social and moral sanctions in order to compel individual reasoners to correct their mistakes not only in deductive inferences but also in matters of observable facts. He holds that when two or more individuals are conscious of the same fact, which is as much as "to know it together . . . it was and ever will be reported a very evil act for any man to speak against his conscience or to corrupt or force another to do so."[9] Much of the *Leviathan* deals with the ways in which equal individuals who are locked in unresolvable conflicts when each insists on his right to use his force can nevertheless reach agreement on shared truths when they learn to reason well and correct each other's errors. But, precisely because reasoning alike and well may not be sustainable over long durations, Hobbes suggests that the multitude decide first to establish the grand arbitrator, the sovereign. Egalitarian individualism and good reasoning combine, according to Hobbes, to establish hierarchy as an instrument serving the citizens who empower it to settle what would otherwise be unresolvable conflicts. The sovereign is, in Hobbes's theory, not a primordial given that warrants that a genuinely superior person can command his subordinates and expect their obedience. It is a legal fiction created through mutually reinforcing individual acts of reasoning from shared axioms about the nature of experience. However, according to Hobbes, radical egalitarian individualism can give rise to hierarchical authority structure, provided the appropriate methods of procedural reason are used. Hobbes's choice of geometry as the model of reasoning that he would like to apply in human affairs stems largely from his search for certainty as a foundation of unchallengeable authority. By comparison, John Locke's disposition to rely on probabilistic empirical reasoning in public affairs is associated with a less rigid conception of authority.

Despite the obvious differences between them, Locke, like Descartes, proceeds through the double moves of negation and construction to constitute the individual as both the anchor and the builder of knowledge. Whereas, following the skeptical decomposition of the given order of ideas, Descartes grounds the construction process in reflexive procedural reason within the framework of Locke's associationist psychology, the process of learning and knowing proceeds from pure sense perceptions registered on an initially empty mental *tabula rasa* and continues through processes of reflection, analysis, and construction to a correct picture of the world. Both Cartesian rationalism and Lockean empiricism thus evolve modes of reasoning that seem to ensure the integrity of the individual as a thinking and knowing agency and the kind of socially shared principles of reasoning that harmonize the ideas and actions of many such individuals. By comparison with geometric-like deductive reasoning, probabilistic empirical reasoning seems to imply different kinds of connections among discrete thinking and reasoning subjects. While deductive reasoning or acts of inferring that proceed from axioms can be performed by an individual independently of other individuals and require minimal social interaction, empirical reasoning seems to depend upon acts of accumulating, comparing, and analyzing testimonies that add up to a much thicker social interaction.

Formal procedural reasoning of the kind used by Descartes or Hobbes is, therefore, compatible with more atomistic insular individualism, while Lockean probabilistic empiricism and associationist reasoning pre-suppose more socially interactive individualism. There are some strong indications that these kinds of differences have been relevant to the selective processes through which mathematical–geometrical styles of reasoning have been adopted and diffused in the French legal–political context and empirical styles of reasoning became so deeply integrated into Anglo-Saxon political and legal thinking.[10]

There is, of course, another distinct category of processes through which the socio-political order is built from the bottom up that does not rest so much on the power of thinking and reasoning to discipline individual actions or social behavior but on the spontaneous or natural actions of individuals as the causes of the social order. Bernard Mandeville stated this idea in a most popular literary form in his *Fable of the Bees* (1723) and Adam Smith later developed it in his influential theory of self-regulating economy.[11] According to this school of thought, when individuals follow their natural disposition to pursue their own selfish interests, their actions and interactions are likely to promote the general welfare, the general social good, even though they neither intend nor even have a conception of this general good. The attractiveness of the idea that a mechanism of self-regulating order may be anchored in dispositions inherent in natural human conduct lies, of course, in the implication that in such circumstances reliance on demanding modes of thought and reasoning may be unnecessary, that order, equilibrium, and welfare may be served without the intervention of the state or the mediation of a potent epistemology. Whereas in Mandeville, the goodness of the system does not depend on the goodness of its parts ("Thus every part was full of vice yet the whole mass a paradise"), in Smith, it is not the intentions of the individual but an external mechanism, "an invisible hand," which leads the actions of individuals who pursue their own interests to contribute to the general welfare. This approach shifts the burden of building the whole, the socio-political order, from behavior directed by what Hobbes called "good principles" of reasoning to behavior driven by individual passions, feelings, and interests. In this approach, the bridges linking the multitude of equal individuals to a stable socio-political order do not rest on the validity of a maximalist epistemology, on the capacity of individuals to think and reason well or to socialize individual behavior by means of effective persuasion.

Because this approach appears more compatible with moral and epistemological pessimism, it is often also perceived as more "realistic." A very influential variant of this approach is found in *The Federalist*, No. 10, where Madison argues that "as long as the reason of man continues to be fallible and he is at liberty to exercise it, different opinions will be formed.'' From this observation, Madison infers that it is foolish to expect even enlightened statesmen to adjust clashing opinions and interests. He suggests, therefore, a constitutional mechanism that does not remove the causes of factions, which flourish under conditions of freedom but control their effects. While Rousseau was not a moral pessimist, he, too, was sufficiently touched by epistemological pessimism, sufficiently anxious about the infirmities of reason as a foundation of the polity to seek reinforcements outside the spheres of human thinking and reasoning. But unlike Mandeville or Smith, Rousseau did not rely on the indirect effects of human passions, vices, or interests as much as on the dogmas of a civil religion and the discovery in the heart of each individual of such social feelings as compassion. But the history of modern political theories and ideologies shows that as a means of cementing the political order, emotions have often been criticized on the grounds of being unstable, prone to provoke violence, and, most importantly for our discussion, incongenial for the kind of detached engagements that Descartes, Hobbes, and Locke thought both possible and necessary for securing the integrity and separateness of the individual in the socio-political context. It is worth noting that while criticism of the premises of Smithian ''free market'' capitalism, on the part of Marxist thinkers for instance, often charges that treating individuals as unthinking forces or causes in the economic–political order dehumanizes the individual as a thinking, self-directing agency, enlightenment thinkers like Condorcet and nineteenth- and twentieth-century liberal thinkers such as J. S. Mill, Karl Popper, and Jurgen Habermas have often criticized the anti-individualistic implications of bonding individuals by means of emotions. Liberal political theory more than Marxist political theory, of course, has tended to stress the links enunciated particularly in Cartesian and Kantian philosophies between the constitution of the individual as a thinking subject and his/her dignity, humanity, and freedom. From this perspective, Rousseau's contribution to nationalism is a source of many reservations.

Modern responses to the dilemma of building the socio-political order from the bottom up seem preoccupied with the twin anxieties of losing the individuals, the ''parts,'' in an all-encompassing whole or losing the whole in a multitude of individuals. I would like to suggest that as ideological resources for modern political world making, modes of reasoning are selected and legitimated in part according to their perceived uses for achieving the desirable balance between the integrity of autonomous, free individuals and the integrity of the socio-political whole. Between these two poles, conservative, order-oriented thinkers like Herder, de Maistre, and Bonald, despite their diverse perspectives, regarded individuals – in one sense or another – as extensions or reflections of an ontologically prior whole, a community, a culture or a society, which, like an organism, is not the result of rational construction or contractual transactions among autonomous individuals. The whole, in this view, is often conceived as inherent in the parts, in individuals who are treated as following, consciously or not, a design immanent in the scheme of things. At the other pole, liberal theorists who privilege the on-

80 YARON EZRAHI

tological status and value of individuals are led either to the notion that egalitarian individuals can generate several variants of liberal and democratic orders or, more recently, to the notion of an order in constant flux, which often amounts to no order at all. In any case, egalitarian individualism seems to ground political orders that lack a deterministic closure although the psycho-political overreaction to such a state of socio-political under-determinism can, under certain circumstances, encourage the rise of totalitarianism (a modern form of holism).[12] In order to impoverish the resources of hierarchy and the legitimation of power, the liberal–democratic tradition tends to assimilate a degree of skeptical thinking whose latent political effect is to sustain a degree of unstructured openness, a measure of benign disorder, uncertainty, or undecidability, which can be resolved neither by reasoning nor legitimate authority. When individualism and egalitarianism are taken seriously, the very possibility of a realized whole, a particular institutionalized whole, which would limit the possibilities of alternative orders, is foreclosed. Hence, skepticism (especially the moderate variants) can be regarded as a mode of thought that can be enlisted to the protection of individualism against the pressures of hierarchy and holism.

6.3 Modes of legal reasoning and structures of modern legal and political authority

Modern theories of sovereignty that anchor the source of power and authority in the people tend to encourage conceptions of the law and of legal reasoning that are consistent with the task of building the socio-political order from the bottom up. Such conceptions of the law and their corresponding practices would tend to vary in different socio-cultural contexts, reflecting, apparently, significant variations in the very definitions of agencies and legitimate methods of order construction. Therefore, the legal context constitutes a particularly illuminating site in which to examine and discern the close relations between specific modes of reasoning and particular models of authority. While differences between legal systems cannot be simply reduced to differences between few principles of reasoning and authority, comparative studies of legal cultures indicate that distinct modes of legal reasoning in Continental and Anglo-Saxon societies, and even, within the latter category, between England and America, relate to distinct notions of orders and different distributions of authority between individuals or voluntary associations and the state.

Mirjan R. Damaŝka suggests that in Continental systems of justice legal reasoning presumes the possibility of conclusive conflict or dispute resolution, of a legal or judicial closure based on the belief that a truth relevant to deciding a case can be found and established. In Continental systems of law, the process of sorting out and using evidence tends to be inquisitorial rather than adversarial and presupposes, therefore, a propensity to rely on the hierarchical authority of the judge, who represents the state rather than on the horizontal authorities of the competing litigants or jurors.[13] Typical of the hierarchical mode of legal reasoning, according to Damaŝka, is also the special influence of professionals whose function is, among other things, to routinize and "typify" situations using broad ordering schemes.[14] Hierarchical perspectives and styles of reasoning that move from top to bottom stress the advantages and requirements of a synoptic gaze from above and, consequently, also of the needs of consistency and uniformity among diverse cases. Hierarchical authorities encourage, in the legal context, the use of intellectual strategies that minimize diversity, contingencies, and uncertainties at the bottom. By contrast, non-hierarchical – what Damaŝka calls the "coordinate" – mode of authority encourages the employment of styles of reasoning that accommodate much greater diversity, contingencies, uncertainties, and inconsistencies. "From the Continental perspective," he writes, "the English Royal judge could appear to be more like the moderator of a judicial conference or perhaps a supervisor of fair proceedings, the announcer of their outcome and the enforcer of judgments rather than the quintessential decision maker. In this perspective, the real adjudicators would seem to be jurors."[15] From a Continental perspective, observes Damaŝka, the real decision makers in the traditional English legal apparatus were laymen. Common law is regarded as the gradual growth of experience from the bottom.[16] Damaŝka, then, sees English and Continental styles of reasoning as corresponding to distinct styles of authority. The relative Anglo-Saxon tendency to moralize, even politicize, legal decisions is associated with the trend to decentralize authority, to rely upon substantive rather than formalistic (and more technical) standards of judicial decision making and tolerate greater pluralism and inconsistencies within the legal system. Also noteworthy is the propensity of decentralized, horizontally coordinate legal structures to be associated with modes of reasoning that can uphold the symmetries of individuals as equal partners in voluntary contracts. Such a system is disposed to stress the use of modes of reasoning to uphold the possibility of reaching agreements or negotiating under the constraints of egalitarian individualism rather than to legitimate or voluntarize obedience to authority.

Despite the obvious exceptions and reservations, from a comparative perspective, the differences between Continental and Anglo-Saxon styles of reasoning deepen when the Continental systems are compared to the American. Even a comparison within the Anglo-Saxon category between English and American legal cultures suggests discontinuities that indicate the extent to which the European features of the English system distinguish it from the American. P. S. Atiyah and Robert S. Summers in their study of the continuities and discontinuities between the English and the American systems suggest that when they are juxtaposed, it is the English system that appears as hierarchic and formalistic and the American that, by comparison, is both more decentralized and disposed to substantive legal reasoning.[17] The much more radically egalitarian American system seems more prone to rely heavily on characteristically anti-hierarchical modes of reasoning that resist the use of formalism to impose uniformities. It is also, therefore, less professionalized, more open to the participation of laymen (juries for instance), and more responsive to the particular contingencies of different situations. By contrast, they indicate, the English legal system is largely based on a traditional concept of the law as a command laid down by the sovereign from above, an approach that tends to minimize risks and errors and displays an elitist distrust and a concomitant pedagogic orientation on the part of the judges toward the wider public. The American system is founded on the very different idea of divisible sovereignty and decentralized, horizontal, and more multiple sources of the law. The law is regarded "as a collaborative human achievement in need of constant renewal."[18] This view is, of course, particularly accommodating to the place of equal individuals in generating binding agreements, authority, and discipline. The particular historical influence of theories of natural rights on the American system reinforces, of course, the notion of the individual as primary and prior to rather than derivative of society.[19] It is as if nature as an extra-social source of norms is necessary in order to repudiate Benthemite notions of rights as deriving from positive law, the product of collective socio-political actions that presuppose the primacy of the whole to the individuals who are conceived merely as its parts. Relative to its English counterpart, the American legal system is, then, more responsive to egalitarian individualism, more open, more deliberately incomplete, more risk taking, and more tolerant of inconsistencies and uncertainties. In others words, it depends on a system of reasoning that sacrifices degrees of holism in order to protect a high degree of decentralized interactive individualism.

The "Critical Legal Studies" school of legal thought in America, which appeared on the scene during the 1970s, tends to go even further in stressing the underdetermined, contingent, and ambiguous character of the law and of judicial decisions.[20] Critical Legal theorists are clearly more deeply driven by anxiety over losing, or constraining, free individuals where they are treated as just parts of a whole, than of losing the whole, thought of as "society" or "polity" in the parts. The radical commitment to the freedom of individuals leads here to the conclusion that no specific legal structure can be established without limiting the range of possible forms of law and order, which diverse individuals have the right to envision and pursue. By stressing the inherent indeterminacy of the whole order, the Critical Legal Studies approach adopts a more extreme variant of decentralized authority as legitimate and of coherent legal structures as arbitrary. Paradoxically, the combined effects of radical individualism, egalitarianism, and decentralized substantive judicial decision making legitimates a wider participation in shaping the socio-political order but, in fact, empties the very notion of participation and the content of the political order as a whole from any particular substantive meaning. Still, the distinction between substantive-content-directed and formalist-rule-directed legal reasoning reflects here different notions of the acceptable balance between the weight ascribed to the value of the individuals as participants and the value ascribed to society or to the state as a collective institution. But, in the final analysis, the kind of criticism leveled by the leaders of the Critical Legal Studies movement against epistemological optimism, authoritative ethical principles, and the separation between legal and political rationales of judging and settling disputes undermines the aspiration to regard legalization as a mode of depoliticization and to ground the power and the authority to resolve conflicts in some objective, universalistic, agreed-upon, and, therefore, non-arbitrary intellectual technical or moral standards. Such an attitude leaves no basis for judging any concentration of power and authority as nonarbitrary. Taking radical egalitarian individualism and freedom seriously leads to the conclusion that the very enterprise of building a legitimate order and authority from the bottom up may, in principle, be impossible. This means, of course, that at least on such grounds, no conception of the whole can legitimate any particular mode of cementing free individuals into a community or a polity.

6.4 Science and democratization in modernist and post-modernist contexts

The discussion of the relations between modes of reasoning and structures of authority in the legal context should not be construed, however, as suggesting that particular forms of thinking and reasoning necessarily support particular forms of authority. As I mentioned previously, the history of political thought and practice may suggest that each mode of reasoning can be enlisted or become integral to several even mutually exclusive forms of politics and authority. Although the characteristics of any mode of thought or reasoning can limit the range of its possible uses as a resource for the construction of a particular order or authority, any given political context equally influences the aspects of that mode of reasoning that become relevant. Thus, Weberian methodological individualism, which was rejected by anti-liberal orientations in the Germany of Weber's time, was perceived as harmonious with mainstream ideas of order and politics in post–World War II Germany and, of course, also in liberal–democratic America.[21] Jamesian pragmatism, which was regarded as deeply responsive to American individualism and the democratic spirit, was regarded by French social theorists like Émile Durkheim as a mode of thinking that is positively dangerous to French culture and society.[22] Similarly, Montaignean skepticism could be enlisted in some contexts to decompose authority as arbitrary while, as Montaigne himself indicated, it could also serve to justify arbitrary order as the only alternative to chaos.

While links between any particular mode of thought or reasoning and a particular form of authority may not be necessary, the specific historical associations between styles of thought and authority may have profound effects on their social and political reputations and, therefore, also on their diffusion in other contexts. Particularly instructive illustrations of these points are the discontinuous associations between scientific modes of reasoning and democratization in seventeenth- and eighteenth-century Western societies and in some of the same societies during the late twentieth century.

Beginning with mid-seventeenth-century England, for example, the historical association between experimental scientific modes of establishing and certifying claims of knowledge were regarded as novel, politically relevant techniques of achieving consensus among individuals of diverse social and religious affiliations taken as equals. According to Bishop Sprat, the first observer-historian of the Royal Society, the enterprise of advancing knowledge is not entrusted to individual men, "not to philosophers; not to devout and religious men alone."[23] In the Royal Society . . . the Soldier, the Trades-man, the Merchant, the Scholar, the Gentleman; the Courtier, the Divine, the Presbyterian, the Papist; the Independent and those of Orthodox Judgment have laid aside their names of distinction and calmly conspired in a mutual agreement of labor and desires. . . ." This, observed Sprat, is a blessing "which seems even to have exceeded that evangelical promise that the Lion and the Lamb shall lie down together."[24] Against a background of violent verbal confrontations in the religious controversies of the time, Sprat insisted that the "silent, effectual and unanswerable arguments of real productions," the reliance on experimental demonstrations and on observations could help remedy the social strife induced by conflicts of opinion and contribute, to use his words, to "the sweetening of such dissentions."[25] Sprat articulated what have since become standard notions of the association of scientific norms and practices of reasoning and persuasion and a decentralized demo-cratic political order. It was along such lines that scientific modes of reason-ing and validating claims of knowledge have been presented as consistent with novel forms of authority based on voluntary agreements among equal individuals. The individuals who, in the context of science, were certified as reliable witnesses of physical facts have gradually emerged also as reliable witnesses of socio-political and economic facts.[26] In both the contexts of science and the "new" politics, authority was presumed to be built from the bottom up. The analogy between nature and society, between the laws of nature and the laws of society, was inspired in no small way by the notions enunciated, for example, by John Locke, that individuals can reach agree-ments and cooperate if, as witnesses of the same natural and social worlds, they, as thinking and reasoning subjects, apply correct reasoning procedures to the materials of their sense experience. Experience analyzed according to the valid canons of reasoning can, in his view, lead discrete individuals to the same conclusions.

While in matters concerning the facts of our physical and social experi-ence, knowledge can only be probabilistic, the assumption about the possi-bility of reaching such agreements on truth was reinforced by the metaphysical ideas of the world as a coherent intelligible whole. The meta-physical idea of the unity and coherence of nature and, by analogy, of society as objects of witnessing, reasoning, and understanding have diminished the anarchistic potential of the democratized epistemology manifest in the prac-tices and echoed in the defense of the new science. The metaphysical foun-dations of early modern science implied, therefore, an idea of democratic epistemology which was compatible with holistic notions of the world as an object of knowledge. The view of the world as a unified, coherent, and in-telligible object of knowledge also reinforced in the scientific tradition the ideas of unity and coherence as ideals of explanation.

These metaphysical theories and their complementary epistemology largely originated from Judeo-Christian theology.[27] In the Western religious traditions, the world is a creation of a supreme, divine intelligence; God imposes order on chaos and makes the world intelligible. An influential Christian variant sees God as a supreme engineer who created the world as a machinelike cosmic clock. Although in many later versions of the mechanical philosophy of the universe, God was removed as a necessary first cause or as the ultimate guardian or synoptic viewer of the world, the persistent idea of nature as a unified and coherent whole, as a system of regularities, has contained the imprint of the initial theological notion of the world as molded by an intelligent divine power. Regardless of its theological origins, however, the unity of nature and, by analogy, of society as an object of knowledge seemed to guarantee that more universally accessible, decentralized, and participatory modes of reasoning, as those indicated by spokesmen of the new science such as Sprat, would be compatible with social consensus on truths. Especially within the empirical–probabilistic mode that allows each person to hope only for experiencing or witnessing a fragment of the world, many individuals, by comparing and analyzing their experience, as the Fellows of the Royal Society appeared to do, were expected to evolve a larger, more comprehensive yet coherent picture of the universe. What started as an individual experience was seen as progressing through demonstrations, experiments, proofs, and the correct use of words into a collective certified body of knowledge. The practice of science exemplified, according to this outlook, the ways by which egalitarian individuals could evolve socially shared authoritative knowledge of nature, and later also of society, as a whole. The new science not only assimilated, then, the religious idea of the world as a unified, coherent, and intelligible object but also turned the witnessing of God's work in nature from a means of reinforcing faith to a procedure for the decentralized participatory certification of a secular, human, yet authoritative body of truths.

The political implications of this more democratic epistemology for legitimizing truths and order from the bottom up did not escape leading theorists like John Locke, who constructed their novel contractual theories of government on the new theory of knowledge. Locke's liberal views are based on an optimistic democratic epistemology according to which discrete yet interacting individuals can reach agreement by means of the application of the "correct" canons of reasoning to "common observations in like cases" and the weight of accumulating testimonies.[28]

Inasmuch as early modern democratic principles and practices had to be justified first in pre-democratic, traditional, mostly monarchic regimes, the guaranteed wholeness of the world as the object of scientific "discoveries" and the expected unity and coherence of scientific knowledge itself were bound to temper the fears that the acceptance of the more democratic, decentralized canons and practices of claiming knowledge and certifying truths would threaten the integrity and stability of the social order. As Bishop Sprat attempted to demonstrate, equality and decentralization in the practices of the Royal Society were congenial for generating consensus, while these were precisely the practices of the theologians engaged in religious disputations that produced strife, unresolvable conflicts, and (as Locke added) intolerance.[29] Science could appear in this context as a bundle of practices of thought, reasoning, and persuasion that substantiate voluntary liberal and democratic rationales or procedures for the establishment of authority and holistic social order. As I indicated earlier, science, as a cluster of modes of reasoning with which egalitarian individuals can evolve authority and create a unified social order, has not been as central to the school of political thought that welded classical economics and liberalism. In this view, a coherent socio-political order depends largely upon the unintended effects of the actions and interactions of self-interested individuals. But, even in this variant of modern social or political theory, there is an implicit conception of the "whole" or a "system" that can have such attributes as "harmony," "balance," "self-regulation," and the like.

In some late twentieth-century democracies, a host of social and cultural orientations commonly lumped together under the category of post-modernism reflect in part a decline in the willingness to assume even a weak version of holism, unity, coherence, and balance as the attributes of clearly bounded wholes like "society" or the "state." Consequently, the decentralized "democratic" epistemological strategies of building up knowledge, strategies associated with the scientific practices of experiments, observations, and probabilistic reasoning from experience, do not seem to sustain their earlier force as a means by which discrete individuals can reach the same conclusions, develop a shared picture of the whole in the respective contexts of nature and society. Post-modernist orientations are distrustful of the possibility of safely moving from discrete individual starting points to shared concepts of a whole. By comparison with modernist orientations, they display deeper appreciation for the limits of scientific knowledge and the subjectivity and incommensurability of values. Post-modernism maintains that there is, therefore, an irremedial underdeterminism of normative standards for deciding on either the "right" or "correct" socio-political order or the legitimate ways of using whatever shared knowledge we have to guide our actions.

Empirical and probabilistic modes of reasoning, to be sure, always left the possibility of gaps in our knowledge and uncertainties in the constructed pictures of nature and society. But, during the second half of the twentieth century, internal developments in the sciences, including mostly the declining relevance of visual phenomenal referents, which are at least partly accessible to laymen and, correspondingly, the increasing importance of esoteric mathematical reasoning in the construction and validation of scientific theories, have eroded much of the early confidence in "science" as a model for the generation of discipline and authority within an egalitarian individualistic social context. As John Dewey anticipated, in a cultural context where a "spectator theory of knowledge" has been discredited and the conception of the world as a fixed, knowable object is replaced by the notion of the world as a being in an interminable process of becoming, the analogy from nature to society is more congenial to the idea of politics as a continual open-ended process of interaction than a series of actions organized and directed by shared, valid procedures or reasoning.[30] Some discernible processes of fragmentation and localization in the politics of late twentieth-century democracies are reinforced by the emergence of new forms of much more radically plastic conceptions of individualism that allow for more internally fluid experiences and externally diverse expressions of identity. Moreover, the decline of various forms of holism has been accompanied by the intensification of reflexive individualism as a mode of thought and, at times, even a psychosocial practice of exploring a plurality of inner forms and identities and their social correlates. These trends further delegitimate limits imposed by internalized or externally projected coherences as normative styles of thought and authority.[31] The fluid-reflexive-undetermined self may nevertheless also be an intended strategy for, or an unintended cause of, rendering the individual too elusive to be counted on as a building block of large-scale projects of political engineering. If, for example, the Hobbesian self-preserving individual or the Smithian "economic man" were sufficiently fixed as agencies whose behavior could be regarded as transparent or predictable enough to warrant models of fitting multitudes of equal individuals into collective structures without violating the principles of liberal democratic individualism, late twentieth-century individualism subverts such models. It suggests images of self and individuality too elusive to substantiate any expectation that under conditions of strict egalitarian individual starting points, patterns of behavior and interaction which add up to bounded socio-political wholes can be generated. In such circumstances, there are no authoritative criteria for selecting from any range of supposed human traits and possibilities those that need special cultivation by means of education and informal social reward systems; no particular modes of reasoning that can be used to generate trust and cooperation among horizontally situated autonomous individuals. No notions of individual thinking, of individual feelings, of individual interests, or of any other individual traits or dispositions can be "naturalized" or otherwise privileged as the basis of desirable and possible models of the socio-political whole and the educational programs deemed instrumental for its production and reproduction.

In many respects, however, such eclectic pluralism[32] can be seen as consistent with a radically decentralized federation of micro-local communities and cultures, a "system" unencumbered by discernible social, political, or even territorial boundaries or hegemonic hierarchies.[33] The implicit negation of holism is compatible in such a context with epistemological pluralism and a concomitant legitimation of non-rational orientations toward experience. In the context of such post-modern socio-cultural environments, science, with its ideals and strategies of reasoning and explanation, appears to imply models of authority too centralized and extensive to be warranted.[34] Thus, while post-modernist thinkers often see science as anti-democratic and an authoritarian mode of knowledge, many scientific intellectuals criticize postmodernism as a form of epistemological anarchism and cultural relativism which can lead to the revival of fascism. In retrospect, it now appears that those who sought to democratize epistemology in order to establish the social or political order on the new principles of voluntary and egalitarian individualism actually opened the way for modes of political imagining and reasoning that could delegitimate order and discredit the very ideas of holism, harmony, and coherence implicit in early "classical" models of democratic politics. Unchecked by the tacit early metaphysical commitment to monistic ontology, decentralized democratic epistemology has increasingly come to be associated with the delegitimation rather than the legitimation of the modern order.

In the final analysis, the post-modernist mood reflects a thorough-going skepticism with regard to the very possibility of building a socio-political order from the bottom up. In the absence of a given or presumed whole or a given hierarchy, no individual can detach him/herself and step outside it in order to have a better view of the larger society or the polity. In such a context, no individual can be seen as a separate part of a given or a potential whole, nor can any form of individual experience or process of reasoning appear to ground actions or interactions that would compose a larger system. The coupling of individualism and science that Machiavelli presupposed and Hobbes, Descartes, and Locke developed has become increasingly questionable as a basis for consolidating a perspective whose authority stems from the fusion of individualism, voluntarism, and intellectual detachment with an idea of order. Perhaps the most compelling insight that can be gleaned from the historical record is that, contrary to the intellectual reductionism and metaphysical monism that underlined the enterprises of Descartes, Hobbes, Locke, and many other modern political theorists, societies give rise to diverse modes of reasoning that constantly and simultaneously participate in constructing and deconstructing the authority frames of the social order. They simultaneously compose and decompose institutional structures, isolate and socialize individuals, cement and fragment collectives, consolidate and undermine patterns of discourse and action.

Notes

1 Machiavelli, Niccolo, *The Prince and the Discourses*, introduction by Max Lerner (New York: Modern Library, 1960), p. 4.

2 Ibid.

3 Dumont, Louis, *Essays on Individualism, Modern Ideology in Anthropological Perspective* (Chicago: Univ. of Chicago Press, 1986).

4 Ibid. (I am particularly indebted to Louis Dumont for his illuminating discussion on holism and individualism as alternative principles of order.) See also Kupferer, Bruce, *Legends of People, Myths of State* (Washington, D.C.: Smithsonian Institution Press, 1988).

5 See Williams, Bernard, "Descartes' Use of Skepticism," and Popkin, Richard H., "Berkeley and Pyrrhonism," in *The Skeptical Tradition,* M. Burnyeat (ed.) (Berkeley: Univ. of California Press, 1983), pp. 337–352, 377–396.

6 See Taylor, Charles, *Sources of the Self, the Making of Modern Identity* (Cambridge, Mass: Harvard Univ. Press, 1989), pp. 143–58.

7 For instrumentalism and its political implications, see Ezrahi, Yaron, *The Descent of Icarus, Science and the Transformation of Contemporary Democracy* (Cambridge, Mass.: Harvard Univ. Press, 1990).

8 Hobbes, Thomas, *Leviathan* (1651) (New York: Collier Books, 1962), Ch. 5, p. 44.

9 Ibid., p. 57.

10 See Ezrahi, *The Descent of Icarus*, pp. 197–216. See also Ezrahi, Yaron, "Sci-

ence and the Problem of Authority in Democracy,'' in *Science and Social Structure: A Festschrift For Robert K. Merton,* Thomas F. Gieryn (ed.), *Transactions of the New York Academy of Sciences, Series II,* 39 (April 1980), pp. 43–60.

11 Smith, Adam, *An Inquiry into the Nature and Causes of the Wealth of Nations* (1776).

12 For the relations between individualism and totalitarianism, see Dumont, *op. cit.*

13 Damaska, Mirjan R, *The Faces of Justice and State Authority, a Comparative Approach to the Legal Process* (New Haven: Yale Univ. Press, 1986).

14 Ibid.

15 Ibid., p. 39.

16 Ibid., p. 42.

17 Atiyah, P. S., and Robert S. Summers, *Form and Substance in Anglo-American Law, Comparative Study of Legal Reasoning, Legal Theory and Legal Institutions* (Oxford: Clarendon Press, 1987).

18 Ibid., p. 47.

19 Ibid., pp. 236–238.

20 See Kelman, Mark, *A Guide to Critical Legal Studies* (Cambridge, Mass.: Harvard Univ. Press, 1987).

21 Max Weber, late in his life, indicated that his motive in pursuing sociology was largely to ''exorcise'' collectivist, organic or spiritual notions of society still dominant in Germany of his time. See Mommsen, W., ''Max Weber's Political Sociology and His Philosophy of World History,'' *International Social Science Journal 17* (1965), pp. 25, 44.

22 Durkheim, Émile, *Pragmatism and Sociology,* J. C. Whitehouse (transl.), J. B. Allcock (ed.) (Cambridge, Mass.: Cambridge Univ. Press, 1983), p. 1.

23 Sprat, T. *History of the Royal Society* (1667), J. Cope and H. W. Jones (eds.) (St. Louis: Washington Univ. Press, 1958), p. 73.

24 Ibid., p. 427.

25 Ibid., p. 426.

26 Ezrahi, *The Descent of Icarus,* pp. 67–127.

27 On the religious sources of the metaphysics of modern science, see Burtt, Edwin Arthur, *The Metaphysical Foundations of Modern Physical Science* (Garden City, N.Y.: Doubleday, 1954), and Manuel, Frank E., *The Religion of Isaac Newton* (Oxford : Clarendon Press, 1974).

28 On the distinct implications of inferences and testimonies in the social validation of knowledge, see Ezrahi, ''Science and the Problem of Authority,'' pp. 111–131.

29 Locke, John, *Letter Concerning Toleration* (Indianapolis: Bobbs-Merrill, 1955).

30 Dewey, John, *The Quest for Certainty* (New York: Putnam's Sons, 1929), esp. p. 291.

31 Ezrahi, *The Descent of Icarus,* pp. 283–290.

32 Ibid.

33 On this issue, see Ezrahi, Yaron, ''Science and Utopia in Late Twentieth-Century Pluralist Democracy,'' in *Science Between Utopia and Dystopia,* Vol. VIII, *Sociology of the Sciences,* E. Mendelsohn and H. Nowotny (eds.) (Dordrecht: Reidel, 1984), pp. 273–290.

34 See, for instance, Lyotard, J. F., *The Post-modern Condition: A Report on Knowledge* (Manchester: Manchester Univ. Press, 1986), and Harvey, David, *The Condition of Post-Modernity* (Oxford: Basil Blackwell, 1989). See also Feyerabend, Paul K., *Against Method* (London: Verso, 1975), and Hannay, Alastair, ''Politics and Feyerabend's Anarchist,'' in *Knowledge and Politics,* Marcelo Dascal and Ora Gruengard (eds.) (Boulder: Westview, 1989), pp. 241–263.

PART II
The anthropology of thought

7
Frames for thinking
WAYS OF MAKING MEANING

Jerome Bruner

I

On 8 February 1672, Isaac Newton presented a paper to the Royal Society of London in which he argued principally on the basis of experiments with prisms that the ambient white light of daylight was not elementary, but composed rather of a mixture of all the hues in the spectrum. The idea came to Newton, so gossipy historians like to tell us, on the basis of observations he made with a prism bought at the Stourbridge Fair in the spring of 1666 when he was twenty-four, shortly before he quit his quarters in Trinity College because of the threat of the plague.[1] Newton regarded his work on color (as he did much else in the 1709 *Opticks*) as simply a matter of empirical demonstration plus a little geometry about angles of incidence and reflection, and he was notably annoyed when another Fellow of the Society, one Dr. Pardies, referred to his 1672 paper in the *Philosophical Transactions* as offering Newton's color "hypothesis."

Newton's explanation of color mixing has endured right into the present and even prompted interesting progeny ranging from last century's Young–Helmholtz theory to yesterday's views of Edwin Land on color mixing. Not only has its explanatory power endured, but it has had an astonishing continuity of development over three centuries. It is a model of explanation in science and provides a paradigm case of an important mode of thought.[2]

But it is only one side of my story, this exemplary scientific achievement. Eventually the relevant volume of the *Transactions* or the *Opticks* itself came into the hands of a charismatic and brilliant young preacher-theologian in the village of Northampton in the Massachusetts Bay Colony, who read it with something more than mere scientific curiosity. The event I wish to relate took place around 1740, around the time of the so-called Great Awakening of that date when there were great social and political stirrings in the colonies, which, as Perry Miller[3] tells us, could as well have been a rising of debtors against creditors or of common men against the gentry or a turning away from the authoritarian Puritanism of a century before. It may even have been exacerbated by an epidemic of sore throat that spread throughout the colonies from Virginia to New England in that year. Or perhaps it was an echo of John Wesley's evangelical, anti-Establishment preaching to the tin miners in far-off Cornwall, who gathered in zealous assemblies of ten thousand at a time to hear the outdoor sermons of that astonishing Nonconformist, who galloped from town to town on horseback to deliver sermons to as many as three such assemblies a day. In any case, the Great Awakening was a veritable frenzy, particularly in the Connecticut Valley, and so alarming was it to the sequestered Harvard faculty, indeed, that they condemned it in terms reserved to only the severest public aberrations: it was "enthusiasm."

The Northampton preacher in question was the well-born young Yale graduate and admirer of John Locke and Isaac Newton, Jonathan Edwards, later to become president of Princeton University. Shortly after reading Newton's publication, Edwards delivered a sermon based upon it to his congregation. After telling his parishioners about Newton's discovery, Jonathan Edwards told them that Newton's unlocking of another of God's secrets gave hope to Everyman, following which he urged upon them that by the exercise of their own efforts they too could do the same.[4] Now what was the difference between how the mind of Jonathan Edwards was working in contrast to the mind of Isaac Newton?

Edwards was smitten with John Locke's ideas about language and thought, to be found in Book III of Locke's *Essay concerning human understanding*. Edwards, while agreeing with Locke that words gain their meaning by referring to ideas, still felt that this was not enough to account for what words communicated. Words, he argued, excite more than ideas. They also arouse passions and convictions and impel us to actions. Edwards could now argue that an idea was "not merely a concept but an emotion."[5] It was a call to appropriate action.

We know what Newton accomplished. What of Edwards? Perry Miller is of the view that he helped break the hold of European deductive rationalism over American religious thought, helped form the American mind with an activist epistemology fit for the New World. He was contributing to the formation of an alternative mode, an interpretive mode of thought, for Edwards was not interested in elucidating Newton's explanation of the composition of light but in *interpreting* it. He was seeking, we would say, a deeper human significance in Newton's work, seeking a meaning behind the meaning. His preoccupation was with how things *should* be rather than with how they *were*, with prescription rather than description: how the mind should be used, how the world should be treated, what should prevail between God and man. And to what end? Unlike Newton, Edwards proved nothing, explained nothing. Yet his interpretive line of thought, perhaps, did bring something powerful into being. By espousing the democracy of mind, by giving a rationale for epistemic self-reliance (echoed a century later by Ralph Waldo Emerson), he helped form the "American ethos." Anomalously, by his own use of mind, he changed the very social reality he was rebelling against.

To understand this accomplishment, we must go beyond Newton's empirical verifiability and beyond formal consistency of the asserting "A and not-A" variety. We might simply say that Jonathan Edwards was a shrewd reader of the Great Awakening and that he used it well as the context for the text he was hawking. Newton, on the other hand, showed no interest in the public rumblings that accompanied the Plague whose erupting drove him from Cambridge in 1667. It was only an annoying interruption of his revolutionary reflections upon the refrangibility of "different sorts of hues." Besides, explanatory standards of the kind that occupied Newton were scarcely affected by the Plague. Whereas the interpretive possibilities open to Jonathan Edwards might well have been shifted toward sympathy for self-reliance by even so trivial an epidemic as the sore throats of 1740. But I think we can put the matter more precisely than that.

II

For reasons both heuristic and expository, I want to focus my discussion more formally upon the contrast between "interpretation" of the J. Edwards type and "explanation" of the Newton type for two reasons.[6] The first is that I think the concept of interpretation may fall outside the reach of conventional computability, *in principle* outside. And it would be useful to explore why that is so and what its implications may be for our ideas about "how the mind works," for it works in many ways employing different rules and principles. The second reason is that I want to show that the interpretive mode is not "outside" the grasp of the human sciences and may indeed be as close to its center as one can get.

Let me take a first step toward our problem. I take it as given that all cognition, whatever its nature, relies upon representation, how we lay down knowledge in a way to represent our experience of the world. I happen to think that representation is a process of construction, as it were, rather than of mere reflection of the world. My version focuses on how human beings *achieve* meanings and do so in a fashion that makes human culture possible and effective.

Let me propose that there are three primitive modes of making meanings, three distinctive patterns of placing events, utterances, particulars of all kinds, into contexts that make possible their construal as "meaning something." Each leads to a form of understanding. I think of them as comprising three distinctive forms of human cognitive activity required for living under cultural conditions. Each is sustained by a body of folk-theoretic beliefs, and not that it matters all that much for our purposes, each is made possible by preadapted cognitive dispositions that reflect the evolution of the primate order. It would be astonishing if man's major modes of meaning making had no assist at all from the human genome.

The first mode of meaning making is directed to the establishment, shaping, and maintenance of *intersubjectivity*. It grows from an initial though primitive human capacity to "read" other minds, a virtual compulsion to do so. From this obligatory simple presumption of consciousness or intentional states in others grows a highly acculturated and complex folk theory of other minds.[7] Without such a folk theory, there could be no presupposition about the intentions of others, including their communicative intentions, or about their beliefs, feelings, or whatever. Without such intersubjectivity, we could not develop the conventions and felicity conditions for managing illocutionary speech acts,[8] nor could we grasp the distinction between what is said and what is meant, nor master the rich lexicon of psychological verbs, nor construe Gricean implicatures.[9] The coherence of our intersubjective meaning making inheres in a more or less internally congruent theory of other minds, about which we are presently learning a great deal. But what also gives it coherence are culturally transmitted strategies for using our presumptions about other minds in discourse, like Sperber and Wilson's "presumption of relevance,"[10] which leads us to presume that whatever an interlocutor says is relevant to the context of the encounter, with the first burden of proof resting on the listener to determine how our interlocutor is expressing her notion of relevance. Intersubjective meaning making, in a word, is an elaborated expression of our recognition of the mental processes of our conspecifics. I can tell you autobiographically that among my own research studies of the last decade, the one that most knocked me for a loop was finding that young infants followed an adult's gaze direction in search of an object of attention and, when they failed to find one, looked back at the adult to re-check on gaze direction – a study with Scaife.[11] Then Anat Ninio and I[12] discovered that infants grasped the distinction between given and new for labels, signaled by the mother's use of rising intonation for new and unsettled matters ("What's *TIup* that?) versus falling intonation for already negotiated labels ("What's *TIdown* that?").

Let me briefly note in passing that intersubjective meaning making is the more interesting for its lack of precise verifiability. It depends enormously upon contextual interpretation and negotiation. This may explain why Anglo-American philosophical theories of meaning, so reliant upon verificationist notions of reference and sense, have paid so little attention to it.

A second form of meaning making is concerned with relating events, utterances, acts, or whatever to the so-called arguments of action: who is the agent of what act toward what goal by what instrumentality in what setting with what time constraints, etc. I refer to it as the *actional* mode.[13] Again, it is a form of meaning attribution that begins very early and appears initially in a surprisingly accomplished form. As I tried to say in my last book, *Acts of Meaning*,[14] it is as if the case structure of language were designed to reflect a "natural" grasp of how action is organized, as if the young child's theory of action were a prelinguistic prerequisite for language mastery.

The third mode of meaning making construes particulars in normative contexts, a matter about which we know altogether too little. Here we are dealing with meanings relative to obligations, general standards, conformities, and deviations. This is the *normative* mode. The adult linguistic vehicle for normative meaning making is the deontic mode, concerned with the nature and limits of obligation, the territory beyond the optative. It has to do with *requiredness*, a matter to which we will return later.

Again, we know from Judy Dunn's work and other studies of "social understanding" that the young child early develops a sense of the canonical status of various ways of doing, of feeling, even of seeming to feel as in pretend play. The child soon learns what is required of her.[15] Normative expectations develop initially in the informal settings of the infant's or young child's intimate world, but they are soon reconstituted and elaborated through encounters with institutionalized forms – as in the law, in religious doctrine and practice, in custom and precedent, even in the poet's tropes ("I could not love thee, dear, so much/Loved I not honor more").

The normative mode is not detached: it expresses itself by imposing constraints on the first two modes. Both intersubjective and actional meanings are shaped by canonical expectations: what is a fit, an appropriate, or a required state of mind, intention, line of action, and so on. Again, language serves powerfully both to transmit and to constitute normative standards through its deontic mode, its distinctions between the obligatory and the optative. The same can be said of the symbolic forms that underlie cultural institutions for controlling the exchange of respect and deference, goods and services, and so on. Normative meaning making delineates a culture's standards of fitness or appropriateness, whether in setting discourse requirements, felicity conditions, or limits on so-called self-interest.

Intersubjective, actional, and normative meaning making are all highly tolerant with respect to verifiability, truth conditions, or logical justification. While meanings relating to intentional states, to human action and its vicissitudes, and to cultural normativity can, within limits, be translated into the propositional forms of a logical calculus (to which I turn shortly), they risk degradation in the process. For although propositional translation always works toward the decontextualization of meanings, intersubjective, actional, and normative meaning making remain stubbornly context dependent. Construing the meaning of the condolence "I know how awful it feels to lose a close friend" is no mere exercise in propositional calculus. It requires pure "psychologism." Its "meaning" lies in its appropriateness. And its appropriateness is context bound. Its context, moreover, is the story into which it can be fitted. And this leads me to an interesting matter that requires immediate attention: the role of story or narrative in meaning making.

A story in its very nature involves action by an agent in a setting where normative expectations have been breached or otherwise brought into question. A story, moreover, is played out on a dual landscape, the landscape of "reality" as set forth by a narrator or as canonically presumed, and a subjective landscape in which the story's protagonists live. Stories are the vehicles par excellence for entrenching the first three modes of meaning making into a more structured whole, a whole that widens the interpretive horizon against which the construal of particulars is achieved. "What's going on here?" is a bid to get the particulars into the diachronic meanings of a narrative.

But stories accomplish something else as well: they provide the means for transcending particularity. Stories are not isolated recountings: they are also instantiations of broader genres. The events and characters of any particular story are, as Vladimir Propp put it, "functions" of a genre of which the particular story is an instance.[16] Nobody has a notion of how many fundamental genres there are, even in a particular culture: all that we know is there are not many and that they both die out and keep getting invented and reinvented by the rare likes of Herodotus, Augustine, Cervantes, Shakespeare, Sterne, Flaubert, and Joyce. Narrative genre – like, say, Northrop Frye's tragedy, comedy, romance, and irony – typically represent canonical human plights, but they also trigger ways of thinking and talking about those plights (and what they "stand for").[17] Genres are, as it were, both in the text and in the reader's head. You can "read" an intended comedy as a tragedy or irony. Genres, in a word, are modes of thought.[18] Whether in the head or on the page, stories have a certain psychological or cultural necessity about them: romantic heroes "deserve" their reward, tragic ones fail of an excess of their own virtues, and so on. Obviously such "necessities" are not of the same order as causal necessities or logical entailments. Yet they have an enormous power in providing coherence and generality to meanings constructed under their contextual control. Such power does not rest on either empirical demonstrability nor upon necessary logical truth, but only on "verisimilitude." And verisimilitude cannot be reduced either to tests of inference or to operations of a logical calculus.

Meaning making, given the narrative condition, is *interpretation*. So when the recipient of the condolence mentioned earlier interprets it as "a hypocritical offering motivated by toadyism," her interpretation involves not only notions about states of mind, ways of striving in the world, and normative expectations, but also certain *necessities* inherent in the culture's ways of dealing with life and death, necessities that derive from the genres on offer in the culture: *narrative* necessities.

This brings us directly to the fourth mode of meaning making, the *propositional* one. In this mode, meaning making is dominated by the formal necessities imposed by the rules of the symbolic, syntactic, and conceptual systems that we use in achieving decontextualized meanings. These include an abundance of rules not only of contingent or causal inference and of logical justification, but also simpler, almost "invisible" ones. These include such rule-bound mundane distinctions as object-attribute, identity-otherness, whole-part, and so on. That something can be treated as an attribute of something else or as part of it or as an instance of a category or as an opposite of something else, these are "simple" rules that compel their own forms of logical necessity.[19] Yet, we identify, place, and define things steadily and easily by hyponymy, meronymy, antinomy, and the like. And we know intuitively that an arm is "part of a body" in a different, more strictly logical sense than, say, an insult is "part" of a plot in a picaresque revenge narrative whose constituents are determined not by strict "logic," but by cultural convention. Indeed, *insult* and *revenge* are themselves constituted by violation of cultural norms and not by the decontextualized necessity that requires a part to be subsumed by a whole. When we subsume such things under a part–whole structure, we leave something crucial behind.

Even granting that formal "logic" may derive from "natural" features of cognition (the Piagetian as well as the Kantian view of the matter), its rules are said to be autonomous and context free. Their application leads to a unique solution, not to alternative interpretations. What justifies a claim of logical "necessity" is an appeal, say, to a syllogism or to *modus ponens* or to a test for contradiction. And in the case of causal "necessity," the appeal is either directly to the rules of inference or indirectly to the logical rules imported into a causal theory from a mathematical model.

It takes boldness and cheek to propose to a logician that logical necessities may grow out of efforts to refine, decontextualize, and universalize the intersubjective, the actional, and the normative modes. Such a proposal would provoke the thundering accusation of "psychologism." But let me speculate on this point, with gratitude to my bold assistant, David Kalmar. It may well be that the three procedures of logic – deduction, induction, and abduction – are directed to the "taming" and decontextualizing of the modes earlier described. That is to say, deduction involves an effort to impose an abstract norm on a set of particulars. "All men are mortal"; therefore it is required that, since Socrates is a man, he too be mortal. Suppose Socrates goes on living longer than Methuselah. The natural language response, of course, is that he *should* be dying, as if there were a hidden deontic in the universal syllogism, as if the syllogism were normative in root. Induction involves, one might speculate, something of the actional. Formally, it includes "all cases of non-demonstrative argument in which the truth of the premises, while not entailing the truth of the conclusion, purports to be a good reason for belief in it."[20] Does this not involve the placement of an array of particulars in a putatively common action context – what a set of things can do, how they can be situated, what agent effected them, in what aspectual point in a sequence they occurred, and so on? As for abduction – the term Charles Sanders Peirce used for hypothesis making – it is a way of externalizing and decontextualizing one's notions about what others (or "other minds") will find believable if tests support them. Peirce once wrote a paper about the if–then query as the essential vehicle for "making our ideas clear," to quote the title of his famous paper.[21] It is how to make the "intersubjective" public, testable, and beyond prejudice. Please take all of this in the speculative sense in which it was offered to me by David Kalmar! The upshot of the proposal is that propositional thinking did not grow out of the blue or spring from the "organ of language," but emerged as a way of going beyond the particularities of the intersubjective, the actional, and the normative modes.

Let me step back for a moment and ask the functional question about decontextualized, propositional meaning making. What function is served by "going Pythagorean" (to use John Bruer's happy expression for it)? Perhaps we save ourselves the trouble of having to learn over and over again, as I once suggested.[22] Or perhaps (to echo an old Basil Bernstein[23] point) we get wider social travel from universals? But does propositional understanding always provide a better guide to the world? Well, the proper answer is "It depends." It depends, for example, on whether you are composing a love letter or writing a paper for the *Philosophical Review*.

A close look at propositional efforts to understand (leaving aside the scientist and the logician) tells us that they are mostly used to tame context effects and to obviate negotiation – with all the risks entailed. Our own work as cognitive psychologists suggests just this. Consider what we have learned these last decades about such seemingly formal matters as category rules. As Douglas Medin[24] notes, concept attainment studies have steadily retreated from formalistic conclusions since the Bruner–Goodnow–Austin book of thirty-five years ago. Back then, it was proposed that categories be envisaged as governed by formal rules for combining the defining attributes of class exemplars.[25] Making sense or meaning had to do with placing events in categories according to such rules. Then Rosch and her colleagues[26] noted that natural-kind categories were not constructed that way, but were organized around the similarity of instances to a good or conventional prototype exemplar (a sparrow is a better bird than an auk). Situating things in categories often seemed less a matter of rule following than similarity matching. But similarities are notoriously protean. Smith and Medin[27] then demonstrated that categories were not "defined" just by a single basic level prototype, but by prototypical exemplars that typified different contexts of encounter – prey birds in the wild, garden bird in the backyard, sea birds on the water, and so on. Finally, both Keil[28] and Carey[29] showed that what held a category or a category system together were neither attribute rules, base-level prototypes, nor context-sensitive exemplars. What mattered was a *theory*: if a paramecium were an animal, for example, it had to have ways of sensing its environment, of eating, of taking up oxygen, of eliminating waste, and so on. It is a theory of "aliveness" that dictates a category's properties, not a formal conjunction of attributes or some exemplifying prototypes. A categorical placement, then, is the terminal step in constructing and applying a theory.

But how, typically, do most theories come into being? It is often by taming and attempting to formalize a narrative, or so we learn from Misha Landau's work[30] on the origins of evolutionary theory or Howard Gruber's[31] on Darwin's way of thinking. "Survival of the fit" is a stock, almost mythic narrative from which Darwin began. Granted there are branches of mathematics, and of the physical and biological sciences that are so formally or propositionally entrenched as to permit derivations without the heuristic support of folktales. But even that is a little dubious. Niels Bohr once told me that the "inspiration" for the Principle of Complementarity grew by analogy with his recognizing that he could not simultaneously understand a petty theft to which his small son confessed both in the light of love and in the light of justice. While this "fact" may not "explain" why you cannot include terms both for a particle's position and its velocity in the same equation, it goes a way toward explicating the interplay of different modes of meaning making in our construction of theories.

The deep issue for the student of cognition is how the meaning seeker proceeds in getting to a final formulation. We get trapped by the ideals of science when we insist on an exclusive role for well-formed computation, verifiability, and truth conditionality. It was a triumph in the propositional mode when Simon and Newell devised a program for proving a Whitehead–Russell theorem from the *Principia*.[32] But how about the more interpretive insight of a myth maker like Homer, honing a story to its intersubjective, actional, and normative meaning essentials?[33] And what of the interpretive activities of a Vladimir Propp in delineating the morphology of the millennia-old folktales in the Helsinki corpus?[34] Or of James Joyce in recognizing that the epiphanies that move us are not the marvels of life, but its very ordinariness?

I am not going literary or antiscience. These are the things we see when we observe how people construct their meanings in the world. These are what compel my excursion around the well formed and propositional. The three primitive modes we have discussed – the intersubjective, the actional, the normative – probably all have biological roots in the genome. They certainly have elaborated support systems in the cultures that humanize us. They yield meanings as forms of intimacy, as requirements of action, as norms of appropriateness, and as knowledge *eo ipso*. Their incorporation into the narrative mode and propositional thinking is no less remarkable as an evolutionary achievement. I want to end with a brief account (as promised) of how this set of meaning making processes might have grown out of human evolution.

III

Let me begin with a brief comment on what might be called the cultural idealization of meaning making. Two have already engaged us: literature and its forms of story and drama; and science with its procedures and proofs. The first "personalizes" meaning by anchoring it in what people do, feel, believe, hope for, and so on. It defines what is expectable and canonical and assures cultural solidarity through myths, legends, genres, and the like. These nourish folk meanings. The propositional idealization of meanings is radically more impersonal. In the guise of truth, it seeks to transcend both the private individuality of the listener and the nature of the occasion on which such meanings are told. Truth is through proof: proof yields unique, aboriginal truth. The meaning of hypotenuse in plane geometry is given by operations performed on an idealized "right triangle," operations indifferent to who carries them out under what circumstances – a king or a commoner, a Hottentot or a Harvard mathematician, whether hypotenuses are ritually holy or repellent. Truths reveal themselves because they are there and/or formally necessary, not because they are sponsored by believable stories or compelling narrators. At least so goes the standard version.

The conflict between the two ideas has sometimes been incendiary, particularly in the nineteenth century, but let us not forget the sixteenth. But the contemporary stance has softened. A modern poet could even proclaim that "Euclid alone has looked on beauty bard." Is this all the swing of a cultural pendulum or can we trace evolutionary roots in this struggle?

Let me take a final moment to sketch a possible evolutionary context. Merlin Donald's recent book[35] reminded us of some relevant matters. Recall there were two explosions in hominid brain size: one coincident with the emergence of *Homo erectus* about a million and a half years ago, the other with *Homo sapiens* three-quarters of a million years later. Both involved disproportionate growth not only of the cerebral cortex but of the cerebellum and hippocampus. The swollen cerebellum ensured bipedal agility. The cortex was the instrument of more abstract intelligence. The best guess about the enlarged hippocampus is that it provided the basis for vastly increased human affectivity. Professor Donald is of the view that the evolutionary step to *H. erectus* witnessed the emergence of self-triggered motor routines, skilled routines called up on command rather than in response to appropriate triggering situations. This "rehearsal loop" made retrieval possible in the interest of practice and play or ritual. Self-mimesis can also serve as the basis for the joint performance of group rituals organized around communally significant skilled actions. What of the enlarged hippocampus in all this? Professor Donald speculates that there was probably a good deal of affect invested in these ritualized skills – throwing rituals, spearing rituals, whatever. And what we know about higher primate immaturity would also suggest that the young of the emerging species performed these motoric skilled routines in play, and immaturity grew longer. In all of this, we have the beginning of enactive representation[36] not only by the individual but by the group. It is a step toward "externalizing" memory and knowledge, to quote Merlin Donald.

We know nothing about early morphophonemic or lexicogrammatic language in *H. sapiens* three-quarters of a million years later, but what we can reasonably suppose is that it was initially used as an adjunct to and a way of further representing skilled action but, more notably, ritualized skilled action sequences. Professor Donald takes speech communication as a major step in the *externalization* of memory; he uses the expression *exogram* to refer to such externally carried memory in contrast to *engram*. One of the chief forms of "externalizing" memory is by story, by shared stories built around performance rituals. This is the classic transition "from ritual to theater" that Victor Turner[37] has so brilliantly described: the emergence of a designated storyteller as a vicar of group ritual. On this account, oral culture's chief "external memory device" becomes the story or narrative. And the story of aboriginal narrative – as in Carol Feldman's paper on genres[38] – reveals that narratives beget genres or perhaps vice versa.

Perhaps the greatest next step forward in memory externalization is crude literacy. For an inscribed record of the past provides the vehicle par excellence[39] for reflection or metacognition, although Scribner and Cole remind us that it is not always used in that way.[40] In any case, on Merlin Donald's account, evolving *H. sapiens* now has three ways of representing the past in an externalized way: through ritualized mimesis of accumulated skill, oral narrative, and external literate representation. Cultural institutions emerge to practice and exploit each of these: those who *do* with artful artisanly skill, those who *tell* narratives of traditional legitimacy, and those who *reckon* by manipulating the externalized record. The three domains remain in chronic overlap – like in Leonardo's notebooks. Contemporary classical historians, like Vernant in France and Geoffrey Lloyd in England, give vivid accounts of this overlap, as when fourth-century Greek thinkers tried to enrich Homeric narrative conceptions of virtue with geometrical concepts for deducing the nature of goodness as forms of harmony and symmetry.[41] But it was not zero-sum: Euclid did not preclude Homer. That was to come later. The Greeks were still tolerant toward all the ways of meaning making that came naturally.

The postmodern view – represented by the likes, say, of Richard Rorty,[42] Paul Ricoeur,[43] Thomas Kuhn,[44] or Nelson Goodman[45] – is rather more akin to the Greeks, though hardly as innocent. They take the view that meanings are always relative to the perspective from which they are derived. Their radical antireductionism and antipositivism seems to live more easily with our evolutionary past. It does not urge that what cannot be proved logically or demonstrated empirically should, in Hume's harsh words, be "cast unto the flames."

Which leads me to end this evolutionary diversion with a proposal and plea. Given human evolution and human history, we cognitive scientists err in insisting on one model of cognition, one model of mind. *Any* one model. And by the same token, we do well to avoid theories of meaning making tied exclusively to the needs and perspectives of science and analytic philosophy. The current cognitive revolution began well: to explain how people came to *understand* something rather than simply how they responded. Time we now turned more vigorously to the *different* ways of understanding, different forms of meaning making. I've suggested several of them. Cognitive science should become the repository of our knowledge about *possible* uses of mind. If it seems at times to reflect literary theory, at times historiography, at times anthropology and linguistics, perhaps that is how it may have to be. When George Miller and I went to our dean at Harvard, McGeorge Bundy, to discuss founding a Center for Cognitive Studies and told him something like that, he replied merrily, "But how does that differ from what Harvard as a whole is supposed to be doing?" In his contribution to this volume, the great Cambridge classicist Geoffrey Lloyd discussed problems in cognitive representation. The most daring law review article on jurisprudence of the last two decades was by the late Robert Cover[46] of Columbia, centering on the issue of how communities convert their norms into presuppositions for guiding legal interpretations, an issue that had occupied a distinguished anthropologist, Clifford Geertz, a few years earlier in his Storrs Lectures at Yale.[47] It is a big world out there and a varied one. No reductionist theory of mind in the old psychological or the new computational style will do it proper justice.

Notes

1 Cohen, I. B. *Franklin and Newton*. Philadelphia, PA: American Philosophical Society.

2 J. B. Conant, in *Two modes of thought: My encounters with science and education* (New York: Trident Press, 1964) takes this empirical mode as contrastive to the theoretical–deductive mode. My contrast, as we shall see, is with an interpretive mode.

3 Miller, Perry (1956). *Errand into the wilderness*. Cambridge, MA: Harvard Univ. Press.

4 I am indebted for this account to my late colleague Perry Miller, who read me accounts of this episode to be included in his masterly volume, *Errand into the wilderness* (ibid.), then in preparation. While much of the history and some of the reasoning in this section can be found in Miller's volume, the story of Edwards's "Newton sermon" was omitted from the final draft of that book.

5 Ibid., p. 179.

6 The reader will readily recognize how indebted I am in this discussion to Georg Henrik von Wright's *Explanation and understanding* (Ithaca, NY: Cornell University Press, 1971).

7 Astington, J. (1994). *The child's discovery of the mind*. Cambridge, MA: Harvard Univ. Press.
8 Austin, J. L. (1962). *How to do things with words*. Oxford: Oxford Univ. Press. Searle, J. (1969). *Speech acts*. Cambridge: Cambridge Univ. Press.
9 Grice, P. (1989). *Studies in the way of words*. Cambridge, MA: Harvard Univ. Press. See particularly chapter 2, "Logic and conversation."
10 Sperber, D., & Wilson, D. (1986). *Relevance: Communication and cognition*. Oxford: Blackwell.
11 Scaife, M., & Bruner, J. S. (1975). The capacity for joint visual attention in the infant. *Nature, 253*(5489), 265–266.
12 Ninio, A., & Bruner, J. S. (1978). The achievement and antecedents of labelling. *Journal of Child Language, 5*, 1–15.
13 Fillmore, C. W. (1968). The case for case. In E. Bach & R. Harms (Eds.), *Universals in linguistic theory*. New York: Holt, Rinehart & Winston.
14 Bruner, J. S. (1990). *Acts of meaning*. Cambridge, MA: Harvard Univ. Press.
15 Dunn, J. (1988). *The beginnings of social understanding*. Cambridge, MA: Harvard Univ. Press.
16 Propp, V. (1968). *Morphology of the folktale*, 2nd ed. Austin: Univ. of Texas Press.
17 Frye, N. (1957). *Anatomy of criticism*. Princeton, NJ: Princeton Univ. Press.
18 Iser, W. (1978). *The act of reading*. Baltimore, MD: Johns Hopkins Univ. Press. See also Feldman, C. (1994). Genres as mental models. In M. Ammaniti & D. Stern (Eds.), *Psychoanalysis and development: Representations and narratives* (pp. 111–121). New York: New York Univ. Press.
19 Beckwith, R., Fellbaum, C., Gross, D., & Miller, G. (1991). WordNet: A lexical database organized on psycholinguistic principles. In U. Zernick (Ed.), *Lexical acquisition: Exploiting on-line resources to build a lexicon*. Hillsdale, NJ: Erlbaum.
20 Edwards, P. (Ed.). (1967). *The encyclopedia of philosophy*. New York: Macmillan, Vol. iv, p. 169.
21 The general reader should not be expected to find her way around in Peirce's *Collected papers*. A brilliant exposition of Peirce's pragmatism is to be found in W. B. Gallie's *Peirce and pragmatism* (New York: Dover, 1966).
22 Bruner, J. S. (1957). Going beyond the information given. In H. Gruber et al. (Eds.), *Contemporary approaches to cognition*. Cambridge, MA: Harvard Univ. Press.
23 Bernstein, B., & Henderson, D. (1973). Social class differences in the relevance of language to socialization. In B. Bernstein (Ed.), *Class, codes, and control, Vol. 2, Applied studies toward a sociology of language*. London: Routledge.
24 Medin, D. L. (1989). Concepts and conceptual structure. *American Psychologist, 44*(12), 1469–1481.
25 Bruner, J. S., Goodnow, J. J., & Austin, G. A. (1956). *A study of thinking*. New York: Wiley. In fact, we proposed three types of categories, formal, functional, and affective, only the first of which was so constituted.
26 Rosch, E. (1978). Principles of categorization. In E. Rosch & B. Lloyd (Eds.), *Cognition and categorization* (pp. 27–48). Hillsdale, NJ: Erlbaum.
27 Smith, E., & Medin, D. L. (1981). *Categories and concepts*. Cambridge, MA: Harvard Univ. Press.
28 Keil, F. C. (1979). *Semantic and conceptual development: An ontological perspective*. Cambridge, MA: Harvard Univ. Press.
29 Carey, S. (1985). *Conceptual change in childhood*. Cambridge, MA: MIT Press.

30 Landau, M. (1991). *Narratives of human evolution*. New Haven, CT: Yale Univ. Press.
31 Gruber, H. E. (1981). *Darwin on man: A psychological study of scientific creativity*, 2nd ed. Chicago: Univ. of Chicago Press.
32 Newell, A., & Simon, H. A. (1972). *Human problem solving*. Englewood Cliffs, NJ: Prentice Hall.
33 For a particularly interesting perspective on this problem, see Auerbach, E. (1953). *Mimesis*. Princeton, NJ: Princeton Univ. Press.
34 Propp, op. cit.
35 Donald, M. (1991). *Origins of the modern mind*. Cambridge, MA: Harvard Univ. Press.
36 Bruner, J., Olver, R., & Greenfield, P. M. (1966). *Studies in cognitive growth*. New York: Wiley.
37 Turner, V. (1982). *From ritual to theater: The human seriousness of play*. New York: Performing Arts Journal Publications.
38 Feldman, op. cit.
39 Olson, D. R. (1994). *The world on paper: The conceptual and cognitive implications of writing and reading*. Cambridge: Cambridge Univ. Press.
40 Cole, M., & Scribner, S. (1974). *Culture and thought: A psychological introduction*. New York: Wiley.
41 Vernant, J. P., & Vidal-Naquet, P. (1988). *Myth and tragedy in ancient Greece*. New York: Zone Books. See also Lloyd. (Chapter 2 of this volume).
42 Rorty, R. (1979). *Philosophy and the mirror of nature*. Princeton, NJ: Princeton Univ. Press.
43 Ricoeur, P. (1984). *Time and narrative*, Vol. 1. Chicago: Univ. of Chicago Press.
44 Kuhn, T. (1962). *The structure of scientific revolutions*. Chicago: Univ. of Chicago Press.
45 Goodman, N. (1978). *Ways of worldmaking*. Hassocks, Sussex: Harvester.
46 Cover, R. (1983). Nomos and narrative: The Supreme Court 1982 term. *Harvard Law Review, 97*.
47 Geertz, C. (1983). *Local knowledge*. New York: Basic Books.

8
Autobiography and fiction as modes of thought

Carol Fleisher Feldman & David A. Kalmar

Until not so very long ago, empirical studies in cognitive development focused chiefly on forms of thinking that were logically organized and synchronic, perhaps because of Piaget's emphasis on the child as little logician. We studied the gradual acquisition of an adult understanding of arithmetic (Gelman and Gallistel, 1978), of physics (Siegler, 1978), and so on. At the same time, we were interested in the child's acquisition of adult linguistic knowledge, which, like adult scientific knowledge, was also characterized as a logical synchronic pattern (Chomsky, 1965). Studies of adult cognition tended to follow this same template, focusing on knowledge of such organized, rule-governed systems as the game of chess (Chase and Simon, 1973) or of economics (Kahneman, Slovic, and Tversky, 1982). In cognitive development and in adult cognition, the aggregate impact of these approaches was to suggest that the human mind had only one way of knowing, namely, a way regulated by a synchronous logical structure. Other cognitive patterns observed in the context of this research were often seen as falls from grace or a failure to master expert rational systems, though equally often they suggested the possibility that people were following a different drummer of a nonscientific kind, for example, there was a realization even as early as 1956 (Bruner, Goodnow, and Austin, 1956) that human materials might elicit a different pattern of understanding than physical shapes.

But, of course, there were many other things going on at the same time in fields quite close by, and bit by bit they began to take shape as suggesting that there might be cognitive instruments of many other kinds: intuition (Westcott, 1968), creativity (Csikszentmihalyi, 1990), and, most notably, narrative (van Dijk, 1980; Schank and Abelson, 1977) and in narrative development (Bretherton and Beeghly, 1982; Bruner, 1983; Dunn and Kendrick, 1982; Miller, 1982; Nelson, 1986, and Stein and Glenn, 1979, inter alia). This is just a beginning, for there were many other developments along these lines in psychology (e.g., Olson's work on literacy, 1986, 1994; Rubin's in memory, 1986; Uleman and Bargh's in social psychology, 1989), in anthro-

We thank the Spencer Foundation for their support with the grant Studies in Cultural Psychology 1991–1995 to our collaborator, Jerome Bruner. We also thank Dr. Bruner for his considerable contribution, including a very helpful reading of an earlier version. Finally, we thank David Olson for providing still another important opportunity to advance this work in interesting company.

pology (Heath, 1983), and in socio-linguistics (Ochs and Schieffelin, 1983) as well; we cannot do them justice here. That there might be narrative as well as paradigmatic modes of thought, as Bruner (1986) put it, came increasingly to be accepted.

But narrative thinking has been a difficult and elusive matter, partly perhaps because of a deeply held, though not well-examined, disposition to think of it as idiosyncratic and even anarchic, whether in whole (a matter of individual points of view freely formed at a particular moment) or in part (comprehension of all the narrative details beyond the bare bones of the event sequence or script within the text). It is only in the last few years that cognitive psychologists have begun to see narrative thinking as part of a cultural psychology, that is, as derived from the culture, and, particularly, as making use of the instruments of the culture, as in the program recommended in Bruner (1990). According to his view, there are many cultural instruments with patterned coherence, generality, and even generativity. Seen this way, grammar and science are two leading cultural instruments, instruments that support thinking of a paradigmatic kind.

But there are also patterned cultural instruments that serve narrative purposes, notably such literary patterns as genre and plot. Within a cultural psychology, these become good candidates for tools that support narrative thinking. And if scientific thought, for example, incorporates the logic of science itself, then narrative thinking might incorporate literary patterns. This opens the possibility that there might be patterned or rule-governed forms of narrative thinking and suggests where to look for them, namely, in narrative cultural models. With this approach in hand, it has become possible to think of narrative thinking as patterned or rule governed (rather than anarchic), as canonical or conventional (rather than idiosyncratic), and as useful coin in human discourse, to borrow a notion from Bourdieu (1991). Since culturally shared instruments are bound to have the Durkheimian (Durkheim, 1965) exteriority and constraint that is the result of social exchange, their interiorization would yield a cognitive tool for conventional modes of narrative thought. Its power and pattern would follow from that of the cultural instrument itself. Since literature and its models have temporal patterns and focus on human intentional states, their power and pattern are bound to be very different from those of science.

What exteriority and constraint is imposed on individual stories, and how do we conventionalize or generalize across them? To answer this, we can ask what cultural instrument is found in literature and literary theory for regularizing understanding. The leading candidate is the notion, central to literary studies, of *genre* (Feldman, 1994). In the study of literature, it is a genre characterization that is used to give an overall and generalized patterning of stories, and a good deal of work has been done on them and with them – their taxonomy or list of types (Hernadi, 1972), their internal structural descriptions (e.g., see Eakin, 1989, for autobiography; and Iser, 1978, and Riffaterre, 1990, for fiction), their conjoint organization (Frye, 1957), and their theoretical construal (Fowler, 1982). The position we take here is that genre patterns are cognitive models that are derived from exposure to texts that embody them but are then imposed on texts by readers who know them as an interpretive lens. They are in the text and in the mind.

The founder of modern genre studies was Northrop Frye (1957). He refocused attention on the existence of genres in literature, developing a two-by-two classification based on the relationship between the reader's activity and the discourse pattern of the text. It yielded four basic genre types: tragedy, comedy, lyric, and epic. He denied the possibility, in principle, of ever discovering a list of genres that was mutually exclusive and exhaustive for several reasons. Specifically, Frye denied that genre could be understood as fixed, since they were modifiable in their mode (e.g., heroic, gothic), divisible into subgenres, and mixable into mixed genres. Moreover, the instances of any one genre could be expected to share at most a family resemblance – there is no defining list of features. Since Frye, there have been tremendous developments in genre theory and a great refinement of notions about the nature of the reader's response as a contribution to the construction of the genre in the text. The literary models themselves have in a sense become cognitive. With these developments has also come a more elaborated theory of what the reader's cultural context contributes and of historical changes in genre patterns. We will return to notions about genre later and consider some important modern views when we come to consider the two genres of interest to us: autobiography and fiction.

According to Tambiah (1990), linguistic genres have an analogue in praxis, particularly in "historically formed culture complexes" (p. 63) such as ritual. Both can be understood as what Wittgenstein (1968) called *forms of life* that bind social interaction into canonical patterns or forms. Oral genres in nonliterate cultures (Rosaldo, 1971) are of the same order. Indeed, they occupy an interesting middle ground between literary genre and ritual praxis, since though they are language forms, they are typically used in ritual contexts, as many students have observed (e.g., Bloch, 1975).

For now, we turn to plot, so we can be clear about what genre is not. Genre is not the same as plot, which is a far better candidate for a structure identifiable in the text itself. And plot is not simply a sequence of plotted events, but rather, as Propp (1968) showed for the folktale, a *pattern* consisting of categorial slots serving particular functions, each of which can be filled with a variety of specific events of the right categorial kind. These functions are distributed across characters in different spheres (hero, villain, helper) and into a typical sequence (beginning with a lack or villainy; to intermediate functions, such as journeys and trials; to marriage; and then to a terminal function, such as gain or escape from pursuit). The category arrangements, in the temporal sequence the tale creates, is what gives interpretable meaning to the particular events selected for each category. For example, the journey of a traveler who goes off on a quest at the start of his tale is in a different category and has a different meaning than the journey of a successful warrior returning home at the end. So an event category has a different meaning depending on its place in the plot sequence or its role in the plot. Moreover, the contingencies go both forward with the time line – a

quest only makes sense because of the prior conditions of the boy who un-
dertakes it, and backward against it, so that what category is selected at, say,
the initial point also depends on what overall plot pattern we are in, the details
of which will all come later.

Moreover, there are category effects at a higher level of organization, say,
to initiate a disruption in a steady state or to repair one. For example, a
category such as "strange news from abroad arrives" could induce or repair
a disruption. And there is a still higher level of patterning that organizes a
sequence of disruptions. A disruption is an important function, perhaps a
metafunction, in the plot, and it can come by many means, but it must always
come after a steady state. Moreover it must always, at least in the folktale,
resolve into another steady state. But the second steady state and the first
have different functions, and this is recognized by the way the second must
both take into account but also somehow transcend the first.

This is all reason to describe plot as structure or structural/functional.
Nevertheless, it operates at a lower level, and in a simpler way than genre,
which is the only good candidate in literary theory for a pattern that could
supply a mode of thought analogous to von Wright's Aristotelian pattern of
scientific thinking, to which we now turn.

If we did find that many people have some modes of thought that are
patterned in the same way as popular genres in this culture, what kind of a
mental process would we be pointing to? These modes of thought are highly
atypical for cognitive psychology, for the nature of the subjects' knowledge
seems to be more interpretive than causal. It is because there seems to be a
need to state some of this in sharper terms that we turn to von Wright's
(1971) important discussion of two kinds of (scientific) theory. Though his
purpose was to describe the scientist's ways of thinking, and though there
are many interesting questions posed for psychological science by the study
of narrative thinking, nevertheless, our interest here is simply in using his
description to understand the cognitive patterns of ordinary people. We are
especially interested in the question of what kind of insight people can expect
to get from narrative modes of thought.

Georg von Wright (1971) points to two forms of scientific explanation,
glossed as Aristotelian and Galilean. But they just as usefully can be seen as
characterizing the modes of thought of ordinary people as the modes of
thought used by scientists. The first is for human action and other intentional
objects and gives teleological explanations organized in the same way as the
temporal explanations in history. The second is for nonintentional objects,
such as human behaviors, and gives synchronic causal accounts. He notes
that scientific psychology was born at a time of great cross pressure between
positivism and antipositivism and so is naturally pulled in both directions –
toward a Galilean account of human behavior given in terms of objective
causes and toward an Aristotelian account of perhaps those same events as
actions, given in terms of human purposes. Nevertheless, virtually all scientific psychology to the present day has been essentially Galilean. And as
the cognition *about* which we have theorized has also been scientific or log-

ical, it too, therefore, has been essentially Galilean. But if people do have modes of thought patterned in the same way as literary genres, that would be, we suggest, cognition patterned along Aristotelian lines.

With von Wright's distinction in mind, let us look at some well-known texts. When we turn to accounts of symbolic action that rise to the level of art – action that is seen to have a complex pattern of meaning by virtue of its interpretability within a complex cultural frame – we eschew the Galilean mode as simplistic and reductive rather than brilliantly distilled, as it so often is in the scientific understanding of the physical world. We do so because the same kind of reduction that can seem to capture the fundamentals underlying a variety of trivial surface variations in the scientific domain can seem forced and unsatisfactory in narrative art, only in part because we tend to consider the true understanding of such matters to be irreducibly complex. For example, the following would not be a "brilliant," nor even an adequate, adult account of Nora's behavior in *The Doll's House*, though many readers see it as an essential theme: Nora became aware of the indignity of her position as a wife and came to find it unacceptable so she left. This nearly Galilean account has a cause (in Nora's construal) and that is, in this case, one source of its inadequacy. For we want to say that the leaving of a husband is a serious matter that is always multiply determined and yet not determined at all, rather chosen and with many countervailing considerations in mind. It may be of some anecdotal interest that Ibsen himself was rather surprised when, in life, feminists took up this play as their own emblem.

Part of the difficulty here is that though this reduction would be too simple even as a report about people's actions in everyday life, it is made even more unsatisfactory by the complex, interpretable texture of its literary expression. For the patterning of the literary artifact that is Ibsen's play planfully triggers understanding by relying on cultural conventions of playwriting (Iser, 1978). The patterning of the play invites a nuanced understanding of the characters and their development, their context, their plight – in short, the discovery or construction (along culturally patterned lines) of meanings beyond those made explicit in the text, though of course the text must contain triggers that invite the reader to discover them. The patterning of text, when it takes place within a cultural literary context, guides discovery of the meanings of the individual actions that occur within it. This process of discovery of meaning through interpretation of patterned cultural artifacts seems to be a central example of Aristotelian understanding. And it seems to be tied up with the patterns of the text that invite it rather than something that can be abstracted away from them.

We will see that the differing textual patterns of three literary tales about women liberating themselves from dull marriages would be at least as important as their common theme for understanding them if we now include a glance at *Madame Bovary* and *The Scarlet Letter*. Despite the common themes, the three novels are entirely different kinds of texts. Some of their differences can be captured by noting that they are of different genres and that their genre differences give such similar events as occur within them very different meanings. The leaving of a husband can be seen as an expression of growth and freedom in *The Doll's House* when it is given its canonical genre assignment as something like the first woman's *Bildungsroman*, whereas in *Madame Bovary*, it can seem to express self-deception, confusion, and even illusionism in the romantic reading of that novel. In contrast, an illicit love affair takes on the dark meaning of a terrible destructive force in the tragic rendering of *The Scarlet Letter*.

Because von Wright's important analysis is so often misunderstood, it may be helpful to describe his picture of the sciences in more detail in order to see what narrative cognition can be expected to yield in the lives of ordinary people.

Von Wright's two types of scientific intelligibility, the Galilean and the Aristotelian, each contain two classes of mental activity that are highly interlinked – the first is explanation, the second understanding. Aristotelian explanation is teleological, Galilean, causal. For von Wright, understanding is an essential process whose importance is not generally recognized. Usually, both processes occur in sequence – we cannot explain anything before it has been appropriately understood; but once we have achieved an explanation, it can serve as the basis of a new understanding for subsequent explanation. In pointing to understanding as a second key constituent of scientific accounts, he makes note of a process, that though inevitable, is often implicit and insufficiently noted or described. So far, von Wright has distinguished two *types* of account and two key and universal constituents of both.

Each form of explanation, causal and teleological, has its own form of coherence. For the causal, the familiar pattern is subsumption under a covering law; causal explanation is usually taken in modern Western culture as the paradigm of true scientific accounts. For the teleological, von Wright recommends the practical syllogism with its derivations of individual actions from antecedent desires and beliefs. This proposal for the teleological pattern has the dual merits of using temporal sequence as its basis and grounding explanation in intentional states. Yet, it is rather unsatisfactory for our purposes, as it explains the bases of individual actions as if they were isolated from any larger model or cultural system, such as a genre frame, that could give them meaning. Moreover, his unsatisfactory management of this issue may be the fundamental reason why Aristotelian explanation is often seen as unequal to the Galilean in power and abstractness, incapable of any real generativity. Once we take advantage of modern developments in psychology and literary theory and situate Aristotelian explanation and understanding within the event-subsuming abstract patterns of genre, we see how Aristotelian accounts can be (temporal) analogues of the (static) Galilean.

Though the two kinds of explanation are distinguished in these ways, the *origin* of their distinction is in the types of objects that they address. Causal explanation is for nonintentional objects, teleological explanation for intentional ones. However, the same existing, singular, human event can often be seen as an objectified behavior or as an (intentional) action. But whichever kind of event we take it to be, it is that decision as to which it is that controls which scientific account will be appropriate, so that von Wright's theory anchors itself in the (stipulative) *object types to be explained*.

Each of the two kinds of *explanation*, causal and teleological, has a corresponding form of scientific *understanding* – the causal of what the thing *is
like*, the teleological of what it *means*. In the matter of explaining human
action within a genre frame, this interpretation that constitutes our understanding seems to be not merely essential, but central. The main thing we
ask of our genre is that it tell us what, say, the leaving of the husband meant
or that it give us an understanding of the event as an intentional action in a
patterned context. Do we then also go on to explain it as caused by desires
in connection with beliefs? Well, yes and no; but in literature, and even in
life, such explanations are seldom really satisfactory and often seem unnecessary. In contrast, no Galilean account is complete without an explanation,
though many would be improved by more attention to understanding, as we
have noted elsewhere (Feldman, 1987).

According to this analysis, von Wright makes three key points:

1. He proposes that there are two (recursively related) constituents of all
   scientific accounts, *explanation* and *understanding*, the second of which
   is often not fully appreciated.
2. He proposes that explanation comes in two forms, *causal* and *teleological*,
   with the importance of the second type often not fully recognized. Each
   of them has a distinctive type of understanding integral to it; for the teleological type, understanding is interpretive.
3. The controlling feature of the selection between these forms is the nature
   (nonintentional or intentional) of the objects to be explained, which can
   be a matter of preference or even a cultural convention.

Since von Wright's book was written, such intention-based psychological
models have come to notice in discussions of "folk" psychology, where
intentional states are taken as basic and explained along patterned lines by
ordinary people. But von Wright's analysis was powerful enough to anticipate
the way Aristotelian folk psychology would generally be seen in a Galilean
context, namely, as illusions that mistakenly elevate mere prejudice about the
insubstantial "irreal" to a world representation that at best simply misleads
and at worst veils the real facts lying behind it. It is seen as contrasting with
a scientific psychology that gives correct explanations of the same matters.
Animism got a very bad name for good reasons in physics, where it was
soundly beaten by Galilean accounts. In the folk psychology literature, it
seems as if animism had been taken, perhaps unthinkingly, for a universal
error, even in the human domain where it has a much more central role – at
very least, we cannot negotiate the social transactions of everyday life without it.

We come now to our studies of genre. The first thing an acculturated adult
reader (or listener) does when hearing a story is to make a guess about its
genre as a condition for further discovery of structure and interpretation. How
does the reader make such attributions? Rarely do book titles have genre
labels as subtitles. For the most part, readers manage without them. In general, we may suppose that readers put prior knowledge about this particular
book and about genres likely to be found there together with clues in the text

itself. These clues may seem to signal the appropriateness of one or another genre assignment. Genre information is, at most, latent in the text. In the studies discussed later, we made use of this normal process, but we controlled *which* genre subjects assigned, simply by telling them how they should view the text. In the first study, the genres were autobiography and fiction.

More basic for modern readers than the Aristotelian distinction between comedy and tragedy or the four-way genre distinction proposed by Frye is the distinction between fiction and autobiography, which, for readers, comes very close to the distinction between story as art and as life. For although autobiography can, and perhaps should, be thought of as a constructed form of artful narration like any other, many ordinary readers see it simply as a report of real-life experiences. It is seen as "found" rather than "made."

Autobiography, for them, means reportage. As such it is not bound by the requirements of crafted art, but by two other constraints. First, it must tell what really happened (that is, be true). In literary theory (Lejeune, 1989), this feature has been noted as well. For Lejeune, two matters related to truthfulness separate the genre of autobiography from fiction: (1) the identity of the proper name shared by author, narrator, and protagonist in autobiography promises a true story about a real person and establishes a relationship with "factors external to the text," and (2) the "autobiographical pact," which is a contract proposed by the author to the reader, "in which the autobiographer explicitly commits himself or herself not to some impossible historical exactitude but rather to the sincere effort to come to terms with and to understand his or her own life" (Eakin, 1989, p. ix).

The "coming to terms with" requirement in Lejeune takes us to the second feature of our subjects' notions about autobiography. Not everything that happens is worth telling, and so autobiography is bound by a discourse requirement that enjoins us to tell each other only about experiences worth telling about, important experiences. Readers of tales seen as autobiographical, then, seek out indicators of the manner of exceptionality. But, for these purposes, important experiences are those that *meant* something, or something special, to the author; they are not the habitual stuff of everyday life.

This way of looking at autobiography focuses attention on the *subjective* life of the reporter. What is "reported" is the writer's *reactions* to events in the world. The events in the world themselves are thus not seen as detached and objectified for the reader's own direct scrutiny, but rather as located in the background of a psychological landscape. And, indeed, this is how our subjects see it as well, as we shall see later.

We turn now to fiction. If what distinguishes autobiography both in literary theory and for our subjects is that it purports in some sense to be a true report, what distinguishes fiction is that it is explicitly not true, but imaginary. Fiction, according to Riffaterre (1990), is a genre that rests on a key convention, namely, that it *excludes the intention to deceive*. For fiction always contains signs that it is imaginary. "Its very name declares its artificiality, and yet it must somehow be true to hold the interest of its readers, to tell them about experiences at once imaginary and relevant to their own lives. ... [T]ruth in fiction rests on verisimilitude, a system of representations that seems to reflect a reality external to the text, but only because it conforms to a grammar'' (pp. xii–xiv). Fiction follows rules.

In a related vein, Iser (1978) notes that fiction opens the horizon of possibilities beyond the normative structures found in life. ''The fictional text makes a selection from a variety of conventions to be found in the real world, and it puts them together as if they were interrelated. This is why we recognize in a novel, for instance, so many of the conventions that regulate our society and culture. But by reorganizing them . . . the fictional text brings them before us in unexpected combinations'' (p. 61). Moreover, the reader of fiction is given a good deal of work to do, for these marked violations of convention are signals for how to unpack the meaning of the text and go ''beyond the information given.'' The reader is ''obliged to work out why certain conventions should have been selected for his attention. . . . In this process the reader is guided by a variety of narrative techniques, which might be called the strategies of the text'' (p. 61). Our fiction readers see it this way, too, as we shall see.

For some years now, our research group has been exploring the ways people interpret literary texts when they have a genre in mind or, how people use genres to guide interpretation or, to put it still another way, what the nature of that patterned knowledge is. In a series of studies, we used an elementary experimental design to explore these matters.

In each study, half of the subjects were told a story was of one genre, half were told it was of another. The story was read aloud individually to each subject after the genre label was given. After the story was read, subjects were asked some interpretive questions and asked to retell the story. Subjects' responses were transcribed from tape and coded.

In one study, thirty-five undergraduates were individually read a 676-word passage from Primo Levi's *The Monkey's Wrench* (1978/1986), which to half of them was described as autobiography and to the other half as fiction. The text is given in Appendix A. As the story opens, a Russian, Nicolai Rasnitsa, is proving his identity to two tourists, the narrator and his friend Falcone. He invites them to come along as his guests on a boat ride. The tourists find themselves participating in a drinking party with Rasnitsa and his two ominous-looking companions. As the story ends, the more they drink, the more the narrator feels himself losing control of the situation. After listening to the story, subjects were asked the questions that are given in Appendix B.

When the text of their interpretive responses is coded, we find that autobiography is seen as true and the events as being reported rather than made. So the basic shape of the ordinary person's understanding of autobiography is as reportage of veridical events and of fiction as crafted construction of the merely possible. Moreover, subjects with an autobiography genre in mind far more often mention the autobiography genre in their interpretations than those with a fiction genre in mind, implying that the mere fact of being an autobiography, with its obligation to report the way things were in life, is highly determinative. In sharp contrast, fiction subjects virtually never mention their genre pattern as an answer, reflecting a very basic underlying generic difference, namely that fiction opens up the horizon of possibilities, as we noted earlier, and, though operating within constraints, is seen as less determinative than autobiography. Taken together, these codes find in ordinary people's thinking key features of the generic patterns of autobiography and fiction found in literature and suggest that they are here operating as modes of thought.

Moreover, as we noted above in our discussion of literary theory, the requirement to tell the truth about a life in autobiography leads, via the autobiographical pact, to a focus on events important or meaningful to the writer. With this focus on the autobiographer's experience, the actual circumstances within which the experience takes place is placed at one remove, in the background. Our subjects also see autobiography this way. When asked to imagine the characters, to describe what "kind of people" they are, autobiography subjects tend not to make note of such important, factual details as the national identities of the characters, specifically that they are Russian (for more on this see Feldman and Kalmar, in press).

Furthermore, we find evidence for Iser's fictional strategies discussed earlier. In autobiography, the characters are seen as "thinly sketched," whereas those same characters are seen in a fictional context as "fully developed." This is related to an important difference between autobiography and fiction that we discussed earlier: that elements within fiction are taken as presuppositional triggers within a crafted universe of meaning, carrying the reader way beyond the information given in the text. To achieve these differences, fiction readers must see certain small details as filled with implied meaning, whereas autobiography readers must construe those same details as just another fact. The thinly sketched characters of autobiography, then, are simply characters about whom we infer nothing more than has been said. The subjects, then, have a fictional mode of thought that corresponds in key respects to the cultural artifact of fiction itself.

To summarize, our subjects have two modes of thought that can be evoked simply by labeling a story as autobiography or fiction, and we have been able to see that they correspond in key respects with the structure of their corresponding literary genres: autobiography is true, uncrafted, and the events within are highly constrained by the genre, whereas fiction is invented, crafted, freer in its possibilities, and triggers presuppositions that make the characters seem more elaborated. It can safely be said that our subjects carry these modes of thought around with them, for a mere label could not have supplied the *pattern* of interpretation they assigned to the genre labels we gave them. In point of fact, they must have learned the patterns by living in an interpretive community and mastering their local community's patterns of interpretation. This is a point that Olson (1986) has made a good deal of in connection with simple literacy. It applies a fortiori at this higher level, too – to what can be thought of as the knowledge that permits us to read not just isolated sentences or even simple stories, but the cultural product that is literature. Moreover, the two modes of thought are generative models that serve as recipes for how to construe (nearly) any tale seen as being in one or the other genre.

And we made an interesting discovery that we had not expected when we

Table 8.1. *Words attributed to*
autobiography and fiction groups

Autobiography	Fiction
another	a
around	birthday
between	each
coming	go
drank	invited
information	little
is	more
men	names
Nicolai	on
picture	people
someone	time
tall	
wrapped	

examined word usage in context: that the two genre labels also affect certain aspects of the plotting of the story seen as being told. Without affecting the elements included in the plot, for they were the same in both groups, the plot pattern was responsive to the genre context. To be more precise, the basic plot type for one of our groups (autobiography) is of an innocent ramble terrifyingly run amok, a near abduction; whereas for the other (fiction) it is of a happy outing at a birthday party, an amusing encounter. The former has its turning point when the (scary) drinking begins, the latter when the party invitation is extended a few minutes earlier.

Words used more frequently by one group than another were examined in their contexts of use. As Olson and Salter (1993) elsewhere correctly note, this is a data-driven process that must be used heuristically and with caution. It helps and is important to have an overall understanding of group differences in interpretive pattern based on reading the transcripts beforehand, so that one approaches the lexical differences with something in mind. In this study, as we described earlier, the codes had richly supplied us with a model of the subjects' differing interpretive frameworks with which to approach the word frequency differences.

The complete list of words used differently by subjects in the two groups is given in Table 8.1. For the fiction group, as our tourist protagonists approach a dock to *go on* a boat trip, they are *invited* to join in a *birthday* party by some *people* (they do or don't know *each* other), whose *names* have been forgotten, where they have a (good or bad) *time, more* or less (*little*). It's *A Day at the Races* – an encounter.

In contrast, the autobiography words mark a bad trip, a near abduction. In the autobiography version, after our travelers (not tourists, for they are in search of *information*) approach the dock, *Nicolai*, who is *someone* unusual, *another* sort of person or from another country, presses them to join him and his friends on the boat. There are two more *men*, one of them *tall*, who produced some food ominously *wrapped* in newspaper and a large quantity of bad wine and sat down with one of the foreigners *between* them. They all *drank* to excess, and they pressed him to drink more, but no one was *coming* to his aid.[1]

Nearly all the words that were differently used by the two groups are used up by this account; there are only five words that did not fit into it, and these are generally too ambiguous to put anywhere. Four of those words, *around* and *is* from the autobiography group and *a* and *on* from the fiction group, were of multiple and therefore indeterminate use. The only other word is the autobiography subjects' use of *picture*, which may have been an echo of something in one of our questions.

Beyond the overall differences in plotting, we can even, we think, make a case for functional substitution within certain word pairs. The ominous *men* of autobiography make an obvious contrast with the friendly *people* of fiction. The non-*coming* of help in autobiography contrasts with the antidepressive, agentive flavor of the characteristic word *go* in fiction. The categorial and alien flavor of *another* and *someone* to describe the Russians in autobiography contrast with the relational use of *each* to describe who knew whom beforehand in fiction. *Nicolai* in the autobiography contrasts with (no) *name* in the fiction. *Information* seems the predatory contrast with the friendly *invited* of fiction. Finally, the autobiography use of *drank* stands out against the whole fiction description, but especially the innocent and jejune *birthday* and the civilized *invited*.

Plainly one important part of the narrative expertise of these normal adult subjects is in knowing how to construe plot events in a way that suits the genre frame where they occur. The autobiography genre demands an unusual experience for it to be worth telling. This is achieved here by seeing the birthday party as a drinking scene that is threatening and scary. The fiction genre has no such requirement, and there the very same birthday party and bootleg liquor are seen as playful and amusing, an adventure that opened up both the protagonists' and the readers' horizon of possibilities.

Subjects, as we have said, all notice the same basic events constituting the story; the difference is a matter of how those events are weighted: what is given, what is new, what the point, and what the background. In a recent paper from this laboratory (Bruner and Feldman, 1993), we described a narrational problem in high-functioning autistic subjects. Though they could understand all the individual events contained in an American Indian folktale about trickery or deceit, they did not see the trick as having the importance it had as the key event on which the story turned. What we didn't see as clearly then, but that the present analysis leads us to believe, is that this would have something to do with weighting, with correctly perceiving what is background and what is noteworthy, and with picking up such textual triggers to unpack meaning as Iser's strategies. In that paper, we also showed a related defect in creating new comments on old topics in conversation in another autistic group. The strategies seem to be at the heart of the ability to tell fictional stories well; they create the meanings that make a story worth telling. But as they are perhaps at the heart of narrative competence for fiction, their absence could also prevent proper weighting of events in comprehension.

A second example will be briefly presented just to give the flavor of the more general claim that we think this first study illustrates. For we believe that these two interpretive patterns are only two important ones among many others that constitute the normal interpretive toolkit of adult members of our culture. In a study currently in progress (Kalmar, 1996), a somewhat longer version of the Primo Levi story is read but characterized as a spy story or a travelogue. A preliminary analysis (subject to revision) finds that words used significantly more often by the spy group are: *happen, information, says, spy, spies, story, what's*. The spy subjects think there's more going on than meets the eye, and they are looking for it (*what's* going on, and something's gonna *happen*). In a context like this, where spies are around, one pays careful attention to what everyone actually *says*. Though they share *information*, this version seems very different from the menacing take of the autobiography subjects. The travelogue subjects focus on the *different culture*, language, places, and facial *features* of their friends. Rather than being out on a romp like the fiction version, the travelers are seriously studying these foreigners (in Russia). They also have a problem with the heavy drinking, but instead of the menace of the autobiography subjects, this time it is a more technical threat to health (*liver*). In short, these two new genres show promise as two more, though less fundamental, modes of thought that crosscut and are different from the ones we have seen before. And there may be any number of other literary genres for which competent adults have a corresponding mode of thought.

These genres have been the subject of our interest here. We believe that they are powerful instruments of adult cognition and, especially, of adult cognition of the Aristotelian type, which is the type suited to accounting for human action. They provide a generative framework for its two constituent activities: teleological explanation of human actions and understanding what they mean in the context. In this chapter, we have tried to show that subjects approach events in stories by applying an interpretive framework that, much as theory does in science, provides a pattern within which otherwise neutral elements take on a determinate meaning and relatedness. These interpretive frameworks are patterned modes of thought that correspond to the genre patterns of the culture, especially its literature, and which must be derived from them as well, perhaps, as contributing to their reconstitution every time a book is read.

Appendix A: Excerpt from Primo Levi's **The Monkey's Wrench**, *as administered*

Rasnitsa, after digging into all his pockets, pulled out a little ID card, all greasy and crumpled; and he showed me and Falcone that the photograph was really of him and that his name really was what he had said: Nicolai M. Rasnitsa. Immediately afterward, he declared that we were

his friends, or rather his guests. In fact, by a lucky coincidence, that day
was his birthday, and he was actually preparing to celebrate it with a
river excursion. Fine, we would all go together to Dubrovka. He was
awaiting the boat, and on it there would be two or three friends from
his village who were also going to celebrate with him. To me, the
thought of a Russian experience, a bit less formal than those connected
with the job, was not unpleasant; but I saw a shadow of misgiving tinge
Falcone's face, usually so inexpressive. And a little later, out of the side
of his mouth, he whispered to me: "Things look bad."

The boat arrived, coming from the direction of the dam, and the two
of us produced our tickets to be checked. Vexed, Rasnitsa told us we
had made a big mistake buying tickets, especially first class and round
trip. Weren't we his guests? He wanted to invite us on the outing, he
was a friend of the captain and the whole crew, and on this line he
never paid for a ticket, for himself or for his guests. We went on board;
the boat, too, was deserted, except for Rasnitsa's two friends, seated on
one of the benches on deck. They were a pair of giants, with jailbird
faces the like of which I've never seen anywhere, in Russia or outside,
except in some spaghetti Westerns. One was obese, and his trousers
hung from a belt fastened tight below his belly; the other was thinner,
with a pock-marked face, and his lower jaw stuck out so that his bottom
teeth closed over the upper ones. Both men stank of sweat and were
drunk.

The boat set off again. Rasnitsa explained to his friends who we
were, and they said that was fine, the more the merrier. They made me
sit between them, and Falcone sat beside Rasnitsa on the opposite
bench. The fat man was carrying a package, wrapped in newspaper,
carefully tied up with a string; he unwrapped it, and inside there were
several rustic sandwiches filled with fatback. He passed them around,
then he went somewhere below deck and came back up carrying a tin
bucket by the handle, obviously a former paint can. From his pocket he
extracted an aluminum cup, filled it with the liquid from the bucket, and
invited me to drink. It was a sweet, very strong wine, something like
Marsala, but harsher, somehow edgy. To my taste it was decidedly bad,
and I saw that also Falcone, who is a connoisseur, wasn't enthusiastic.
But the two were indomitable: in the bucket there was at least three li-
ters of wine, and they declared we had to finish it up during the outward trip; otherwise what kind of birthday would it be? And moreover,
never fear: in Dubrovka we would find more, and even better.

In my scant Russian, I tried to defend myself: the wine was good,
but this was enough for me, I wasn't used to drinking, I was seriously
ill, bad liver, stomach. But there was nothing for it: the two, supported
by Rasnitsa, produced a compulsive conviviality that bordered on menace, and I had to drink again and again. Falcone drank, too, but he was
in less danger than I, because he can hold his wine, and also because,
since his Russian was better, he could make more articulate excuses or
change the subject. He showed no signs of discomfort; he talked and

drank; every now and then my eye, more and more clouded, would catch his clinical glance, but whether through distraction or deliberate determination to be superior, he made no effort, throughout the trip, to come to my aid.

(*The Monkey's Wrench* by Primo Levi, pp. 89–91. Copyright © 1978, Giulio Einaudi editore s.p.a., Torino. English language translation copyright © 1986 by Simon & Schuster, Inc. Reprinted by permission of Simon & Schuster, Inc.)

Appendix B: Interview schedule

1. First, I'd like you to tell it back to me, using your own words, and filling in all the details of how you saw it.
2. What do you think came *before* this?
3. And why do you think that came before?
4. What do you think will come next?
5. And why do you think so?
6. How do you imagine these characters? What kind of people are they?
7. What do you think they are after in this scene? What do they want?
8. What do you think the *author* was trying to accomplish with this scene?

Note

1 This picture derived from the word count analysis is also reported in Feldman and Kalmar (in press), where its educational implications are discussed.

References

Bloch, M. (Ed.). (1975). *Political language and oratory in traditional society*. London: Academic Press.

Bourdieu, P. (1991). *Language and symbolic power* (G. Raymond & M. Adamson, Trans.). Cambridge, MA: Harvard Univ. Press.

Bretherton, I., & Beeghly, M. (1982). Talking about internal states: The acquisition of an explicit theory of mind. *Developmental Psychology, 18*, 906–921.

Bruner, J. S. (1983). *Child's talk: Learning to use language*. New York: Norton.
    (1986). Two modes of thought. In *Actual minds, possible worlds* (pp. 11–43). Cambridge, MA: Harvard Univ. Press.
    (1990). *Acts of meaning*. Cambridge, MA: Harvard Univ. Press.

Bruner, J., & Feldman, C. (1993). Theories of mind and the problem of autism. In S. Baron-Cohen, H. Tager-Flusberg, & D. J. Cohen (Eds.), *Understanding other minds: Perspectives from autism* (pp. 267–291). Oxford Univ. Press.

Bruner, J. S., Goodnow, J. J., & Austin, G. A. (1956). *A study of thinking*. London: Wiley.

Chase, W. G., & Simon, H. A. (1973). The mind's eye in chess. In W. G. Chase (Ed.), *Visual information processing* (pp. 215–281). New York: Academic Press.

Chomsky, N. (1965). *Aspects of the theory of syntax*. Cambridge, MA: MIT Press.

Csikszentmihalyi, M. (1990). *Flow: The psychology of optimal experience*. New York: Harper & Row.

van Dijk, T. A. (1980). *Macrostructures: An interdisciplinary study of global structures in discourse, interaction, and cognition*. Hillsdale, NJ: Erlbaum.

Dunn, J., & Kendrick, C. (1982). *Siblings: Love, envy and understanding*. Cambridge, MA: Harvard Univ. Press.

Durkheim, E. (1965). *The elementary forms of the religious life* (J. W. Swain, Trans.). New York: Free Press.

Eakin, P. J. (1989). Foreword. In P. Lejeune, *On autobiography* (K. Leary, Trans.). Minneapolis: Univ. of Minnesota Press.

Feldman, C. F. (1987). Thought from language: The linguistic construction of cognitive representations. In J. Bruner & H. Haste (Eds.), *Making sense: The child's construction of the world* (pp. 131–146). London: Routledge.

(1994). Genres as mental models. In M. Ammaniti & D. N. Stern (Eds.), *Psychoanalysis and development: Representations and narratives* (pp. 111–121). New York: New York Univ. Press.

Feldman, C. F., & Kalmar, D. A. (in press). Some educational implications of genre-based mental models: The interpretive cognition of text understanding. In D. Olson & N. Torrance (Eds.), *Handbook of Education and human development: New models of learning, teaching, and schooling*. Cambridge: Cambridge Univ. Press.

Fowler, A. (1982). *Kinds of literature: An introduction to the theory of genres and modes*. Cambridge, MA: Harvard Univ. Press.

Frye, N. (1957). *Anatomy of criticism: Four essays*. Princeton: Princeton Univ. Press.

Gelman, R., & Gallistel, C. R. (1978). *The child's understanding of number*. Cambridge, MA: Harvard Univ. Press.

Heath, S. B. (1983). *Ways with words: Language, life, and work in communities and classrooms*. Cambridge: Cambridge Univ. Press.

Hernadi, P. (1972). *Beyond genre: New directions in literary classification*. Ithaca, NY: Cornell Univ. Press.

Iser, W. (1978). *The act of reading: A theory of aesthetic response*. Baltimore, MD: Johns Hopkins Univ. Press.

Kahneman, D., Slovic, P., & Tversky, A. (1982). *Judgment under uncertainty: Heuristics and biases*. Cambridge: Cambridge Univ. Press.

Kalmar, D. A. (1996). *The effect of perspective on recall and interpretation of stories: An extension of Anderson and Pichert*. Unpublished doctoral dissertation, Yale University, New Haven, CT.

Lejeune, P. (1989). *On autobiography* (K. Leary, Trans.). Minneapolis: Univ. of Minnesota Press.

Levi, P. (1986). *The monkey's wrench* (W. Weaver, Trans.). New York: Summit Books. (Original work published 1978.)

Lloyd, G. E. R. (1990). *Demystifying mentalities*. Cambridge: Cambridge Univ. Press.

Miller, P. J. (1982). *Amy, Wendy, and Beth: Learning language in South Baltimore*. Austin: Univ. of Texas Press.

Nelson, K. (1986). *Event knowledge: Structure and function in development*. Hillsdale, NJ: Erlbaum.

Ochs, E., & Schieffelin, B. B. (1983). *Acquiring conversational competence*. London: Routledge & Kegan Paul.

Olson, D. (1986). The cognitive consequences of literacy. *Canadian Journal of Psychology, 27*(2), 109–121.

(1994). *The world on paper: The conceptual and cognitive implications of writing and reading.* Cambridge: Cambridge Univ. Press.

Olson, D. R., & Salter, D. J. (1993). Commentary. *Human Development, 36*(6), 343–345.

Propp, V. (1968). *Morphology of the folktale,* 2nd ed. (L. Scott, Trans.). Austin: Univ. of Texas Press.

Riffaterre, M. (1990). *Fictional truth.* Baltimore, MD: Johns Hopkins Univ. Press.

Rosaldo, M. (1971). Context and metaphor in Ilongot oral tradition. Unpublished doctoral dissertation, Harvard University, Cambridge, MA.

Rubin, D. C. (1986). *Autobiographical memory.* Cambridge: Cambridge Univ. Press.

Schank, R., & Abelson, R. (1977). *Scripts, plans, goals and understanding: An inquiry into human knowledge structures.* Hillsdale, NJ: Erlbaum.

Siegler, R. S. (1978). The origins of scientific reasoning. In R. S. Siegler (Ed.), *Children's thinking: What develops?* (pp. 109–149). Hillsdale, NJ: Erlbaum.

Stein, N. L., & Glenn, C. G. (1979). An analysis of story comprehension in elementary school children. In R. O. Freedle (Ed.), *New directions in discourse processing* (pp. 53–120). Norwood, NJ: Ablex.

Tambiah, S. J. (1990). *Magic, science, religion, and the scope of rationality.* Cambridge: Cambridge Univ. Press.

Uleman, J. S., & Bargh, J. A. (Eds.). (1989). *Unintended thought.* New York: Guilford Press.

Westcott, M. R. (1968). *Toward a contemporary psychology of intuition: A historical, theoretical, and empirical inquiry.* New York: Holt, Rinehart & Winston.

Wittgenstein, L. (1968). *Philosophical investigations,* 3rd ed. (G. E. M. Anscombe, Trans.). New York: Macmillan.

Wright, G. H. von (1971). *Explanation and understanding.* Ithaca, NY: Cornell Univ. Press.

9
Inference in narrative and science

Keith Oatley

Introduction: narrative thinking

"Happy families are all alike; every unhappy family is unhappy in its own way." So wrote Tolstoy (1877/1901) in the famous opening sentence of *Anna Karenina*. We are prompted to think: are we going to read about a happy family? No – if the author has written a sentence with a first part about happy families and a second part about every unhappy family, this story must be about a family that is unhappy in a distinctive way. So: with this sentence Tolstoy prompts our minds into motion. Further thoughts may occur: perhaps there is a brief frisson of emotion or flash of memory. "Will this unhappy family be unlike mine?"

Another famous first sentence is by I. A. Richards (1925): "A book is a machine to think with." What kind of thinking do books enable us to do? In particular, what do books of fiction enable us to do as compared with books of science? Bruner's (1986) proposal that there are two modes of thought, a narrative mode for thinking about human action and a paradigmatic mode for thinking about mechanisms and natural science is a productive one (in Chapter 7 of this volume Bruner calls them agentive and epistemic). Here I suggest that the narrative mode is useful in many domains, not just in fiction. It is based on distinctive psychological processes, and it is used widely in explanation, including scientific explanation.

One of the properties of the narrative mode is that objects expressed in this mode, that is to say, stories about agents, slip easily into the mind. The story of *Anna Karenina* is an example. The mind is more resistant to objects based on the paradigmatic mode. At least such objects need elaborate cultural assistance to allow them to enter the mind, for example, knowledge about how to reason mathematically, how to understand statistical data presented in tables or diagrams, or how to draw inferences validly from scientific experiments.

Scientists do not restrict themselves to mathematics, diagrams, and experiments. They use narrative too. Here are a few sentences from Richard Feynman's famous textbook of physics (1963). They are from his introduction to

Thanks to David Olson and Tom Trabasso for their helpful comments on a draft of this chapter and to the Social Science and Humanities Research Council of Canada for supporting the research under Grant 410-93-1445.

Newton's third law of motion: For every action there is an equal and opposite reaction. Feynman introduces his discussion in narrative mode with a story about two agents called particles:

> Suppose we have two small bodies, say particles, and suppose that the first one exerts a force on the second one, pushing it with a certain force. Then, simultaneously, according to Newton's Third Law, the second particle will push on the first with an equal force, in the opposite direction. (p. 10–2)

A little further down the page, Feynman switches to the paradigmatic mode, with an equation for these equal and opposite forces:

$$dp_1/dt = -dp_2/dt$$

In this equation, the momentum of Particle 1 is p_1 and the momentum of Particle 2 is p_2, force is the rate of change of momentum (dp/dt), and the equation expresses the idea that these two forces are equal and opposite, but the equation or indeed the reason why one might wish to write it are incomprehensible without knowledge of calculus, a Western cultural product. What Feynman is doing, of course, is to begin his explanations in narrative mode in order to connect with our ordinary human intuitions, which will then be formalized by means of the cognitive prostheses of differential equations, from which a whole set of new inferences can be made that are unavailable to people who are naive in mathematics.

Let us now take an example from fiction: Sherlock Holmes has just examined two ears sent in a cardboard box to a lady in Croydon. Lestrade, the inspector of police, thinks that the ears must have been sent as a practical joke by some medical students. Holmes speaks first, then Lestrade:

> "... this is not a practical joke."
> "You are sure of it?"
> "The presumption is strongly against it. Bodies in the dissecting rooms are injected with preservative fluid. These ears bear no sign of this. They are fresh, too. They have been cut off with a blunt instrument, which would hardly happen if a student had done it.... We are investigating a serious crime." (Doyle, 1981, p. 892)

Soon after this speech Holmes notices that the ears of the recipient of the gruesome package have similar conformations to those of one of the ears in the box and infers that this ear belonged to a close relative of hers. He explains to Watson that he noticed this ear's characteristics because he had studied ears and written two articles in the previous year's *Anthropological Journal* on their idiosyncratic shapes.

Having given examples from science and from fiction, let me add one further example: from autobiography. In 1907 the founder of American pragmatism and semiotics, C. S. Peirce, wrote an article for the *Atlantic Monthly* in which he recounted the following incident. The article was rejected, but an account of the incident, published posthumously, was reproduced in an article by Sebeok and Umiker-Sebeok (1983), which has served as inspiration for my chapter, also both a source and a key for some of Peirce's writings. (They use Peirce, 1935–1966, as their source; for quotations from Peirce here, I give the page numbers in their article.)

In 1879 Peirce had sailed in a steamship from Boston to New York to attend a conference. After disembarking he discovered he had left behind a valuable watch that had been given him by the U.S. Coast and Geodetic Survey as well as his overcoat. He went immediately back to the ship to find his things gone. He arranged to have all the ship's waiters lined up before him:

> I went from one end of the row to the other, and talked a little to each one, in as *dégagé* a manner as I could, about whatever he could talk about with interest, but would least expect me to bring forward, hoping that I might seem such a fool that I should be able to detect some slight symptom of his being the thief. When I had gone through the row I turned and walked from them, though not away, and said to myself, "Not the least scintilla of light have I got to go upon." But thereupon my other self (for our communings are always in dialogues) said to me, "But you simply *must* put your finger on the man. No matter if you have no reason, you must say whom you will think to be the thief." I made a little loop in my walk, which had not taken a minute, and as I turned toward them, all shadow of a doubt had vanished. (Sebeok and Umiker-Sebeok, 1983, p. 11–12)

Peirce took one of the men aside but could not persuade him by reason, threat, or the offer of 50 dollars to give up the lost objects. Then he had the man followed. After a complex pursuit, Peirce regained his possessions. The man he picked out had indeed stolen them.

In "The Adventure of the Cardboard Box" shortly after inferring that the parcel containing the two ears could only be explained by a crime, Sherlock Holmes gave one of the best definitions of this kind of inference that Peirce had made to identify the thief: "to reason backward from effects to causes" (Doyle, 1981, p. 895). Though Holmes claimed that his inferences were "as infallible as so many propositions of Euclid" (Doyle, 1981, p. 23, *Study in Scarlet*), Peirce was more candid: such an inference is always a guess, "a singular salad . . . whose chief elements are its groundlessness, its ubiquity, and its trustworthiness" (Sebeok and Umiker-Sebeok, 1983, p. 16). Peirce saw the ability to make such inferences, which he called "abductions," as part of our given mental equipment: the human mind "having been developed under the influence of the laws of nature, for that reason naturally thinks somewhat after nature's pattern" (Sebeok and Umiker-Sebeok, 1983, p. 17). Abductive guesses are not always correct, but they are correct far more frequently than would occur by chance.

In 1878 Peirce had proposed that there are only three forms of inference. Abduction is one of these. He expressed the idea in terms of syllogistic figures about drawing beans from a bag, like this (Sebeok, 1983, p. 8).

Deduction

Rule:	All the beans from this bag are white.
Case:	These beans are from this bag.
∴ *Result*:	These beans are white.

Induction

Case:	These beans are from this bag.
Result:	These beans are white.
∴ *Rule*:	All the beans from this bag are white.

Abduction

Rule:	All the beans from this bag are white.
Result:	These beans are white.
∴ *Case*:	These beans are from this bag.

Deduction is inference in which we reason from a rule, generalization, or theory to some particular instance, or "case" as Peirce calls it. Johnson-Laird (1993) has written that in deduction there is no gain of semantic information. When we reason in the opposite direction, there is a gain of semantic information. One form of semantically increasing information is induction: reasoning from several instances (such as the observed cases of beans from the bag) to a generalization (about all the beans). The other form is abduction to an explanation of how something came about (for instance, how a particular set of beans was chosen). Peirce also referred to abduction as "hypothesis," or "retroduction," and sometimes as "speculative modelling." Abduction is always guessing, but as Peirce said, "we must conquer the truth by guessing, or not at all" (Sebeok and Umiker-Sebeok, 1983, p. 11).

We can, however, perhaps make a more specific proposal about the grounds of abduction than Peirce's "singular salad." Generally abductive inferences are made from two elements: an observation and a relevant base of knowledge. In "The Adventure of the Cardboard Box," Holmes inferred that the severed ears were not from a medical dissecting room because there was no preservative other than rough salt (observation) and because he had general knowledge of what goes on in medical schools.

Of course, Holmes is mythological rather than a realistic character, and Conan Doyle is a crafty storyteller. His stories are heroic, allowing us to identify with Holmes. Though there is a representation of a potential critic in Dr. Watson, his commentary is always supportive of Holmes's inferences, allowing extra links to be added to chains of reasoning rather than questioning any of them. In detective stories of the kind that Edgar Allan Poe invented and Conan Doyle made popular, certainty of such inferences can be claimed – and of course in the story the inferences do turn out to be correct. We have to exert ourselves and step outside the frame of "The Adventure of the Cardboard Box" to make inferences other than Holmes's. Holmes infers the ears were cut from dead people, but there is nothing in the first part of the story to prevent an inference that the ears were cut from living people and that a ransom note would shortly be delivered. To make such a different inference would be to start writing a different story. So we stay in Conan Doyle's story, and Holmes's abduction that the old lady's sister had been murdered slips into our minds with ease and satisfaction. The story is about Holmes's intentions and actions with which we easily identify. We follow it as if we were Holmes, as if these inferences were popping into our own minds.

Generally, in order to understand any narrative we do make a range of inferences (Graesser, Singer, and Trabasso, 1994). Principal among these are inferences from actions and events in the story to explanations in terms of the goals and plans of characters (Wilensky, 1978).

Human life, as many social scientists have observed, is founded on being able to act purposefully in the world, using information in planning processes to work out how to act. In understanding a story, we run these planning processes, as it were, backward: finding explanations in terms of an agent's goals and plans for the actions and events that we read about. As Wilensky (1978) has put it, when we read a story, we are not trying to work out what will happen next. Rather, we summon up a range of explanations for what does happen. The genre of the detective story or mystery involves us in focusing specifically on explanations of the actions of one character – the murderer.

The effect of prompting explanations of action is not confined to narratives of detection. It is characteristic of all narrative, from the recounting of one's own actions, as Peirce did, to the highest art. In *Anna Karenina*, for instance, Anna and Vronsky fall in love near the beginning of the novel. Why? Tolstoy goes to considerable lengths to provide the reader with the background information that they had both led lives of inner conflict. He shows us Vronsky going to the station to meet his mother, not because he wanted to, but because he would always act in obedience to her. Thus, we are prepared for him to notice Anna getting off the train, because he is not fully engaged in what he is doing. As to Anna, she acts respectably although married to someone whom she does not love. When Anna and Vronsky fall in love, then, this does not come exactly as a surprise. Rather it grows out of their characters, goals, and life situations. Without being able to make the inferences about the roots of their actions in their characters and life situations, we would probably not enjoy the novel. As Henry James (1884) asked: "What is character but the determination of incident? What is incident but the illustration of character?" In the nineteenth-century novel, then, what we abduce in explaining action is character. By contrast, in scientific exposition, narrative typically gives way to other forms of discourse and to inferences about how things work.

What individual human minds can't do

Suppose that Wilensky (1978) is right in proposing that a basic process of reading narrative is summoning up explanations, that is to say, making abductive inferences, about what is going on. This may happen either because, in a detective story, the protagonist with whom we identify makes inferences that will later be corroborated by events or more subtly because characters' actions allow us to infer character, as in the novels of Tolstoy and Henry James.

Perhaps, indeed, abduction is a kind of inference that is characteristic of fiction. Readers are easily led into abductive inferences. Perhaps a distinctive attribute of fiction – what makes it fiction rather than science – is that the inferences seldom stand realistic scrutiny, let alone scientific scrutiny. Abduction is nowadays defined as reasoning toward the best explanation. In a story, because the writer constructs a closed world he or she can make sure an inference is indeed the best explanation. But in real life, looking forward from any event into the future, we usually do not know which explanation will be the best one: a guess may be better than a random shot as Peirce argued, but it will be a guess. Perhaps abduction is only for fiction and other domains that need no firm anchor in fact. Perhaps climbing through a web of abductions allows us merely to escape into fanciful but nonexistent universes. Perhaps science depends on different forms of inferencing. Perhaps it depends, as Bacon proposed, on inductions from sets of cognate instances to generalizations and laws. Perhaps, when information is to be increased scientifically, induction is the heart of the paradigmatic (epistemic) mode of thought.

Brown and Clement (1987) have shown, however, that induction to a scientific generalization is very difficult. Their subjects were high-school students who might subsequently take physics but had not yet done so. There was a pretest with three questions about Newton's third law (the one mentioned earlier in discussing Feynman's textbook). One question was about a book on a table: does the table exert an upward force on the book? In a posttest, after instruction on Newton's third law, the same three questions were asked again together with two more. From 14 students who could not correctly answer the question about the book on the table in the pretest, the experimenters randomly selected two groups of 7 students each.

One group was instructed using the best available high-school physics textbook. It was an innovative and well-written book. The section used for instruction on Newton's third law was an exposition that dealt explicitly with whether a table on which a book is resting exerts an upward force on the book. It started straight out by saying that the table does exert a force on the book. Then came a set of other examples of action and reaction, including a finger pressing on a stone (Newton's own example), a rifle kick, an athlete running. Then the text returned to the example of the book on the table. The message to this group of students was that they should, under guidance of the text, make an inductive inference from a set of examples of Newton's third law.

The second group of students was not encouraged to do induction. Instead they were offered a bridging concept that offered an explanation of why Newton's third law worked – a concept that would allow them to do abduction. Here is the concept they were offered: first think of pushing down with your hand on a spring resting on a table; notice how the spring would push back on your hand. Then think of a book resting on a long springy plank that has been laid across a gap between two sawhorses. Imagine the plank's springiness pushing back on the book. Next imagine the plank becoming thicker and thicker. The springiness of the plank has not gone away, but as the plank gets thicker it needs more force to let us see it bending. The thicker plank's springiness is stiffer. All materials have springiness, dependent on the bonds between the molecules, so that even when no deformation of a plank or any other material is visible, this springiness is still there. So it is in a table; its springiness pushes back on a book resting on it.

So: the students in the second group were offered an explanation that could enter their minds. It was the missing half, as it were, of the abduction: observation – the book rests on the table; explanation – its downward force is exactly opposed by an equivalent force of the springiness of the table. In the posttest, seven out of the seven of the students who were given the explanation about the springiness of materials answered correctly the question about the book on the table, significantly more than the two out of seven students from the induction group. The abduction group also gave correct answers for the other examples in the posttest and in this also they did significantly better than the induction group.

There is a growing number of indications that induction to productive generalizations is difficult for humans. Brown and Clement's (1987) study is one such. Others are shown in Case's (1991) extensive studies of how children who have skills in one domain, though they involve comparable procedures to problems in adjoining domains, do not transfer these skills. They do not on their own make the generalizing induction, though they can be instructed to acquire central conceptual structures that do generalize across domains.

In an early and important paper on artificial intelligence, Newell (1972) made a related point about psychology, which had tied itself to an inductive model of science. Newell argued that in psychology one cannot hope to perform a set of experiments, each yielding one small piece of empirically established knowledge and then by induction from these observations arrive at general principles of mental functioning.

Simulation

Newell was in the forefront of introducing into the study of mind the methodology of design. We do not have to rely solely on experiments; we can also see what principles are involved by trying to design mental-like processes. The cognitive design methodology can be thought of as simulation. Notice how the term *simulation* carries a distrustful connotation of falsehood, just as does the term *fiction*. Despite this, it has been the computational exploration of the design of mental-like processes that has formed the intellectual center of the cognitive revolution in psychology. The idea is that if one really understands something, one can write a program to simulate it, and that if one does not understand it, then computational explorations will be profoundly important in understanding underlying principles and in providing new metaphors.

Simulation need neither start nor stop with computers. In *Best Laid Schemes* (Oatley, 1992), I made the case that novels in the narrative mode are not descriptions of action, but simulations of action that run on the minds of readers. The idea derives, I hope without anachronism, from the *Poetics*, in which Aristotle (c. 355 B.C./1970) discusses how drama is *mimesis* of human action. *Mimesis* is usually translated into English as "imitation" or "representation." But, I suggest, what Aristotle really meant was closer to what we now mean by *simulation*. A play is a simulation of action by the actors. But there is an extra step beyond this and beyond the idea of simulation on computers: the step is that a play as it is performed, or a narrative as it is read, only really becomes a simulation in the sense that Aristotle meant when it runs on the minds of an audience or readers. Is it the music or the ways in which the actors are dressed that make a play moving? No, says Aristotle, they are the least important elements. It is the plot that is "the heart and soul, as it were, of tragedy . . . it is the *mimesis* of an action and [simulates] persons primarily for the sake of their action" (p. 28). So simulations must concentrate on what is essential, and in the case of narrative this includes action. The action of the play is taken up into our own cognitive planning mechanisms. We sit in the theater and run these actions as if they were our own. Comparable processes occur, I believe, in watching sports. Rather than being used to decide what to do – the way these processes are mostly used in real life – these planning processes are guided by the plot as we identify with a protagonist in a story or by the flow of action as we identify with an athlete in a sporting event.

Just as cognitive scientists write simulations (programs) to run on computers, it follows from this argument that it should be equally appropriate for a cognitive scientist to write simulations (novels) to run on minds. Cognitive scientists who write programs see abduction as central to their activities. It occurred to me that this could be a central issue in a novel. *The Case of Emily V.* (Oatley, 1993) is such a novel about the nature of truth and the search for it. In it both Sherlock Holmes and Sigmund Freud (unbeknown to each other at first) investigate the same person. The question is how might ideas about abduction resolve the tension between empirical (Holmesian) and hermeneutic (Freudian) thinking. In this novel, it is not just a matter of reading about such issues as in an academic article, the reader finds him- or herself making such inferences and thereby being able to experience something of the possibilities of discovering truth within each kind of thinking.

EMOTIONS DURING READING

One of the features of reading narrative, as Aristotle pointed out, is that we ourselves are affected by emotions as the plans and actions of a protagonist meet vicissitudes. Although the action is simulated, the emotions that occur when we run the actions of the drama on our planning systems are real. They are our own emotions. Aristotle in *Poetics* discussed the significance of experiencing emotions such as fear and pity in tragedies, and of undergoing the process of *katharsis*, which may best be translated as clarification. I have discussed this more extensively elsewhere (Oatley, 1992).

As one reads or watches a performance in the theater, emotions occur. The occurrence of such emotions, I take it, is evidence that a reader is personally connected to the story; one seldom hears about people experiencing emotions (except perhaps anxiety and exasperation) when reading scientific textbooks. When we identify with agents in a story, when we run their actions on our own planning processes, the emotions produced as the protagonist's actions meet with events in the story world happen to us, the readers or members of the audience. They do not merely happen to the characters in the story. (An alternative theory of the emotions of narrative, due to Tan, 1994, is that in the story world, we are invisible observers. Emotions we experience are those of human sympathy. I have discussed this alternative theory and its relation to my theory of understanding narrative as a form of simulation in [Oatley, 1994].)

According to Peirce, an emotion is itself a kind of abduction. This formulation – consistent with the theory of emotions that Oatley and Johnson-Laird (1987) have proposed – enables us to see how the reader, not just the story character, makes such abductions. The argument is that during evolution certain recurring kinds of events have occurred. By natural selection, organisms have evolved to recognize such events and to deal with them. As Peirce put it, without such abductions, "the human race would long ago have been extirpated for its utter incapacity in the struggles for existence" (Sebeok and Umiker-Sebeok, 1983, p. 17). Thus, fear is a kind of inference that occurs in response to events of certain kinds. It is an explanation, as it were, that these events are dangerous, and pragmatically it prompts a distinctive repertoire of action: to interrupt the current behavior, to seek safety, to fight. During evolution such mechanisms of recognition and repertoires of appropriate response have been compiled into the nervous systems of animals including ourselves. When reading a thriller, for instance, exactly this kind of abduction occurs to us, and we read quickly to reach the point when the protagonist is again safe.

What kind of emotions occur during reading? Oatley and Biason (forthcoming) had 59 high-school students read a short story about identity. There were two such stories, each in the first person, each with an adolescent narrator. One by Alice Munro is called "Red Dress": it is about a girl who goes to a school dance, fearing she looks dreadful in the dress her mother has made for her and fearing that she will be a wallflower. The other, by Carson McCullers, called "Sucker," is about a boy whose young cousin lives with him like a younger brother. The protagonist, who has largely ignored the younger boy, starts to treat him better when a girl to whom the protagonist is attracted starts reciprocating his attention. We randomly assigned students to one of the two stories, asked them to read it as they would ordinarily, and, adapting the method of Larson and Seilman (1988), we asked that they mark an *E* in the margin at any point where they experienced an emotion and to mark an *M* where a personal memory came to mind. After reading their story, they gave some details about the emotions and memories they had marked. We related measures derived from these incidents of emotion and memory to other variables, such as liking for the story and amount of out-of-school

Table 9.1. *Mean numbers of emotions reported by male and female high-school students (numbers of students are in parentheses) reading a story with a male protagonist (''Sucker'') and a female protagonist (''Red Dress'')*

	Story		
	"Sucker"	"Red Dress"	Combining both stories
Numbers of emotions			
For males	4.88 $(n = 17)$	2.88 $(n = 17)$	3.88* $(n = 34)$
For females	6.77 $(n = 13)$	6.67 $(n = 12)$	6.72* $(n = 25)$

*The main effect of gender difference in analysis of variance is $p < 0.02$.

reading. We also asked two teachers of English literature at their school to discuss between themselves criteria they used for marking and then to mark the students' summaries of the stories. I will present one observation and two sets of data from the study.

The observation is this: all the students had both emotions and memories during their reading of the stories. All, therefore, connected themselves to the text in a personal way – not just analyzing it without involvement of the self. Obviously we created a demand characteristic: we asked the students to have emotions and memories, but none of them had any problem with this task.

The data were as follows. We counted how many emotions each student recorded, and in Table 9.1 the result is shown: the data are presented as a function of the gender of the reader and the story that was read. If we take the number of these emotions as a measure of identification with the protagonist, the girls were significantly more involved than the boys and were equally able to identify with either a female or a male protagonist. To those versed in the psychology of gender differences, this result may be unsurprising. What we concluded was that the ability to identify with (or perhaps have sympathy for) a character in a story can be measured. (G. Cupchik, P. Vorderer, and I have subsequently run, but not yet analyzed, a study of reading in which we distinguish the hypothesis of identification from Tan's 1994 hypothesis of sympathy.) Second, we found that these measures of involvement with the story, though they were associated with the extent to which the students liked the story, were not associated with their academic achievements: their expected marks in English literature or the marks given to them anonymously by two teachers for their summaries. The somewhat dispiriting conclusion is that although literature in both school and university is thought to be the subject in which there can be involvement of self in the domain of personal values, students' abilities to do what is required of them by the curriculum (e.g., giving details of the story and understanding its theme – the criteria on which the teachers marked the summaries) were independent of the students' personal involvement in the story.

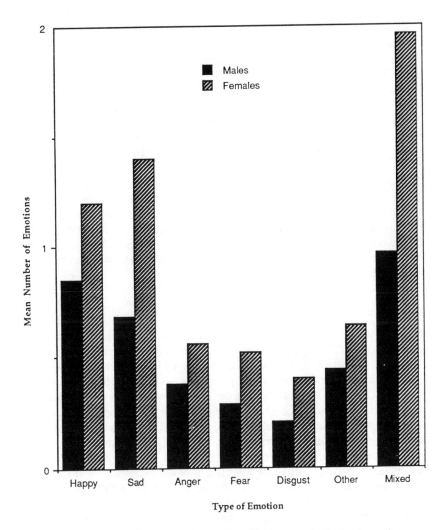

Figure 9.1. Mean numbers of emotions of specific types and of mixed emotions, reported by male and female high-school students reading a short story (either "Sucker" by Carson McCullers or "Red Dress" by Alice Munro).

The second set of data concern what emotions the high-school subjects experienced. These are shown in Figure 9.1. We asked the subjects to say what they called each emotion and then whether it was a kind of any of the following: happiness/joy, sadness/grief, anger/irritation, fear/anxiety, disgust/hatred, and we found that the students experienced a variety of these emotions.

There is now a substantial amount of research to indicate that whenever each distinct kind of basic emotion (happiness, sadness, anger, fear, disgust) is aroused, it produces a distinctive kind of cognitive process. Thus Isen

(1990) has shown that when they are happy people are more generous to others, they make more creative word associations, they more easily solve certain kinds of problems, and so on. When they are sad or depressed, people tend to have previous sad episodes from their lives coming to mind (Williams, Watts, MacLeod, and Mathews, 1988). When they are fearful, attention is strongly constrained toward issues of safety and danger (Mathews, 1993). When they are angry, certain kinds of plans begin to be formed to get even. My colleagues and I are now investigating how each emotion mode is aroused by reading, then operates in the interpretation of the text. I predict the same distinctive effects of emotions will be found. What I propose from the preliminary data of Table 9.1 and Figure 9.1 is that specific emotions are typically produced while reading narrative and that, as elsewhere, each kind of emotional state gives rise to a distinctive mode of thought with identifiable characteristics. By contrast, when reading science, even in narrative passages, there is not the same degree of identification, hence not the same opportunity for emotions to occur. And, as many would claim, scientifically we might try to avoid entering into emotional modes, though I have some more to say about this later.

Abduction and its relation to other forms of inference

Although abduction is guessing, this form of thought occurs in science too. As Peirce put it: ''not the smallest advance can be made in knowledge beyond the stage of vacant staring, without making an abduction at every step'' (Sebeok & Umiker-Sebeok, 1983, p. 16). So how does fiction differ from science? One way, I believe, is that fiction, like other kinds of simulation, is concerned mainly with coherence. Though fiction has multiple meanings for different people, each ensemble of meanings must cohere within itself. More interestingly too, for each narrative that is read, the meaning must cohere with the reader's beliefs and emotional responses: this is a step toward what we mean by personal truth, the kind that promotes insights about ourselves and others. This, I believe, is part of the significance of finding that emotions and memories are stirred by narrative.

By contrast, science has procedures from which the personal is, in a sense, factored out and by which consensual truths may be transmitted. It involves a more elaborate set of inferences. Peirce proposed that doing scientific research needs to use his three kinds of reasoning in a specified order. First, one uses abduction from observations to a possible explanation or hypothesis. From this, one deduces a fact not yet observed. Then several tests of such facts are put together with the original observation to make a generalizing induction (Sebeok and Umiker-Sebeok, 1983, pp. 49–50, note 9).

Peirce said that before the turn of the century he more or less mixed up abduction and induction: then he made the distinction clearly in a number of metaphors. Here (somewhat modified from Peirce's complex formulation) is one of these. Suppose you have two pieces of paper: on one is a typed letter, the other bears a signature. Suppose it is important to know if the signature belongs to the typed letter. If there are irregularities in a pattern of tearing, such that the typed piece of paper and the piece with the signature exactly match, you could make an abduction: the signature belonged to the typed letter and was torn from it. If, however, we wish to confirm this, we need to make inductions: "the two pieces of paper which matched in such irregularities as have been examined would be found to match in other, say slighter, irregularities" (Sebeok and Umiker-Sebeok, 1983, p. 25). Peirce continues in this passage: "The inference from the shape of the paper to its ownership is precisely what distinguishes hypothesis from induction, and makes it a bolder and more perilous step."

INDIVIDUAL AND DISTRIBUTED MODES OF THOUGHT
Most researchers conceptualize thought as a process of the individual mind. There is another possibility: as Vygotsky (1930/1978) and Harré (1983) have suggested, thought may first of all be social; later in development we can do it individually, while maintaining its social quality in inner dialogue as Peirce mentioned in his anecdote about discovering who had stolen his watch and overcoat. This idea is appealing because it makes it easy to see how the social, for example, in the form of culturally elaborated methods of using inferences, enters into thinking.

Individual and social thinking in narrative. In genres such as the detective story, the author has thought individually to create a closed world with a protagonist. Readers run the protagonist's action on their own minds and think the protagonist's thoughts. In this case reading too is individual: readers engage in what Barthes (1975) has called a readerly reading, becoming somewhat passive receivers of the author's text.

Barthes (1975) has argued that with the polysemous nature of literary narrative, particularly in texts that are considered good literature, because of the different levels of meaning that are involved, readers can also engage in "writerly" readings. Readers do not just receive the text, they transform it, becoming writers of the understandings that they create. Writerly readings are constructive of a constrained but open set of meanings to be discovered by the reader interacting with the text. Whenever a writerly reading occurs, the reader is active, and we can say that the thought associated with the book is no longer just individual. A genuinely social event, a dialogue between writer and reader, has occurred. Cognition is distributed between writer and reader.

Individual and social thinking in scientific inference. Not only is induction hard for individuals to do productively, as I have suggested earlier, but even if more or less forced to do it, they still find it hard to make generalizations converging on truth in ways that are characteristic of science.

Here is a study to this point by Wason (1960) on university student subjects who were asked to consider the three digits 2, 4, 6 and find what general rule he had in mind that connected the digits. Each was asked to write down new examples of strings of digits, noting also why each example was offered.

Wason then said whether each example obeyed his general rule or not. Subjects were to go on proposing examples until they thought they knew what the general rule was. Then they had to write this generalization down, and Wason told them if it was what he had in mind.

Most subjects announced at least one incorrect general rule before finding the correct one and 28 percent failed to discover the rule at all. They proceeded mainly by offering examples that could confirm their current hypothesis. If they thought that the rule was "three successive even numbers in ascending order," they might offer "6, 8, 10," then "22, 24, 26," and so on. After deducing several such examples, they would announce their hypothesis as the general rule. Much less frequently did they offer examples that might disconfirm the hypothesis they were entertaining such as "1, 3, 7."

The rule that the experimenter had in mind was this: "any three numbers in ascending order." To discover it, subjects had both to vary their hypotheses and generate examples contrary to them. In this way, one subject offered "10, 6, 4," giving as her hypothesis: "the highest number must go last." After entertaining several hypotheses and generating nine examples, one (just given) negative to the hypothesis she was entertaining, she announced the rule correctly in 17 minutes. The tendency to perseverate on positive instances has been called the *confirmation bias:* people seldom follow the procedure that Popper (1962) regards as basic to science, of generating instances that might disconfirm hypotheses. In Peirce's terms, they were working inductively but were using induction upon unhelpful examples.

The issue is this. When we think of modes of thought as individual, experiments such as Brown and Clement's or Wason's, showing that people find induction to scientific generalizations very hard, seem discouraging. What is required, I believe, are three steps, all of potential significance for educators in understanding thinking.

The first step is to recognize and understand the processes of inference. As Peirce has proposed, there are only three forms: abduction, deduction, induction.

The second step is to inquire whether there are natural barriers in humans to any of these three forms of inference. I do not believe there are. I have already argued that abduction is a fundamental mode of human thinking, as indicated by its ease and by its use in the universal human activity of understanding stories. I suggest deduction too is universal. Here is an example from Homer (c. 850 B.C./1987). At the beginning of the *Iliad*, the Greek army is beset by a pestilence (observation). It is explained (abduction) in terms of Apollo being angry with them (theory). From this theory, an inference is drawn (deduction) that they should do something to placate Apollo. This deduction is of a kind easily made by anyone hearing this story or a similar episode from another culture; theories that illness is due to personal agency occur in many cultures (Foster, 1976), including our own, for instance, Koslowski (1978, #176) found that 40 percent of patients who had a heart attack thought it was due to the will of God, and 20 percent thought it was punishment for their own misdeeds. All theories of health, including folk theories, allow deductions to be drawn: these take the form of predictions and recommendations. As to induction, there is no reason to believe that it is beyond any ordinary human being. It would be eccentric to doubt that in every society people have been able to induce on the basis of previous days that the sun will rise tomorrow or that like other people each of us will die.

The third step: what does Western culture offer by way of scientific thinking and the paradigmatic (or epistemic) mode of thought? My proposal is that like writerly reading, science depends on two things: the availability of writing, as Olson (1994) has so elegantly shown, and the use of Peirce's three forms of thinking in carefully orchestrated, socially distributed ways. So, in science, to paraphrase Newton, in order to see far we must stand on the shoulders of giants. We read the writings of those who have gone before, acquire intellectual prostheses from the tradition of scientific research. And, if we are producers of science, we think not individually, but socially. Shortcomings of individual inference making are overcome by distributed cognition (Oatley, 1991): one person proposes a hypothesis, another who has a different interest in the matter proposes inductive tests that could disconfirm it. Though we humans are not good at generating examples to disconfirm our own theories, because theories are the spectacles through which we see the world, we are good at seeing what is wrong with other people's ideas. Here emotion and its modes of thinking enter science. People can behave aggressively to defeat a scientific opponent and to achieve scientific status. Convergence on truth is a fortunate by-product.

The distributed process of science has been recently studied by Dunbar (1993), a cognitive psychologist who spent a year learning molecular biology and cell biology and then a year as an observer in four major U.S. cell and molecular biology laboratories that work on mechanisms of cancer, AIDS, and so on. Dunbar found that much of the conceptual change that occurs in the laboratories he studied is traceable to the meetings of 7 to 30 people that are held weekly or so. In these meetings postdoctoral fellows and graduate students present what they have been working on, and the results are discussed within the group. One of the processes that leads to conceptual change is what Dunbar calls "regional analogy." Such analogies are made within a region of understanding, but from some other part of the region. When there is some result that is difficult to understand, analogies to what is known in another biochemical system, from some other subfield, or from some other organism are suggested by members of the research meeting. The problem and data can then be reconceptualized.

In three of the four laboratories that Dunbar studied, the members all have different backgrounds and training; in biochemistry, molecular biology, cell biology, developmental biology, and so on. Collectively they are well placed to see results from different viewpoints. These three laboratories generate and make frequent use of regional analogies – new insights occur, and new discoveries are made. In the fourth laboratory, all the members have similar backgrounds. Though the group is respected, it has made less progress recently; its work occurs largely by varying parameters.

Second, Dunbar found that confirmation bias is counteracted by one person presenting results and others at the meetings seeing different interpretations of them. One example, described by Dunbar in colloquia he is now giving, occurred when a scientist presented to a laboratory meeting some of his recent results that he said he could not understand in terms of the explanation he offered. Another scientist, quickly joined by some others, proposed an interpretation that was different from his. Dunbar says this new explanation has become the basis of a very important scientific advance. But it took the person who had done the experiments two weeks before he understood it, let alone accepted it.

Science would not work with individual knowers and doers. Its cognition is necessarily distributed. Each participant has a role in the process of approaching truth. No one embodies, let alone reaches, the truth as a whole. In the history of science, there are some apparent counterexamples of people who worked largely individually. An instructive one was Darwin in his discovery of evolution by means of natural selection.

Although Darwin's observations from his voyage on the *Beagle* may seem to have been an individual and atheoretical gathering of examples, this was not their provenance. As shown by Gruber and Barrett (1974, see especially his diagrams on p. 127), Darwin's observations were collected to test a theory. At first the theory was that the physical world had changed, but species are fixed and adapted to it. Then as he began to believe that species also changed, he reconsidered his observations to test his new idea. He formulated his theory of evolution by natural selection in 1838. So the question for biographers and biologists is: what was Darwin doing in the 20 years before he published *The Origin of Species* in 1859? The answer is that Darwin, more than most scientists, was not interested in merely publishing an abduction, a hypothesis. He saw the problem as a rhetorical one, in Aristotle's nonpejorative sense of this term. He wanted to have evidence for his hypothesis that would come as close to the irrefutable as possible. What Darwin did was what Peirce later recommended. He cycled round the loop: abduction, deduction, induction. He was able to maintain within himself the social element: he had both his own new hypothesis of natural selection, and he held on clearly to the counterhypothesis from which the attacks on his theory would come, that humans and all other species had been separately created and had remained fixed. What Darwin did, and what he wrote about in *The Origin of Species* and in his later books on evolution, derived from a comparison of the deductions from his hypothesis and from the counterhypothesis. When his books were published and the actual social process of criticism began, the scales were so heavily weighted in Darwin's favor by his having thought through the arguments and generated extra examples over which to make inductive generalizations that the outcome was assured, at least among scientists.

Nowadays, science conforms closely to its explicitly social format. To publish reputably, for instance, one person takes the role of author; others review each submitted manuscript and take the role of seeing it from the point of view of different hypotheses, abducing to different explanations than the one the author is proposing. Different people act in different phases of Peirce's cycle, so truths based on the correspondence between hypotheses and empirical reality are approached.

The success of our human adaptation is that humans, more than any other vertebrate species, can join together to do things that are too difficult to do alone. A great deal of thinking is of this kind. It includes thinking the thoughts prompted by reading a novel in a writerly way, and it includes scientific thinking. It is not so much that certain kinds of thinking are difficult in themselves. Rather, some of the overall patterns of thinking are too difficult for individuals: therefore we do them together, each of us taking on from time to time a different role in larger, distributed, inferential processes.

References

Aristotle (c. 355 B.C./1970). *Poetics* (G. E. Else, Trans.). Ann Arbor: University of Michigan Press.

Barthes, R. (1975). *S / Z* (R. Miller, Trans.). London: Cape.

Brown, D. E., & Clement, J. (1987). Overcoming misconceptions in mechanics: A comparison of two example-based teaching strategies. In *American Educational Research Association*, Washington, DC, April 20–24.

Bruner, J. (1986). *Actual minds, possible worlds.* Cambridge, MA: Harvard Univ. Press.

Case, R. (1991). *The mind's staircase.* Hillsdale, NJ: Erlbaum.

Darwin, C. (1859). *On the origin of species by means of natural selection.* London: Murray.

Doyle, A. C. (1981). *The complete adventures of Sherlock Holmes.* London: Penguin.

Dunbar, K. (1993). How scientists really reason: Scientific reasoning in real-world laboratories. In R. J. Sternberg & J. Davidson (Eds.), *Mechanisms of insight* Cambridge, MA: MIT Press.

Feynman, R. P., Leighton, R. B., & Sands, M. (1963). *The Feynman lectures on physics, Vol. 1, Mainly mechanics, radiation, and heat.* Reading, MA: Addison–Wesley.

Foster, G. M. (1976). Disease etiologies in non-Western medical systems. *American Anthropologist, 78,* 773–781.

Graesser, A., Singer, M., & Trabasso, T. (1994). Constructing inferences during narrative text comprehension. *Psychological Review, 101,* 371–395.

Gruber, H. E., & Barrett, P. H. (1974). *Darwin on man: A psychological study of scientific creativity, together with Darwin's early and unpublished notebooks.* New York: Dutton.

Harré, R. (1983). *Personal being: A theory for individual psychology.* Oxford: Blackwell.

Homer (c. 850 B.C./1987). *The Iliad.* Harmondsworth: Penguin.

Isen, A. (1990). The influence of positive and negative affect on cognitive organization. In B. Leventhal, T. Trabasso, & N. Stein (Eds.), *Psychological and biological processes in the development of emotion* (pp. 75–94). Hillsdale, NJ: Erlbaum.

James, H. (1884). The art of fiction. *Longman's Magazine,* September.

Johnson-Laird, P. N. (1993). *Human and machine thinking*. Hillsdale, NJ: Erlbaum.

Koslowski, M. (1978). Perception of the etiology of illness. *Perceptual and Motor Skills, 47,* 475–485.

Larson, S. F., & Seilman, U. (1988). Personal meanings while reading literature. *Text, 8,* 411–429.

Mathews, A. (1993). Biases in emotional processing. *The Psychologist: Bulletin of the British Psychological Society, 6,* 493–499.

Newell, A. (1972). You can't play 20 questions with Nature and win. In W. G. Chase (Ed.), *Visual information processing*. New York: Academic Press.

Oatley, K. (1991). Distributed cognition. In M. W. Eysenck (Ed.), *Dictionary of cognitive psychology* (pp. 102–107). Oxford: Blackwell.

(1992). *Best laid schemes: The psychology of emotions.* New York: Cambridge Univ. Press.

(1993). *The case of Emily V.* London: Secker & Warburg.

(1994). A taxonomy of the emotions of literary response and a theory of identification in fictional narrative. *Poetics, 23,* 53–74.

Oatley, K., & Biason, A. (forthcoming). Emotions and memories in high-school students' understanding of two short stories.

Oatley, K., & Johnson-Laird, P. N. (1987). Towards a cognitive theory of emotions. *Cognition and Emotion, 1,* 29–50.

Olson, D. R. (1994). *The world on paper*. New York: Cambridge Univ. Press.

Peirce, C. S. (1935–1966). *Collected papers of Charles Sanders Peirce*, C. Hartshorne, P. Weiss, & A. W. Burks (Eds.). Cambridge, MA: Harvard Univ. Press.

Popper, K. R. (1962). *Conjectures and refutations*. New York: Basic Books.

Richards, I. A. (1925). *Principles of literary criticism*. New York: Harcourt Brace Jovanovich.

Sebeok, T. A. (1983). One, two, three spells UBERTY. In U. Eco & T. A. Sebeok (Eds.), *The sign of three: Dupin, Holmes, Peirce* (pp. 1–10). Bloomington: Indiana Univ. Press.

Sebeok, T. A., & Umiker-Sebeok, J. (1983). "You know my method": A juxtaposition of Charles S. Peirce and Sherlock Holmes. In U. Eco & T. A. Sebeok (Eds.), *The sign of three: Dupin, Holmes, Peirce* (pp. 11–54). Bloomington: Indiana Univ. Press.

Tan, E. S. -H. (1994). Film-induced affect as a witness emotion. *Poetics,* 7–32.

Tolstoy, L. (1877/1901). *Anna Karenina* (C. Garnett, Trans.). London: Heinemann.

Vygotsky, L. S. (1930/1978). Tool and symbol in child development. In M. Cole, V. John-Steiner, S. Scribner, & E. Souberman (Eds.), *Mind in society: The development of higher mental processes* (pp. 19–30). Cambridge, MA: Harvard Univ. Press.

Wason, P. (1960). On the failure to eliminate hypotheses in a conceptual task. *Quarterly Journal of Experimental Psychology, 12,* 129–140.

Wilensky, R. (1978). "*Understanding goal-based stories*," Department of Computer Science, Research Report No. 140, Yale University.

Williams, J. M. G., Watts, F. N., MacLeod, C., & Mathews, A. (1988). *Cognitive psychology and emotional disorders*. Chichester: Wiley.

10
Literate mentalities
LITERACY, CONSCIOUSNESS OF LANGUAGE, AND
MODES OF THOUGHT

David R. Olson

The question I propose to address in this chapter is the role that writing
played and continues to play in the evolution and development of the form
or mode of thought, the mentality, if you will, that we in the West describe
as scientific. I will conclude with some comments on how children acquire
this more specialized model of thought.

Goody and Watt (1963) first suggested that the Greek invention of logic
was a by-product of the invention of an alphabet. They argued that the existence of a permanent representation of speech allowed readers, unlike
speakers, to reflect on the linguistic and logical properties of their own speech
and so to detect the relations we continue to this day to describe as logical.
While they were careful not to identify logic with rationality, they did infer
that the invention of logic was an important step in the evolution of that
formal mode of thought we dignify by the term *scientific*.

Although the hypothesis is entirely plausible, it suffers from a critical
defect, namely, the lack of evidence. Three widely cited criticisms must be
acknowledged. Lloyd (1979) showed that the evolution of analytic arguments
evolved in the marketplace, in oral argument and counterargument rather than
in the private scrutiny of written documents. True, the Greeks could write,
but there is little evidence that writing was the primary mode of discourse;
writing was sometimes used to record speech, but the primary mode of discourse remained oral. Even the notion of proof, Lloyd argued, had more to
do with silencing the opposition than with strict logical deduction. Thomas
(1992), in her more extensive analysis of ancient Greek literacy, found that
literacy had many forms and functions, was intimately connected with oral
discourse, and reflected as much as shaped Greek culture. As a result, it is
impossible to state in any simple and direct way how literacy contributed to
classical Greek thought.

Second, Scribner and Cole's (1981) widely cited study of the uses and
consequences of literacy among the Vai of Liberia compared three groups of
subjects: those who were schooled and literate in English, those unschooled
but literate in Vai, an indigenous syllabic script, and those who had neither
been to school nor were literate in Vai. To their dismay, being literate in Vai
had little effect on cognitive performances while being schooled in English
had marked effects. Greenfield (1983), in reviewing the book, expressed the
general view by saying that the Scribner and Cole volume "should rid us
once and for all of the ethnocentric and arrogant view that a single technology

suffices to create in its users a distinct, let alone superior, set of cognitive processes'' (p. 219).

Third, no satisfactory basis has been found for clearly distinguishing the oral from the written because writing has been related to speaking in so many different ways. Writing is sometimes used to record speech; other times it provides a written script for subsequent oral performance. Writing, until recently at least, has been closely tied to speaking. Finnegan (1988), among others, has noted the complete interdependence of the two, and Carruthers (1990) has shown that even in a highly literate society, the monastic society of the late medieval period, scholars did their thinking and composing almost exclusively in oral form. Even Saint Thomas Aquinas is said to have composed his magisterial *Summa* by dictating orally to a fleet of scribes. The boundary between the oral and the written, like the distinction between oral and literate cultures, therefore, has been blurred considerably.

My suggestion is that the focus on the modality of expression, the oral and the written, may have obscured a more important underlying fact, namely, how writing and the literate tradition contributes to the formation of a set of concepts about language that have turned out to be extremely important in the evolution of what we think of as scientific thought. The virtue of the hypothesis is that it escapes the criticisms mentioned earlier. It is not critical that Aquinas did his composing orally so long as he did it in terms of the categories and distinctions evolved for creating and interpreting written texts. And it does not matter that those competent in the Vai script showed few of the capabilities of those schooled in English for only the latter explicitly marked the metalinguistic distinctions that were tested for. And it does not matter that the Greeks did their disputations in the agora so long as those arguments could be scrutinized in literate terms, specifically, in terms of their ``actual linguistic meanings'' as Epicurus insisted (Long and Sedley, 1987).

Actual linguistic meanings

Lloyd (1990) pointed out that some forms of argument, especially those of syllogism, axiomatic deductions, and proof, depend upon the univocal meanings of expressions. Yet the concept of ``actual linguistic meanings'' like the concept of ``literal meaning'' is extremely difficult to analyze. Lloyd (1990) points out that Aristotle's conception of natural science necessarily excluded the metaphorical; ``metaphors . . . are disastrous in scientific explanations and they make a nonsense of syllogistic'' (p. 22). Metaphor, while acceptable in poetry and rhetoric, took on a pejorative tone when applied in science. But what is that ``actual linguistic meaning''? It cannot be identified with intended meaning because either literal or metaphorical meaning could be intended. Furthermore, no meaning is free from metaphor.

Yet it is useful to distinguish the literal from metaphorical if for no other reason than to use these categories to criticize one's own and other's arguments. Lloyd (1990) puts it this way: ``it is evident that where *there are no such explicit categories as these*, statements of ideas and beliefs are less liable to a certain type of challenge'' (p. 25). One such challenge was that leveled at Empedocles, who claimed that the salt sea is the sweat of the earth. Aristotle dismissed the claim, arguing that while that may make good poetry, it made poor science. An important part of writing is the invention and learning of devices for indicating how a statement is to be taken; literal and metaphorical ways of taking an utterance are importantly different. But such a distinction is neither absolute nor universal.

Seventeenth-century writers such as Galileo and Thomas Brown drew an equivalent distinction between speaking strictly and speaking roundly or "largely" (Olson, 1994, p. 270) in order to reconcile biblical texts with the newly discovered facts of nature. When the Bible said, or at least implied, that the earth was at the center of the universe with stars arrayed above it, that was taken as speaking largely. The correct relations could be expressed in careful language, preferably mathematics.

In our own time, Grice (1989) usefully distinguished "sentence meaning" from "speaker's or utterer's meaning," the former a meaning expressed by lexicon and syntax, the latter a meaning intended by a speaker and conveyed sometimes by what is said and sometimes by what is not said. We recall Grice's famous, if invented, example of the music reviewer who wrote "Miss X produced a series of sounds that corresponded closely to the score of 'Home Sweet Home.'" The listener would ask him or herself why had the reviewer said all that instead of simply *sing*; the answer is presumably to indicate some striking difference between Miss X's performance and the activity usually described as *singing*. The listener may infer that "Miss X's performance suffered from some hideous defect" (Grice, 1989, p. 37).

Now my hypothesis is simple: Literacy has a distinctive influence on how language, in particular meaning, is conceptualized. The meaning tied to the form of an expression is the literal meaning; the form of an expression is what is brought into consciousness by writing and literacy. Criticism of an argument in terms of its form is therefore a literate form of thinking. Epicurus' talk of "actual linguistic meanings" marks him as literate.

Some caveats. Literacy, being able to read and write, is not responsible for bringing "language into consciousness" in any general sense. Each aspect of language comes into consciousness to the extent only that one has a model or theory or concept for representing that aspect of language. Furthermore, some other activities bring aspects of language into consciousness just as well as writing does – rhyme and alliteration are cases in point. Distinctions between "straight" and "crooked" speech (Feldman, 1991), between story and song, or between questions and statements are marked in many, perhaps all, languages, written or not. Hence, my suggestion is rather that writing brings some distinctions into consciousness, among them, the notion of literal meaning. I will elaborate this hypothesis by appeal to some historical data and some experimental data of my own and others.

The invention of writing systems

The implications of writing for cognition have been overlooked, in part, because of a faulty theory of writing. The Aristotelian assumption, accepted until quite recently, is that writing is the transcription of speech. That assumption has informed the histories of writing as well as the theories of reading. Some recent writers, Harris (1986) prominent among them, have suggested that the Aristotelian view is based on an anachronism. To assume that writing is putting down speech assumes that the writers already have a concept or concepts of speech that they try to honor in their script. Historical evidence is just the opposite. Early scripts show no sign of an awareness of language as a series of sentences, words, or sounds. Earliest scripts represented, for example, "three sheep" with three tokens, one for each sheep, rather than two tokens, one for each word (Schmandt-Besserat, 1992). The inference is that writing represented things, not words; the discovery of a word was, and continues to be, for children growing up in a literate society, one of the great cognitive achievements. Again, this may require a qualification. Words, as lexical entities, are part of the cognitive competence of speakers. What is to be learned is a concept of word, a concept that includes not only "sheep," but also "three" and "what." This is the concept that was and is so difficult to achieve. The very idea that speech could be inventoried in the way that objects can be inventoried is a remarkable insight indeed.

A similar story can be told, indeed has been told (Olson, 1993; Sampson, 1985), for the discovery of the phoneme as represented by a letter of the alphabet. The problem was not one of representing sounds by letters, but of coming to hear words as composed of constituents that could be represented by letters. Again the story is complex and not completely relevant here, but simplifying brutally, we could say that rather than the alphabet being a product of the "genius" of the Greeks, it was the simple product of attempting to use a Semitic script, a script well suited to represent Semitic languages, to represent the Greek language, for which it was ill suited with the consequent attempt to "hear" Greek in terms of the categories provided by the letters of the script. The uninventoried sounds discovered by the Greeks were what we now think of as the vowels. We shall see how this works when we consider how children learn to spell.

The upshot of this story is that the history of writing is not one of learning to transcribe speech, but rather of learning to "hear" and think of language in terms of the categories and distinctions provided by the writing system. The history of writing is, in large part, the history of bringing speech into consciousness. Not all aspects of speech, of course, but at least those aspects marked in the writing system. Sentences, words, and phonemes are such aspects. (Illocutionary force is not well represented by an alphabetic writing system, and recovery of force has remained one of the largely unresolved aspects of language, a point that figures centrally in Olson, 1994.)

I want now to turn to some of the experimental data on consciousness of language as it develops in children, again, to show that ways of thinking about language are influenced in important ways by familiarity with a script. Again, a caveat is in order. Since Levy-Bruhl (1926), at least anthropologists have been leery of the comparisons between adult members of traditional (sometimes unlettered) cultures and child members of literate Western cultures. And rightly so; the assumption invites domination and sometimes conquest. But corresponding changes have occurred in our thinking about cognitive development. We no longer think of conceptual development simply as an unfolding, but rather we see children as constructing for themselves many of the same concepts that we recognize as having been constructed historically. Among them are some particular concepts of language to which I now turn.

Children's metalinguistic development

Consider first children's knowledge of phonemes. Phonemes are subsyllabic constituents of speech. To be a speaker is to "know" in some sense the phonology of the language. Isolating phonemes and knowing about phonemes is quite a different thing, for that involves bringing phonemic constituents into consciousness and turning these constituents into objects of reflection. It is the relation between knowledge about phonemes and writing systems that concerns us here.

The traditional assumption, the one traceable to Aristotle's view that writing is transcription, and one still common in some theories of reading, is that as children know the phonology of their language, the problem in reading is learning how to express that knowledge with letters of an alphabet. The problem with the traditional view is that there is no basis for saying that speakers know *about* their phonology independently of the scripts invented for representing speech. Harris (1986) pointed out that the Greek inventors of the alphabet never succeeded in developing a phonological theory for the simple reason that they mistakenly took the alphabet as that theory, ignoring phonological distinctions not represented by the alphabet. An example in English is the distinction between long and short /a/. At and ate differ only in the length of the vowel yet both are expressed by the same letter form *a*. To claim that a letter was invented to "represent" an otherwise known sound involves an anachronism; rather it was the invention of the letter that allowed the sound to be heard *as a sound*. The letter invites the formation of a new equivalence class.

Complexities of the relation between sounds and letters have led some "whole language" writers to claim that reading can proceed without regard to the relations between phonology and alphabet by focusing on the "meaning." Left unanswered, however, is what precisely they are making sense of. In my view, what they are making sense of when they learn to read is how writing relates to speech.

I shall mention two lines of evidence that indicate how writing systems influence the perception of speech. Some two decades ago, Read (1971) examined children's invented spellings, that is, how children who did not know "correct" spellings made up spellings for words. Notable among his findings were the following invented spellings, characteristic of most of the children he studied:

day DA   lady LADE   feel FEL

and

bait, bet, bat BAT

but also

igloo EGLIOW   fell FALL

He interpreted the findings as indications of children's implicit phonological knowledge, which surely it must be. But the evidence may be viewed in another way, namely, as a matter of analyzing one's speech in terms of the categories offered by the writing system.

Consider how this would work. The children all knew the alphabet, that is, the names of the letters and how to draw them. Their task, as they saw it (if I may be so bold as to speak for these preschool children), was to interrogate their pronunciation of words in terms of the letter names they knew. Thus, knowing the letter *a* was called /a/, they listened to their pronunciation of such words as *day* and *lady* and hearing that sound represented it by *a*, producing DA and LADE. The same is true for all so-called tense vowels for which the name of the letter corresponds to the sound it represents. So too for *bait*, *bet*, and *bat*, for which the sound of the letter name /a/ is closest to the vowel sound in the word and so is written as *a* to produce BAT in all three cases.

The more complex are children's inventions for so-called lax vowels, the short *a*, *e*, *i*, *o*, and *u*. These are the sounds that the letter supposedly represents, rather than simply the letter name. It is the difference between *hat* and *hate* or between *beet* and *bet*. Whereas adult spellers use *a* for both long and short /a/ as above, children inventing spellings write the short /i/ with an *e* so that *fish* is spelled FES and the short /e/ with an *a* so that *fell* is spelled FALL, and so on. As Read points out, children detect the phonetic relationship, the similarity in sound, rather than the phonemic relationship. In my terms, the children hear their speech in terms of a similarity relation between the names of the letters and the sounds in their speech.

The relation between speech and writing may be stated more generally. It is that the alphabet provides a model, a set of constituent forms and sounds, in terms of which the children analyze their speech. The units of speech they detect are not the phonemes of the language, but rather the sounds corresponding to the names of the letters. The writing system provides a model for speech and thereby brings that speech into consciousness. Note that it is not that one becomes conscious of one's speech generally, but rather that one comes to hear one's speech as composed of those constituents represented by the alphabet. Incidentally, this would help to explain the well-known fact that knowledge of the alphabet is a good predictor of children's progress in learning to read.

One criticism that may be leveled against the more general claim that learning an alphabet is learning a model for the sound patterns of one's speech is that these findings may be simply "developmental," that is, a characteristic that children grow out of rather than a reflection of a particular form of knowledge. This possibility has been ruled out by recent cross-cultural findings.

It is well known that people familiar with an alphabet "hear" words as composed of the sounds represented by the letters of an alphabet. People tend to think that there are more sounds in the word *pitch* than in the word *rich*, although linguists assure us that there are not (Ehri, 1985). Similarly those familiar with an alphabet are able to delete the sound /s/ from the word *spit* to yield /pit/ or to add an /s/ to /pit/ to make the word *spit*. Morais, Bertelson, Cary, and Alegria (1986) and Morais, Alegria, and Content (1987) found that Portuguese fishermen living in a remote area who had received even minimal reading instruction were able to carry out such segmentation tasks, whereas those who had never been exposed to the alphabet could not. Similarly, Read, Zhang, Nie, and Ding (1986) found that Chinese readers of traditional character scripts could not detect phonemic segments, whereas those who could read Pinyin, an alphabetic script representing the same language, could do so. Thus, to learn to read any script is to find or detect aspects of one's own implicit linguistic structure that can map onto or be represented by that script. In this way, the script provides the model for thinking about the sound structure of speech. The model provides the concepts that make these aspects of speech conscious.

Knowledge of phonology may have little impact on thinking. I detailed it only because it shows in a clear way how the writing system brings an aspect of speech into consciousness. I want now to show that writing serves the same role in bringing meaning and, in particular, sentence meaning into consciousness. To anticipate our conclusion, it is an awareness of sentence or linguistic meaning that gives literate thinking its particular properties.

Members of traditional cultures have been shown to treat alternative expressions having the same sense as being "the same." In contrast, members of literate cultures tend to use the stricter criterion of verbatim repetition as being "the same" (Finnegan, 1977; Goody, 1987). The very notion of *verbatim*, according to the wording, is medieval in origin, suggesting that the concept is a relatively modern one.

Some recent work on children's understanding of the relations between "what is said" and "what is meant" has shown that preschool children have particular difficulties with just this set of concepts. Hedelin and Hjelmquist (1988) showed preschool children a collection of animals including a black dog and a white dog, all of which were fed in turn except for the white dog, which remained standing outside the barn. Children were told to pass on to the newly arriving zookeeper the message "The dog is hungry." The children successfully relayed the message. Then the zookeeper asked, "Did you say the white one was hungry?" to which children under five replied, "Yes," whereas those over five replied, "No." These findings are similar to those reported earlier by Robinson, Goelman, and Olson (1983).

Our research (Torrance, Lee, and Olson, 1992) tested preliterate children on their ability to distinguish a verbatim repetition from a paraphrase. We asked children, the youngest of which were three years of age and the oldest, ten, to make judgments as to whether or not "Teddy Bear" should be awarded a sticker on the basis of how well Teddy responded to various requests. In one series of trials Teddy's task was to say *exactly* what a story character, Big Bird, had said when he came into the kitchen. These were the verbatim trials. In a second series of trials, Teddy's task was to say what Big Bird wanted – he did not have to "use the same words." These are the paraphrase trials. Practice trials involving correction preceded the experimental trials. In each trial the child was asked to judge whether or not Teddy got it right and so deserved a sticker. If so, the child was given the privilege of rewarding Teddy with a sticker or saying "No sticker, Teddy." Needless to say, children delighted in their role as judges.

As predicted, children under five years succeeded with the paraphrase items while failing the verbatim item. What they found difficult was to withhold a sticker from Teddy when Teddy was to say the same words, for example, "Big Bird is hungry," but had actually said, "Big Bird wants food." Thus although they can repeat a sentence from an early age, only when they are about six – becoming readers in Canadian schools – do they succeed in rejecting paraphrases when asked exactly "what was said." Interestingly, the pattern can be reversed if one uses well-practiced nursery rhymes in which wording becomes the critical factor. On these trials, children succeed on the verbatim items, correctly rejecting paraphrases. However, they now fail the paraphrase items; they fail to acknowledge that the paraphrase expresses the same meaning as the original expression.

Although it remains to be shown, the distinction between verbatim repetition and paraphrase, we suggest, is not merely "developmental," that is, something that will be overcome with age. Rather, we suggest that it reflects a new consciousness of the semantic properties of language, the notion of fixity of wording that comes from reading and otherwise dealing with written texts.

Thinking

Unlike knowledge about phonology, knowledge about "actual linguistic meanings," that is, the meaning tied to the actual linguistic form, the "very words," does have implications for the evolution of a literate mode of thought.

The relations between writing, literal meaning, logical form, deduction, and proof are, it goes without saying, extremely complex. But is seems safe to say that logical proof depends upon the form of an expression, not its content. Deciding on the truth of a belief on the basis of evidence is presumably universal to the human species, if not to lower creatures. But deciding on the validity of an argument depends upon judgments of necessity holding between words and statements. Proof involves the notion that something follows necessarily from what was said. It requires some distinction between an inference and an implication. But if something is to be derived from a statement (rather than the situation described), some means must be available for preserving and referring to that statement. This is where, by hypothesis, writing comes in; writing is "closed" (Barthes, 1977) in a way that speech is not. The implication is seen as following from the statement as fixed and as distinguished from its paraphrase.

Fixity is not enough. Proof requires the meaning to be fixed as a literal meaning as well. Metaphor is incompatible with proof. Proof assumes literal meaning. Logic and literal meaning seem to be mutually defining. Literal meaning is that meaning for which rules of logic hold. To return to Lloyd (1990, p. 22): "metaphors . . . are disastrous in scientific explanations and they make a nonsense of syllogistic."

Systematically applied, this way of taking expressions results in a new genre, scientific or philosophical discourse. Such discourse is not only intended to be taken literally, it tends to control how it is taken by restricting the type of speech acts involved to a single type, namely, assertives. Expressions not even labeled as assertives are known to be such by their position in the genre.

These rules do not easily apply to ordinary expressions, for ordinary expressions may not specify how they are to be taken, whether as statements, promises, predictions, or the like. To illustrate, an utterance such as "Dinner is at eight" could be taken as a statement, a promise, an invitation, or even an admonition – if one were late.

Implication depends upon how utterances are taken. Consciousness of the fact or possibility that utterances can be taken literally – according to the very words – is at the heart of literate thinking.

That ways of taking utterances determines how we reason from them is nicely shown in some research by Cheng and Holyoak (1985). Adult subjects were to judge the truth of a logical rule by testing examples against that rule. However, subjects' responses tended to reflect their interpretation of that rule. Although intended as a logical premise *If p, then q*, subjects tended to translate it into a pragmatic statement suitable for granting permission. Thus in testing the validity of the rule "If one is to drink alcohol, then one must be over eighteen," subjects were likely to think of two implications, one valid, namely, *p only if q (one can drink alcohol only if one is eighteen)*, and one invalid, namely, *if q (one can), p* (if eighteen, then one can drink alcohol). The latter, although congruent with a permission statement, makes the logical error of treating the conditional as a biconditional.

But not all ways of taking utterances are available to everyone. The option of taking utterances literally according to the very form of the expression seems itself to be a literate enterprise. Consider the famous studies of reasoning among the unlettered peasants of Uzbekistan in the 1930s. A sample from one of the interviews is as follows:

> In the far North, where there is snow, all bears are white. Novaya Zemlya is in the far North and there is always snow there. What color are the bears there?

> To which a non-literate subject, not untypically, responded: "I don't know . . . There are different sorts of bears. (Luria, 1976, pp. 108–109)

Luria called such responses failures to infer from the syllogism. In general, when subjects had no knowledge of the facts alleged in the story, they were unwilling to draw any inferences from it; if the alleged facts contradicted their beliefs, they based their conclusions on what they knew rather than on what the questioner has intended as the premise.

Of course, there is nothing wrong with such reasoning. The problem comes from the researcher failing to indicate how to take the statements in the story. He intended it as a premise; the subject took it as hearsay. But that is not the whole story. The legacy of Western literacy is the ability, on occasion, to take utterances literally according to the narrow meaning of the words employed.

Taking an expression literally was not a problem only for Luria's illiterate subjects; it is a problem extensively discussed in the anthropological literature. Since Levy-Bruhl, anthropologists have been puzzled by some expressions that seem to be characteristic of at least some traditional societies: "Twins are birds" of the Azande or "Corn is deer" of the Huichol. Western literate cultures provide two mutually exclusive ways of taking such expressions as literal or as metaphorical. The problem is that these options seem not to be available in traditional societies. But why should members of another culture be forced to choose between the alternatives valued in our culture? This is a theme carefully developed in Lloyd (1990) and Frye (1982).

Perhaps the conclusion is that it is never possible to deal with expressions in ordinary language as if they were verbal formula. For that reason, science has increasingly come to rely on mathematics and other formal models. But that does not take away from the point that a consciousness of the verbal form and its attendant sentence meaning is what allows discourse to achieve the explicitness and formality distinctive of modern science and the distinctive mode of thought that it entails.

Furthermore, it is this role that underwrites the importance of literacy in education. In this context, literacy is to be thought of as a particular way with words, their meanings, and their roles in expressions and not merely as the ability to inscribe. The very meaning of literacy has to, indeed already has begun to, change.

References

Barthes, R. (1977). *Image-music-text* (S. Heath, Trans.). Glasgow: Fontana Collins.
Carruthers, M. J. (1990). *The book of memory: A study of memory in medieval culture.* Cambridge: Cambridge Univ. Press.
Cheng, P., & Holyoak, K. (1985). Pragmatic reasoning schemas. *Cognitive Psychology, 17,* 391–416.
Ehri, L. C. (1985). Effects of printed language acquisition on speech. In D. R. Olson, N. Torrance, & A. Hildyard (Eds.), *Literacy, language, and learning: The nature and consequences of reading and writing* (pp. 333–367). Cambridge: Cambridge Univ. Press.
Feldman, C. F. (1991). Oral metalanguage. In D. R. Olson & N. Torrance (Eds.), *Literacy and orality* (pp. 47–65). Cambridge: Cambridge Univ. Press.
Finnegan, R. (1977). *Oral poetry: Its nature, significance, and social context.* Cambridge: Cambridge Univ. Press.
   (1988). *Literacy and orality: Studies in the technology of communication.* Oxford: Blackwell.
Frye, N. (1982). *The great code.* Toronto: Academic Press.
Goody, J. (1987). *The interface between the oral and the written.* Cambridge: Cambridge Univ. Press.

Goody, J., & Watt, I. (1963). The consequences of literacy. *Contemporary Studies in Society and History, 5,* 304–345.

Greenfield, P. M. (1983). Review of "The psychology of literacy" by Sylvia Scribner and Michael Cole. *Harvard Educational Review, 53,* 216–220.

Grice, P. (1989). *Studies in the way of words.* Cambridge, MA: Harvard Univ. Press.

Harris, R. (1986). *The origin of writing.* London: Duckworth.

Hedelin, L., & Hjelmquist, E. (1988). Preschool children's mastery of the form/content distinction in spoken language. In K. Ekberg & P. E. Mjaavatn (Eds.), *Growing into the modern world.* Trondheim: University of Trondheim, Norwegian Centre for Child Research.

Levy-Bruhl, L. (1926). *How natives think.* London: George Allen & Unwin. (Original work published 1910.)

Long, A. A., & Sedley, D. N. (1987). *The Hellenistic philosophers.* Cambridge: Cambridge Univ. Press.

Lloyd, G. E. R. (1979). *Magic, reason and experience.* Cambridge: Cambridge Univ. Press.

(1990). *Demystifying mentalities.* Cambridge: Cambridge Univ. Press.

Luria, A. R. (1976). *Cognitive development: Its cultural and social foundations.* Cambridge, MA: Harvard Univ. Press.

Morais, J., Alegria, J., & Content, A. (1987). The relationships between segmental analysis and alphabetic literacy: An interactive view. *Cahiers de Psychologie Cognitive, 7,* 415–438.

Morais, J., Bertelson, P., Cary, L., & Alegria, J. (1986). Literacy training and speech segmentation. *Cognition, 24,* 45–64.

Olson, D. R. (1993). How writing represents speech. *Language and Communication, 13*(1), 1–17.

(1994). *The world on paper: The conceptual and cognitive implications of writing and reading.* Cambridge: Cambridge Univ. Press.

Read, C. (1971). Pre-school children's knowledge of English phonology. *Harvard Educational Review, 41*(1), 1–34.

Read, C. A., Zhang, Y., Nie, H., & Ding, B. (1986). The ability to manipulate speech sounds depends on knowing alphabetic reading. *Cognition, 24,* 31–44.

Robinson, E., Goelman, H., & Olson, D. R. (1983). Children's relationship between expressions (what was said) and intentions (what was meant). *British Journal of Developmental Psychology, 1,* 75–86.

Sampson, G. (1985). *Writing systems.* Stanford, CA: Stanford Univ. Press.

Schmandt-Besserat, D. (1992). *Before writing.* Austin: Univ. of Texas Press.

Scribner, S., & Cole, M. (1981). *The psychology of literacy.* Cambridge, MA: Harvard Univ. Press.

Thomas, R. (1992). *Literacy and orality in ancient Greece.* Cambridge: Cambridge Univ. Press.

Torrance, N., Lee, E., & Olson, D. (April, 1992). *The development of the distinction between paraphrase and exact wording in the recognition of utterances.* Poster presentation at the meeting of the American Educational Research Association, San Francisco, CA.

11
Mythology and analogy

Cameron Shelley & Paul Thagard

11.1 Introduction

The term "myth" is commonly applied to an untrue story or a false or incredible belief, implying that myths represent some sort of primitive epistemological inadequacy. Yet myths lie at the foundations of the mental and social background of every human culture. The incongruity of these two facts naturally raises a number of questions including

(a) In what way do members of a culture understand their myths?
(b) In what way should researchers seek to understand myths?

Many theories concerning the meaning of myths address these questions by ranking one form of understanding over the other. However, these same theories often conflate the conceptual content of myths with possible interpretations, that is, the significance a myth has for its subscribers.

A common intuition about myths is that they are, in some way, analogous to established ways of thinking and perceiving. Plato felt that myths constitute a deficient form of explanation, although he recognized their pedagogical usefulness. Euhemerus held that myths are a confused and exaggerated form of history. Müller felt that myths represent a form of allegorical thought hostile to, and eventually overcome by, philosophy. Also, myth has been compared to poetry, ciphers, primitive science, cultic liturgy, and many other things. What is so disconcerting about myth is that all these comparisons produce apparently valid interpretations in some cases.

In order to overcome this apparent chaos in mythology, researchers have resorted to a number of simplifying assumptions. The most ubiquitous of these assumptions are

(1) The content of any myth permits exactly *one* interpretation.
(2) All myths are interpretable within exactly *one* theoretical framework.

These assumptions have the advantages that they permit a researcher to focus completely on some salient aspect of a myth, and they facilitate making theoretical generalizations of such an aspect over a large corpus of myths. The disadvantages that come with these assumptions are that they encourage

This research was supported by the National Science/Natural Sciences and Engineering Research Council of Canada.

oversimplification of analyses, and they lead inevitably to unenlightening logomachies about the one essential aspect of myth.

These points may be made concrete by looking at a simple example of the problems just mentioned. One such example is the now discredited mythological theory of Müller (1873, 1897). Müller holds that myths are allegorical stories about solar phenomena, for example, sunrise and sunset (see also Cohen, 1969, p. 339; Dowden, 1992, pp. 25–7). He supposes that the allegorical aspect of myth arises because of errors in word usage overcoming facts about the natural phenomena to which the words actually refer (Müller, 1873, p. 353). The effect of these errors is to lead primitives into odd or superstitious beliefs in an attempt to reconcile the way they speak with the way things actually are, for example:

> But the curious part, as showing again the influence of language on thought, an influence more powerful even than the evidence of the senses, is this, that people who speak of life or soul as the *shadow* [emphasis added] of the body, have brought themselves to believe that a dead body casts no shadow, because the shadow has departed from it. (Müller, 1873, p. 336)

This analysis seems reasonable enough, as far as the usage of the word *shadow* is concerned. Yet Müller uses the same paradigm of "language infecting thought" as his theoretical framework (required by assumption 2 above) for the analysis of myths.

Müller (1873, pp. 378–81) applies his theory, in accord with assumption 1 earlier, to the myth of Daphne and Apollo. The story is a typical one concerning Greek gods. Apollo is smitten with the beauty of the mountain nymph Daphne and attempts to ravish her. While fleeing, Daphne calls upon her mother – Earth – who turns Daphne into a laurel tree or spirits her away, leaving a laurel tree in her place. This foils Apollo, who, apparently considering the ravishment of a tree to be unworthy of him, consoles himself by fashioning a wreath from its leaves. For Müller, the true meaning of this myth is revealed largely by substituting the names Apollo and Daphne with their true, etymologically solar meanings. He claims that Apollo, more particularly in his aspect as Phoibos Apollo, is one of "the mythic disguises of the sun" and that Daphne, while meaning "laurel" in Greek, is cognate with the Sanskrit word for "dawn." Replacing the proper names with these meanings, Müller (1873, p. 380) reconstructs the myth as an allegory of natural phenomena:

> The story of Phoibos and Daphne is no more than a description of what one may see every day; first, the appearance of the Dawn in the eastern sky, then the rising of the Sun as if hurrying after his bride, then the gradual fading away of the bright Dawn at the touch of the fiery rays of the sun, and at last her death or disappearance in the lap of her mother, the Earth.

According to Müller's approach, the meaningful content of the myth is no more than his interpretation of it. Thus, any concepts the myth embodies are identified with its proper interpretation, and its original guise must be considered cognitively empty. Anyone, such as the ancient Greeks themselves, subscribing to the myth but unaware of Müller's analysis is therefore engaging in a rather meaningless act – not a very charitable ascription on Müller's part! Müller was sensitive to this problem but attempted to overcome it by a repeated assertion of dogma, for example, "people do not tell such stories . . . unless there is some sense in them" (1873, p. 379), and "A fact does not cease to be a fact, because we cannot at once explain it" (1873, p. 381).[1]

A methodologically sounder approach would be to place the identification of the cognitive content of a myth logically prior to its interpretation. In this way, the issue of how to legitimately interpret myths may be usefully separated from the issue of how the conceptual content of myths may be represented. The aim of this chapter is to proceed in this direction by proposing an analytical framework for myth in which *analogy* is examined as a means for representing conceptual content in myths and both assumptions 1 and 2 regarding interpretations are rejected. Instead, the following revised assumptions are adopted:

(1') Any myth may have more than one valid interpretation.
(2') All myths are interpretable by consideration of their analogical content.

Assumption 1' is roughly what Kirk (1974, pp. 39–42) calls *multifunctionalism* and reflects the view that a myth is capable of more than one way of being significant. Assumption 2' reflects the view, for which we argue in this chapter that analogy is an indispensable – though not exclusive – means of representing the content of myths.

This leaves the question of what it is to interpret a myth. We return to this question in section 11.4 by which point the analytical framework developed in sections 11.2 and 11.3 can be used to address it. At this point, we claim that the answer requires a response to both questions a (how subscribers understand their myths) and b (how researchers understand myths) posed at the outset of this introduction.

To accomplish these objectives, in section 11.2 we give a brief overview of the multiconstraint theory of analogy proposed by Holyoak and Thagard (1995) and apply this theory to the reanalysis of structuralist, psychoanalytic, and functional theories of myth in section 11.3. This sets the groundwork for our discussion of the role of analogy in myth in section 11.4 and our assessment of the prospects for future research into the issues raised in this chapter.

11.2 The multiconstraint theory of analogy

The theory of analogy presented by Holyoak and Thagard (1995) sets out a means of explicitly identifying the connections between patterns from two domains of knowledge. The basic idea of the theory is to pick out and juxtapose the parallels or mappings between the two patterns in question. A common example of analogy is the "proportional" analogy frequently found in IQ test questions such as "A hand is to an arm as a foot is to what?"

Source	Target
feast	life
courses	events
guest	Time
waiters	age
caretaker	Death
consist-of$_0$(feast,courses)	consist-of$_1$(life,events)
eat(guest,courses)	expend(Time,events)
serve(waiters,courses)	mark(age,events)
clean-away(caretaker,feast)	discontinue(Death,life)
conclude$_0$(clean-away,feast)	conclude$_1$(discontinue,life)
cause$_0$(eat,conclude$_0$)	cause$_1$(expend,conclude$_1$)

Figure 11.1. Barnfield's comparison of a feast to life. The attributes *events* and *caretaker* are interpolated from the poem's context. Subscripts are used to distinguish repeated occurrences of otherwise identical predicates, for example, *cause$_0$* and *cause$_1$*.

This may be symbolically represented in the form A : B :: C : X, where X is the missing term (cf. Holyoak and Thagard, 1995, ch. 2, p. 11). But this way of symbolizing analogy may be inadequately detailed to represent the conceptual structure of analogy in the general case.

Consider the analogy developed in the following poem, entitled "A Comparison of the Life of Man," written by Richard Barnfield c. 1598:

Man's life is well compared to a feast,
Furnished with choice of all variety:
To it comes Time; and as a bidden guest
He sits him down, in pomp and majesty:
The threefold age of Man the waiters be.
    Then with an earthen voider, made of clay,
    Comes Death, and takes the table clean away.

The analogy Barnfield elaborates between life and a feast could be represented by the conceptual parallels given in Figure 11.1. Each row gives the mappings from the items in the *source* (feast) domain to the corresponding items in the *target* (life) domain.

It can be seen from Figure 11.1 that the mappings from the source domain to the target domain fall into three different categories (cf. Holyoak and Thagard, 1995, ch. 2, pp. 7–14). The first category is the *attribute* mapping, represented in this instance by the parallels between *feast* and *life, courses* and *events, guest* and *Time, waiters* and *age,* and *caretaker* and *Death*. These are called attribute mappings because they connect atomic concepts or attributes. The second category is the *relational mapping*, represented by the parallels between *consist-of$_0$* and *consist-of$_1$, eat* and *expend, serve* and *mark,* and *clean-away* and *discontinue*. These are called relational mappings because they connect simple, two-place relations between attributes. The third category is the *system* mapping, represented by the parallels between $conclude_0$ and $conclude_1$, and $cause_0$ and $cause_1$. These are called system mappings because they connect systemic relations between propositions (rather than attributes).

This theory of analogy is described as a *multiconstraint* theory for two reasons: (1) each mapping is interpreted as a constraint on the overall "fit" of the analogy and (2) each mapping need not be strictly one-to-one, homological, or homomorphic. The analogy in Figure 11.1 is largely one-to-one because most attributes in the source domain each correspond to only one attribute in the target domain and *vice versa*. The exceptions are the attributes *events* and *caretaker*, which were interpolated from context to be paired with *courses* and *Death*, respectively. The analogy is homological since corresponding predicates in each row have equal numbers of slots. The analogy is also homomorphic because corresponding slotholders for predicates in each row are themselves corresponding predicates in another row. For these reasons, Barnfield's analogy has a high degree of fit.[2]

Before proceeding to apply this theory to mythology, it is instructive to see how it applies to a simple example from a related area of study: magic (see also Tambiah, 1973). Sir James Frazer (1913) proposed two laws to describe the practice of "sympathetic" magic: the law of *similarity* and the law of *contact*. The law of similarity states that an effect resembles its cause. The law of contact states that objects that have been in contact continue to act on each other after contact is over. The law of similarity can be seen at work in the use of voodoo dolls and can be captured in an analogical analysis (Holyoak and Thagard, 1995, ch. 9, p. 29):

> [T]he sorcerer's use of an effigy in the attempt to harm a person depends on similarities between relations as well as attributes: The action (sticking needles in the doll) does not directly resemble the desired effect (pain in the enemy). However, the doll and the person resemble each other, and the action of sticking needles in the doll resembles sticking a spear in the person.

The analogy by which the magic is conceived to work is represented in Figure 11.2. In this example, the system mappings $cause_0$ and $cause_1$ relate a proposition to a state of affairs.

There are a couple of important ways in which this example differs from the previous one. First, the difference between the source and target domains is not that of a better-understood domain to a less-understood one. Instead, they have been selected largely out of convenience for a particular purpose for which they are most salient: causing injury. This gives rise to a second distinction of the voodoo analogy: the conflation of the two domains into a single concept. In this case, the concepts in the source domain are taken to be substitutable for the corresponding concepts in the target domain. The result is the identification at the functional level of the system mappings $cause_0$ and $cause_1$ to produce the *metasystem* mapping:

$cause_2$ (insert-into, injured)

Source	Target
doll	person
needle	spear
mutilated(doll)	injured(person)
insert-into(doll,needle)	stab-with(person,spear)
$cause_0$(insert-into,mutilated)	$cause_1$(stab,injured)
$cause_2$(insert-into,injured)	

Figure 11.2. The belief in the effectiveness of a voodoo doll is represented by an analogy between the *doll* domain and the *person* domain. The metasystem mapping *$cause_2$* appears in the bottom row.

Here, a causal relation is constructed by taking the first argument to *$cause_0$* (insert) and the second argument from *$cause_1$* (injured). This hybridization is a form of induction whereby a hidden regularity between analogs is conceived in order to satisfy some goal in analogy construction. Such inductively produced mappings we will call *metasystem* mappings to indicate their relationship to the analogical system as a whole. This inductive procedure must be considered to be risky in a normative theory of analogy (cf. Holyoak and Thagard, 1995, ch. 9, pp. 27–8).

The theory of analogy presented by Holyoak and Thagard (1995) provides, among other things, a rich and explicit way of describing the conceptual aspects of analogical thinking. The applicability of this theory to the description of sympathetic magic suggests that it could be useful in describing conceptual aspects of the related study of mythology. Also, the concept of a metasystem mapping has been introduced. In section 11.3, we undertake a conceptual analysis of myth by applying the multiconstraint theory of analogy described here.

11.3 Analogy in mythological theory

As mentioned in section 11.1, frameworks for the analysis of myth have generally proceeded under some rather austere assumptions (labeled a and b). The alternative, it is implicitly supposed, is some form of groundless eclecticism through which myths might be analyzed on any basis the mythologist cares to select. The purpose of this section is to demonstrate that assumptions 1 and 2 can be relaxed without such a retreat into arbitrariness. This is done by reanalyzing three prominent approaches to mythology in terms of the analogical theory presented in section 11.2.

The development of an analogical framework for mythology is intended as an argument in favor of assumptions 1' and 2' given in section 11.1. One consequence of these assumptions is that one myth may be expected to yield to more than one method of interpretation. This amounts to the construal of mythological analysis as an analysis of *motifs* – thematically coherent elements – within a single mythic narrative. We suggest that this property is inherent in myth, that any single myth persists in a culture in part *because* it has more than one motif and therefore more than one valid interpretation. Such a property undoubtedly contributes to the myth's relevance within a culture (Cohen, 1969, pp. 349–53). To support this contention, the mythological example used to demonstrate different approaches in this section is the Oedipus myth. This is not done to give what we contend to be the ultimate analysis of that myth but rather to make plausible the idea that the myth has more than one valid level of significance.[3]

The theories of myth reanalyzed in this section are *structuralism, psychoanalysis*, and *functionalism*. These theories have been chosen not out of ignorance of other approaches but because they focus the most closely on the cognitive aspects of myth. Other approaches such as *historicism* (e.g., Grant, 1973; Sourvinou-Inwood, 1987; Brilliante, 1990; Dowden, 1992, pp. 23–4, 49–51) and *myth-ritualism* (e.g., Kluckhohn, 1942; Raglan, 1955; Fontenrose, 1966; Kirk, 1970, pp. 8–31; Versnel, 1990; Dowden, 1992, pp. 27–8, 34–5) would very likely respond to the sort of reanalysis presented here.

11.3.1 STRUCTURALISM

The structuralist study of myth, founded by Claude Lévi-Strauss, is probably the most influential mythological theory proposed in this century. What is paradoxical in this situation is that the theory was never fully stated by Lévi-Strauss himself (Cohen, 1969, p. 345; Leach, 1976, pp. 25–7; Sperber, 1979). In spite of this, Lévi-Strauss's ideas have been advanced and discussed in both his own examples and the criticism of others so that it is possible to get a reasonable picture of the structuralist approach to myth in both its theoretical and practical aspects. In order to assess the cognitive content of the structuralist approach, this section presents an overview of it, followed by a number of criticisms that address its implicit use of analogy.

The structuralist analysis of myths includes three components: a Hegelian/ Marxist notion of a system of logical oppositions between signs and relations between oppositions (Burridge, 1967), a functional component relating the logical component of a myth to the culture in which it occurs (Douglas, 1967, p. 52; Cohen, 1969, p. 348; Kirk, 1970, pp. 43–5; Leach, 1974, pp. 57–8), and a linguistic component through which mythical thought lends itself to narrative expression as part of a system of cultural communication (Burridge, 1967, pp. 97–102; Leach, 1974, pp. 59–60). Lévi-Strauss (1969, p. 14) himself sometimes talks as if the first, logical component were his only concern:

> I had tried to transcend the contrast between the tangible and the intelligible by operating from the outset at the sign level. The function of signs is, precisely, to express the one by means of the other. Even when very restricted in number, they lend themselves to rigorously organized combinations which can translate even the finer shades of the whole range of sense experience. . . . Our task, then, is to use the concept of the sign in such a way as to introduce these secondary qualities into the operations of truth.

I	II	III	IV
(i) Cadmus-Europa		(ii) Cadmus-dragon	
	(iii) Spartoi		(ix) Labdacus
	(iv) Oedipus-Laius		(x) Laius
		(v) Oedipus-sphinx	
(vi) Oedipus-Jocasta			(xi) Oedipus
	(vii) Eteocles-Polyneices		
(viii) Antigone-Polyneices			

Figure 11.3. A structural description of the Oedipus myth. The narrative order of events may be read from left to right, top to bottom.

Lévi-Strauss claims, then, that myths may be understood solely as structures in which signs are organized in logical, truth-laden combinations that supervene sensory experiences. Although, fortunately, Lévi-Strauss does not strictly adhere to this impoverished model, the analysis of structure in myth remains the most significant contribution of his theory.

An explanation of what Lévi-Strauss (1955, pp. 89–94)[4] means by structure is best given by illustration. His analysis of the Oedipus myth, although more a brief advertisement of his approach than a serious analysis (Vernant, 1980, pp. 228–30), is sufficient for this purpose. The plot of the Oedipus myth, largely as it exists in Sophocles' play, may be summarized as follows:

(i) Cadmus seeks his sister Europa carried off by Zeus.
(ii) Cadmus kills a dragon.
(iii) The Spartoi (the men who are born from the dragon's teeth as a result of Cadmus planting them) kill one another on a ruse by Cadmus.
(iv) Oedipus kills his father, Laius.
(v) Oedipus kills the Sphinx (actually, it commits suicide when he solves the riddle it poses).
(vi) Oedipus marries his mother, Jocasta.
(vii) Eteocles kills his brother Polyneices (both are Oedipus' sons/half-brothers).
(viii) Antigone buries her brother Polyneices despite a prohibition against doing so.

In addition to these events, Lévi-Strauss inserts the following etymologies into his analysis:

(ix) Labdacus (Oedipus's grandfather) = "lame."
(x) Laius (Oedipus's father) = "left-sided."
(xi) Oedipus = "swollen-foot."

These elements, i through xi, are then arranged into four columns, the narrative sequence being laid out from left to right and top to bottom, as in Figure 11.3. Each column collects together items from the Oedipus myth that have similar significance. Column I signifies an *overrating of blood relations*, that is, relations that "are subject to a more intimate treatment than they should be'' (Lévi-Strauss, 1955, p. 90). In contrast, column II signifies an *underrating of blood relations*. Column III refers to monsters that are slain, while column IV refers to a remarkable common trait in the male line of Oedipus' family (the Labdacids).

For Lévi-Strauss, the structure of the myth consists in the relationships that hold among the meanings of each column. Columns I and II both deal with blood relations but do so in converse, or opposite, ways. What is not so obvious is that columns III and IV, on Lévi-Strauss's analysis, both relate to the *autochthonous* view of human origin – that humans emerged whole from their native soil rather like plants. Since the monsters (the dragon and the sphinx) both represent challenges to this view, the common element of column III is the denial of the autochthonous theory (Lévi-Strauss, 1955, p. 91) represented by the death of the monsters. Conversely, or oppositely, column IV represents the *persistence* of the autochthonous theory of human origin because "in mythology it is a universal character of men born from the earth that at the moment they emerge from the depth, they either cannot walk or do it clumsily" (Lévi-Strauss, 1955, p. 91).

The meaning of the myth, as Lévi-Strauss has it, can now be summarized by explicitly stating an analogical relationship between the oppositions: that the overrating of blood relationships (column I) is to the underrating of those relationships (column II) as the denial of the autochthony theory (column III) is to the persistence of that theory (column IV). Symbolically, Lévi-Strauss's interpretation can be represented by the following notation, reminiscent of the proportional analogies mentioned in section 11.2[5]

I : II :: III : IV

Taking Lévi-Strauss literally, this expression would be the result of the analysis of the Oedipus myth. A verbal explication of this structure is roughly as follows. The conflict between ratings of *actual* blood relations identified by columns I and II somehow resolves or replaces the conflict between ratings of *theories* of blood relations identified by columns III and IV (Lévi-Strauss, 1955, pp. 91–2). Thus, the outcome of conflict in column I and in column II mirrors the outcome of conflict between the sexual theory of descent in column III and the autochthony theory of descent in column IV. Lévi-Strauss (1955, pp. 91–2) does go on, as we would expect, to state what function the myth might actually have for the ancient Greeks:

> The myth has to do with the inability, for a culture which holds the belief that mankind is autochthonous, to find a satisfactory transition between this theory and the knowledge that human beings are actually born from the union of man and woman. Although the problem obviously cannot be solved, the Oedipus myth provides a kind of logical tool which, to phrase it coarsely, replaces the original problem.

In the final analysis, then, the meaning of the myth is identified with the way its logical structure relates a theoretical dichotomy (autochthony vs. sexual reproduction) to a practical problem (underrating blood relations vs. overrating blood relations). In fact, Lévi-Strauss holds this to be a general property of myth: that it deals with difficulties in reconciling aspects of culture, for example, the autochthony theory, with aspects of nature, for example, sexual reproduction.

There are many criticisms that can be brought against this style of analysis, aside from the cursory nature of this particular example.[6] The most cogent criticisms relevant to this chapter concern the real status of Lévi-Strauss's "logical" oppositions and the assessment of oppositions that are discernible in any particular myth. Whereas the latter issue is of concern,[7] it is the former, epistemological issue that needs to be further considered here. Specifically, Lévi-Strauss's "logical" oppositions are conceptual rather than logical, and the : and :: notation obscures the nature of the relationships uncovered by structuralist analysis. This issue is addressable in terms of the theory of analogy presented in section 11.2.

Lévi-Strauss's (1955, pp. 85–6) conviction that myth functions in terms of logical oppositions is based on his belief that myths of any culture should be recognizable as such by members of any other culture, unlike other forms of expression like poetry:

> [T]he mythical value of the myth remains preserved, even through the worst translation. . . . It is language, functioning on an especially high level where meaning succeeds practically at "taking off" from the linguistic ground on which it keeps rolling.

Whatever Lévi-Strauss means by "mythical value," his assertion is untrue of his own example of the Oedipus myth. If it were true, the provision of translations of Labdacus', Laius', and Oedipus' names to their etymologies (in column IV) would be quite unnecessary; the structure of the myth itself would reveal their true values to the unimpaired reader or listener. A more likely explanation would come from a knowledge specifically of ancient Greek culture.[8] Thus, the correspondences that Lévi-Strauss calls "logical oppositions" are really conceptual contraries. This is revealed by any attempt to equate the denial of one with its "opposite." Although it is reasonable to say that one cannot both underrate *and* overrate a blood relation at the same time, it cannot reasonably be said that not underrating a blood relation *is* to overrate it and vice versa. Thus, these facts about such oppositions reveal that their differences are conceptual rather than logical in nature. This does not serve to deny that structure of the sort Lévi-Strauss supposes is present and detectable in myths; rather, it shows that more information is needed to properly characterize and understand such correspondences.

In turn, this calls into question the usefulness of the notations : and :: when applied to the analysis of different myths. If these are used to symbolize the relationship of arbitrary conceptual differences, as the preceding argument might suggest, then how could they legitimately indicate any similarity of structure from one myth to another? For example, in the analysis of the Oedipus myth, the : symbol represents a difference in the estimation of a blood relation, whereas in other cases, it represents the difference between cooked food and raw food (Lévi-Strauss, 1969). On the whole, the : and :: notations are insufficient to represent the analogical structure of a myth and are likely to lead to unnecessary confusion in understanding and applying structuralist ideas. This problem can be overcome by using a richer analogical theory to represent a myth's structure explicitly.

Lévi-Strauss's structuralist analysis of the Oedipus myth may be reanalyzed into an explicit analogy by taking the blood-relations area as the source domain and the autochthony area as the target domain of an overarching analogical structure. To proceed, it is necessary to specify the concepts embodied in each area (in each column) and how the instances of the concepts within those areas are both similar to and different from their contraries.

Lévi-Strauss's description of column I as representing an overrating of blood relations is rather superficial. It might equally well be said that each item represents an impious act: Cadmus' pursuit of Europa is a challenge to Zeus, her abductor, while Oedipus' marriage to Jocasta and Antigone's burial of Polyneices contravene religious prohibitions. However, it is possible to stay much closer to Lévi-Strauss's analysis by noting that each event in column I is primarily about the efforts of men to *retain* women within the family group. Specifically, the men in question act to keep women from leaving their immediate family. (In the case of Polyneices, his death incites Antigone to break the prohibition against burying his body. As a result, she is imprisoned and commits suicide and therefore never marries.)

In contrast, the common element in column II concerns the killing of men by their rivals from within the family group. In the case of Cadmus and the Spartoi, the dragon Cadmus killed was a son of Ares; Cadmus makes up this affront to the deity by marrying Ares' daughter Harmonia, thus becoming an uncle of the Spartoi by marriage as well as their king (Burkert, 1985, pp. 168–70). This underrating of blood relations may therefore be more exactly stated as the *rejection* of men from the kinship group. Thus, the analogical relation between columns I and II can be given as in Figure 11.4. The meta-system mapping of this analogy is represented in the final row of Figure 11.4 by the functional relationship that retaining women in the intimate family *requires* that potential male rivals within that family be killed. This mapping, in turn, participates in the overall interpretation of the myth.

According to Lévi-Strauss, the slaying of each monster (in column III) represents the *denial* of the autochthony theory of human origin. The physical defects in the gait of each character (in column IV) similarly represents the *affirmation* of that theory. The analogical relationship between these two columns is summarized in Figure 11.5. Following Lévi-Strauss's analysis, the functional mapping, given in the bottom row of Figure 11.5, is that the overcoming of the monsters *warrants* a continuing belief in the autochthonous theory of human origin.

The obvious question at this stage is: What is the result of this demonstration? The answer, if analogical theory has been applied felicitously, is that the result of this analysis should be an important function of the myth itself. Lévi-Strauss, quoted earlier, states that the function of the myth is to "replace" the paradox of contradictory theories of descent represented by columns III and IV with the problem in family dynamics represented by

I	II
Europa, Jocasta, Antigone Cadmus, Oedipus, Polyneices	Spartoi, Laius, Polyneices Cadmus, Oedipus, Eteocles
$sister_0$(Europa,Cadmus) mother(Jocasta,Oedipus) $sister_1$(Antigone,Polyneices)	uncle(Cadmus,Spartoi) son(Oedipus,Laius) brother(Eteocles,Polyneices)
pursue(Cadmus,Europa) marry(Oedipus,Jocasta) invite(Polyneices,Antigone)	decimate(Cadmus,Spartoi) $kill_0$(Oedipus,Laius) $kill_1$(Eteocles,Polyneices)
$retain_0$(Cadmus,Europa,Labdacid) $retain_1$(Oedipus,Jocasta,Labdacid) $retain_2$(Polyneices,Antigone,Labdacid)	$reject_0$(Cadmus,Spartoi,Labdacid) $reject_1$(Oedipus,Laius,Labdacid) $reject_2$(Eteocles,Polyneices,Labdacid)
require(retain,reject)	

Figure 11.4. The male attempts to retain related women (column I) are compared with their attempt to annihilate their male rivals (column II). Attribute mappings have been compressed in the top row; the metasystem mapping (*require*) is given in the bottom row.

III	IV
dragon, sphinx	Labdacus, Laius, Oedipus
$monster_0$(dragon) $monster_1$(sphinx)	lame(Labdacus) left-sided(Laius) swollen-foot(Oedipus)
$descent_0$(dragon,sexual) $descent_3$(sphinx,sexual)	$descent_1$(Labdacus,autochthony) $descent_2$(Laius,autochthony) $descent_4$(Oedipus,autochthony)
slay(Cadmus,$monster_0$) kill(Oedipus,$monster_1$)	$born_0$(Labdacus,lame) $born_1$(Laius,left-sided) $born_2$(Oedipus,swollen-foot)
$deny_0$(slay,$descent_0$) $deny_1$(kill,$descent_3$)	$affirm_0$($born_0$,$descent_1$) $affirm_1$($born_1$,$descent_2$) $affirm_2$($born_2$,$descent_4$)
warrant(deny,affirm)	

Figure 11.5. The denial of the autochthony theory of human origin (column III) is compared to the affirmation of that theory (column IV). The metasystem mapping (*warrant*) is given in the bottom row.

columns I and II. But how, exactly, can such a conclusion be formally related to the structure elucidated?

An explicit conclusion to the structural argument may be stated in terms of an overarching function, or metasystem mapping, relating the analysis of columns I and II to the analysis of columns III and IV. Effectively, this amounts to identifying a conceptual relationship between the metasystem mappings *require* and *warrant*. Oversimplifying a little, it may be said that the systemic requirement for conflict in the family *permits* the continued warrant given to the autochthony theory of descent. In other words, it seems that the observed and persistent requirement for conflict in familial male–female relations permits persistent belief that the sexual theory of descent can be denied in favor of the autochthony theory. Given this analysis, a reasonable overall metasystem mapping for the Oedipus myth is

permit(require,warrant)

Although this analysis is still crude, it is suggestive. In fact, it suggests that the Oedipus myth is an exploration of divine and mortal roles in defining human familial descent. In that sense, it is conceptually similar to the Garden of Eden myth from the Old Testament, which can be construed as an attempt to resolve Eve's relation to Adam in such a way that she is of the same race as Adam without being his sister (Leach, 1974, pp. 57–8). The result of impiousness is similarly devastating in both cases.

The greatest advantage of Lévi-Strauss's structuralist theory of myth is that it takes myths seriously as sophisticated mental and cultural phenomena. A significant difficulty with the theory is Lévi-Strauss's construal of the structure he uncovered as "logical oppositions" rather than as concepts participating in analogical relationships. As a result, the : and :: operators become an obstacle to the full understanding of a myth due to their highly nonspecific nature.

The analogical theory discussed in section 11.2 is well suited to addressing this problem because it requires the analyst to be explicit about the relationships that are being attributed to the myth under analysis. Also, it requires the analyst to distinguish different levels of analogical relationships.[9] In addition, the formal nature of the multiconstraint theory of analogy permits a fairly precise evaluation of the fitness of analogies proposed in structuralist analyses. Although the analogical interpretation of the Oedipus myth given in this section does not significantly expand the scope of ideas about that particular myth, it does illustrate how the conceptual difficulties of structuralist analysis become apparent and does suggest how these difficulties may be overcome. Also, this example indicates how the structures generated in a structuralist approach are relevant to the cognitive apprehension of myth.

11.3.2 PSYCHOANALYSIS

The structuralist theory of Lévi-Strauss suggests an analysis of myths according to what they indicate about the anthropological aspects of a culture: roughly, its kinship, economic, or political systems. Recast as an analogical theory, structuralist analysis reveals the manner in which superficially disparate but anthropologically significant concepts are embedded in myths. But is this enough to explain the emotional interest that people commonly invest in their myths? It is likely that the capacity of myths for conveying views

on things like autochthony is insufficient as an account of the pervasive
fascination with myths.

The most obvious available candidate for an account of the psychological
significance of myths is psychoanalysis. What is not so obvious is the potential affinity between Freudian psychoanalysis and Lévi-Straussian structuralism, but this potential is nicely summarized by Segal (1979, p. 133):

> At the risk of some violence to both Freud and Lévi-Strauss, we may
> suggest that the internal stability of psychodynamics, that balance of op-
> posing forces of the psyche which allows us to function according to a
> socially accepted standard of healthy, non-neurotic behavior, has some
> analogy, *grosso modo*, with the structuralist model of myth's mediation
> of polarities in the social order.

So, if there is any truth to the claim that "psychodynamics" can be construed
as Segal has it, then we may expect some appropriate psychological account
of mind to be applicable to myth in a structuralist manner.

Although Freud never took up the analysis of myths per se himself, he
certainly accepted the relevance of his psychoanalytic theories to the study
of mythology. The application of psychoanalysis to mythology was carried
out by several of his followers, among them Jung (Jung, 1953; Jung and
Kerényi, 1970) and Rank (1914, 1932), and has proven popular in studies of
classical mythology.[10] Freud set the stage for the psychoanalytic approach by
comparing myths and folklore to dreams. For Freud (1952, p. 5), mythology
is the "prescientific" counterpart of psychology and provides a system of
interpretation similar to his own system of dream interpretation. This is motivated by Freud's (1952, p. 74) view that dream symbols also have a direct
influence on the symbolism of myths.

Dreams occur, according to Freud, as attempts to derive acceptable symbolic structures from the workings of the unconscious mind during sleep
(Cohen, 1969, pp. 340–1). The unedited wishes and fantasies of an individual are freely expressed by the unconscious but are usually censored and
reconstructed in the mind by symbolic operations such as condensation, dis-
placement, distortion, dramatization, and splitting. Myths are rather like day-
dreams in that they deal in the same unconscious concerns but are subject to
a higher degree of rearrangement by the wakeful, conscious mind.

There is some plausibility to this view. It would help to account for the
obvious element of fantasy and unreality that myths often reflect, as Kirk
(1970, p. 270) notes:

> Dreams, like myths, present us with a fantastic *mélange* of subjects,
> places, periods, sequences, and styles. Their emotional tone is liable to
> change disconcertingly from tranquillity to terror, from deep involve-
> ment to passionless observation. Like myths they have an odd propen-
> sity for switching from minute detail, or a kind of visual brilliance and
> heightened realism, to a colorless detachment and abstraction.

Kirk goes on to point out that the members of many cultures, such as the
Australian aborigines, describe myths as occurring during a "dreamtime."[11]

If dreams traffic in consciously unacknowledged desires, myths must also, according to Freud. Thus, the job of the mythologist is to analyze myth in a manner similar to the analysis of dreams in order to uncover its unconscious motivations. As Rank (1914, p. 9)[12] puts it: "The manifestation of the intimate relationship between dream and myth . . . entirely justifies the interpretation of the myth as a dream of the masses of the people."

But here, one can accuse Freud and Rank of a bad analogy. If unconscious desires motivate dreaming, why need they additionally motivate myth making? Furthermore, although an individual may have an unconscious, do "masses of the people" have anything truly similar? It does not seem warranted to suppose a collective unconscious simply to support the hypothesis of people having collective dreams (see Kirk, 1970, p. 274).

However, it may be possible to retain some of the desirable aspects of psychoanalytic interpretation while addressing some of its difficulties. The tactic of relating psychoanalysis to structuralism has been pursued by Caldwell (1973, 1976, 1990) and Segal (1979). In this approach, the psychological significance of a myth is construed as being conveyed by the *same mechanism* as in structuralist theory but is construed as providing a *complementary interpretation*. That is to say, the psychological content of a myth can be analyzed in the structuralist manner – through analogy – but contains different terms and relationships. On this view, the essential difference between structuralist and psychoanalytic theories is that "in the former it is an *intellectual* impulse which is 'exhausted,' while in the latter an *emotional* impulse is 'exhausted' " (Caldwell, 1976, p. 216).

As an example of this kind of analysis, Caldwell gives an account of the Oedipus myth (see also Caldwell's [1976, 1990] analysis of the Orestes myth). His summary of the plot for the analysis is as follows:

(i) Labdacus dies when Laius is one year old.
(ii) Laius rapes Chrysippus.
(iii) Laius refuses a sexual relationship with Jocasta.
(iv) Laius is killed by Oedipus.
(v) Oedipus is exposed and later kills Laius.
(vi) Oedipus flees from Corinth.
(vii) Oedipus kills the sphinx and marries Jocasta.
(viii) Oedipus learns of his incest and blinds himself.
(ix) Oedipus is exiled.
(x) Polyneices leaves Thebes; Eteocles disregards curse.
(xi) Eteocles is a misogynist; Polyneices marries Aegeia, is enabled to return to Thebes.
(xii) Eteocles and Polyneices kill one another.

The structural arrangement of this plot is given in Figure 11.6.

In Caldwell's (1973, pp. 211–24) analysis, column I represents the absence of a father in the three generations of the family, column II represents the attempt made by the males to avoid their fate, column III represents the responses of the males to a "female who is both feared and desired," and column IV represents the realization of the family curse in each generation.

I	II	III	IV
(i) Labdacus		(ii) Laius-Chrysippus	
	(iii) Laius-Jocasta		(iv) Laius-Oedipus
(v) Laius	(vi) Oedipus-Corinth	(vii) Oedipus-Jocasta	(viii) Oedipus-Oedipus
(ix) Oedipus	(x) Polyneices-Thebes	(xi) Eteocles-misogynist	(xii) Eteocles-Polyneices

Figure 11.6.   The psychological structure of the Oedipus myth. Column I represents the absence of fathers; column II, the men's avoidance of fate; column III, the men's response to women; and column IV, the realization of the family curse.

The absence of a father in column I is psychologically important because it gratifies the wish of the son to take the father's place (Caldwell, 1973, p. 212). The significance of column II is that it represents a projection of the fear of women onto the female characters (Caldwell, 1973, pp. 213, 215). The attitude of the male characters to the female characters in column III is a "decomposition," whereby enough characters are provided to be the unique objects of each man's fear or desire of a woman (Caldwell, 1973, p. 218). Caldwell is less clear on the psychoanalytic meaning of column IV, except that "its common element is simply the conclusion of all that's gone before, the justification of fear, and the realization of the Curse in all three generations" (Caldwell, 1973, p. 224), which makes column IV sound somewhat redundant.

Also, Caldwell does not clarify in what way these columns form a structure, but it is no doubt organized in imitation of Lévi-Strauss's analysis of the same myth. A more detailed comparison of psychoanalytic themes is given in Figures 11.7 and 11.8. Column I gives evidence for occurrences of classic Freudian castration anxiety, in this case by the *fulfillment* of a wish on the part of each male to replace his father (Caldwell, 1989, pp. 37–41). Column II shows how each male member of the Labdacid family manifests a fear of women. This seems to be consistent with another aspect of the Freudian Oedipal complex, the realization by young boys that they are ill equipped to satisfy their mothers, whom they desire. Caldwell (1974a, p. 211) refers to this as the "infantile limitation" (Caldwell, 1989, pp. 41–48). In the Oedipus myth, this fear is *projected* into the form of a curse on the family line. The relationship between the columns can also be inferred from Caldwell's (1974a, p. 211) discussion. The realization of one's own limitations, represented in column II, can be palliated by instead attributing the failure to possess one's mother to aggression and threatening by one's father. Thus, one is the victim rather than the author of one's own misfortune.

Column III provides examples of the difficulty the Labdacid men experience in forming normal, reproductive relationships. They are either homosexual, misogynistic, or, if heterosexual, end up in incestuous or childless marriages. From Caldwell's comments, this is due to a decomposition of their sexual preferences into contrary objects of desire (Caldwell, 1989, pp. 62–5). Thus, for example, Laius marries Jocasta but prefers Chrysippus, the young son of Pelops. Column IV shows behavior that is consistent with Rank's

I	II
$dead_0$(Labdacus) $dead_1$(Laius) exiled(Oedipus)	$cursed_0$(Laius) $cursed_1$(Oedipus) $cursed_2$(Polyneices)
displace(Laius,Labdacus) kill(Oedipus,Laius) repudiate(Polyneices,Oedipus)	refuse(Laius,Jocasta) flee(Oedipus,Periboea) leave(Polyneices,Aegeia)
$wish_0$(Laius,$dead_0$) $wish_1$(Oedipus,$dead_1$) $wish_2$(Polyneices,exiled)	$fear_0$(Laius,Jocasta) $fear_1$(Oedipus,Periboea) $fear_2$(Polyneices,Aegeia)
$fulfill_0$($dead_0$,$wish_0$) $fulfill_1$($dead_1$,$wish_1$) $fulfill_2$(exiled,$wish_2$)	$project_0$($fear_0$,$cursed_0$) $project_1$($fear_1$,$cursed_1$) $project_2$($fear_2$,$cursed_2$)
palliate(fulfill,project)	

Figure 11.7. The analogy of the wish for the absence of the father (column I) is compared to the anxiety of possessing the mother (column II). The fulfillment of the wish palliates the anxiety. Some additional details from the narrative have been inserted.

III	IV
homosexual(Laius) $heterosexual_0$(Oedipus) misogynistic(Eteocles) $heterosexual_1$(Polyneices)	$paternophobic_0$(Laius) $paternophobic_1$(Oedipus) $paternophobic_2$(Eteocles) $paternophobic_3$(Polyneices)
rape(Laius,Chrysippus) flee(Oedipus,Periboea) rebuke(Eteocles,Theban-women) leave(Polyneices,Aegeia)	curse(Pelops,Laius) blind(Oedipus,Oedipus) $kill_0$(Polyneices,Eteocles) $kill_1$(Eteocles,Polyneices)
$marry_0$(Laius,Jocasta) $marry_1$(Oedipus,Jocasta) king(Eteocles,Thebes) $marry_2$(Polyneices,Aegeia)	friend(Pelops,Laius) father-in-law(Oedipus,Oedipus) $brother_0$(Polyneices,Eteocles) $brother_1$(Eteocles,Polyneices)
$decompose_0$(homosexual,rape,$marry_0$) $decompose_1$($heterosexual_0$,flee,$marry_1$) $decompose_2$(misogynistic,rebuke,king) $decompose_3$($heterosexual_1$,leave,$marry_2$)	$compose_0$($paternophobic_0$,friend,curse) $compose_1$($paternophobic_1$,father-in-law,blind) $compose_2$($paternophobic_2$,$brother_0$,$kill_0$) $compose_3$($paternophobic_3$,$brother_1$,$kill_1$)
confirm(decompose,compose)	

Figure 11.8. The analogy of Labdacids' difficulty in forming normal heterosexual relationships (column III) is compared to their fear of their offspring (column IV). The difficulty confirms the Labdacids' hesitancy to become fathers. Some additional details from the narrative have been inserted.

(1932, pp. 303–12) contention that each male is *paternophobic* – afraid of becoming a father. This is because to become a father is to acknowledge the facts about family descent and the inevitability of one's own death. In Freudian terms, this seems to be realized by the composition of this paternophobia by contrary facts about the men's relations with their contemporaries and competitors (Caldwell, 1974a, p. 215; Buxton, 1980). The relationship between columns III and IV is one of complementarity: The difficulties in forming the usual reproductive relationships with women *confirms* or is explained by the fear of becoming a father and having to face the fact of mortality.

The connection of the motifs represented in Figures 11.7 and 11.8 is essentially that proposed by Rank (1932, pp. 303–12). The analogy between columns I and II concerns the nature and potential consequences of *inter*generational conflict. The analogy between columns III and IV emphasizes the possibilities for *intra*generational conflict. The point Caldwell seems to indicate is that intergenerational conflict is the model and cause of conflict within a generation, which may be represented by the overall metasystem mapping:

cause(palliate,confirm)

where the metasystem mapping *palliate* represents the influence of intergenerational conflict and the metasystem mapping *confirm* represents the intragenerational conflict thus caused.

There are several aspects to this sort of analysis that may be brought into question, aside from the crudity of this particular example. One might ask whether or not the "emotional impetus" of a myth can really be captured by giving an explicit analogical structure as above. But such a question mistakes the purpose of analysis, which is not to *be* a myth, but rather to *represent* the content of a particular motif. Thus, although the emotions themselves are certainly not *present* in an analogical interpretation, their participation in structuring a myth may still be *represented* by concepts such as *fear and desire*. With an adequate store of such basic terms, the psychological relations provided by Freudian theory or another relevant theory, for example, *decompose, wish, project, and compose*, may be understood as high-level mappings in the analogical framework.

The advantages of applying analogical theory to the psychological analysis of myth are similar to the advantages discussed with regard to structuralism in section 11.3.1. The necessity of making analogical relationships explicit requires a thorough consideration of the relationships among diverse elements of a myth. Furthermore, the framework requires each interpretation to be carried through to its logical conclusion. Also, the sorts of relationships available to any analysis are directly restricted by the theory being applied. In the case of Freudian psychoanalysis, the system mappings must be drawn from the mechanisms posited for the interpretation of dreams, for example, decomposition and projection. By the same token, the utility of the psychoanalytic approach can be evaluated by its ability to provide such means for the representation of observable, psychological phenomena in myths.

Caldwell's application of psychoanalysis to mythology as a form of structuralism is motivated by the observation that each theory addresses a different aspect of myth, roughly, the emotional and anthropological aspects. If true, then the unified experience represented by a myth is well reflected by the use of analogy in representing that experience. The difference among motifs then arises from the different domains, for example, anthropological and psychological, from which mappings are drawn. However, neither theory examined so far addresses the issue of what domain the metasystem mappings are drawn from. Section 11.3.3 presents a brief examination of the functionalist approach to myth analysis, which helps to resolve this problem.

11.3.3 FUNCTIONALISM

The functionalist approach to myth is most closely associated with the work of Malinowski (1926). This approach emphasizes the role that myths play in the society of their subscribers. Malinowski presents the mythological classification system he gathered from his studies of the Trobriand islanders. The islanders divide myths into three categories: *kukwanebu*, fairy tales intended to be entertaining and not taken seriously (Malinowski, 1926, p. 25); *libwogwo*, legends about events and figures that are taken to be historically accurate (p. 33); and *liliu*, myths that are taken to be both true and sacred (pp. 35–6).

Malinowski's (1926, p. 36) main concern is with the third category, which he associates closely with ritual and religion:

The *myth* comes into play when rite, ceremony, or a social or moral rule demands justification, warrant of antiquity, reality, and sanctity.

Whether or not myths must always be associated with ritual and religious practice is a debatable issue that is not covered here.[13] What is important to understand for present purposes is Malinowski's claim that myths serve to justify or warrant certain beliefs and attitudes.

One example of such a myth, which concerns the origin of humankind in the Trobriand islands, may be paraphrased as follows (Malinowski, 1926, pp. 46–8):

The world was originally peopled from underground where humanity had led an existence similar in all respects to the present life on earth. For an unspecified reason, the totem ancestors of the human tribes, including the Dog and the Pig, came to the surface via a special hole called Obukula near the village of Laba'i. The Dog ate the fruit of the *noku* plant, whereupon the Pig said, "Thou eatest noku, thou eatest dirt; thou art a low-bred, a commoner; the chief, the *guya'u*, shall be I." And ever since, the Malasi clan, descendants of the Pig, have outranked the Lukuba clan, descendants of the Dog.

This myth, explains Malinowski, serves as a charter for the social superiority of the Malasi clan over the others. This myth clearly does give a justification for the social state of affairs among the Trobrianders, just as Malinowski claims. The analogical structure of the myth consists simply in the relationship between the actions of the animal totems, represented in the left table of Figure 11.9, and the current situation of the human clans, represented in the right table of Figure 11.9. The crucial point of the totem-animal domain is the contrast between the Dog's eating of the noku and the Pig's act of speaking, whereas the crucial point of the human-clans domain is their descent from the totem animals.

It is also interesting to note that the content of the Pig's decree is essentially to express its relationship with the Dog, as it is set out in the left table of Figure 11.9. This appears to constitute a metonymic relation between the Pig's decree and the analogical motif within which it occurs. The presence of such metonymic relations can be expected to provide clues as to the analogical structures underlying important motifs.

This notion of a mythical *warrant* is the same as that employed in section 11.3.1 as the metasystem mapping in Lévi-Strauss's analysis of the Oedipus myth (in Figure 11.5). This is not a coincidence; such functional rules constitute the natural endpoint of the analogical analysis of myth. In other words, the process of analyzing a myth as described so far has its natural conclusion in a general relationship such as *warrant (x, y)* – the licensing of some analog *x* by the corresponding analog *y*. Although Malinowski felt there was little more than this to be said about myths in general, the *analogical* framework presented in this chapter provides a definite procedure that connects the analogy among facts represented in myths to the level of *function*, thus tying the two approaches together. This is effectively done by identifying mythological functions (as Malinowski has them) with the metasystem mappings under discussion in this chapter.

One objection that might be raised at this point is whether functions such as *warrant* should relate two analogical structures or relate a person to an analogical structure. In other words, perhaps warranting is something a mythological structure does for a person, which might be represented as *warrant (x,John)*, where myth *x* warrants something for its subscriber named John. But this has the obvious problem that it conflates the interpretation of a myth with assenting or subscribing to that message. As a result, it also leaves the "something" (the message) to be understood implicitly. If John subscribes to the myth, this fact would, provisionally, be better represented as

subscribe(John,warrant(x,y))

This, however, is clearly a step further than understanding the function of the myth itself and is further discussed in section 11.4.

One shortcoming of Malinowski's approach is his narrow focus on myths that do provide social charters and his rejection of myths that might be better described as explanations (Kirk, 1970, pp. 19–23). It is more accurate to say that myths may serve a variety of functions of which warranting is one. Kirk (1970, pp. 253–61) offers a more elaborate "typology" of mythological functions, which may be summarized as follows:

• Entertainment, including myths primarily intended to be burlesque, farcical, or pornographic.

Dog totem	Pig totem	Lukuba clan	Malasi clan
Dog	Pig	Lukuba	Malasi
noku	decree	Dog	Pig
common(Dog)	chief(Pig)	inferior(Lukuba)	superior(Malasi)
eat(Dog,noku)	proclaim(Pig,decree)	totem-of$_0$(Dog,Lukuba)	totem-of$_1$(Pig,Malasi)
cause$_0$(eat,common)	cause$_1$(proclaim,chief)	cause$_2$(totem-of$_0$,inferior)	cause$_3$(totem-of$_1$,superior)
confirm$_0$(cause$_0$,cause$_1$)		confirm$_1$(cause$_2$,cause$_3$)	

Figure 11.9. The analogical structure of the Lukuba–Malasi origin myth. The left table illustrates the analogical structure of the actions of the Dog and Pig totems. The right table illustrates the analogical structure of the contemporary social situation between the Lubuka and the Malasi clans. The former analogy is the conceptual basis for the latter, thus giving the overall metasystem mapping: *warrant(confirm$_0$,confirm$_1$)*.

- Operative or validatory, including myths that model, confirm, warrant, or etiologize objects, situations, and practices.
- Explanatory or speculative, including myths that explain, resolve, palliate, or evaluate difficult phenomena and beliefs.
- Eschatological, including myths that describe the afterlife and the underworld.

While Kirk's arrangement of categories is debatable, his proposed typology at least suggests a reasonable division of metasystem mappings suitable for myth analysis.

What is left, then, is an inventory of functional relationships that may be applied in the process of mythological analysis presented here. These functions include *warrant, confirm, validate, explain, resolve, palliate, evaluate,* and *sanction* among others. The issue of how to more carefully define these notions is further discussed in section 11.4.

11.4 Cognitive analysis of myth

It is now possible to return to the question raised at the end of section 11.1: What is it to interpret a myth? For present purposes, this question can be restated as follows: What is the justification for taking the theoretical framework developed in sections 11.2 and 11.3 as a basis for interpreting myths? If there is a justification, then a further question naturally arises: Is this framework *sufficient*, in some sense, to support legitimate interpretations of the significance of myths? We address these questions in this section. Section 11.4.1 reviews and clarifies the analytical methodology proposed in this chapter, and section 11.4.2 gives a discussion of further cognitive aspects of this application of analogical theory. A brief evaluation of our proposal is given in section 11.5.

11.4.1 METHODOLOGY
The analytical framework used in section 11.3 is realized as a method for deriving an overall function or metasystem mapping from a consideration of the basic characters and events provided by a myth motif. To recapitulate, this method consists of the following steps:

1. Identifying the attributes, relations, and system mappings present in the myth.
2. Grouping the results of step 1 according to domain, for example, kinship or wish fulfillment.
3. Pairing the analogically related domains resulting from step 2.
4. Assigning an appropriate metasystem mapping between the pairs from step 3.
5. Repeating steps 1 through 4 as appropriate until a single system is constructed.

Although analogy occupies the central position in this procedure, it is worth noting that other cognitive abilities, for example, abstraction and induction, are importantly involved.

A definitive characteristic of myth is that significant attributes and relationships are repeated several times in the course of a narrative. Thus, items
grouped into one domain in step 2 do not occur singly but in sets. For
example, there are three occurrences of the relation *retain* in the Oedipus
myth as given in column I of Figure 11.4. These three occurrences, sub-
scripted 0, 1, and 2, are abstracted to form the predicate *retain* that is given
later in the same figure. When analogies are constructed in step 3, the analogical correspondences may hold between sets of items rather than the
strictly one-to-one correspondences given in the simple examples in section
11.2. This is because it may be difficult to say exactly which items in the
myths are given in corresponding pairs.[14] It might equivalently be said that
the analogy holds between the abstractions derived from each set. For this
reason, abstraction is an important cognitive ability in the framework proposed here.

Another contributing cognitive ability, mentioned in section 11.3.3, is induction. A simple example of induction arose in section 11.2 in discussing
the workings of magic in the case of the voodoo doll. In that example, the
desired function of injuring a person is accomplished by "identifying" or
"conflating" the highest-level mappings in the analogy: $cause_0$ and $cause_1$
(see Figure 11.2). All the correspondences in the analogy, by virtue of the
law of similarity, seem to justify the formation of a single concept relating
the source and target items into a single system. The result of this sort of
induction is captured by a metasystem mapping. More complex examples of
the same process are evident in myth. For example, the domains represented
by columns I and II in Figure 11.4 are given an explicit functional relationship by the metasystem mapping *require(retain,reject)*. Obviously, this is
more general than a simple conflation of predicates but is rather a means of
subsuming the analogy under a single concept. This is necessary if step 5 is
to be possible, a process that calls for more explicitness than Frazer's law of
similarity.

The step that most extends the theory of analogy presented in section 11.2
is step 5. By virtue of this step, analogies themselves may effectively be
placed in analogical relations with other analogies. This kind of structural
complexity is unexplored by Holyoak and Thagard (1995) but does not violate any of the constraints they discuss. The systems subsumed inductively
under explicit rules in step 4 form the input to further iterations of abstraction,
analogy, and induction. It is by this unified procedure that representations of
mythical motifs are derived from the evidence given in myth narratives.

The way in which the analogical method improves upon the structuralist
method can be demonstrated by contrasting their differing use of analogical
notation. A typical occurrence of the : and :: notation for proportional analogies (see section 11.2) is given by Leach (1974) in his evaluation of Lévi-
Strauss's analysis of the Oedipus myth, (see section 11.3.1):

I : II :: III : IV

In fact, the structuralist analysis is not adequately described as an analogy
in this manner. A proportional analogy occurs in a form like: A hand is to

Source	Target
hand	foot
arm	leg
$terminate_0(hand, arm)$	$terminate_1(foot, leg)$

Figure 11.10. A proportional analogy of limbs.

I:II	III:IV
overrate(blood-relation)	deny(autochthony)
underrate(blood-relation)	affirm(autochthony)
$contrary_0$(overrate, underrate)	$contrary_1$(deny, affirm)
replace($contrary_0$, $contrary_1$)	

Figure 11.11. Incomplete representation of the Oedipus myth structure.

an arm as a foot is to what? This analogy has the structure given in Figure 11.10. This structure is equivalent to the proportional structure

hand:arm::foot:leg

From a comparison of the two representations, it is obvious that each : is equivalent to the presence of the relational mapping *terminate*. The :: indicates that the relational mapping recurs in both source and target domains.

Clearly, the structuralist analysis of the Oedipus myth does not follow this pattern. If it did, it would be the structure given in Figure 11.11. Two problems with this representation are immediately apparent. First, the actual evidence for the analysis does not even appear, that is, there is no indication of the items or relationships from the Oedipus myth given in Figure 11.11. Thus, the reasoning behind the structuralist analysis is left unrepresented. Second, the relational mappings, *contrary*$_0$ and *contrary*$_1$, are *not* part of the analysis of the Oedipus myth per se but are rather inherent in the structuralist analytical paradigm. In effect, their appearance in Figure 11.11 is simply redundant; but they are needed in order for the conclusion, *replace*, to be statable at all.

This underrepresentation of structuralist analysis leads to the following conclusions. First, the notation of proportional analogy is an inadequate means of describing structuralist analysis. Second, structuralists, probably as a result of this inadequacy, have not fully explored the significance of analogy in mythological structures. One of the main purposes of this chapter is to indicate how an enriched theory of analogy can broaden the scope and consistency of the analysis of myths.

Of course, the application of Holyoak and Thagard's (1995) theory of analogy does not resolve all issues of mythological analysis. But, in addition to what we have already addressed in this chapter, the theory does facilitate further research into related areas of importance to myth, especially *subscription* and *metaphor*.

11.4.2 SUBSCRIPTION AND METAPHOR

The problem of subscription is discovering in what way members of a culture believe in or relate to their myths (see section 11.3.3). In the past, this has been the limit of the cognitive consideration of myths and has not yielded convincing results.

For example, Pettazzoni (1954b) discusses the nature of the belief that some North American Indians have in some of their myths by equating their claim that the myths are true histories to their behavior after hearing the myths retold, for example.

> Among the south-eastern Yavapai of Arizona, anyone listening to the story of the dying god ran the risk of falling ill, with the result that when the narrative was ended every listener would get up, stretch and shake himself, with the intention of freeing himself in this way, as he believed he could, from the besetting malady. (Pettazzoni, 1954b, pp. 103–4)[15]

Pettazzoni cites several similar examples from other cultures. The problem with Pettazzoni's theory is that a belief in the historical truth of a myth narrative does not explain the apparent belief in the contagion that may be caught from hearing it. In effect, Pettazzoni is stretching the notion of "truth" too far. A better assessment of this situation would be to say that the Yavapai subscribe to the myth in at least two different ways: one in which the myth is an historical account and another in which the hearer is so sympathetic with the protagonist as to undergo an analogous experience upon hearing the myth.

In section 11.3.3, we stated that subscription is a relationship between a member of a culture and the analogical structure of a mythological motif. Malinowski's example of a Trobriand myth, represented in Figure 11.9, seems to be a good example of how a human member of a contemporary clan can view his situation as analogous to that of nonhuman beings. Members of the Lukuba clan will be sympathetic with the Dog, whereas members of the Malasi clan will be sympathetic with the Pig. If sympathy with a narrative character means adopting a relationship between oneself and that character, then subscription to this myth implies, at least, the willingness to substitute some term involving oneself for that character in the analogical structure given by the myth. In the case of the Trobriand or Yavapai myths cited, the relationship is one of being like the character. In the Oedipus myth, by contrast, the relationship is one of being unlike Oedipus and therefore learning from his misfortunes.

In general, subscription to a myth may be viewed as a commitment to a particular interpretation of it. Motifs may be informed by a variety of principles, for example, historical, social, or pedagogical, in addition to the anthropological and psychological principles discussed earlier. The legitimacy of each such interpretation depends on the degree of fitness of the analogical

structure underlying the interpretation. As conceptual structures to which people may subscribe, myths lend credence to certain habits of action or of
thought.

Since subscription would seem to be a relationship between a person and
a metasystem mapping, two things must be further explored in order to specify what the various modes of subscription are: the conditions for applying
metasystem mappings to analogies and the way in which analogies are a
natural means of providing support for modes of subscription. The first point
requires much more consideration and is outside the scope of this chapter.
The second point may be addressed by noting the way in which mythical
structures resemble the concept of a *schema* as discussed by Holyoak and
Thagard (1995, ch. 5, pp. 32–5). A schema, in this sense, is an analogical
structure stripped of the specifics of any particular example. Because of this
abstract quality, schemas are conceptual tools for understanding many, potentially heterogeneous situations. A commonality between this sort of
schema and a myth is that both are instantiated by repeated examples of a
certain type of analogical structure. Thus, the apparent tendency of myths to
contain repeated instances of parallel structures may be explained as the result
of a cognitive requirement for apprehending the underlying schema. Lévi-
Strauss (1955, p. 105) notes that the multiplication of some component of a
myth serves to "make the structure of the myth apparent." It is beneficial
to see, however, that this fact follows from cognitive aspects of analogy and
need not stand as an extra theoretical assumption. Also, since both myths and
schemas serve, in a sense, as recipes for thought and action, it is not surprising that the analogical schemas contained in myths should be the objects
of subscription.

Another aspect that analogies and myths may have in common is their
relationships with the phenomenon of metaphor. Myths are often supposed
to embody metaphorical thinking (in addition to simply containing metaphors), for example, as claimed by Cassirer (1946, p. 92):

> Here one is reminded forcefully of the principle which might be called
> the basic principle of verbal as well as mythic "metaphor" – the princi-
> ple of *pars pro toto*. It is a familiar fact that all mythic thinking is gov-
> erned and permeated by this principle.

Here, Cassirer suggests that myth shares with metaphor some basic principle
of the nonliteral use of symbols. If true, this could be significant when the
relationship of analogy to metaphor, discussed by Holyoak and Thagard
(1995, ch. 9, pp. 4–15), is considered.

Without engaging in undue speculation, some of the potential similarities
between myth and metaphor are worthwhile pointing out for future consideration. These points of comparison include the following (Holyoak and Thagard, 1995, ch. 9, pp. 7–14):

- As noted above, neither the use of a myth nor the use of a metaphor
  necessarily indicates a literal belief. Someone who says "Socrates was a
  lion" may not subscribe to the proposition literally asserted anymore than

someone citing or reciting a myth may subscribe to its "historical" veracity.

- Myth, like metaphor, involves the "conflation," or comparison, of items from two domains.
- Both myths and metaphors appear to create analogies that efface the source/target distinction present in simple analogies, that is, the created analogies do not necessarily contrast a well-understood domain with a less well-understood domain.
- Myths do *not* have the asymmetry of metaphors. In metaphors, information flows in one direction, from source to target, so that, for example, information about lions is being mapped to the human domain in the expression "Socrates was a lion" and not the other way around. In myth, by contrast, both source and target may be information rich.
- Myths and metaphors both permit more than one possible interpretation; the interpretation understood may be the one most relevant to a particular context.

Although these points are addressed within the analogical framework, their explication as *metaphorical* phenomena remains to be completed.[16] Further research in the relationship between analogy and metaphor should produce more insight on this issue.

11.5 Conclusions

The purpose of this chapter has been to explore the participation of analogical thought in the structure and interpretation of myth. The multiconstraint theory of Holyoak and Thagard (1995) has been applied as the representation of analogical structures evident in mythic motifs. In this paradigm, an interpretation of a myth is the derivation of the functional attributes (metasystem mappings) of mythic motifs from the items and relations present in the narrative. A substantial amount of work remains in order to flesh out the approach outlined here, but there do appear to be sufficient reasons for proceeding.

On the one hand, this paradigm subsumes many of the features of structuralist, psychoanalytic, and functionalist approaches to myth. Therefore, it constitutes a method for making explicit the cognitive content of mythological motifs without the necessity of dogmatically adopting a single theoretical framework. On the other hand, this paradigm constitutes an extension to the analogical theory presented in Holyoak and Thagard (1995). In supporting a particular interpretation of a myth, analogical thinking is required to participate in an overall process that includes other cognitive mechanisms such as abstraction and induction. One of the consequences of this fact is that analogies may end up standing in analogical relationships with other analogies. This sort of embedding, although not inconsistent with the theory provided by Holyoak and Thagard (1995), is nevertheless a new consideration. It is quite possible that embedding of this kind has a more general role to play in analogical thinking than has been realized so far.

Returning to the issues raised at the outset of this chapter, it can be seen that analogical analysis of myth has the desired properties specified in section 11.1:

(1') Any myth may have more than one valid interpretation.
(2') All myths are interpretable by consideration of their analogical content.

As demonstrated in section 11.3, the Oedipus myth has more than one possible interpretation, but these need not be considered as necessarily exclusive. What is important in the analysis of myth is that the attribution of a motif to a myth should be motivated by and derived from the material present in the narrative itself.

The proposed method for interpreting myths, in turn, permits the discussion to return to the questions that motivate this chapter, as stated at the outset of section 11.1:

(a) In what way do members of a culture understand their myths?
(b) In what way should researchers seek to understand myths?

The answer to these questions is deceptively simple: in the *same* way. We have, in the course of this chapter, developed a method for a researcher to derive an interpretation of a myth from its narrative, in answer to question b. But, to address question a, such an interpretation is also ascribable to a member of the culture in which the myth occurs. The mechanisms of analogy, abstraction, and induction are all independently motivated cognitive faculties and capable of being explicitly modeled. A primary object of research in mythology, then, is to identify interpretations of a myth that are methodologically tenable and also plausibly ascribable to those who subscribe to the myth in a particular mode. The approach demonstrated in this chapter constitutes a tool for satisfying both requirements. Certainly, however, further research into the cognitive aspects of myth, including the relationship between myth and metaphor, is called for.

It may, at first glance, seem perverse to imply that the interpretations of a myth produced by researchers are effectively variants of those possible to the subscriber's culture, but this is not the case. Both researchers and subscribers are in roughly the same position with respect to the interpretation of a myth; both have about the same narrative material at hand. The subscriber has the advantage of the cultural background necessary to make discerning the significant elements of a myth effortless or unconscious. The researcher has the advantage of having to justify interpretations *explicitly*, if advantage it is. But both are in the business of producing interpretations of myths. Also, the presence of myth variants indicates the fact that different cultural groups have varying requirements of their myths.

Finally, the cognitive approach to mythology might also shed some light on two further interesting facts about myths. First, myths are universally distributed. Just as no human culture has been discovered that lacks a fully realized language, no human culture has been discovered that lacks a fully realized mythology. All primitive cultures and, very likely, all modern cultures have what are recognizably myths. This fact is certainly no accident, and it militates against the impulse to regard myths as simply the products of some largely savage or prerational mode of thought. Rather, the universality of myths calls for an account that includes a cognitive component of adequate complexity and universality, which the multiconstraint theory of analogy provides. In so far as analogical reasoning is concerned, there is no cause to distinguish the cognitive abilities of "primitives" from those of modern people. Second, myths are widely regarded as opposed to logic or as attempts to "deliberately cultivate ambiguity" (Lloyd, 1990, p. 23). Any conclusions drawn from reasoning in which myths participate are felt to be inherently unverifiable, whereas conclusions drawn from logic can be based on evidence that may be effectively scrutinized (Lloyd, 1990, pp. 45–7). This is rather similar to the situation of analogical thinking, which is often dismissed as fallacious. If the theory presented in this chapter is correct, then the reputation of mythical inscrutability may be explainable partly by the tendency to dismiss analogy as illogical. Thus, the multiconstraint theory of analogy should help to clarify the nature of myth without mistaking the complexity and ambiguity that are the intrinsic qualities of this cultural phenomenon.

Notes

1 See Lang (1897) for a thorough attack on Müller's theory.

2 This is not, however, a measure of the work's poetical qualities.

3 Also, it has been examined by mythologers from a variety of approaches, which makes it a convenient point of comparison. See Bremmer (1987) for a useful summary of the Oedipus myth. N.B. Throughout this chapter we use the Latinized spellings of the characters' names for the sake of consistency.

4 All page references for Lévi-Strauss (1955) are from Sebeok (1958).

5 This notation is used by Lévi-Strauss (1969) and is essentially that used by Leach (1974, p. 65) in connection with the Oedipus myth. In section 11.4, we argue that this is inadequate.

6 For example, see Vernant (1981) and Lloyd-Jones (1985, pp. 168–9) for structuralist critiques of the Oedipus myth.

7 See Kirk (1970, pp. 57–8) and Lévi-Strauss's (1987, pp. 100–1) response.

8 For example, Lloyd (1990, pp. 45–6) cites a note from an ancient medical text referring to the "Amazonian" practice of dislocating the hip or knee joints of male offspring to prevent them from fomenting insurrection, which might explain why the ancient Greeks would accept an account of systematic lameness in a royal family.

9 Vernant (1980, pp. 168–85), who distinguishes *formal, semantic,* and *sociocultural* levels of structuralist analysis.

10 See Caldwell (1974b) and Glenn (1977) for detailed bibliographies.

11 In addition, native informants sometimes give Freudian-style interpretations of their myths; see Cohen (1969, pp. 341–2).

12 All page references to Rank (1914) are from Freund (1932).

13 See especially Kirk (1970, pp. 8–31) for further discussion.

14 The Trobriand myth described in section 11.3.3, as it lacks a repetition of plot elements, is simple enough that corresponding pairs can be discerned.

15 All page references to Pettazzoni (1954b) are from Dundes (1984).
16 See Lloyd (1966, pp. 192–209) and Leach (1976, pp. 68–70) for relevant comments on myth and metaphor.

References

Bremmer, J. (1987). Oedipus and the Greek Oedipus complex, in *Interpretations of Greek mythology*, J. Bremmer, (ed.), Croom Helm, London, chapter 3, pp. 41–60.

Brilliante, C. (1990). History and the historical interpretation of myth, in *Approaches to Greek myth*, L. Edmunds (ed.), Johns Hopkins Univ. Press, Baltimore Md., chapter 2, pp. 91–140.

Burkert, W. (1985). *Greek religion*. Harvard Univ. Press, Cambridge, Mass. Translation of *Griechische Religion der archaischen und Klassischen Epoche* by J. Raffan, Kohlhammer: Stuttgart 1977.

Burridge, K. O. L. (1967). Lévi-Strauss and myth, in *The structural study of myth and totemism*, No. 5 in *Association of Social Anthropologists Monographs*, E. Leach (ed.), Tavistock, Publications, London, chapter 4, pp. 91–118.

Buxton, R. G. A. (1980). Blindness and limits: Sophokles and the logic of myth, *Journal of Hellenic Studies* **100**: 22–37.

Caldwell, R. S. (1973). The misogyny of Eteocles, *Arethusa* **6**(2): 197–231.

  (1974a). The blindness of Oedipus, *International Review of Psycho-Analysis* **1**: 207–18.

  (1974b). Selected bibliography on psychoanalysis and classical studies, *Arethusa* **7**(1): 115–34.

  (1976). Psychoanalysis, structuralism, and Greek mythology, in *Phenomenology, structuralism, semiology*, No. 1 in *Brucknell review series*, Garvin H. R. (ed.), Associated Univ. Presses, Cranbury N.J., chapter 12, pp. 209–30.

  (1989). *The origin of the gods: A psychoanalytic study of Greek theogonic myth*, Oxford Univ. Press, Oxford.

  (1990). The psychoanalytic interpretation of Greek myth, in *Approaches to Greek myth*, L. Edmunds (ed.), Johns Hopkins Univ. Press, Baltimore, Md., chapter 7, pp. 342–92.

Cassirer, E. (1946). *Language and myth*, Dover Publications, New York. Translation of *Sprache und Mythos: Ein Beitrag zum Problem der Götternamen* by S. K. Langer, 1925.

Cohen, P. S. (1969). Theories of myth, *Man: The Journal of the Royal Anthropological Society* **4**: 337–53.

Douglas, M. (1967). The meaning of myth, with special reference to 'La geste d'Asdiwal,' in *The structural study of myth and totemism*, No. 5 in *Association of Social Anthropologists Monographs*, E. Leach (ed.), Tavistock Publications, London, chapter 2, pp. 49–70.

Dowden, K. (1992). *The uses of Greek mythology. Approaching the ancient world series*, Routledge & Kegan Paul, London.

Dundes, A. (ed.) (1984). *Sacred narrative: Readings in the theory of myth*, Univ. of California Press, Berkeley.

Fontenrose, J. (1966). *The ritual theory of myth*, No. 18 in *Folklore studies series*, Univ. of California Press, Berkeley.

Frazer, J. G. (1913). *The golden bough: A study in magic and religion*, 3rd ed., Macmillan, London.

Freud, S. (1952). *On dreams*, Standard edition of the complete psychological works of Sigmund Freud, Norton, New York. Translation of *Über den Traum* by J. Strachey, 1901.

Freund, P. (ed.) (1932). *Otto Rank: The myth of the birth of the hero and other writings*, Vintage Books, New York. Reprinted in 1964.

Glenn, J. (1977). Psychoanalytic writings on classical mythology and religion: 1909–1960, *Classical World* **70**(3): 225–47.

Grant, M. (1973). *Roman myths*, Penguin Books, Harmondsworth.

Holyoak, K. J., and Thagard, P. (1995). *Mental leaps: Analogy in creative thought*, MIT Press, Cambridge, Mass.

Jung, C. G. (1953). *Psychological reflections: An anthology of the writings of C. G. Jung*, No. 31 in *The Bollingen library*, Harper & Row, New York. Translation of *Psychologische Betractungen: Eine Auslese aus den Schriften von C. G. Jung*, 2nd ed. by J. Jacobi, 1949.

Jung, C. G., and Kerényi, C. (1970). *Introduction to a science of mythology: The myth of the divine child and the mysteries of Eleusis*, Routledge & Kegan Paul, London. Translation of *Einführung in das Wesender Mythologie* by R. F. C. Hull.

Kirk, G. S. (1970). *Myth: Its meaning and functions in ancient and other cultures*, Vol. 40 of *Sather classical lectures*, Cambridge Univ. Press, Cambridge.

——— (1974). *The nature of Greek myths*, Penguin Books, Harmondsworth.

Kluckhohn, C. (1942). Myths and rituals: A general theory, *Harvard Theological Review* **35**(1): 45–79.

Lang, A. (1897). *Modern mythology*, AMS Press, New York.

Leach, E. (ed.) 1967. *The structural study of myth and totemism*, No. 5 in *Association of Social Anthropologists Monographs*. Tavistock Publications, London.

——— (ed.) (1974). *The structure of myth*, in *Lévi-Strauss*, E. Leach (ed.), 2nd ed. William Collins Sons, Glasgow, chapter 4, pp. 54–82.

——— (1976). *Culture and communication: The logic by which symbols are connected. Themes in the social sciences series*, Cambridge Univ. Press, Cambridge.

Lévi-Strauss, C. (1955). The structural study of myth, *Journal of American Folklore* **78**: 428–44. Reprinted in Sebeok (1958, pp. 81–106) and Lévi-Strauss (1963, pp. 206–31).

——— (1969). *The raw and the cooked*, No. 1 in *Introduction to a science of mythology*, Harper & Row, New York. Translation of *Le cru et le cuit* by J. Weightman and A. Weightman, Paris: Plon, 1964.

——— (1987). *Anthropology and myth*, Basil Blackwell, Oxford. Translation of *Paroles donée* by R. Willis, Paris: Plon, 1984.

Lloyd, G. E. R. (1966). *Polarity and analogy*, Cambridge Univ. Press, Cambridge.

——— (1990). *Demystifying mentalities, Themes in the social sciences series*, Cambridge Univ. Press, Cambridge.

Lloyd-Jones, H. (1985). Psychoanalysis and the study of the ancient world, in *Freud and the humanities*, P. Horden (ed.), Duckworth, New York, chapter 7, pp. 152–80.

Malinowski, B. (1926). *Myth in primitive psychology, Psyche miniatures series*, Kegan Paul, Trench, Trubner, London.

Müller, F. M. (1873). *Introduction to the science of religion: Four lectures delivered at the Royal Institution, with two essays on false analogies, and the philosophy of mythology*. Longmans, London.

——— (1897). *Contributions to the science of mythology*. Longmans, London.

Pettazzoni, R. (1954a). *Essays on the history of religions*, number 1 in *Studies in the history of religions, supplements to Numen series*, E. J. Brill, Leiden, the Netherlands.

Pettazzoni, R. (1954b). *The truth of myth*, in *Studies in the history of religions, supplements to Numen series* (Pettazzoni, 1954a). Translation of *Verità del mito*, Studi e materiali di storia delle religioni **21**: 104–16, 1948. Reprinted in Dundes, (1984, pp. 98–109).

Raglan, F. (1955). Myth and ritual, in *Myth: A symposium*, T. A. Sebeok (ed.), Indiana Univ. Press, Bloomington, chapter 6, pp. 122–35. A reprinting of a special issue of the *Journal of American Folklore* **78**, 1955.

Rank, O. (1914). The myth of the birth of the hero: A psychological interpretation of mythology, *Journal of Nervous and Mental Diseases* **18**: 1–100. Translation by F. Robbins and S. E. Jelliffe. Reprinted in Freund (1932, pp. 3–96) and Segal (1990, pp. 3–86).

— (1932). *Forms of kinship and the individual's role in the family*, Knopf, New York. Reprinted in Freund (1932, pp. 296–315).

Sebeok, T. A. (ed.) (1958). *Myth: A symposium*, Indiana Univ. Press, Bloomington. A reprinting of a special issue of the *Journal of American Folklore* **78**, 1955.

Segal, C. (1979). Pentheus on the couch and on the grid: Psychological and structuralist readings of Greek tragedy, *Classical World* **72**(3): 129–48.

Sourvinou-Inwood, C. (1987). Myth as history: The previous owners of the Delphic oracle, in *Interpretations of Greek mythology*, J. Bremmer (ed.), Croom Helm, London, chapter 10, pp. 215–41.

Sperber, D. (1979). *Claude Lévi-Strauss*, in *Structuralism and since: From Lévi-Strauss to Derrida*, J. Sturrock (ed.), Opus series, Oxford Univ. Press, Oxford chapter 1, pp. 19–51.

Tambiah, S. J. (1973). Form and meaning of magical acts: A point of view, in *Modes of thought: Essays on thinking in Western and non-Western societies*, R. Horton and R. Finnegan (eds.), Faber & Faber, London, chapter 8, pp. 199–229.

Vernant, J.-P. (1980). *Myth and society in ancient Greece*, No. 5 in *European philosophy and the human sciences*, Harvester Press, Brighton, U.K. Translation of *Myth et société en Grèce ancienne* by J. Lloyd, Paris: F. Maspero, 1974.

— (1981). *Ambiguity and reversal: On the enigmatic structure of Oedipus Rex*, in *Tragedy and myth in ancient Greece*, No. 7 in *European philosophy and the human sciences*, J. P. Vernant and P. Vidal-Naquet (eds.), Harvester Press, Brighton, U.K., chapter 5, pp. 87–119. Translation of *Mythe et tragedie en Grèce ancienne*, by J. Lloyd, Paris: F. Maspero, 1972.

Versnel, H. S. (1990). What's sauce for the goose is sauce for the gander: Myth and ritual, old and new, in *Approaches to Greek myth*, L. Edmunds (ed.), Johns Hopkins Univ. Press, Baltimore, Md., chapter 1, pp. 23–90.

PART III
The development and education of thought

12
Cognitive domains as modes of thought

Susan Carey

Many authors argue that cognition is structured by distinct cognitive domains. Since each cognitive domain is characterized by a distinct form of reasoning, positing cognitive domains is one instantiation of positing distinct modes of thought. In this chapter,[1] I distinguish two quite different proposals for the nature of cognitive domains (innate cognitive modules and framework theories), consider whether intuitive biology is a cognitive domain on either proposal, and speculate on the mechanisms by which people create new framework theories.

12.1 Innate cognitive modules as components of basic cognitive architecture

One construal of domain-specific cognition is articulated most clearly by Chomsky (1980). In Chomsky's view, humans are endowed with a number of systems of knowledge, such as knowledge of language, knowledge of physical objects, and knowledge of space. Each system of knowledge applies to a distinct set of objects and phenomena. For example, knowledge of language applies to sentences and their constituents; knowledge of physical objects applies to material bodies and their behavior; knowledge of space applies to places in the layout and geometrical relations among them. More deeply, each knowledge system is organized around a distinct set of core principles. For language, these are the principles of universal grammar; for physical objects, the principles might include Newton's axioms or the principles of continuity and cohesion; for space, the principles might include the axioms and postulates of Euclidean geometry.

Many writers have applied Chomsky's notion of an innate domain to cognitive modules. Some, like Sperber (1994) and Leslie (1994), are explicit that theirs is a proposal about basic cognitive architecture. In Sperber's view, the mind has two tiers: (1) a single thick layer of perceptual input modules, which have information provided by sensory receptors as input and a conceptual representation categorizing the object perceived as output, and (2) a complex network of conceptual modules, which have conceptual representations both as input and output.[2] Leslie's (1994) account of ToBy (theory of bodies) and ToMM (theory of mind module) are worked out examples of cognitive modules with exactly the properties Sperber specifies, as is Spelke's characterization of the module for physical reasoning (see Carey and Spelke,

1994, for example). Spelke (1988) argues that perceptual analysis yields a representation of the surface layout, which the physical reasoning module analyzes to establish the objects in the array, their location, and certain of their causal interactions. Spelke proposes three principles that determine the entities in this domain and constrain reasoning about them: cohesion (objects are bounded, coherent wholes that maintain their boundaries as they move through space), continuity (objects trace spatiotemporally continuous paths as they move through space), and contact (objects interact causally only if in contact).

Space permits just a taste of the argument for innate cognitive modules; the evidence has been extensively reviewed elsewhere (cf. Carey and R. Gelman, 1991; Hirschfeld and Gelman, 1994; Sperber, Premack, and Premack, 1995). Part of the argument is based on learnability considerations. For example, Leslie (1994) argues that it is not possible to derive causal concepts from spatiotemporal relations, so the perception of causality in some situation must be provided by a cognitive module. The bulk of the evidence is empirical – data that indicate that young infants perceive and reason about the world in terms of the hypothesized principles. These data derive from studies that exploit the robust finding that babies will look longer at events that violate some expectancy they have established than at events that conform to what they expect. This fact enables studies of looking time patterns to establish how the baby represents the events he or she observes.

Consider, for example, a study that demonstrates that babies' reasoning is guided by the continuity principle (Spelke and Kestenbaum, 1986, reported in Spelke, 1988; see Xu and Carey, in press, for a replication). According to the continuity principle, objects travel on precisely one connected path; objects do not go out of existence at location A and reappear at a later time at a spatially distinct location B. Spelke and Kestenbaum showed babies an event involving two screens placed on a stage floor, placed side by side with a gap between them. Babies observed one object emerging from the right side of the right screen and then returning behind it, followed by another physically identical object emerging from the left side of the left screen and then returning behind it. No object ever appeared in the gap between the screen, and the baby never saw two objects at once. Note that the continuity principle requires that the baby (and the adult) establish a representation of two numerically distinct objects in this event; one object cannot go from one screen to the other without passing through the intervening space. After babies had become bored watching this event, the screens were removed, revealing either the expected outcome (two objects) or an unexpected outcome (one object). Babies looked reliably longer at the unexpected outcome. A variety of control experiments established that this expectancy was based on the babies' analysis of the discontinuity of the path traced by the object(s) and not some other aspect of the situation.

Evidence of this sort has supported claims for at least three early emerging cognitive modules that support reasoning about the physical world, about people, and about number. It is important to see that on the module view of cognitive domains, perception and reasoning are very closely interrelated.

Carey and Spelke (1994) distinguish two general ways in which the tasks of apprehending the entities in the domain and reasoning about them could be related. Consider, for example, the domain of reasoning about human action and experience, which requires identifying people in the environment. It is possible that perceivers single out human beings by virtue of a face recognizer, a voice recognizer, a gait recognizer, and the like (all exploiting spatiotemporal information). Whenever the perceiver is confronted by eyes, hair, and other features in the proper configuration, her face recognizer would signal the presence of a person. This signal would then trigger the operation of the theory of mind module, whereby the actions of the person are understood in terms of the person's goals and intentions. Alternatively, perceivers may single out persons by analyzing the behavior of entities, asking whether an entity's behavior appears to be directed to some goal, to be guided by perceptions or beliefs about its environment, to be colored by emotions, and the like. On the second account, processes of perceiving and reasoning about psychological beings are intimately connected: they are guided by the same system of knowledge.

Carey and Spelke (1994) reviewed the evidence concerning the solution to the perception problem in each of the well-established infant cognitive modules: physical reasoning, reasoning about people, and number. In each case, the weight of evidence favors the second possibility, that perception and reasoning are guided by a single knowledge system. To continue with the example of person perception: infants use contingent response as a way of identifying the people in their environment. For example, infants attempt to interact socially with a mobile that moves in response to a leg kick (Watson, 1979). And infants do not attempt to interact socially with dolls in spite of a doll's face matching the configuration of a human face.

In sum, research on infants suggests that the human mind is articulated in terms of distinct modules, at least for language, numerical reasoning, physical reasoning, and reasoning about people. In these domains, the principles that guide reasoning in the domain also guide categorization of entities as falling in the domain.

12.2 Cognitive domains as intuitive theories

A second, quite different characterization of cognitive domains identifies them with intuitive theories. Before discussing this view, let me note that not all adherents of domain-specific cognition endorse it. Atran (1994), for example, argues that it is fundamentally misleading to construe cognitive domains as theories and excoriates those philosophers (e.g., Quine and Putnam) who see ordinary cognition as continuous with scientific thought, claiming that such a view would seem ludicrous, on its face, to any anthropologist.

Before this issue can be joined, some agreement on what a theory is must be reached as well as some agreement on which aspects of scientific theories are being claimed for intuitive theories. Scientific theories are often formalized and are always the result of institutionalized, self-aware, cognitive activity. These aspects of scientific theories are not presumed to characterize intuitive theories (hence, *intuitive*), but it is not these aspects that make a scientific theory a *theory* either. Philosophers differ in their rational reconstruction of the concept *theory*,[3] but the analysis offered by those cognitive scientists who believe that intuitive theories constitute cognitive domains is that which sees theories as *explanatory* structures. Theories are those cognitive structures that characterize the causal mechanisms at work in the world and that therefore provide fodder for explanation. (See Salmon, 1989, for a review of the considerations in favor of viewing explanation in terms of providing causal mechanisms that account for why some phenomenon to be explained came to pass.) This characterization is true both of scientific theories and intuitive theories and distinguishes theories from other cognitive structures (e.g., scripts, Schank and Abelson, 1977, or pattern abstraction mechanisms, Posner and Keele, 1968).

Wellman (1990) makes an important distinction between framework theories (or foundational theories; Wellman and Gelman, 1992) and specific theories. Framework theories are those that determine the basic ontology a person is committed to and the most general explanatory notions a person represents. Four-year-olds' theory of mind is an example of a framework theory; their theories of belief fixation and morality being specific theories constrained by their framework theory. Behaviorism is an example of a framework theory; the behaviorist account of language acquisition is a specific theory. All theories (specific and framework) determine a domain of phenomena involving a theory-specific ontology and articulate causal mechanisms at work in the domain. Wellman convincingly argues that when cognitive scientists write about intuitive theories (e.g., Carey, 1985), they usually mean framework theories.

At any rate, in this chapter I mean by *intuitive theory* a cognitive structure that embodies a person's ontological commitments (i.e., specifies the basic kinds of things there *are* in the world) and provides modes of explanation for the phenomena in its domain. The notion of a *domain,* in this view, is a domain of phenomena involving the entities recognized by the theory; the central components of an intuitive theory are its ontology and the causal mechanisms it exploits in explanation. (See Carey, 1985; Gopnik and Wellman, 1994; Keil, 1989; Murphy and Medin, 1985; Wellman, 1990; Wellman and Gelman, 1992, for related characterizations of intuitive theories and the role they play in conceptual structure.)

Examples in the literature of intuitive framework theories include the 4-year-old's theory of mind (Perner, 1991; Wellman, 1990), the 10-year-old's theory of matter (Carey, 1991; Piaget and Inhelder, 1941; Smith et al., 1985), the infant's theory of physical bodies and their interactions (Baillargeon, Kotovsky, and Needham, 1995; Leslie, 1994; Spelke, 1991; Spelke et al., 1992), high school student's intuitive mechanics (Clement, 1982; McCloskey, 1983), an intuitive cosmology constructed in the early elementary school years (Vosniadou and Brewer, 1992), and an intuitive biology (constructed by age 7 to 10; Carey, 1985, or even earlier; Hatano and Inagaki, 1994; Keil, 1992; Wellman and Gelman, 1992). In each case, attribution of an intuitive theory to the child requires establishing that the child distinguishes entities in the domain of the theory from those not in its domain and appeals to theory-specific causal mechanisms to explain the interactions among the entities in the domain.

It is not clear what Atran is denying when he denies that ordinary cognition relies upon theorylike representational structures. If he denies that ordinary folk formalize their knowledge, explicitly marshal evidence for it, or are part of the institutions that construct Western scientific and technological knowledge, nobody would quarrel. Nor would anybody quarrel with his speculation that "the structures of ordinary conceptual domains may strongly constrain, and thereby render possible, the initial elaboration of corresponding scientific fields." Indeed, those who believe that scientific thought is continuous with everyday cognition see that speculation as one way of *stating* the continuity hypothesis. The ontological commitments of ordinary folk, the phenomena they represent, are part of the starting points for institutionalized science, as is their causal understanding and their intuitive theories.[4]

12.3 Relations between the two views of cognitive domains

On both views, cognitive domains pick out a set of entities in the world and are responsible for processing privileged sorts of information about those entities. The two views are further confused by the fact that both claim the young child's intuitive theory of mind and theory of bodies as examples of cognitive domains. Indeed, Leslie (1994) even names his innate cognitive modules "theory of bodies" and "theory of mind module." Nonetheless, the two conceptions of cognitive domains are genuinely different. The intuitive theory view does not take innateness as a necessary property of a cognitive domain; intuitive theories can function as cognitive domains even if they are constructed during the course of development. Conversely, the innate module view does not take causal/explanatory structure as a necessary property of cognitive domains; folkbiology, for example, is posited by Atran (1994) to be a pretheoretical cognitive module. In sum, the intuitive theory view claims young children's theories of bodies and mind as cognitive domains because they meet the criteria for intuitive theories; it is accidental that they also may be innate. In contrast, the view of cognitive modules as a fundamental aspect of cognitive architecture claims these domains because they meet the criteria for innate domain-specific reasoning; it is accidental that they also embody causal mechanisms.

12.4 Folkbiology as a cognitive module

The differences between the two views become focused in discussions of folkbiology as a cognitive domain. Atran (1994) and Sperber (1994) view folkbiology as an innate core module that is not theorylike even among adults in most cultures. Others view folkbiology as an intuitive theory, although there is controversy as to when it first emerges. Carey (1985, 1988) claimed that biology did not emerge as an autonomous domain until the end of the first decade of life; others (Hatano and Inagaki, 1994; Keil, 1992, 1994) argue that preschoolers have constructed an autonomous intuitive biological theory. Wellman and Gelman (1992) are agnostic as to whether preschoolers have constructed biology as an intuitive theory; they argue that preschoolers certainly recognize animals and perhaps plants as ontologically distinct from other entities in the world, but that it is unclear whether preschoolers understand any biology-specific causal mechanisms.

The literature raises several possibilities, then, as to the status of intuitive biology as a cognitive domain:

1. Folkbiology is an innate core module, not theorylike (Atran, 1994; Sperber, 1994).
2. Folkbiology is an innate module, and like physical reasoning also an intuitive theory from the beginning (Keil, 1992, 1994).
3. Folkbiology is not an innate module; folkbiology is a framework theory constructed sometime during the first decade of life, at least in contemporary American culture (Carey, 1985).

If the third possibility is correct, there are several options as to the source of an intuitive biology. First, the first and third possibilities could *both* be correct. As Atran (1994) suggests, the innate core folkbiology may constrain and make possible the construction of explicit causal biological theories. Alternatively, there may be no innate core folkbiology, but a different module may determine the ontological type animal, namely, an innate folk psychology. The emergence of an autonomous folk biology would then require conceptual change in the innate concept *animal* (Carey, 1985, 1988). Finally, there may be no innate core folkbiology, and the emergence of an autonomous biology may exploit only domain general concept formation and explanation-building capacities.

In order to evaluate these alternatives, we must look at how folkbiology has been characterized by their adherents as well as at the evidence that has been offered for each.

12.5 Critique of the Sperber/Atran view

Although Sperber (1994) and Atran (1994) believe that folkbiology is an innate cognitive module, the evidence they offer for this view is very different from that appealed to in support of numerical reasoning, physical reasoning, and psychological reasoning as cognitive modules. Rather than specifying the principles of an innate folkbiology and then seeking evidence that babies' identification of and reasoning about animals is guided by these principles, Sperber and Atran point to cross-cultural universality among *adult* folkbiology as their main evidence. The cross-cultural universality Atran and Sperber offer as evidence that folkbiology is a core cognitive domain has two components: universality in taxonomic organization of categories of animals and plants[5] and an essentialist view of why animals and plants have certain of their properties.

Atran (1990, 1994) has shown that all cultures divide the living world into two kingdoms (animals and plants), that each of these is taxonomically subdivided into major life forms (e.g., fish, bird, and mammal), and that these are further subdivided into (sometimes unnamed) subcategories (e.g., ungulates and rodents). Finally, the taxonomy bottoms out in all cultures at the level of primary taxa (species/genus; e.g., mouse, dog, wolf, and deer). Furthermore, Atran (1994) claims, "Invariably, humans presume each primary taxon to uniquely possess an inherent physical nature or underlying essence, which determines the kind's teleological growth, its characteristic behavior, morphology and ecological proclivity."

The Sperber/Atran position has the following empirical and conceptual problems: first, those aspects of folkbiology (as they characterize it) that emerge early in childhood are most probably not domain specific; second, those aspects of folkbiology (as they characterize it) that are domain specific are probably not innate, nor are they theory neutral; third, Sperber and Atran fail to confront the full implications of the problem of perception; and fourth, Sperber and Atran run into what I will call "the problem of theory-laden attribution."

12.5.1 TAXONOMIC ORGANIZATION AND ESSENTIALISM: PLAUSIBLY INNATE BUT NOT LIKELY SPECIFIC TO FOLKBIOLOGICAL CLASSIFICATION

Taxonomic organization is a property of the conceptual/linguistic system in general, especially the nominal system, both in the adult final state and early in development. I believe that this is also true of essentialism, although the argument in the latter case is harder to make.

Natural language nominal systems are built on the backbone of an ontological hierarchy (Keil, 1979; Sommers, 1963) of which biological classification is just a small part. Furthermore, children set up hierarchical relations among categories very early in cognitive development (Smith, 1979; Markman, 1989: 2- to 3-year-olds) and do so equally within categories of animals and within categories of artifacts and food. The earliest lexicalized hierarchies include animal/dog, cat, bird, . . . , toy/doll, car, block, . . . , food/cracker, cookie, cereal, apple . . . (Markman, 1989). Each of these hierarchies include intermediate levels that are not lexicalized by the child (e.g., toy/*building toy*/ Legos, blocks, Lincoln Logs; animal/*mammal*/dog, cat, bird), a feature that is also universal in folkbiological taxonomies (Atran, 1994).

Essentialism, like taxonomic structure, derives from the logical work nouns do. The child has a default assumption that count nouns are substance sortals, that is, naming concepts that provide conditions of identity during the maximal life line of an entity. (See Hirsch, 1982; Macnamara, 1986; Wiggins, 1980, for related characterizations of substance sortals; see Hall and Waxman, 1993, for evidence that young children expect count nouns to be substance sortals.) Indeed, every count noun provides criteria for identity that distinguish property changes that signal that the entity referred to ceases to exist from property changes that leave the entity in existence. That is, the application of every count noun carries with it the idea that the identity of the entity picked out by the noun is unchanged in the face of surface changes.

I submit that biological essentialism is the theoretical elaboration of the logical/linguistic concept, substance sortal.

The mutual exclusivity assumption (Markman, 1989) that very young children make concerning *all* count nouns (not just animal terms) can be seen as reflecting this basic essentialism. Young children assume, for every entity, that it is a member of just one kind, and therefore, that it will have just one kind label.[6] That is, at the outset of language learning, children assume each entity can have only one essence, only one criterion for identity.

Finally, at least some experimental demonstrations that very young children have essentialist expectations about living kinds have also shown that they have essentialist expectations about other kinds. For example, Gelman and Markman (1986) showed that 4-year-olds expect shared kind membership rather than shared appearances to determine unobservable properties. That is, a bird that looks like a bat will have unobservable properties of other birds rather than unobservable properties of bats. However, they found this equally true of substance kinds; gold that looks like silver will have unobservable properties of gold, not silver.

Atran (1994) argues convincingly that folkbiology's commitments to taxonomy and essentialism go deeper than in any other cognitive domain. This I freely grant. But these are characteristics of the adult system. According to the view I am developing here, these aspects of universal folkbiology are due to a match between the world and important domain general constraints on the nominal system that get exploited and developed in the course of universal theory building in this domain. The empirical evidence is that in development the roots of these aspects of folkbiology are not initially tied to children's expectations about animals and/or plants.

12.5.2 ASPECTS OF ATRAN'S FOLKBIOLOGY THAT ARE DOMAIN SPECIFIC BUT PROBABLY NEITHER INNATE NOR THEORY NEUTRAL

When Atran (1994) characterizes the cross-culturally universal essentialist expectation concerning biological taxa, he characterizes the underlying essence as determining characteristic morphology and behavior, teleological growth, and characteristic ecology. Characteristic morphology and behavior are not domain-specific notions. Other natural kinds such as oceans and rivers and celestial objects have characteristic morphology and behaviors. However, teleological growth and characteristic ecologies certainly are domain-specific properties; only living kinds have these.[7] But it is doubtful that knowledge of animals' growth and ecology are part of an innate concept of animal. (See section 12.6.1 and also Carey, 1985; Keil, 1989, for a review of evidence that preschool children fail to understand people's growth and that coming to understand patterns of teleological growth as a core property of animal kind reflects theoretical elaboration of the concept of animal during years 6 to 10 and beyond.)

12.5.3 THE PERCEPTION PROBLEM

Sperber's two-tier vision of cognitive architecture includes input modules that take spatiotemporal information and output a categorized entity (as it were, *animal*), which is then input to a cognitive module (as it were, folkbiology), which processes information relative to it. The folkbiology module will be useless unless the cognitive system can identify the animals in the world. As mentioned in section 12.1, Carey and Spelke (1994) reviewed the evidence concerning the well-documented cognitive modules and argued that the principles that determine the entities in the domain and constrain reasoning about them are identical. If innate cognitive modules always have this property, then folkbiology, as characterized by Atran (1994) and Sperber (1994), cannot be an innate module. This is because having an essential nature or being part of a taxonomic structure, the key features of the folkbiology Atran has identified, are not conceivably identifiable from any spatiotemporal analysis. The only solution to the perception problem for folkbiology would be that animals are identified on the basis of some properties unrelated to the information that guides reasoning about them.

A plausible solution to the perception problem is that animals are identified by the module that picks out beings with intentional states, that is, beings capable of attention to the environment and of goal-directed activity. But these are the features that identify entities in the theory of mind module. This line of argument suggests that animals are initially in the domain of a cognitive module that is not a folkbiology, but rather a folkpsychology (Carey, 1985).

12.5.4 THE PROBLEM OF THEORY-LADEN ATTRIBUTION

In describing the cross-cultural universality in taxonomic organization of living kinds, Atran sometimes uses the term *folktaxonomy* and sometimes the term *folkbiology*. These are very different. The term *folktaxonomy* makes no commitment to how the entities in taxonomy are construed, but *folkbiology* does. Indeed, the very characterization of the taxonomy as one of *living kinds* also presupposes a concept of "living," a concept that must go beyond having an essential nature and being part of a hierarchy. Gold has an essential nature and is part of a hierarchy: gold/precious metal/metal/element/substance, but gold is not in the domain of folkbiology. And, as pointed out earlier, Atran (1994) includes biology-specific features in his characterization of the domain. For example, he includes an understanding that a kind's essential nature determines patterns of teleological growth and characteristic ecology as part of universal folkbiology. The problem here is wanting it both ways – wanting folk*biology* to be both biology and pretheoretical.

Sperber's (1994) explicitly extensionalist view of the domain of a cognitive module contains the same tension. Sperber explicitly denies that the internal structure of a module is its core, *all* the internal structure providing a mode of construal. But it is the mode of construal that makes the module a "biology."[8] Without a biological mode of construal (i.e., specifically biological causal mechanisms explaining biological phenomena), the entities in the extension of the concept *animal* may not be part of a biology at all. This is not merely a logical point; as already mentioned, there is ample empirical evidence for an innate cognitive module with animals in its domain that is not a biology, but is rather a psychology (a theory of mind, Sperber's metacognitive module).

The problem of theory-laden attribution is ubiquitous in hermeneutic disciplines such as anthropology, developmental psychology, and history of science. In developmental psychology, we find evidence that children represent a concept whose extension largely overlaps some adult concept. To communicate that concept, we must use some word in our lexicon, but that word names a concept that plays some particular inferential role in our conceptual system. We must be very careful not to attribute our concept to the child unless we provide positive evidence that the child's concept plays largely the same inferential role within his/her conceptual system. Otherwise, the problem of theory-laden attribution becomes the fallacy of theory laden attribution.

I conclude that there is at present no good arguments to consider folkbiology an innate module in the sense in which language, number, reasoning about objects, and reasoning about persons are.

12.6 Folkbiology as a framework theory

I have argued against the Sperber/Atran vision of folkbiology as a cognitive module that is both innate and not theorylike. The question then arises whether folkbiology is a cognitive module in the sense of a framework theory, and if so, when, during development, children first construct it.

A framework theory is characterized by ontological commitments, a set of phenomena in its domain, and causal mechanisms that explain these phenomena. Carey (1985), Keil (1992, 1994), and Wellman and Gelman (1992) all offer related analyses of biology as a framework theory and marshal evidence that bears on the question of when children first represent an intuitive biology. Keil argues that preschool children do. Wellman and Gelman argue that preschool children certainly make the ontological distinction between animals and inanimate objects and thus have a separate ontology of biological kinds. They further argue that while it is unclear whether preschoolers understand any biology-specific causal mechanisms, the weight of evidence suggests they do. Hatano and Inagaki (1994) argue that 6-year-olds have constructed a first framework theory of biology, a vitalist biology. Carey (1985) argued that a first intuitive biology is not constructed by American children until around age 10.

Wellman and Gelman (1992) raise the possibility that preschool children may draw the ontological distinction between animate and inanimate entities while not representing any biology specific causal mechanisms. This possibility embodies the fallacy of theory-laden attribution. That is, evidence that children represent a concept animal distinct from other concepts is not tantamount to evidence for an ontological commitment *of the child's* (Keil, 1979; Carey, 1985). To join this issue, we need an analysis of ontological concepts and some hint of what evidence we could draw on to assess whether some concept of the child has this status.

Keil's (1979) analysis of ontological commitments draws on the distinction between predictability and truth. It is a category mistake to assert "The rock is hungry," whereas it is merely false to assert "Grass is red." A rough and ready test of the ontological distinctions a person draws is provided by their judgments of category mistakes; the categorical distinctions across which we judge category mistakes to occur reflect our ontological commitments (Keil, 1979; Sommers, 1963). Unfortunately, children under age 5 or so cannot be probed for judgments of category mistakes (Keil, 1979), so we must appeal to other types of evidence to judge whether a conceptual distinction made by younger children is an ontological distinction for them. Carey (1985) argued that ontological concepts are simply those that are the core concepts in framework theories, those that articulate our most basic modes of construal and explanation. If we accept this analysis, then the question of whether a concept represented by a child is an ontological concept becomes the same question as whether the concept is central to a framework theory.

There are at least two ways in which children could represent a distinction between animals and nonanimals without that distinction constituting an ontological distinction between biological and nonbiological entities. First, the distinction could result from domain-general concept formation capacities, reflecting domain-general similarity computations, and could thus fail to be an ontological distinction at all. Domain-general prototype abstraction mechanisms have been documented in adults (e.g., Posner and Keele, 1968), young children (e.g., Diamond and Carey, 1990), and infants (e.g., Cohen and Younger, 1983). Infants who have been trained to distinguish one random pattern from another would not be credited with an *ontological* distinction between those two patterns. Second, the distinction might be an ontological distinction, but the framework theory in which the concept *animal* is embedded might be an intuitive psychology, not an intuitive biology. The distinction could be one between entities with intentional states and entities without intentional states. As argued earlier, I favor the second possibility. That is, I do believe that the distinction between animals and nonanimals is an ontological distinction for babies, but I see no evidence that it is a biological distinction. An example of the fallacy of theory-laden attribution in action: Wellman and Gelman (1992) point to the fact that infants communicate with humans and not inanimate objects as evidence against a "domain general understanding of the *biological* world" (emphasis added).

12.6.1 THE SEARCH FOR BIOLOGY SPECIFIC EXPLANATORY STRUCTURES

Wellman and Gelman (1992), Keil (1994), and Hatano and Inagaki (1994) all maintain that preschoolers have constructed an intuitive biology. The characterization each gives of the preschoolers' intuitive biology differs. Wellman and Gelman and Keil concur with Atran and Sperber in attributing an essentialist understanding of animals to children of these ages, but as argued earlier an essentialist understanding of animals does not, by itself, constitute a biological understanding of animals. More is needed.

Wellman and Gelman (1992) suggest (as does Keil, 1994) that preschool children have knowledge of at least three specifically biological causal mechanisms: maturational growth, inheritance of physical properties, and disease transmission and contagion. Carey (1995) argues that the evidence in each of these cases actually supports the claim that it is only after age 7 or older that children have constructed an understanding of each of these as part of a folkbiological framework theory. Here, for a flavor of the argument, I discuss the case of maturational growth.

Rosengren et al. (1991) showed that preschool children understand that growth is unidirectional (i.e., animals and plants increase in size rather than decrease in size), and growth is a property of animals and plants but not artifacts. Preschool children also know that growth is inevitable, not subject to a person's desires (Inagaki and Hatano, 1987). And finally, preschool children understand that a baby pig will become an adult pig rather than a cow, even if raised by a cow mother together with other of the mother cow's cow babies. (Gelman and Wellman, 1991, refer to this as knowledge of "innate potential.") Similarly, Hirschfeld (1994) showed that preschool children know that a black baby will grow into a black adult, even if adopted by white parents and raised in a family with white children.

That preschool children have such knowledge about growth is part of the evidence that they have an essentialist understanding of animals and plants: an entity's being an animal or plant means that it is inevitable that it starts out small and gets bigger, and its kind determines what properties it will have as an adult (i.e., determines the outcome of the growth process). And that preschool children have such knowledge is part of the evidence that they distinguish bodily phenomena (such as growth, the heart's beating, breathing, sleeping, and bodily symptoms of illness) from other phenomena involving humans and animals as not subject to intentional causation. But that they have such knowledge does *not* constitute evidence of knowledge of biology-specific causal mechanisms.

What do preschool children think is the cause of growth? Two things: birthdays and food. One 3-year-old combined these ideas into the theory that birthday cake is essential for growth (Carey, 1985). Focus on birthdays reflects confusion between "getting older" and "getting bigger."[9]

But doesn't knowledge about the relation between eating and growth constitute evidence of knowledge of a biology-specific causal mechanism? It is very important to distinguish knowledge of a *cause* from knowledge of a *causal explanatory mechanism*. Consider the child's knowledge that flipping a light switch will cause the light to go on or off. Toddlers know this; we would not want to credit them with any understanding of the mechanism by which the switch causes a change of state in the light. Similarly, knowledge that food causes you to grow may be a knowledge of a simple input–output causal relation, certainly acquired by direct tuition ("If you don't eat your vegetables, you won't grow into a big strong girl"). Simple causal relations are distinguished from causal explanatory mechanisms along two dimensions: complexity (mechanisms involve intermediate steps) and coherence (interrelations with other causal mechanisms which mutually constrain each other). The preschool child has no clue as to any bodily mechanism that mediates between eating and growing.

Finally, a closer look at the data on preschoolers' understanding of growth reveals conceptual change, both in the concept of growth and of animal kind.

Keil's (1989) transformation studies show that preschool children do *not* consider it essential to an animal's kind that the animal get its properties through a process of natural growth, whereas by age 9 or 10, children have constructed this understanding. Preschool children believe that a skunk can be turned into a raccoon through surgery; by age 9 (and in some studies age 7 or 8), children believe that the animal that results from such a transformation is still a skunk that just looks like a raccoon (Keil, 1989). It is not the case, however, that preschool children think that anything that looks like a raccoon is a raccoon; a skunk with a raccoon costume on, pictured to look identical to a raccoon, is judged to still be a skunk (Keil, 1989); a dog with all its insides removed (the blood and bones and stuff like that) is judged not to be a dog anymore (Gelman and Wellman, 1991). These data suggest that to preschool children the core of the notion of animal kind includes bodily structure: the body must have the right structure, including internal structure, in order for the entity to be an animal or a particular kind of animal. It is not enough to look just like an animal (as in stuffed dog) or a particular kind of animal (as in a raccoon-costumed skunk). But these data also show that 10-year-olds have constructed a deeper notion of how that bodily structure must come to be: for 4- to 6-year-olds, surgery will do it; for 10-year-olds, it must be a natural growth process.

In a related study, Keil (1992) showed children pictures of two animals that looked identical as adults and indicated that one had a life cycle that began as an egg, metamorphosed into a worm, and then again into the adult form, whereas the other was born as a small version of the adult and merely grew. The question was whether they were the same kinds of animals. Only children older than 9 or 10 thought that they could not both be the same kind of animal. These developmental differences between 4- and 9-year-olds reflect changes in the principles that determine the entities in the domain; by age 9, aspects of the life cycle have become part of the core principles.[10]

In sum, there is excellent evidence that by age 10 American children have constructed a construal of animals whereby their kind-determining bodily properties are achieved through a process of maturational growth, a construal Atran (1994) claims is an important aspect of universal folkbiology. Further, Jeyifous (1986) used Keil's tasks to study the development of understanding of biological kinds among rural, unschooled Yoruba in Nigeria, and found the same developmental pattern at roughly the same ages. These data support Atran's (1994) claims that this understanding is part of universal folktaxonomy but conflict with his vision that this understanding is part of an innate cognitive module. For the preschool child, knowledge that animals and plants grow appears to be one fact among many that they have acquired, probably through domain-general learning mechanisms. Only later (by age 10 in rural Nigeria and rural United States) does this fact become incorporated into an intuitive biology.

Carey (1995) reviews the evidence concerning preschool children's understanding of biological inheritance and disease and concludes that, just as in the case of preschool understanding of growth, understanding is restricted to knowledge of simple causal relations. Young children know, for example, that dirt, poisons, going outside with no coat on, and germs cause disease. Also, they know that diseases can be caught from other people. Such knowledge can serve as the input to the construction of a first biology, but there is no evidence in this literature that preschool children have yet constructed any understanding of biologically specific causal mechanisms underlying these phenomena.

12.6.2 WHAT IS THE FIRST FOLKBIOLOGY?

What are the principles that constitute the first biology? Keil (1992, 1994) proposes that the mode of explanation that characterizes the earliest biology is functional/teleological. That is, the child explains the properties of animals, at least in part, in terms of what they are for. Put this way, this mode of explanation is not sufficient to determine a biology, for functional explanation is important in other domains as well (want/belief explanation is functional, as is our reasoning about artifacts). In order for a functional analysis to be part of a biology, the goal must be a *biological* goal. The most fundamental biological goals are maintaining life and avoiding death and perhaps maintaining health, and these goals are not seen in biological terms until age 6 or 7 or even later (Carey, 1985, 1988, 1995).

Indeed, Keil has demonstrated functional explanation in the service of biological goals at least by age 7. For example, he shows that children at this age judge that plants are green "because being green is good for plants, being green helps there be more plants," whereas emeralds are green "because emeralds are made of little bits which mix together to make the emerald green" (Keil, 1992). Another study (Jaakkola and Carey, in preparation) shows that by age 6 or 8 children organize their functional explanations of bodily processes in terms of the basic goal of maintaining life.

Inagaki and Hatano (1993) present evidence that by age 6 the child (at least the modern Japanese child) has constructed an autonomous biology surrounding this goal – a vitalist biology. Vitalist biologies have been independently constructed in many different cultures, including Western ones (see, for example, Toulmin and Goodfield, 1962). As the children Inagaki and Hatano are studying are Japanese, they place their studies in the context of Japanese vitalism, which is built around the concept *ki*, or life force. *Ki* is roughly analogous to Western biology's (prior to the late 19th century) *entelechy*, or vital force, the extra something a body must have to be alive. When an animal or person dies, the vital force leaves the body. In Western vitalism, this was often conceptualized as the vital force (soul) leaving with the last breath. Also common to both Japanese and Western vitalism is the idea that the air is one source of vital energy and that breathing is in the service of replenishing and sustaining life through obtaining vital energy from the air. Another aspect of vitalism is a "balance" theory of disease: diseases result from separate components of the life force (humors, *Ying-Yang*) becoming out of balance. Japanese vitalism elaborates a theory of the workings of internal organs, whereby they are endowed with agency and work to maintain bodily function by playing a role in the transmission and exchange of vital force. This vital force, *ki*, is undifferentiated (from modern science's point of view) between a substance, energy, and information.

Inagaki and Hatano present two sorts of evidence that Japanese children have constructed a vitalist biology by age 6. First, in free explanations for bodily phenomena, children of this age (or 7- to 8-year-olds) sometimes elaborated vitalist ideas. For example, when asked what would happen to one's hands if blood circulation were to stop, one child said, "If blood does not come to the hands, they will die, because the blood does not carry energies to them" (Inagaki and Hatano, 1993). In a similar vein, Crider (1981) documented the "container theory" of the workings of the human body constructed by American children between ages 8 and 10, whereby the stomach and lungs are conceptualized as containers for vital substances that are obtained from the outside, and the role of the blood is to transport these vital substances all over the body. Most probably, the vital substances in the American child's container theory are similarly undifferentiated between substance/energy/information.

Inagaki and Hatano (1993) suspected that free explanation tasks, such as those Crider based her characterization on and such as those that yielded the relatively small number of vitalist explanations from their own subjects, may underestimate the attractiveness of a vitalist construal of animals for young children. They therefore devised an explanation preference task, the second source of evidence for their claim. Subjects (6- and 8-year-old children as well as adults) were asked to choose which of three explanations for each of a variety of phenomena they preferred. For example, the question might be: Why do we eat food every day? and the three explanations offered:

1. Intentional: Because we want to eat tasty food.
2. Vitalistic: Because our stomach takes in vital power from the food.
3. Mechanistic: Because we take the food into our body after its form is changed in the stomach and bowels.

Inagaki and Hatano (1993) found the 6-year-olds to prefer the vitalistic explanations (54 percent of choices), followed by the intentional explanations (25 percent of choices). Eight-year-olds preferred the mechanistic explanations (62 percent of choices) but also showed a substantial preference for vitalistic explanations (34 percent). Adults overwhelmingly preferred mechanistic explanations (96 percent).

Inagaki and Hatano's (1993) data provided interesting evidence that a vitalistic construal of bodily processes is psychologically intermediate between an intentional construal and a mechanistic construal. They showed that the 6-year-olds confused the vitalistic and intentional explanations and virtually never confused either with the mechanistic explanations, whereas the 8-year-olds confused the vitalistic and mechanistic explanations and virtually never confused either with the intentional explanations.

The data in support of Inagaki and Hatano's (1993) conjecture that a vitalistic biology is the first autonomous biology constructed by young children and that it is constructed by age 6 is suggestive but not conclusive. The main problems are that only few children spontaneously produce vitalist explanations, and the choices in the explanation choice task are confounded. For example, the intentional explanations in the study are often little more than tautologies, as in "We eat food each day because we want to eat tasty food." More informative intentional choices could have been provided, such as "We eat food every day because we get hungry and eating gets rid of the feeling of hunger." And the mechanistic explanations often included detailed information and vocabulary that 6-year-olds were unlikely to know, as in people take in air, because the lungs take in oxygen and change it into useless carbon dioxide.[11] My point here is that such explanation choice tasks are very difficult to carry out; making different explanation types comparable with respect to informativeness of the explanation and familiarity with the information in it is no easy matter.

Inagaki and Hatano's (1993) conjecture is plausible and should be followed up in several ways. Scholarly work is needed to establish whether vastly different cultures have indeed independently constructed vitalist biologies, and whether vitalist ideas are of the sorts that spread from culture to culture. That is, we need an analysis of the epidemiology of vitalist representations (Sperber, 1985). A more thorough study of vitalist biologies would yield an analysis of what they have in common – the core principles of vitalism. If such core principles are forthcoming and if research with children in different cultures revealed that young children universally construct a biology that embodies some (all) of those core principles, then we should conclude that vitalist biologies are closely related to construals of the world embodied in first-order cognitive modules.

Such a state of affairs would not establish that a vitalist biology is itself an innate cognitive module for all the reasons already outlined in this chapter. Inagaki and Hatano's (1993) evidence is that a vitalist biology is constructed by age 6, and there is still good reason to deny an autonomous biology to children age 4 or under. Specifically, 4-year-olds cannot have constructed a vitalist biology, for they have not constructed the concept of life (Carey, 1985, 1988; Carey and Spelke, 1994).

Keil's (1992, 1994) proposal that the earliest biology relies on functional/ teleological explanation and Inagaki and Hatano's (1993) proposal that the earliest biology is a vitalist one are not incompatible. The two modes of explanation are complementary and could well be aspects of the child's first framework theory of biology, constructed around age 6. We now turn to the problem of how the child might possibly make the transition from a conceptual state in which *animal* is in the domain of an intuitive psychology to a conceptual state in which *animal* is also the main ontological type in the domain of an intuitive biology.

12.7 The origin of new framework theories; the problem of conceptual change

It is natural to propose that humans learn about the world by observing it: we learn that bodies fall by watching them fall; we learn that insults make people angry by watching people react to insults; we learn that $2 + 2 = 4$

by observing two sets of two things combine into one set of four things. Variants of this proposal may be offered. Children may learn by actively manipulating things (e.g., releasing or throwing objects, insulting people, and combining sets) or by interacting with other people (e.g., tossing balls around, participating in social exchanges, and playing number games).

If any of these proposals are correct, then children and adults will learn only about the things they perceive. A child who cannot perceive any object that falls, any person who is moved to anger, or any sets of two things that combine into a set of four things will never learn about these entities, however much she observes the surrounding layout, manipulates portions of the layout, or interacts with other people within the layout. Perception therefore limits the development of knowledge.

The consequences of this limit depend on the nature of the perceptual processes that single out the objects about which we reason. If reasoning depends on domain-specific systems of knowledge, then cognitive development within a domain is constrained by the principles governing the perceptual process for that domain. Whether cognitive development can bring conceptual change depends, then, on the relation between the principles governing perception and those governing reasoning.

If in a certain domain, perception and reasoning are guided by distinct principles, experience may undermine the original principles governing reasoning. For example, suppose that perception of persons depends on a face recognizer, whereas initial reasoning about persons depends on notions that action is governed by choice and that choices accord with beliefs and desires. Encountering a doll, the child would recognize the doll to be a person. The behavior of this person would not, however, appear to result from choices but from the blind operation of the laws of mechanics. Since the doll must be admitted to the class of persons (we are assuming that the face recognizer, not the psychological reasoner, makes this decision), the child is now in a position to learn that his initial psychology is false: not all persons choose their actions. With increased exposure to dolls, stuffed animals, portraits, and the like, this learning will grow and be extended. Learning therefore will bring changes to the child's initial system of knowledge.

In contrast, if the same system of knowledge guides perception and reasoning, the child cannot learn by observing the world that his initial system of knowledge is false. For example, suppose that both perception and reasoning about persons are guided by notions of freely chosen action in accord with beliefs and desires. When the child encounters an object that does not act freely, he will not conclude that his psychological notions are false, but rather that this object does not fall within the domain of his psychology: it is not a person.

In any domain in which perception and reasoning depend on the same system of knowledge, learning from observation, from action, or from social interchange will preserve the initial system of knowledge. Knowledge will grow by a process of enrichment, whereby core principles become further entrenched. The initial system of knowledge cannot be overthrown by a process of learning from experience, because only objects that conform to that system are available to be experienced. Cognitive development will be a process of enrichment around unchanging core principles.

Studies of mature, commonsense reasoning seem to support the view that knowledge of physical objects, persons, and number develops by enrichment. That is, the principles that determine the entities in the domain and guide reasoning about those entities in infancy remain at the core of these concepts. In the domain of physics, principles such as cohesion, contact, and continuity appear central to mature intuitions about objects persistence (see Hirsch, 1982) and object motion (see Spelke, 1991, for discussion). In the domain of psychology, the conception of people as goal-driven agents in perceptual contact with the world appears to be deeply ingrained in mature common-sense reasoning (Wellman, 1990). And in the domain of number, Gallistel and Gelman (1992) argue that the most intuitive mature conceptions of number are those that derive from the principles of one-to-one correspondence and succession.

These examples are taken from innate modular domains, but the argument for enrichment as the only form of learning applies equally to learning constrained by framework theories. Indeed, the argument sketched earlier is exactly that developed by Kuhn (1962) in his characterization of normal science. Framework theories also provide criteria for determining the entities in the domain and for interpreting phenomena involving those entities.

Nevertheless, this reasoning leads to a contradiction. Conceptual change in the domains of physics, psychology, number, and geometry is not only possible, but actual. In the history of science and mathematics, it has occurred with the development of quantum mechanics; with the attempt to construct a purely behavioristic or mechanistic psychology; with the discovery of rational, real, and complex numbers; and with the development of non-Euclidean geometries. In each of these cases, development has led to the abandonment of principles that formerly were central to knowledge in the domain in favor of new principles. The existence of these changes poses a major challenge to the view that knowledge develops by enrichment around a constant core. In addition, in the history of science and mathematics, new framework theories have been developed: evolutionary and molecular biology, chemistry, economics. Representations of new core principles determining new ontological categories have come into being.

In sum, there must be learning mechanisms other than enrichment. How might conceptual change be possible?

12.8 Conceptual change

The nature and existence of conceptual change has been extensively analyzed and debated since Feyerabend (1962) and Kuhn (1962) independently adopted the mathematical term *incommensurability* (no common measure) to refer to mutually untranslatable theoretical languages (see Suppe, 1977, for a comprehensive critique of the early Kuhn/Feyerabend positions). These debates have led to a softening of Kuhn's and Feyerabend's early claims. In particular, current analyses of conceptual change in science deny that the meanings of all terms in a theory change when some do, that theories completely determine evidence and therefore are unfalsifiable, or that theory change is akin to religious conversion. These analyses nevertheless hold that the core insight of the Kuhn/Feyerabend early work stands: the history of science is marked by transitions across which students of the same phenomena speak incommensurable languages.

Carey (1991) summarizes the recent analyses of conceptual change that have been offered by philosophers of science (Kitcher, 1988; Kuhn, 1982; see also Hacking, 1993; Nersessian, 1992) and by cognitive scientists (Thagard, 1988; Vosniadou and Brewer, 1992). Conceptual change consists of conceptual differentiations, such that the undifferentiated parent concept plays no role in subsequent theories (Carey, 1991; Kuhn, 1977), and the creation of new ontological categories (Thagard, 1988). Conceptual change involves change in the core principles that define the entities in a domain and govern reasoning about those entities. It brings the emergence of new principles, incommensurable with the old, which carve the world at different joints.

12.9 Cognitive science and the history of science

Some doubt the relevance of historical analyses of conceptual change to cognitive science and especially to cognitive development. Scientific reasoning and concepts, one might argue, are different from ordinary reasoning and concepts. Only the former undergo changes in core principles. No matter what one's initial response to this argument, it is important to note that the existence of conceptual change in science challenges the argument given above that learning can occur only by enrichment. If domain-specific learning is constrained by the same principles that determine the entities in the domain and constrain reasoning about them, then no person at any level of expertise is in a position to learn that his or her present system of knowledge is false.

Those who emphasize the differences between intuitive theories and explicit scientific theories often imply that those differences in themselves *explain* conceptual change. In particular, the community of scientists, the self-reflective nature of explicit theory construction, and the instructional institutions that create scientists are often credited as engines of conceptual change (e.g., Spelke, 1991). I grant that developed science differs from intuitive knowledge in these three ways. Nonetheless, communication among scientists, reflection, and instruction do not themselves provide a mechanism for conceptual change.

First, processes that occur within an interactive community of scientists cannot, in themselves, bring about conceptual change, because the interactions within a community can only be as effective as the conceptions of its individual members permit. Communication between scientists succeeds only insofar as two scientists can single out the same things to talk about. The arguments against the possibility of conceptual change therefore apply to the community of scientists as well as to the individual scientist.

Next, consider the possibility that reasoners use "disciplined reflection" to revise conceptions within a domain. Many have argued that metacognitive abilities enable human intelligence to extend itself beyond its initial limits (e.g., Sperber, 1994). By itself, however, reflection can do nothing to extricate developing conceptions from the self-perpetuating cycle just described. We as humans can only reflect on the entities we conceptualize. If these are determined by domain-specific principles, we will be able to reflect only on entities whose behavior accords with our initial conceptions. Reflection by itself will not produce conceptual change.

Finally, instructional institutions that create science cannot in themselves account for conceptual change for two reasons. Instruction cannot account for individual discovery or invention. Also, instruction, like all communication, is limited by the student's ability to apprehend the objects to which it applies. If a student is not able to apprehend the entities in a to-be-learned theory, he or she may mouth the correct words but will assign to them meanings licensed by his or her own concepts (cf. the literature on misconceptions in science education reviewed in Carey, 1986).

In sum, we do not dispute that Western science is a social process, the product of self-reflective, metaconceptually sophisticated adults, and that systematic instruction is required to form these adults. These facts, however, do not provide an account of conceptual change. We require such an account: an explanation of how a reasoner can move beyond the core principles in a system of knowledge. Once such an account is provided, we may ask how it tempers the generalization that knowledge develops by enrichment around a constant core.

12.10 Mechanisms of conceptual change

12.10.1 MAPPINGS ACROSS DOMAINS

The formal reflections of scientists provide one source of evidence concerning the processes of conceptual change. We begin with the reflections of the physicist, historian, and philosopher of science Pierre Duhem. Duhem (1949) suggested that scientific physics is not built directly upon commonsense understanding of physical phenomena but depends instead on translation between the language of ordinary experience and the language of mathematics. According to Duhem, the objects of science are not concrete material bodies but numbers. To provide explanations for physical phenomena, physicists first translate from a physical to a mathematical description of the world, and then they look for generalizations and regularities in the mathematical description. These generalizations, when translated back onto the language of everyday objects, are the physicists' laws.

In our terms, scientists who effect a translation from physics to mathematics are using their innately given system of knowledge of number to shed light on phenomena in the domain of their innately given system of knowledge of physics. Scientists do this by devising and using systems of measurement to create mapping between the objects in the first system (number) and those in the second (bodies). Once a mapping is created, the scientists can use conceptions of number to reason about physical objects. They therefore may escape the constraints imposed by the core principles of physical reasoning. In effect, the mapping from physics to number creates a new ontology for the domain of physics which need not be commensurate with that in the old domain of physics.

How do scientists construct mappings across domains? Science's informal documents (lab notebooks, journals) provide an excellent source of data concerning this process. Recently, cognitive scientists as well as historians and philosophers of science have begun to mine this source (e.g., Gruber, 1974, on Darwin; Nersessian, 1992, on Maxwell; Tweney, 1991, on Faraday). Nersessian (1992) concentrates on two interconnected pairs of processes that recur in historical cases of conceptual change: (1) the use of physical analogy and (2) the construction of thought experiments and limiting case analyses. These processes serve both to reveal tensions and inadequacies within a system of knowledge and to restructure that system through the construction of mappings across knowledge domains.

12.10.2 PHYSICAL ANALOGIES
Nersessian's (1992) analysis of Maxwell's use of physical analogies provides a worked example of the productive use of such mappings in the process of conceptual change. According to Nersessian, Maxwell himself used the term *physical analogy* in explaining his method. A physical analogy exploits a set of mathematical relationships as they are embodied in a source domain so as to analyze a target domain about which there is only partial knowledge. In Maxwell's case, the source domain was fluid mechanics as the embodiment of the mathematics of continuum mechanics, and the target domain was electromagnetism. By constructing the analogy between these two areas of physics, Maxwell was able ultimately to construct an effective mathematical theory of electromagnetism.

Nersessian notes several important lessons from this case study. First, the analogy from fluid mechanics to electromagnetism did real inferential work: important mistakes in Maxwell's first characterization of the electromagnetic field are traceable to points at which this analogy breaks down. Second, the process of constructing mappings across domains is difficult: each mapping must be explored and tested in depth to determine its usefulness. Third, "imagistic representations" play an important part in constructing the mapping from physics to number: they express mathematical relationships in a directly comprehensible way and thus serve as a good bridge between domains. Fourth, the process of constructing a mapping across domains is not one of transferring the relations from source domain to target domain in one fell swoop by plugging in and testing values. Rather, a scientist explores different possible mappings from the source domain onto the target domain, imposing different conceptualizations of the target domain in so doing. Finally, the mapping thus created can produce conceptual change in both domains. By using the Newtonian mathematics of continuum mechanics to understand electromagnetic fields, Maxwell constructed a mathematics of greater generality than that of this source domain (Nersessian, 1992).

12.10.3 THOUGHT EXPERIMENTS AND LIMITING CASE ANALYSES
Another modeling activity is the construction of thought experiments, including limiting case analyses. Philosophers of science have often discussed

how (or whether) thought experiments can be *experimental*: can they have empirical content even though they involve no new data? Kuhn (1977), analyzing a thought experiment that figured in the process by which Galileo differentiated instantaneous velocity from average velocity, argued that one function of thought experiments is to show that current concepts cannot apply to the world without contradiction. Nersessian (1992) extended Kuhn's analysis by arguing that thought experiments involve mental model simulations, which are part of the source of their empirical content.

Nersessian's example is Galileo's famous thought experiment showing that heavier objects do not fall faster than lighter ones. Galileo imagined two objects, a large, heavy one and a small, light one, in free fall. According to Aristotelian and scholastic physics, the heavier object should fall faster. He then imagined joining the two objects with an extremely thin rod, creating a composite object. This thought experiment suggests two contradictory outcomes (as in Kuhn's analysis of the function of thought experiments): (1) the composite object is heavier still and therefore should fall even faster, and (2) the slower speed of the smaller object should impede the speed of the larger object, so the composite object should fall more slowly. Galileo went on to construct a limiting case analysis concerning the medium in which objects fall to resolve the contradiction. He concluded that in a vacuum objects of any weight will fall at the same speed. This thought experiment and limiting case analysis played a role in constructing a differentiated, extensive conception of weight. That conception, in turn, depends on the mathematical distinction between a sum and an average.

12.11 Conceptual change in intuitive theories

If processes such as those discussed by Nersessian are necessary components of the engine for conceptual change, we can account for the plausibility of the intuition that conceptual change results from the cooperative activity of a scientific community, from reflection, and from instruction. Galileo, Maxwell, Faraday, Einstein, and Darwin left writings, diaries, and notebooks showing that they used the heuristic processes Nersessian describes and that they were fully conscious of doing so. They used these processes in the context of a self-reflective understanding of the goal of constructing new scientific theories. When one constructs a mapping across domains for the first time, one never knows how useful or deceptive it will prove to be. Thought experiments, physical analogies, and limiting case analyses serve as devices to communicate new conceptualizations to the scientific community, but these new conceptualizations will be adopted only insofar as they provide resolutions to standing puzzles and promote a productive research program. The jury is the social institutions of science.

But do heuristic processes of the kind Nersessian describes and the mappings that result from them also occur outside of developed science? Carey and Spelke (1994) argue that they probably do and that they play a role in the documented conceptual changes of childhood and early adolescence in several domains: number, matter, mechanics, and thermal phenomena. Smith et al. (1988) and Wiser (1988a) have developed curricula to effect conceptual change in the classroom based on the same principles enunciated in Nersessian's analysis (imagistic representations of the mathematical principles that underlie physical analogies from source domains to the target domain, limiting case analyses, thought experiments). Not only are these curricula effective, they are more effective than carefully constructed matched curricula that do not embody these heuristics. Such results lend support to the supposition that analyses such as Nersessian's will be applicable to understanding conceptual change on the part of normal junior and senior high school students. The literature on child philosophy is also filled with examples of elementary-aged children spontaneously engaged in reasoning of this form (for example, Matthews, 1980).

12.12 The search for other mechanisms underlying conceptual change

To sum up the argument so far: two construals of what kind of structure might constitute a cognitive domain have been developed in the literature – an innate module and a framework theory. Folkbiology is not a good candidate for an innate module but is a paradigm example of a framework theory. Its domain-specific ontology (animals, plants) and phenomena (disease, family resemblance, reproduction, growth, bodily processes, death) are explained by a rudimentary theory that exists in skeletal form by age 6 and is elaborated thereafter. My reading of the evidence leads me to conclude that folkbiology is not constructed as a framework theory until age 6 or 7 (this is a lowering of the estimate in Carey, 1985, which put the age at 9 or 10). If this picture is right, then the preschool child's concept of animal must be different (in the strong sense of conceptual change) from that of the older child and adult. Indeed, Carey (1985, 1988) argues that this is so: the preschool child has an undifferentiated concept alive/active/real/existent that plays no role in the 10-year-old's conceptual system, the status of people as animal is different for preschool children and 10-year-olds, the core of the concept of animal kind differs, and so on.

Of course, this is not the only example of conceptual change during these years. (See also Vosniadou and Brewer, 1992, for evidence of conceptual change within intuitive cosmology and Carey, 1991, for evidence of conceptual change within an intuitive theory of matter.) And, as argued earlier, there is at least one candidate set of mechanisms that can underlie conceptual change through analogical mappings between domains.

At this point in the argument, we arrive at a crucial stumbling block. Analogical mapping cannot be the only source of conceptual change involved in the formation of biology as a framework theory. Unlike the relation between physics and mathematics, there is no mapping between the core principles in the first framework theory of biology and any antecedently existing domain. That is, there is no source domain for the concepts of the life cycle, a vitalist conception of the workings of the human body, or the other principles that articulate the first framework folkbiology. Thus, although exploring partial isomorphisms between domains is one source of conceptual change, it cannot be the only one.

Besides the exploitation of isomorphisms between distinct domains, two other types of processes contribute to conceptual change. First, new framework theories are often differentiated from earlier ones (cf. Carey, 1985, 1995, for evidence that folkbiology is differentiated out of folkpsychology). In the course of such differentiations, mappings between emerging core concepts and those of the original domain are exploited. For example, it is likely that a vitalist construal of animals is built on the core notion of animals as agents. As Gelman (1990) stressed, one of the core principles that guides identification of and reasoning about animals is that they have an internal source of movement (she dubs this "the innards principle"). This internal causal power makes animals capable of action, and evidence of an internal source of action is one of the fundamental ways we (and babies) differentiate animals from nonanimals. Initially the internal causal power is a source of action, not of life. *Life* is not the same as *agency*, even though there may be a common source via the innards principle. Nothing from the base domain of psychology, with intentional causation as its core explanatory mechanism, can serve as the source of ideas about the life cycle, reproduction, death, and the body-as-machine.[12]

The problem, then, is how the child constructs the skeletal notion of life to map onto the innards principle. Another process exploits the child's prodigious fact-learning capacities, especially causal facts (the simple input–output causal relations discussed earlier). Sometimes these are learned simply because the child is told them; sometimes they are inferred. For example, Springer (1995) taught preschool children two facts: babies grow in their mommy's tummies, and when inside, babies are not subject to any external causal influences. Just learning these two facts lead children to perform better on a range of tasks that diagnose an understanding of biological inheritance. Such causal facts are place holders for causal mechanisms – they alert the child to search for explanatory understanding. More importantly, they are interrelated and mutually constraining (causal facts about birth constrain causal facts about inheritance; causal facts about the body and growth constrain facts about birth). A framework theory is born through a process by which a network of causal facts becomes interrelated and mutually constraining (the coherence aspect of how causal mechanisms differ from causes). This process leads to changes in a concept's core and supports the formation of new ontological types (e.g., *living thing*) that articulate new framework theories.

I admit that these last speculations are extremely sketchy, and I offer them as a place holder for a worked-out proposal for mechanisms of conceptual change to supplement those offered by Nersessian (1992). The view elaborated in this chapter – that cognition is articulated in terms of framework theories and that new framework theories are constructed during development – ultimately will stand or fall on the success of the project of explaining how framework theories come into being. But however they are formed, these framework theories provide the basis for distinct modes of thought.

Notes

1 Much of the argument in this chapter is drawn from Carey and Spelke (1994) and Carey (1995).

2 In Sperber's account, one of the innate conceptual modules, a metarepresentational module, is sufficiently important that he deems it a third tier, although he stresses that initially it is just one conceptual module among many.

3 For example, theories can be analyzed as sets of sentences from which predictions can be logically derived, these predictions then tested against empirical data. This is not the view of theories adopted here.

4 There are several case studies of lay intuitive theories in which it has been found that these are largely the *same* as the first theories developed by institutionalized science that are close to the phenomena (thermal phenomena: see Wiser and Carey, 1983; Wiser, 1988b; intuitive mechanics: see McCloskey, 1983; matter: see Carey, 1991; folkbiology: see Hatano and Inagaki, 1994; Atran, Chapter 13 of this volume).

5 Especially animals; in one of the cultures Atran has studied, the Itzaq-Maya, fungi and lichens are not considered alive (Atran, 1994). An interesting issue is the theoretical significance of such examples of *lack* of cross-cultural universality. Do Itzaq-Maya have different criteria for life, or do they simply lack evidence that fungi and lichens meet their criteria for life? For present purposes, I grant Atran's point that folktaxonomies are largely universal.

6 Of course, establishing a hierarchy of kinds entails violating the mutual exclusivity assumption. My point here is that the mutual exclusivity assumption applies equally to biological and nonbiological kinds, as does the ability to overcome this assumption and set up hierarchies.

7 This depends, of course, on what is meant by *ecology*. If a kind's characteristic ecology includes only where it is typically found – fish in rivers and lakes, moose in forests, buffalo on plains – then other kinds have characteristic ecologies as well. Celestial objects are found in the heavens, rivers, and lakes on the surface of the earth, furniture in houses, etc. But if *ecology* includes more biology-relevant information – how animals shelter themselves from the cold, how they protect their young, what they eat – then these properties are domain specific. But then they are not theory neutral, at least in the adult's conceptual system.

8 Or "zoology," as Sperber also characterizes the domain.

9 This same child believed that on her mother's birthday, her mother (a few months older than her father) would become taller than her father, because her mother would be 38 while her father would only be 37.

10 This deepening continues beyond age 10; 10-year-olds judge that a skunk, accidentally given an injection of a chemical shortly after birth that caused it to grow into an animal that looks just like a raccoon, has indeed become a raccoon; adults judge it still to be a skunk (Keil, 1989).

11 This explanation is defective as a functional explanation as well. Why would the body want to change air into something useless?

12 It is possible that the young child's understanding of complex artifacts serves as a source domain for the last of these biological explanatory structures

References

Atran, S. (1990). *Cognitive Foundations of Natural History*. Cambridge: Cambridge Univ. Press.

(1994). Core domains versus scientific theories: evidence from systematics and Itzaj-Maya folk biology. In L. A. Hirschfield & S. A. Gelman (Eds.), *Mapping the Mind: Domain Specificity in Cognition and Culture*. New York: Cambridge Univ. Press.

Baillargeon, R., Kotovsky, L., & Needham, A. (1995). The acquisition of physical knowledge in infancy. In D. Sperber, D. Premack, & A. J. Premack (Eds.), *Causal Cognition: A Multidisciplinary Debate*. Oxford: Clarendon Press, pp. 79–116.

Carey, S. (1985). *Conceptual Change in Childhood*. Cambridge: Bradford/MIT Press.

(1986). Cognitive science and science education. *American Psychologist 41*, 1123–1130.

(1988). Conceptual differences between children and adults. *Mind and Language 3*, 167–181.

(1991). Knowledge acquisition: Enrichment or conceptual change? In S. Carey & R. Gelman (Eds.), *Epigenesis of Mind: Studies in Biology and Cognition*. Hillsdale, NJ: Erlbaum.

(1995). On the origin of causal understanding. In D. Sperber, D. Premack, and A. J. Premack (Eds.), *Causal Cognition: A Multidisciplinary Debate*. Oxford: Clarendon Press, pp. 268–302.

Carey, S., & Gelman, R. (Eds.) (1991). *Epigenesis of Mind: Studies in Biology and Cognition*. Hillsdale, NJ: Erlbaum.

Carey, S., & Spelke, E. (1994). Domain specific knowledge and conceptual change. In L. A. Hirschfeld & S. A. Gelman (Eds.), *Mapping the Mind: Domain Specificity in Cognition and Culture*. New York: Cambridge Univ. Press, pp. 169–200.

Chomsky, N. (1980). *Rules and Representations*. New York: Columbia Univ. Press.

Clement, J. (1982). Students' preconceptions in introductory mechanics. *American Journal of Physics 50*(1), 66–71.

Cohen, L. B., & Younger, B. A. (1983). Perceptual categorization in the infant. In G. K. Scholnick (Ed.), *New Trends in Conceptual Representation*. Hillsdale, NJ: Erlbaum, pp. 197–200.

Crider, C. (1981). Children's conceptions of the body interior. In R. Bibace & M. Walsh (Eds.), *Children's Conceptions of Health, Illness and Bodily Functions*. San Francisco: Jossey–Bass.

Diamond, R., & Carey, S. (1990). On the acquisition of pattern encoding skills. *Cognitive Development 5*(4), 345–368.

Duhem, P. (1949). *The Aim and Structure of Physical Theory*. Princeton: Princeton Univ. Press.

Feyerabend, P. (1962). Explanation, reduction, empiricism. In H. Feigl & G. Maxwell (Eds.), *Minnesota Studies in the Philosophy of Science*, Minneapolis: Univ. of Minnesota Press, Vol. 3, pp. 41–87.

Gallistel, C., & Gelman, R. (1992). Preverbal and verbal counting and computation. *Cognition 44*, 43–74.

Gelman, R. (1990). First principles organize attention to and learning about relevant data: number and the animate-inanimate distinction as examples. *Cognitive Science 14*, 79–106.

Gelman, S. A., & Markman, E. M. (1986). Categories and induction in young children. *Cognition 23*, 183–208.

Gelman, S. A., & Wellman, H. M. (1991). Insides and essences: Early understandings of the nonobvious. *Cognition 38*, 213–244.

Gopnik, A., & Wellman, H. M. (1994). The theory theory. In L. Hirschfeld & S. Gelman (Eds.), *Mapping the Mind: Domain Specificity in Cognition and Culture.* New York: Cambridge Univ. Press.

Gruber, H. E. (1974). *Darwin on man: A psychological study of scientific creativity.* New York: Dutton.

Hacking, I. (1993). Working in a new world: The taxonomic solution. In P. Horwich & J. Thomson (Eds.), *World Changes.* Cambridge, MA: MIT Press.

Hall, D. G., & Waxman, S. R. (1993). Assumptions about word meanings: Individuation and basic-level kinds. *Child Development 64,* 1550–1570.

Hatano, G., & Inagaki, K. (1994). Young children's naive theory of biology. *Cognition 50,* 171–188.

Hirsch, E. (1982). *The Concept of Identity.* New York: Oxford Univ. Press.

Hirschfeld, L. A. (1994). Is the acquisition of social categories based on domain-specific competence or on knowledge transfer? In L. A. Hirschfeld & S. A. Gelman (Eds.), *Mapping the Mind: Domain Specificity in Cognition and Culture.* New York: Cambridge Univ. Press, pp. 201–233.

Hirschfeld, L. A., & Gelman, S. A. (Eds.) (1994). *Mapping the Mind: Domain Specificity in Cognition and Culture.* New York: Cambridge Univ. Press.

Inagaki, K., & Hatano, G. (1987). Young children's spontaneous personification as analogy. *Child Development 58,* 1013–1020.

(1988). "Young Children's Understanding of the Mind–Body Distinction." Paper presented at the Meeting of the American Educational Research Association, New Orleans.

(1993). Young children's understanding of the mind–body distinction. *Child Development 64,* 1534–1549.

Jaakkola, R., & Carey, S. (in preparation). Children's body knowledge: The structure and content of a first biological theory.

Jeyifous, S. (1986). Atimodemo: Semantic and conceptual development among the Yoroba. Unpublished doctoral dissertation, Cornell University, Ithaca, NY.

Keil, F. C. (1979). *Semantic and Conceptual Development: An Ontological Perspective.* Cambridge, MA: Harvard Univ. Press.

(1989) *Concepts, Kinds and Cognitive Development.* Cambridge, MA: MIT Press.

(1992). The origins of an autonomous biology. In M. R. Gunnar & M. Maratsos (Eds.), *Modularity and Constraints in Language and Cognition. The Minnesota Symposium on Child Psychology 25,* 103–137.

(1994). The birth and nurturance of concepts by domains. In L. A. Hirschfeld & S. A. Gelman (Eds.), *Domain Specificity in Cognition and Culture.* New York: Cambridge Univ. Press, pp. 234–256.

Kitcher, P. (1988). The child as parent of the scientist. *Mind and Language 3,* 217–228.

Kuhn, T. S. (1962). *The Structure of Scientific Revolutions.* Chicago: Univ. of Chicago Press.

(1977). A function for thought experiments. In T. S. Kuhn (Ed.), *The Essential Tension.* Chicago: Univ. of Chicago Press.

(1982). Commensurability, comparability, communicability. *PSA 1982, 2.* East Lansing: MI: Philosophy of Science Association, pp. 669–688.

Leslie, A. (1994). ToMM, ToBy, and Agency: Core architecture and domain specificity. In L. A. Hirschfeld & S. A. Gelman (Eds.), *Mapping the Mind.* New York: Cambridge Univ. Press, pp. 119–148.

Macnamara, J. (1986). *Border Dispute: The Place of Logic in Psychology.* Cambridge, MA: MIT Press.

Markman, E. M. (1989). *Categorization and Naming in Children: Problems of Induction.* Cambridge, MA: MIT Press.

Matthews, G. B. (1980). *Philosophy and the Young Child.* Cambridge MA: Harvard Univ. Press.

McCloskey, M. (1983). Naive theories of motion. In D. Gentner & A. Stevens (Eds.), *Mental Models.* Hillsdale, NJ: Erlbaum.

Murphy, G. L., & Medin, D. (1985). The role of theories in conceptual coherence. *Psychological Review 92,* 289–316.

Nersessian, N. J. (1992). How do scientists think? Capturing the dynamics of conceptual change in science. In R. N. Giere (Ed.), *Cognitive Models of Science. Minnesota Studies in the Philosophy of Science,* Vol. 15, pp. 3–44. Minneapolis: Univ. of Minnesota Press.

Perner, J. (1991). *Understanding the Representational Mind.* Cambridge, MA: Bradford/MIT Press.

Piaget, J., & Inhelder, B. (1941). *Le development des quantites chez l'enfant.* Neufchatel: Delchaux et Niestle.

Posner, M. I., & Keele, S. W. (1968). On the genesis of abstract ideas. *Journal of Experimental Psychology 77,* 353–363.

Rosengren, K. S., Gelman, S. A., Kalish, C. W., & McCormick, M. (1991). As time goes by: Children's early understanding of growth in animals. *Child Development 62,* 1302–1320.

Salmon, W. C. (1989). *Four Decades of Scientific Explanation.* Minneapolis: Univ. of Minnesota Press.

Schank, R. C., & Abelson, R. (1977). *Scripts, Plans, Goals, and Understanding.* Hillsdale, NJ: Erlbaum.

Smith, C. (1979). Children's understanding of natural language hierarchies. *Journal of Experimental Child Psychology 27,* 437–458.

Smith, C., Carey, S., & Wiser, M. (1985). On differentiation: A case study of the development of the concepts of size, weight, and density. *Cognition 21,* 177–237.

Smith, C., Snir, Y., Grosslight, L., & Unger, C. (1988). "Using Conceptual Models to Facilitate Conceptual Change: Weight and Density." Educational Technology Center Technical Report, Harvard University, Cambridge, MA.

Sommers, F. (1963). Types and ontology. *Philosophical Review 72,* 327–363.

Spelke, E. S. (1988). The origins of physical knowledge. In L. Weiskrantz (Ed.), *Thought Without Language.* Oxford: Clarendon Press, pp. 168–184.

   (1991). Physical knowledge in infancy: Reflections on Piaget's theory. In S. Carey & R. Gelman (Eds.), *Epigenesis of Mind: Studies in Biology and Cognition.* Hillsdale, NJ: Erlbaum.

Spelke, E. S., Breinlinger, K., Macomber, J., & Jacobson, K. (1992). Origins of knowledge. *Psychological Review 99,* 605–632.

Spelke, E. S., & Kestenbaum, R. (1986). Les origines du concept d'objet. *Psychologie Française 31,* 67–72.

Sperber, D. (1985). Anthropology and psychology: Towards an epidemiology of representations ([the Malinowski Memorial Lecture, 1984]). *Man* (N.S.) *20,* 73–89.

   (1994). The modularity of thought and the epidemiology of representations. In L. A. Hirschfeld & S. A. Gelman (Eds.), *Domain Specificity in Cognition and Culture.* New York: Cambridge Univ. Press, pp. 39–67.

Sperber, D., Premack, D., & Premack, A. J. (1995). *Causal Cognition: A Multidisciplinary Debate.* Oxford: Clarendon Press.

Springer, K. (1995). Acquiring a naive theory of kinship through inference. *Child Development 66*, 547–558.

Suppe, F. (1977). *The Structure of Scientific Theories*. Urbana: Univ. of Illinois Press.

Thagard, P. (1988). *Conceptual Revolutions*. Princeton, NJ: Princeton Univ. Press.

Toulmin, S., & Goodfield, J. (1962). *The Architecture of Matter*. Chicago: Univ. of Chicago Press.

Tweney, R. D. (1991). Faraday's notebooks: The active organization of creative science. *Physics Education 26*, 301.

Vosniadou, S., & Brewer, W. F. (1992). Mental models of the earth: A study of conceptual change in childhood. *Cognitive Psychology 24*(4), 535–585.

Watson, J. (1979). Perception of contingency as a determinant of social responsiveness. In E. Tohman (Ed.), *The Origins of Social Responsiveness*. Hillsdale, NJ: Erlbaum, pp. 33–64.

Wellman, H. M. (1990). *The Child's Theory of Mind*. Cambridge, MA: MIT Press.

Wellman, H. M., & Gelman, S. A. (1992). Cognitive development: Foundational theories of core domains. *Annual Review of Psychology 43*, 337–375.

Wiggins, D. (1980). *Sameness and Substance*. Oxford: Basil Blackwell.

Wiser, M. (1988a) "Can Models Foster Conceptual Change? The Case of Heat and Temperature." Educational Technology Center Technical Report, Harvard University, Cambridge, MA.

Wiser, M. (1988b). The differentiation of heat and temperature: History of science and novice-expert shift. In S. Strauss (Ed.), *Ontogeny, Philogeny, and Historical Development*. Norwood, NJ: Ablex, pp. 28–48.

Wiser, M., & Carey, S. (1983). When heat and temperature were one. In D. Gentner & A. Stevens (Eds.), *Mental Models*. Hillsdale, NJ: Erlbaum, pp. 267–297.

Xu, F., & Carey, S. (in press). Infants' metaphysics: The case of numerical identity. *Cognitive Psychology*.

13
Modes of thinking about living kinds
SCIENCE, SYMBOLISM, AND COMMON SENSE

Scott Atran

Introduction: Modes of thought

Two decades ago Robin Horton and Ruth Finnegan (1973) edited a synthesis of anthropological speculation on *Modes of Thought: Essays on Thinking in Western and Non-Western Societies*. In that volume, authors debated the defining intellectual and practical aspects of: (1) everyday common sense, (2) Western science, and (3) the symbolism of myth, magic, and religion. Something of a consensus emerged, with most contributors granting that people in "traditional" non-Western societies function in a more or less "logical" and "rational" manner as we do, at least in mundane contexts of ordinary life. There was also considerable support for the view that there is a measure of similarity and historical continuity between at least some aspects of common sense, on the one hand, and science and symbolism, on the other.

But opinion diverged over the apparent differences between science and symbolism. For example, Horton (1973) claimed that magic reflects an "erroneous" extension of commonsense rationality to understanding causal processes that operate in the cosmos at large. By employing rash inductions or faulty deductions, magical rites simply fail as scientific experiments. By contrast, Tambiah (1973) argued that people do not ritually invoke magical relationships to elaborate inductively or instantiate deductively some causal theory. Rather, in magic people seek to involve body and mind more intimately in what is going on in the world around.

Current work in cognitive anthropology, psychology, and philosophy suggests a much more fragmented view of the diverse domains that constitute "common sense" and of the various ways these domains may be treated scientifically or symbolically. Still, the issues originally raised in *Modes of Thought* may be pertinent to this work, provided they can be constrained to the terms of cognitive science today. In an endeavor to meet the constraint, this chapter briefly tracks the ways peoples in different cultures think about living things.

Cross-cultural and developmental studies indicate that folkbiology, which at a minimum includes the categorization of kinds of animals and plants as well as reasoning about them, may be one of the core domains of ordinary human cognition. In the West, biology (or natural history as it is known historically) was the first science to emerge. Concepts of ordinary and extraordinary living things play key roles in all religions, myths, and magical practices. Thus, by exploring various thoughts about living kinds in these pervasive modes – common sense, science, and symbolism – we might hope to learn something about the profound unity of human nature and its marvelous cultural possibilities.

13.1 Folkbiology

Ethnobiology is a branch of cognitive anthropology concerned with studying the ways members of a culture understand and utilize the local flora and fauna. A century of enthnobiological research has shown that even within a single culture there may be several different sorts of "special-purpose" folk-biological classifications that are organized by particular interests for particular uses (e.g., beneficial versus noxious, domestic versus wild, edible versus inedible; cf. Hough, 1897). Only recently, however, has intensive empirical and theoretical work revealed a cross-culturally universal general-purpose taxonomy that supports the widest possible range of inductions about living kinds.

13.1.1 DOMAINS OF CAUSAL SCHEMA
Human minds seem to be endowed with fundamentally *distinct domains of causal schema for thinking about the world*. A distinct causal domain is a distinct way of thinking about (necessary and sufficient) conditions that relate causes to effects. The focus here is on one particular natural-category domain: non-human living things, that is, kinds of animals and plants.[1]

Geoffrey Lloyd (1990) suggests that the unitary notion of "cause" in Western science, like that of "nature," may have no directly corresponding notions in classical China or in other historical traditions and are thus unlikely concepts of universal common sense. Although modern science strives to unify all kinds of causal processes under a single system of contingent, mechanical relationships (push/pull, clockwork, etc.), recent work in cognitive anthropology and developmental psychology suggests that even people in our own culture initially do not spontaneously reason this way and may never do so. Thus, people from a very early age and through all of their adult lives seem to think differently about different domains (Hirschfeld and Gelman, 1994), including the domains of naive physics (Baillargeon, 1986; Spelke, 1990; Carey et al., 1992), naive biology (Keil, 1989; Gelman and Wellman, 1991), naive psychology (Leslie, 1990; Astington and Gopnik, 1991; Avis and Harris, 1991), and naive sociology (Turiel, 1983; Cosmides and Tooby, 1992). People attribute *contingent* motions to inert object substances; spontaneous actions and *teleological* developments to species of animals and plants (e.g., internally directed growth and inheritance of related parts and whole); *intentional* relationships to one another's beliefs, desires, and actions; and group assignments (e.g., kinship, race) that specify a range of *deontological* obligations and contractual actions.

Teleo-essentialism: The schema for living kinds. Each of these conceptual modules – folkphysics, folkbiology, folkpsychology, and folksociology – targets a somewhat different database as input in order to structure it in a distinct way as output (i.e., as domain-specific representations). For example, the categorization of an organism as a kind of living thing, such as a dog, involves selective attention to certain perceptible features of the world. The selected features may involve various aspects of the object's shape, size, movement, texture, sound, and smell. But the selection process itself is driven, at least in part, by a set of causal presumptions to the effect that the living world categorically divides into well-bounded types, regardless of the degree of morphological variation that may actually exist or be observed within or between different kinds: for example, DOG (including puppies, poodles, and huskies), TOAD (including tadpoles), OAK (including acorns, saplings, and bonsais), and TIGER (including cubs, dwarfs, and three-legged albino mutants).

Even very young children tend to attribute the rich characteristic structure of living things to very abstract, informationally poor stimuli that clearly go beyond the information given. For example, they will readily take as representations of living things closed two-dimensional figures that have irregular protruding parts. For a given drawing, children will ask what the protruding part is purposively "for" if they are primed to believe that the drawing represents a prickly plant rather than, say, a prickly mineral (Keil, 1994). The teleological presumption of living things as organized hierarchies of complementary functions that serve the species is a psychologically crucial element to understanding relations between physiology and morphology, disease as the derangement of function, and systematic relations between living kinds.

The cognitive impetus that drives the learner to this naive appreciation of the relationship between a largely unknown (and perhaps unknowable) genotype and its various phenotypic expressions is likely a naturally selected endowment of evolution. It enables every person to quickly apprehend particularly salient aspects of the biological reality of how genotypes and their environments jointly produce phenotypes without that person having to be immediately aware of the precise causal mechanisms involved (an awareness that only now emerges after two millenia of concerted scientific effort). On this account, it is not surprising that urban American children and rural Yoruba children (Nigeria) learn about allowable morphological and behavioral transformations and variations among folk species in nearly identical ways and at nearly identical ages (Jeyifous, 1985).

The folk species concept: Its bearing on cognitive evolution. From the standpoint of human evolution, this presumption of essence represents a balancing act between what our ancestors could and could not afford to ignore about their environment. The ontological concept of a "natural kind" with a deep essence is very much like Laplace's conception of probability, that is, a compromise between innate knowledge and congenital ignorance. For God, by contrast, would leave nothing to chance, nor would an all-knowing divinity have to research the underlying natures of the world's limited varieties – they would be prima facie evident. The concept of the folk species allows us to perceive and predict many important properties that link together the members of a biological species *that are actually living together at any one time* and to categorically distinguish such nondimensional species from one another (cf. Mayr 1969). This is adequate for apprehending the biological makeup of local environments, such as those in which our hominid ancestors evolved and in which many "traditional" cultures have developed.

But from a scientific vantage, the concept of folk species is woefully inadequate for capturing the graded relationships that characterize the evolution of species over geologically vast dimensions of time and space – dimensions for which human minds were not directly designed (naturally selected) to comprehend.

Only by painstaking, culturally elaborated conceptual strategies, like those of science, can minds transcend the innate bounds of their phenomenal world and begin to grasp nature's graded subtleties. To do so, however, requires continued access to the intuitive categories of common sense, which anchors speculation and allows more sophisticated knowledge eventually to emerge.

13.1.2 FOLK TAXONOMY

All human beings, then, classify animals and plants into basic groupings that are "quite as obvious to [the] modern scientist as to a Guaraní Indian" (Simpson, 1961:57). This is the concept of the (folk) species. It is the primary locus for thinking about biology among layfolk the world over. Historically, it provided a trans-theoretical basis for scientific speculation about the biological world in that different biological theories, including evolutionary theory, have sought to account for the apparent constancy of species and for the apparent similarities and differences between species (Wallace, 1889:1; cf. Mayr, 1969:37).

In addition to the spontaneous arrangement of local fauna and flora into specieslike groupings, these basic groupings have "from the most remote period in . . . history . . . been classed in groups under groups. This classification is not arbitrary like the grouping of stars in constellations" (Darwin, 1859:431). This further taxonomic arrangement of species into higher-order "groups under groups," which is common to folk the world over, provides the principle framework for thinking about the similarities and differences between species and for exploring the varied nature of life on earth (Berlin et al., 1973; Brown, 1984).

(Folk) biological ranks. Folkbiological taxonomy supports indefinitely many inductions about the plausible distributions of initially unfamiliar biologically related traits over organisms given the discovery of such traits in some organism or the likely correlation of known traits among unfamiliar organisms given the discovery of only some of those traits among the organisms. For example, the discovery of breast cancer in monkeys could warrant the initial induction that mammals are susceptible to breast cancer but not birds or fish, because only mammals have mammary glands. And the knowledge that wom-

bats have mammary glands would warrant the induction that they also have many of the other external and internal traits associated with mammals, such as fur and warm blood (cf. Rips, 1975; Osherson et al., 1990).

This ''default'' taxonomy serves as an inductive compendium of biological information. It is composed of a fairly rigid hierarchy of inclusive classes of organisms, or taxa. At each level of the hierarchy, the taxa, which are mutually exclusive, partition the locally perceived biota in a virtually exhaustive manner. Lay taxonomy is universally composed of a small number of absolutely distinct hierarchical levels, or *ranks* (Atran 1990; Berlin 1992): such as the level of *folk kingdom* (e.g., ANIMAL, PLANT),[2] *life form* (e.g., BUG, FISH, BIRD, MAMMAL, TREE, GRASS, BUSH, MUSHROOM),[3] *folk species* (e.g., GNAT, SHARK, ROBIN, DOG, MAPLE, WHEAT, HOLLY, TOADSTOOL),[4] and *folk sub-species* (COLLIE, RETRIEVER; SUGAR MAPLE, RED MAPLE).[5]

Intermediate levels also exist between the levels of the folk species and life form. Taxa at these levels usually have no explicit name (e.g., rats + mice but no other rodents), although sometimes they may (e.g., felines, legumes). Such taxa, especially unnamed covert ones, tend not to be as clearly delimited as folk species or life forms, nor does any one intermediate level always constitute a fixed taxonomic rank that partitions the local fauna and flora into a mutually exclusive and virtually exhaustive set of broadly equivalent taxa. Still, there is a psychologically evident preference for forming intermediate taxa at a level roughly between that of the scientific family (e.g., canine, weaver bird) and order (e.g., carnivore, passerine) (Atran, 1983).

The rank of folk species vs. Rosch's basic level. By far, the majority of taxa in any folkbiological system belong to the folk-species level. Comparing the relative salience of folkbiological categories among Tzeltal Maya and other small-scale societies around the world, anthropologist Brent Berlin and his colleagues (Berlin et al., 1974) find that folk species are the most basic conceptual groupings of organisms (cf. Hays, 1983, for New Guinea). Folk species represent the cuts in nature that Maya children first name and form an image of (Stross, 1973) and Maya adults most frequently use in speech, most easily recall in memory, and most readily communicate to others (Hunn, 1977). Correspondence of folk species to scientific species or genera is not isomorphic and varies according to patterns of species distribution within biological families and other factors. Nevertheless, folk species usually encompass single biological species and usually do not extend beyond biological genera for larger vertebrates and flowering plants.

In experiments conducted by psychologist Eleanor Rosch and her colleagues (Rosch et al., 1976), the most salient category cuts in the folkbiological classification of urban American folk do not uniformly correspond to the level of folk species (see Zubin and Köpcke, 1986, for Germany). Thus, TREE, BIRD, and FISH are themselves treated as basic categories. These life form categories – and not subordinate folk species like OAK, ROBIN, and SHARK – turn out to be the most inclusive category for which a concrete image of the category as a whole can be formed, the first categorization made during perception of the environment, the earliest category named by American children (Dougherty, 1979), and the categories most codable, most coded, and most prevalent in ordinary (urban) English. Only the MAMMAL life form is not coded at the basic level. This is because mammalian folk species, like HORSE and DOG, retain appreciable cultural importance in industrial societies (e.g., via story books, nature programs on television).

In contrast to the basic level, cross-cultural evidence indicates that the folk-species level is an absolute phenomenon that does not shift as a function of cultural significance or individual familiarity and expertise. In a series of inference studies, American subjects perform much as do Maya subjects in maximizing inductive potential at the folk-species level. Both midwestern Americans and Itzaj Maya are much more likely to infer that, say, oak trees have a disease (or a given enzyme, protein, etc.) that white oak trees have than to infer that trees have a disease that oak trees have (Coley et al., submitted). This result cannot simply be attributed to the fact that subjects are more likely to generalize to a more specific category. Indeed, subjects in both cultures are no more likely to infer that, say, white oak trees have a disease that spotted white oak trees have, than to infer that oak trees have a disease that white oak trees have. The same findings apply in cases of inferences to particular folk species of fish or birds as opposed to inferences to fish or birds in general.

These findings cannot be explained either by appeals to cross-domain notions of perceptual similarity or to the structure of the world "out there." On the one hand, if inferential potential were a simple function of perceptual similarity – or the basic level in Rosch's sense – then Americans should inductively privilege the life form level. Yet, Americans privilege folk-species just as Maya do. On the other hand, objective reality, that is, the actual distribution of biological species within groups of evolutionarily related species, does not substantially differ in the natural environments of midwesterners and Itzaj Maya. But unlike Maya, the Americans perceptually discriminate life forms more readily than folk species.

True, there are more locally recognized species, say, of trees in the Itzaj Maya area of Peten, Guatemala, than in the Midwest United States. Still, the readily perceptible evolutionary "gaps" between species are roughly the same in the two environments (e.g., a clear majority of tree genera in both environments are monospecific). If anything, one might expect that having fewer trees in the American environment allows each species to stand out more from the rest (Hunn, 1976). Also for birds, the relative distribution of evolutionary related species also seems to be broadly comparable across temperate and rainforest environments (Boster, 1988).

Finally, Maya privileging of induction at the folk-species level cannot be attributed to greater cultural significance or individual expertise, for the most culturally salient taxa, those for which there is greatest expertise, are folk-specifics and varietals. These do not privilege induction over folk species. This also suggests that patterns of induction among American folk do not simply owe to degeneration, or devolution, of folkbiological knowledge through gradual attrition of cultural saliency at lower levels of taxonomy.

Although the heuristic knowledge summarized at Rosch's basic level may devolve in this way, folkbiological presumptions and patterns of inference do not.

The findings support the idea that fundamental categorization processes in folkbiology are rooted in domain-specific conceptual presumptions and not in domain-general perceptual heuristics. People in small-scale versus high-technology cultures may differ in terms of the level at which names readily come to mind or knowledge about biological kinds but still privilege the same absolute level of reality for biological reasoning, namely, the folk-species rank. This is because they presume the biological world to be fully partitioned at that rank into non-overlapping kinds, each with its own unique causal essence or inherent underlying nature (Atran, 1987). By contrast, a partitioning of artifacts (including those of organic origin, such as foods) is neither mutually exclusive, virtually exhaustive, nor inherent: some mugs may or may not be cups; an avocado may be a fruit or vegetable depending on how it is served; a given object may be a bar stool or waste bin depending on the social context or perceptual orientation of its user; and so on.

The significance of rank. Classes of organisms, or taxa, are identified by clusters of readily perceptible features. These taxonomic clusters of features are maximally covariant, with each such cluster separated from others of its rank by a readily perceptible gap where clusters share few, if any, features (Hunn, 1976). Ranking is a cognitive mapping that places taxa in a structure of *absolute levels*, which may be evolutionarily designed to correspond to fundamentally *different levels of reality*. Thus, the rank of folk kingdom – the level at which organisms are classified as ANIMAL or PLANT – may be determined, a priori, by our innate ontology (cf. Donnellan, 1971). In other words, we can only know that something is an organism if and only if we know it is either ANIMAL or PLANT.

The rank of folk species – the level at which organisms are classified as DOG, OAK, and so on – corresponds to the level at which morphological, behavioral, and ecological relationships between organisms maximally co-vary. It is the rank where people are most likely to attribute biological properties. This includes characteristic patterns of inheritance, growth, and physiological function as well as more hidden properties, such as hitherto unknown organic processes, organs, and diseases. The rank of folk sub-species – the level at which organisms are classified as BEAGLE, SUGAR MAPLE, and so on – corresponds to ranges of natural variation that humans are most apt to appropriate and manipulate as a function of their cultural interests.

The level of life form – the level at which organisms are classified as BIRD, TREE, and so on – may correspond to a partitioning of the local ecological landscape, to which we assign species roles in the "economy of nature" as a function of the way their specific morphology and behavior is fitted to those roles. For example, the morphology and behavior of different birds corresponds to a partitioning of the ways vertebrate life competitively accommodates to the air. The morphology and growth pattern of different trees corresponds to a partitioning of the ways single-stem plants competitively access sunlight in the earth's gravitational field (a 100-foot-tall multiple-stem bush would be physically impossible on earth). These divisions not only share readily perceptible features and behaviors that are related to habitat, but they also structure inductions about the distribution of underlying properties that presumably relate biology to the local ecology.

The significance of rank is to allow generalizations across classes of taxa at any given level. For example, the living members of a taxon at the level of the folk species generally share a set of biologically important features that are functionally stable and interdependent (homeostasis) and can generally interbreed with one another but not with the living members of any other taxon at that level (reproductive isolation). Taxa at the life form level generally exhibit the broadest fit (adaptive radiation) of morphology (e.g., skin covering) and behavior (e.g., locomotion) to habitat (e.g., air, land, water).

The generalizations that hold across taxa of the same rank (i.e., a class of classes) are thus of a different logical type than generalizations that apply to only this or that taxon (i.e., a class of organisms). Termite, pig, and lemon tree are not related to one another by virtue of any simple relation of class inclusion or connection to some common hierarchical node but by dint of their common rank – in this case the level of folk species.

Notice that a system of rank is not simply a system of hierarchy. Hierarchy, that is, a structure of inclusive classes, is common to many cognitive domains, including the domain of artifacts. For example, CHAIR is often included under FURNITURE but not VEHICLE, and CAR is included under VEHICLE but not FURNITURE. Nevertheless, there is no ranked system of artifacts: there is no inferential link or inductive framework that spans both CHAIR and CAR or FURNITURE and VEHICLE by dint of a common rank, such as the artifact SPECIES or the artifact FAMILY. In other words, in many domains there is hierarchy without rank, but only in the domain of living kinds is there always rank.

Since Darwin, taxonomic induction is no longer based on a presumption of ranks as fixed levels of reality. For example, there is no special set of biological laws that applies to all and only species, as opposed to genera or varieties. Neither is any kind of organism still essentially defined by a fixed bundle of underlying properties. There is no set of properties whose members are severally necessary and jointly sufficient to determine what taxon an organism belongs to. Nevertheless, the conception of taxonomy as an inductive compendium and ranking of biologically important information remains "the foundation of the scientific method in biology: To most biologists, the 'best' classification must be the one that maximizes the probability that statements known to be true of two organisms are true of all members of the smallest [i.e., lowest ranked] taxon to which they both belong" (Warburton, 1967).

Full activation of this principle of category-based induction for all higher-order taxa and for the whole of the living kind taxonomy would require support from a unifying causal theory of the sort science was to provide. For

224   SCOTT ATRAN

example, upon finding that the bacteria *E-scheriehia coli* shares a hitherto unknown property with turkeys, it may take a Nobel Prize-winning insight and belief in the underlying genetic unity of living kinds to ''safely'' make the inference that all creatures belonging to the lowest-ranked taxon that contains both turkeys and *E. coli* also share that property. In this example, the lowest-ranked taxon just happens to include all organisms.

13.1.3 A COMPARISON WITH ITZAJ MAYA FOLKBIOLOGY

The Itzaj are the last Maya Indians native to the Petén tropical forest, once an epicenter of classic Maya civilization. Although the Itzaj cosmological system was sundered by the Spanish conquest and subsequent oppression, Itzaj folkbiological knowledge, including taxonomic competence as well as practical application, remains strikingly robust (Atran, 1993). This is not surprising; for if the core of folk knowledge about the biological world is spontaneously emitted and transmitted by minds, then it should be largely independent of (historically and culturally specific) institutionalized modes of communication.

Itzaj taxonomy. Itzaj Maya folkbiology provides evidence for generalizations about the specific taxonomic structure that delimits the universal domain of folkbiology but also for the influence of local ecology and culture. There is no common lexical entry for the plant kingdom in Itzaj; however, the numeral classifier *teek* is used with all and only plants. Plants generally fall under one of four mutually exclusive life forms: *ché* (trees), *pok-ché* (undergrowth-herbs, shrubs, bushes), *ak'* (vines), and *su'uk* (grasses). Each life form is distinguished by a particular stem habit, which is believed to be the natural outgrowth of every primary kind of *pu (k) sik'al* (species essence) included in that life form. A number of introduced and cultivated plants, however, are not affiliated with any of these life forms and are simply denoted *jun-teek* (lit. ''one plant''), as are many of the phylogenetically isolated plants, such as the cacti. Arguably, some may be thought of as *monospecific life forms*, in much the same way that the aardvark is the only known species representing its scientific order. All informants agree that mushrooms (*xikin˜che'*), lit. ''tree-ear'') have no *pu (k) sik'al* and are not plants but take life away from the trees that host them. Lichens and bryophytes (mosses and liverworts) are not considered to be plants to have an essence or to live.

The Itzaj term for animals (*b'a'al˜che'* = ''forest-thing'') polysemously indicates both the animal kingdom as a whole (including invertebrates, birds, and fish) and also a more restrictive grouping of quadrupeds (amphibians, reptiles, and, most typically, mammals). The quadrupeds are divided into two mutually exclusive life forms: walking animals (*b'a'al˜che' kuximal* = mammals except bats) and slithering animals (*b'a'al˜che' kujiltik ub'aj* = herpetofauna, i.e., amphibians and reptiles). Birds (*ch'iich'* including *sotz'* = bats) and fish (*käy*) exhibit patterns of internal structure that parallel those of the mammals (Coley et al., submitted).

For the life form of invertebrates (*mejen b'a'al˜ché*), whose morphology and ecological proclivity is very different from that of humans and other vertebrates, correspondence of folk to modern systematics blurs as one descends the ranks of the scientific ladder, and violations of scientific taxonomy tend to be more pronounced. Still, in this respect as in others, the categorical structure of Itzaj folkbiology differs little from that of any other folkbiological system, including that which initially gave rise to systematics, including evolutionary systematics.[6]

Like other folk around the world, Itzaj also have a number of relatively stable intermediate categories, both named and unnamed. Examples of named intermediate categories include *aak* (turtle), *kan* (snake), *kab'* (bee), *'xa'an* (palm trees). Examples of unnamed intermediate categories include locally occurring fragments of biological families, such as Cebidae (monkeys), Dasypractidae (agoutis and pacas), and Meliaceae (mahogany and tropical cedars). A number of intermediate categories are also polysemously named after a protoytpical species: *b'alum* (jaguars, in particular, and large felines, in general), *juj* (iguanas, in particular, and lizards, in general), *ya'* (chicle tree, in particular, and Sapotaceae trees, in general).

What follows is a brief account of findings in regard to all mammals represented in the local environments of the Itzaj and Michigan groups, respectively. For Itzaj we included bats, although Itzaj do not consider them mammals. For the students we included the emblematic wolverine, although it is now extinct in Michigan. Each group was tested in its native language (Itzaj and English) and included six men and six women. No statistically significant differences between men and women were found on the following tasks, which were designed to probe two general questions.

To WHAT EXTENT ARE DIFFERENT FOLKBIOLOGICAL TAXONO-MIES CORRELATED WITH ONE ANOTHER AND WITH A CORRE-SPONDING SCIENTIFIC (EVOLUTIONARY) TAXONOMY OF THE LOCAL FAUNA AND FLORA? Elsewhere (Atran, 1994), I describe the sorting procedures for eliciting individual taxonomies as well as mathematical techniques for aggregating individual taxonomies into a "cultural model" of the society's folkbiological system. Results indicate that the individual folkbiological taxonomies of Itzaj and students from rural Michigan are all more or less competent expressions of comparably robust cultural models of the biological world. To compare the structure and content of cultural models with one another, and with scientific models, we mathematically correlated each group's aggregate taxonomy with an evolutionary taxonomy (for details, see López et al., forthcoming).

The overall correlations were quite high both between evolutionary taxonomy and Itzaj taxonomy ($r = .81$) and between science and the folk taxonomy of Michigan students ($r = .75$). Somewhat surprisingly, Itzaj come even closer to a scientific appreciation of the local mammal fauna than do Michigan students. A comparison of higher-order taxa only (i.e., excluding folk species) still shows a strong correlation both for Itzaj ($r = .51$) and Michigan subjects ($r = .48$).

The overwhelming majority of mammal taxa in both cultures correspond to scientific species, and most of these taxa also correspond to monospecific genera: 30 of 40 (75 percent) basic Michigan mammal terms denote biological species, of which 21 (70 percent, or 53 percent of the total) are monospecific genera; 36 of 42 (86 percent) basic Itzaj mammal terms denote biological species, of which 25 (69 percent, or 60 percent of the total) are monospecific genera. At higher levels, Itzaj and Michigan folk taxonomic trees compare favorably to one another and to science, both in terms of number of nodes and levels at which nodes are formed. Agreement between the higher-order folk taxonomies and science is maximized at the level of the scientific suborder (i.e., the level between family and order), both for Itzaj and Michigan subjects, indicating that there is indeed an intermediate level in the folk taxonomies of both cultures (López et al., forthcoming).

A closer comparison of the folk groupings in the two cultures suggests that there are at least some universal cognitive factors at work in folkbiological classification that are mitigated or ignored by science. For example, certain groupings, such as felines + canines, are common to both Itzaj and Michigan students, although felines and canines are phylogenetically further from one another than either family is to other carnivore families (e.g., mustelids, procyonids). These groupings of large predators indicate that size and ferocity are salient classificatory dimensions in both cultures (cf. Henley, 1969; Rips et al., 1973). These are dimensions that a corresponding evolutionary classification of the local fauna does not markedly exhibit.

Other factors in the divergence between folk taxonomies and science are related both to science's incorporation of a worldwide perspective in classifying local biota and to its reliance on biologically "deep," theoretically weighted properties of internal anatomy and physiology. For example, the oppossum is the only marsupial present in North and Central America. Both Itzaj and the students relate the oppossum to skunks and porcupines because it shares with them numerous readily perceptible features of morphology and behavior. From a scientific vantage, however, the oppossum is taxonomically isolated from all the other locally represented mammals in a subclass of its own. Thus, if we exclude the oppossum from the comparison between the folk taxonomies and science, the correlation rises notably for Itzaj (from $r = .51$ to $r = .60$) and the students (from $r = .48$ to $r = .55$).

One factor mitigating the ability of Itzaj or Michigan students to appreciate the oppossum as scientists do is that there are no other locally present marsupials to relate the oppossum to. As a result, the most readily perceptible morphobehavioral difference between the oppossum and other local mammals – carrying its young in a pouch – cannot be linked to discoverable differences that would connect the oppossum to other marsupials and help to differentiate them from non-marsupials. The oppossum's pouch appears as just another characteristic morphobehavioral feature, like the porcupine's quills or the skunk's smell. Both Michigan students and Itzaj are apparently unaware of the deeper biological significance of the oppossum's lack of a placenta.

To what extent do the culturally specific theories and belief systems, such as science, shape folkbiological taxonomy? A striking folk bias is evident in Itzaj classification of snakes (*kan*). Questioning shows that people fear certain snakes. Only some of these are actually poisonous, but all those feared are nevertheless thought to sprout wings and extra heads and to fly off to the sea with their last victims – a likely cultural survival of the pre-Columbian cult of *kukul˜kan* ("feathered serpent"). In-depth interviews suggest that supposed danger is an overriding factor in preliminary snake sortings and supports one interpretation of a multi-dimensional scaling of these sortings (Atran, 1996).

A first interpretation of the phenomenon might be that in some cases the biological target is more determined by culturally specific interests than by readily perceptible phenotypic gaps in the distribution of local biota. Evidence from biology and social history, however, indicates a more complex story. Humans everywhere, it seems, are emotionally disposed to fear snakes (Seligman, 1971) and to socially ritualize this phobia (Marks, 1987) in recurrent cross-cultural themes, such as "the cult of the serpent" (Munkur, 1983).

The fact that people are spontaneously more inclined to exhibit and express fear of snakes than fear of much more lethal cultural artifacts – like swords, guns, and atom bombs – intimates an evolutionary explanation: such naturally selected phobias to resurgent perils in ancestral environments may have provided an extra margin for survival, whereas there would be no such direct natural selection of cognitive responses to the more recent dangers of particular cultural environments. To some extent, then, Itza snake classification seems an exception that proves the rule: folktaxonomies are more or less naturally selected conceptual structures – "habits of mind" – that are biologically pretuned to capture relevant and recurrent contents of those natural environments – "habits of the world" – in which hominid evolution occurred.

The best candidate for the cultural influence of theory in American folkbiology is science of course. Yet, the exposure of Michigan students to science education has little apparent effect on their folk taxonomy. From a scientific view, the students taxonomize no better than do Itzaj. Science's influence is at best marginal. For example, science may peripherally bear on the difference in the way Itzaj and Michigan students categorize bats. Itzaj deem bats to be birds (*ch'iich'*), not mammals (*b'a'al˜che'*).

Like Michigan students, Itzaj acknowledge in interviews that there is a resemblance between bats and small rodents. Because Itzaj classify bats with birds, they consider the resemblance to be only superficial and not indicative of a taxonomic relationship. By contrast, Michigan students "know" from schooling that bats are mammals. But this knowledge can hardly be taken as evidence for the influence of scientific *theory* on folk taxonomy. Despite learning that bats are mammals, the students go on to relate bats to mice and shrews just as Itzaj might if they did not already "know" that bats are birds. From an evolutionary stand, however, bats are taxonomically no closer to rats than to cats. The students, it seems, pay little or no attention to the deeper biological relationships science reveals. In other words, the primary influence of science education on folkbiological knowledge may be to fix category labels, which in turn may affect patterns of attention and induction.

The influence of science education on folk induction may also reflect *less actual knowledge* of theory *than willing belief* that scientific theory supports folk taxonomy. The high concordance between folk taxonomy and science, especially at the level of the folk species, provides Michigan students prima facie support for believing that their folk taxonomy is more or less on a scientific track. Given their belief that science has a causal story to tell, they assume that the same story pretty much holds for their folk taxonomy. This belief steers them into inductive errors but also to the realization that eliminating such errors leads to a closer accord with science – albeit a modest one.

For example, given that a skunk and oppossum share a deep biological property, Michigan students are less likely to conclude that all mammals share the property than if it were shared by a skunk and a bear. From a scientific standpoint, the students are using the right reasoning strategy (i.e., diversity-based inference) but reaching the wrong conclusion because of a faulty taxonomy (i.e., the belief that skunks are taxonomically further from bears than from oppossums). But if *told* that oppossums are phylogenetically more distant from skunks than bears are, then the students readily revise their taxonomy to make the correct inference. Still, it would be misleading to claim that the students thereby use theory to revise their taxonomy, although a revision occurs *in accordance with* scientific theory.

American students from rural Michigan and Itzaj Maya both project biological properties from typical taxa to superordinate groups, as determined by lowest mean taxonomic distance (calculated in terms of the intervening number of hierarchical nodes between a given taxon and every other taxon in the superordinate group). Thus, when people learn that an unknown biologically related property, such as a disease, is possessed by a typical species that shares many properties with other members of the same taxonomic category, then they are more likely to generalize than if the same fact had been learned about some atypical species (cf. Rips, 1975). Nevertheless, the Itzaj and Michigan students differ in their appreciation of what counts as typical taxa.

For example, large felines appear at the bottom of American typicality ratings and at the top of Itzaj ratings, although the actual frequency of occurrence and encounter with large felines is nowadays roughly comparable in rural Michigan and central Peten (López et al., forthcoming). By contrast, frequently encountered squirrels and raccoons appear toward the top of the American typicality ratings but toward the bottom of Itzaj typicality ratings. This is so for typicality ratings indirectly derived from the taxonomy itself (mean taxonomic distance) or from direct subject ratings of how "typical" (on a seven-point scale for Americans) or how "true a representative" (*jach* for Itzaj) each species is of the mammals in general. Similarly birds at the top of Rosch's (1975) typicality list for Americans (e.g., plain-colored passerines such as sparrows) are never considered "true representatives" (*jach*) of BIRD (*ch'iich'*) for Itzaj, whereas birds at the bottom of Rosch's typicality list are (e.g., Galliformes such as turkeys). This is the case despite the fact that the frequency of occurrence and encounter with plain-colored passerines is about the same in rural Michigan and central Peten and always greater than the frequency of occurrence and encounter with Galliformes.

In one study, we asked both midwestern Americans and Itzaj to indicate the "truest" birds among a series of 104 scaled color drawings of the birds of Peten. The Americans invariably placed passeriformes, such as flycatchers and orioles, at the top of their list and Galliformes, such as the ocellated turkey, crested guan, and great curassow, at the bottom. Itzaj did just the reverse. When asked which birds were more likely to share a disease with other birds, Americans and Itzaj both strongly preferred their respective truest birds. In justifying choices, Americans argued that the less remarkable and more frequently encountered passeriformes were more like most other birds than the remarkable galliformes were like most other birds. In other words, the passeriformes had a higher maximum average similarity to the birds as a whole. By contrast, Itzaj tended to argue that diseases of the galliformes would have greater impact on other living things in the forest, including other birds. This is supposedly because of their remarkable size, behavior, and value (in the food chain) to other salient birds (predators), mammals (large carnivores), trees (large nut and fruit trees), and humans.

In each case for which we have Itzaj typicality measures, the most typical folk representatives are large, perceptually striking, culturally important, and ecologically prominent: the jaguar and its allies for the mammal life form, the ocellated turkey and its allies for the bird life form, the fer-de-lance and its allies for the named intermediate category of snakes, and the cabbage palm and its allies for the named intermediate category of palms. Each can grow large but is not the largest of its category (coup are bigger than jaguars, certain vultures are bigger than ocellated turkeys, boa constrictors are bigger than fer-de-lance, and corozo palms are bigger than cabbage palms).

The three dimensions of perceptual, cultural, and ecological salience are all seemingly necessary to a determination of typicality, but none alone appears to be sufficient. Nor is there any one criterion or well-defined group of criteria that determines any one dimension. Each typical representative is otherwise physically striking, but in a different way (the jaguar's luxuriant coat, the ocellated turkeys magnificent feathers, the fer-de-lance's yellow throat, the young cabbage palm's broadleaf cover of the forest floor, and the mature cabbage palm's strikingly tall and leafless trunk). Each is culturally important but in a different way (jaguars are lords of the forest, ocellated turkeys define the country's bounty, fer-de-lance is the most feared creature of all, and cabbage palms provide the thatch for all types of shelter).

Each is salient to the forest's ecological composition and to people's place in it, but in a different way (the jaguar's habitat – some 50 square kilometers – determines the extent of a forest section, the ocellated turkey's presence indicates where game is abundant, where the fer-de-lance strikes determines where people should fear to tread, and where there are cabbage palms human settlement is possible). Indeed the three dimensions seem to be so bound up with one another that it is difficult, if not impossible, to completely distinguish them for any particular case. In other words, typicality for the Itzaj appears to be an integral part of the human (cultural relevant) ecology.

ECOLOGICAL UNDERSTANDING THROUGH FOLKTAXONOMY. Concern with ecology is also likely one reason for Itzaj "failure" to apply the so-called diversity principle to biological reasoning. According to this principle, when things are equal (e.g., when taxa are equally typical), then a biological property shared by two taxonomically close taxa (e.g., a wolf and a coyote) is less likely to be shared by a superordinate group of taxa (e.g., mammals) than a property shared by two taxonomically distant taxa (e.g., a wolf and a gopher). The diversity principle corresponds to the fundamental principle of induction in scientific systematics: a property shared by two organisms (or taxa) is likely shared by all organisms falling under the smallest (or lowest ranked) taxon containing the two.

Thus, American folk seem to use their biological taxonomies much as scientists do when given information that is unfamiliar to infer what is likely in the face of uncertainty: if informed that goats and mice share a hitherto unknown property, they are more likely to project that property to mammals than if informed that goats and sheep do. By contrast, Itzaj tend to use similarly structured taxonomies to search for a causal ecological explanation as to why such an unlikely event should occur: for example, bats may have passed on the property to goats and mice by biting them, but a property would not likely need an ecological agent in order to be shared by goats and sheep.

In the absence of a theory – or at least the presumption of a theory – of causal unity underlying disparate species, there is no compelling reason to consider a property discovered in two distant species as biologically intrinsic or essential to both. In such circumstances it may make more sense to consider the counter-intuitive presence of a property in dissimilar species as the likely result of an extrinsic or ecologically "accidental" cause. It is not that Itzaj do not understand the diversity principle. In tests involving diversity-based reasoning in other domains, Itzaj performed successfully as a group. For example, when asked whether a person should spend a fixed amount of time visiting one part of a forest or many parts in order to determine if that forest should be settled or cultivated, Itzaj invariably opted for the latter alternative.

Note that in both the American and Itzaj cases similarly structured taxonomies are providing the distance metrics over which biological induction takes place. For the Americans, taxonomic distance indicates the extent to which underlying causes are more likely to predict shared biological properties than are surface relationships. For Itzaj, taxonomic distance suggests the extent to which ecological agents are likely to be involved in predicting biological properties that do not conform to surface relationships. A priori, either stance might be correct. For example, diseases are clearly biologically related; however, the distribution of some hitherto unknown disease among a given animal population could well involve epidemiological factors that essentially depend on both inherent biological susceptibility and ecological agency.

More generally, what "counts" as a biological cause or property may be different for folk, like the Itzaj, who necessarily live in intimate awareness of their biological surroundings, and those, like American folk, whose awareness is less necessary and intimate. For most Itzaj, awareness of biological causes and properties may be directly related to ecology, whereas for most American folk the ecological ramifications of biological causes and properties may remain obscure. Historically, the West's development of worldwide scientific systematics explicitly involved disregard of ecological relationships and of the colors, smells, tastes, and textures that constitute the most intimate channels of recognition and access to the surrounding world of organic beings.

If this scenario is anywhere near correct, then an integrative (folk)biological theory – however rudimentary – *cannot be* the cognitive mechanism responsible for the ontology of living kinds, as some researchers have proposed (Carey, 1985; Murphy and Medin, 1985; Keil, 1989; Gelman and Coley, 1991). In other words, it is not the elaboration of a theory of biological causality that progressively distinguishes people's understanding of the (folk) species concept as it applies to (non-human) animals and plants from their understanding of concepts of inert substances, artifacts, or persons. Rather, there seems to be *a universal, a priori presumption* that species constitute "natural kinds" by virtue of their special (initially unknown and perhaps unknowable) teleological natures, and that species further group together naturally into ranked taxonomies. This spontaneous arrangement of living things into taxonomies of natural kinds thus constitutes a prior set of constraints on *any and all possible theories* about the causal relations between living kinds.

13.1.4 SCIENCE AND COMMON SENSE

Aristotle was the first in the West (or anywhere else, it seems) to advance the theoretical presumption of overarching causal unity and underlying lawful uniformity for domains of "natural kinds," including biological kinds as well as kinds of inert physical substances (Atran, 1985). This strategy eventually enabled Western science to extend these natural domains from just local relationships among their respective kinds to the whole planet and cosmos. In the history of biology, or natural history, a series of taxonomic types emerged to provide a system of reference for the comparative study of organisms. It is by developing notions of species, genera, families, and classes that natural historians managed to progressively standardize what was already – at least to some extent – common to the viewpoints of ordinary folk everywhere. Ultimately, this framework would provide a practical basis for the comprehensive survey of beings the world over and a conceptual foundation for the theoretical elaboration of their interrelations. This elaboration would finally embrace all living kinds – including humankind – into a *theory* of biology.

Proto-theory to scientific theory: Taxonomic constraints. Readily perceptible properties of taxa (morphotypes) are generally good predictors of deeper, underlying shared properties and may originally provide the basis for living kind categories. Initially, the underlying essential structures are unknown and merely presumed to (teleologically) cause the observable regularities in biological categories. Attention to this causal link and a cognitive endeavor to know it better leads to awareness that this correlation between surface and deep features is not perfect. Added knowledge about these deeper properties may then lead to category modification. For example, most adult Americans categorize whales and bats as mammals despite the many superficial properties shared with fish and birds, respectively.

Despite the ''boot-strapping'' revision of taxonomy implied in this example, notice how much did not change: neither the abstract hierarchical schema of folk taxonomy nor – in a crucial sense – even the kinds involved. Bats, whales, fish, mammals, and birds did not just vanish from common sense to arise anew in science like Athena springing from the head of Zeus. Rather, there was a re-distribution of affiliations between antecedently perceived kinds. What had altered was the construal of the underlying natures of those kinds, with a consequent re-distribution of kinds and a re-appraisal of properties pertinent to reference.

Vitalism's enduring nature and the taxonomic tree of life. Vitalism is the belief that biological kinds – and their maintaining parts, properties, and processes – are not reducible to the contingent relations that govern inert matter. Its cultural expression varies (cf. Hatano and Inagaki, 1994). Within any given culture, people may have varying interpretations and degrees of attachment to this belief: some who are religiously inclined may think that a ''spiritual'' essence determines biological causality; others of a more scientific temperament might hold that systems of laws that suffice for physics and chemistry do not necessarily suffice for biology. Many, if not most, working biologists (including cognitive scientists) implicitly retain at least a minimal commitment to vitalism: they acknowledge that physico-chemical laws should suffice for biology but suppose that such laws are not adequate in their current form and must be enriched by further laws whose predicates (i.e., natural kinds) are different from those of inert physics and chemistry.[7]

Moreover, it is not at all clear how complete elimination of teleological expressions (concepts that are defined functionally) from biological theory can be pursued without forsaking a powerful and fruitful conceptual scheme for understanding physiology, morphology, disease, and evolution. In cognitive science, the belief that biological systems, such as the mind/brain, are not wholly reducible to electronic circuitry, like computers, is a pervasive attitude that implicitly drives considerable polemic but also much creative theorizing. Thus, even if this sort of vitalism represents a lingering folk belief that science might seek to ultimately discard, it remains an important and perhaps indispensable cognitive heuristic for regulating scientific inquiry – a ladder that must first be climbed before being thrown away.

Similar considerations apply to the use of taxonomic hierarchies in systematics. By tabulating the ranges of extant and extinct genera, families, classes, and so on, systematists are able to provide a usable compendium of changing diversity throughout the history of life. For example, recent comparisons of the relative numbers of families of insects and flowering plants reveal the surprising fact that insects were just as taxonomically diverse before the emergence of flowering plants as after. Consequently, evolutionary effects of plant evolution on the adaptive radiation of insects are probably less profound than previously thought (Labandeira & Sepkoski, 1993).

Again, the heuristic value of (scientifically elaborated) folk-based strategies for cosmic inquiry is compelling despite the fact that evolutionary theorists are well aware that there are no "true" distinctions between these various taxonomic levels. Such basic "common sense" may remain *psychologically valid* for everyday understanding of the world but perhaps not *epistemically valid* for the vastly extended or reduced dimensions of modern science. In Kantian terms: although common sense no longer *constitutes* true knowledge of the cosmos, it still *regulates* how we come to know anything at all about the world.

13.1.5 SUMMARY: THE COGNITIVE UNIVERSALITY OF BIOLOGY

Humans everywhere, it appears, have similar folkbiological schema composed of essence-based species and ranked ordering of species into lower-order and higher-order groups. To some extent, these groups within groups represent the routine products of innate "habits of mind," naturally selected to grasp relevant and recurrent "habits of the world." They are not as arbitrary and hence not as variable across cultures as, say, the gathering of stars in constellations.

In the history of biology or natural history, a series of taxonomic types emerged to provide a reference system for the comparative study of organisms. Developing notions of species, genera, families, and classes, naturalists progressively standardized what was already common to ordinary folk ways of thinking. Ultimately, this framework would provide a basis for the comprehensive survey of beings the world over and a conceptual foundation for the theoretical elaboration of their interrelations. This elaboration would finally embrace all living kinds – including humankind – into a theory of biology.

Accordingly, an integrative (folk)biological theory – however rudimentary – cannot be the cognitive mechanism responsible for the ontology of living kinds. Rather, the spontaneous arrangement of living things into ranked taxonomies of essentialistic species constitutes a prior set of constraints on any and all possible theories about the causal relations between living kinds. Recent cross-cultural evidence among Maya and American folk indicates this is the case.

Itzaj Maya and American students use similarly structured taxonomies in somewhat different ways in order to extend understanding of the world in the face of uncertainty. In principle, either way might succeed. For centuries, Itzaj have managed to so use their folkbiological structures to integrate and maintain a fairly stable, context-sensitive ecological order. In a different way, scientists who use taxonomies as heuristics for reaching a more global, context-free understanding of biological relationships generate important new discoveries of properties that do not conform to surface appearances. American folk unwittingly pursue a compromise of sorts: maintaining ecologically valid categories but reasoning about them as if they were theory based. Irrelevancy often results.

13.2 Natural causality and the supernatural

This part examines the notion that people who live in "traditional" cultures – where magic, myth, and religion are interdependent and socially prominent – live in conceptual worlds that are profoundly different from our own world (or each other's worlds). To the contrary, our work and that of other psychologists and cognitive anthropologists indicates that

(a) There is striking recurrence of symbolic content across historically isolated cultures (e.g., incorporeal spirits, immortal beings, monstrous species hybrids, metamorphosis and reincarnation, animated substances).
(b) This recurrence owes almost entirely to universal cognitive mechanisms that process cultural input (information) in ways that are variously triggered but subsequently unaffected by the nature of that input (e.g., spirits and immortals are not mindless and so have memories, beliefs, desires, sufferings, etc.; monsters and reincarnates still eat and grow; animated objects don't pass through walls, whereas angels and ghosts may do so but likely not through each other).
(c) These universal mechanisms are the very same core set of cognitive modules that are responsible for the sorts of factual, commonsense beliefs about the everyday world that are intuitively obvious to everyone in the world (naive physics, naive biology, naive psychology, naive sociology).

As for supernatural beliefs:

(d) They are just as counter-intuitive for the people who think them true as for those who think them false (e.g., wine as the blood of Christ, a wafer as his body).
(e) People who believe such counter-intuitive beliefs to be true do so by ritually proscribing situations of conflict with intuitively mundane beliefs (e.g., devout Catholics are not routinely cannibals); such people routinely invoke non-conflictual aspects of intuitive belief systems to give mundane content to "impossible worlds" (e.g., God is everywhere but likely not in the trash and ought to behave like a good family man, except in bed).
(f) Belief in the supernatural does not involve causal thinking that is misapplied or distinctive (e.g., there is no sense in which shaman, sorcerer, or priest believe their actions or sayings will initiate a chain of material causes that will change the matter of the world, only its cultural ecology).

13.2.1 SPURIOUSLY INCOMMENSURABLE WORLDVIEWS
By and large, anthropologists seeking to show deep cultural differences do so by attempting to show how curious native life is in terms of:

joking, punning, promising, metaphor, irony, gossip, lying, cheating, insult, skepticism, deceit, conceit, pride, sacrifice, prayer, magic, religion, storytelling, betting, marriage, cooking, classifying nature, reckoning time, counting, navigation and landscape, mapping, litigation, gift exchange, etiquette, hospitality, feasting, mourning, interpretation of dreams, sex and food taboos, food sharing, morality, crime, punishment, medicine, nosology, disaster-relief routines, common defense, self-defense, murder, warfare, political negotiation, property, marriage, family, kinship, song, dance, architecture, painting, and so on.

The most discerning anthropologists have convincingly argued that it is fruitless to attempt a definition of *any* such synthetic notion in terms of necessary and sufficient conditions (Needham, 1975; Geertz, 1983; Shweder, 1991). For example, activity interpreted as sacrifice or marriage in one society might be interpreted as murder or the violation of a sex taboo in another. Contrary to earlier proponents of evolutionary and diffusionist models of culture, anthropology today holds that systematic differences between "our" notions and corresponding "native" notions are not simply matters of more or less of something. Even within our own culture, there may be no hard and fast boundaries between many such notions, such as warfare and politics, magic and religion, marriage and property, and so forth.

Nevertheless, when anthropologists use these synthetic notions (or others like them) to show cross-cultural differences – as they invariably do – they also invariably assume that each such useful notion expresses at least some family resemblance of cross-cultural reality (cf. Brown, 1991). The anthropologist creates these terminological tools of the trade precisely in order to translate and synthesize what to the casual observer would otherwise seem to be a diverse and disjoint array of native notions. Indeed, a studious endeavor to so paraphrase and digest a native notion in synthetic terms is the only way anthropologists have devised so far of conveying to us their understanding of what "the natives" think and do.

Hedges to the effect that the natives do not mean what we mean about something requires at least some overlap in what we both mean (i.e., local commensurability). To give a rather mundane but revealing example: Suppose that you make your first visit to France. You visit the Versailles Palace and remark, *"Regardez cette belle chaise."* By this you mean to translate your thought, "Look at that beautiful chair," while pointing to the armchair of Louis XVI. Suppose your fellow English-speaking tourists understand about as much French as you do and do not see you pointing. They would not know, then, whether you had referred to Louis' armchair or to the nearby armless chair of Marie Antoinette. But if your French tour guide does not see you pointing and if your accent intimates a good command of French, then she might think you are referring only to the nearby armless chair of Marie Antoinette. She would likely rule out your referring to Louis' armchair because the word for armchair in French is *fauteuil* and not *chaise*. In contrast to most English speakers, for whom *armchair* is merely a subordinate category of the basic category *chair*, most French speakers consider *fauteuil* and *chaise* to be contrasting basic categories. But if your guide saw you pointing, then she probably would think that you had mistranslated your thought. Even if she corrected you, however, by answering, *"C'est un beau fauteuil"* (It is a beautiful armchair), you might simply infer that she was only confirming what you said with some added precision, namely, that the chair, or more precisely the armchair, was indeed beautiful. Increased exposure to French language and culture might eventually convince you that you had made a linguistic mistake. Or it might convince you that the French were simply unnecessarily nitpicking about certain things in their culture, especially if you were to find out during a visit to Canada that people in Quebec use *chaise* to refer to chairs with and without arms.

Even within our own culture, there is a constant if implicit negotiation of meaning of a similar sort. For example, someone's use of *cup* might overlap with someone else's use of *mug*. True, Maya statements such as *aj-waay k-u-tz'ik u-yol*, which the anthropologist might paraphrase as "witches take souls," allow much greater latitude in negotiations over meaning: ranging from positivist interpretations of native utterances and beliefs as generalized or as mistaken explanations of diseases to romantic interpretations of a more convoluted, hermeneutical sort. But even in such cases: "Charity is forced on us; whether we like it or not, if we want to understand others, we must count them right in most matters" (Davidson, 1984:197). This is so whether our negotiations over meaning lead us to conclude that there is simply a difference of opinion over our respective meaning boundaries or a difference over what in fact each of us holds to be true or false.[8]

Notice, however, that *any* of these negotiations over meanings presuppose a general agreement on what statements both we and our interlocutors take to be sensible (true or false) and a vast agreement in our beliefs. If not for this common "something," it would be inconceivable that an anthropologist would be able to penetrate the worldview of a native group in the year or two it usually takes to do so (about the same time it takes an infant to learn a language). This is not to say that the anthropologist learns all there is to know about the native culture (indeed, neither the anthropologist nor the native may ever learn all there is to know about their own respective cultures). But even the dullest anthropologist quickly intuits that, in most respects, the native thinks pretty much like the anthropologist. Because this fact is intuited so rapidly and effortlessly, the anthropologist is then able to leisurely search for the profound *differences* that will earn a dissertation, tenure, or renown as "The Sorcerer's Apprentice."

13.2.2 SOME IMAGINARY ITZAJ MAYA ENTITIES

Across cultures throughout the world people can readily identify beliefs that they consider religious, mythical, or magical. In most cultural settings where such beliefs arise, they arise together. Anthropologists and psychologists have customarily regarded such networks of beliefs as "symbolic systems" or "cosmological theories" that pervade or determine a culture's worldview. The apparent diversity of worldview is the main support for cultural relativism – the doctrine that peoples in different societies think differently about how the world is constituted and conceive different ranges of empirical knowledge and ways of attaching meaning to things.

The most striking support for cultural relativism is thought to come from those "primitive," "exotic," or "traditional" societies where, from a Western standpoint, natural and supernatural phenomena are so seemingly intermeshed that the people in those societies just live in "another world." Consider, for example, the sorts of symbolic propositions typically stated by Itzaj Maya speakers and recorded in field notes:

I.   "The sorcerer" (*aj waay*) "transformed himself" (*tusutk'esaj ub' aj*) "into a dog" (*ti pek'*). The *waay* "makes bad sickness" (*kumentik k'ak'as koja'anil*) and "steals" (*kuyoklik*) "one's soul" (*uyol mak*). You need a *waay* to catch and kill a *waay*. I remember a *waay* who turned into a "pig" (*k'ek'en*) and another into a "shadow biter" (*chib'il˜b'o'oy* = "small gekko"), but all the other sorcerers I heard about turned into "village animals" (*b'a'a˜che'il kaj*) to be near the [victim's] house.

II. "A person" (*kristyaanoj*) "ensouls" (*kutz'ik uyol*) "a house" (*ti naj*) and the house "has a soul" (*yan uyol*). A person "can ensoul" (*patal utz'ik uyol*) "what he makes" (*ta' b'a'ax kumentik* = artifacts). "A bad wind" (*k'ak'as ik'*) brings sickness and takes its soul. Then you need "a curer" (*aj pul˜yaj*) to make a "sacrifice" (*sakrifiisyoj*) with "incense" (*pom* = copal resin).

III. Some "persons" (*krityaanojoo'*), the "*k'änte'* family" (*k'änte'*), say their name is "howler monkey" (*aj b'aatz'*) because they were howler monkeys before; the "spider monkey" (*aj tuuchaj*) is *tesukun* (another family).

IV. "One-animate wood fairy" (*juntuul arux*), follows you "into the forest" (*ti k'aax*). Sometimes you can feel it because it comes as "the possessor of the wind" (*uyumil ik'*). Sometimes you can tell it's there because it turns itself into "a small child" (*mo'nok paal*). But once it stole my mocassins just before I caught a glimpse of it. You have to catch it before it turns to wind. . . . Now when an *arux* comes all you have to do is turn on a radio; they hate listening to radios. You don't see them much in the forest any more; they don't like the [newcomers] who are felling the forest.

V.   "One-round *sas˜tun*" (*jun kuul sas˜tun*), you can hear it whirl as it flies by. I saw one on the table in [a curer's house], a clear stone. It flies when it's looking for a curer who will treat it well, bathe in it in "strong water" [*yek ja'*] = drinking alcohol]. Once the *sas˜tun* came to a curer but left the next day. The curer looks into the *sas˜tun* to see if a sick person will live or die, seeing the way lines lie [that form in the clear center]. It can tell who stole your pig. Nobody, not even a curer, can ever find the *sas˜tun*; it finds you.

VI. "The fer-de-lance and its companions" (*uyet'ok k'ok'o*, i.e., vipers, coral snakes, and other snakes considered poisonous), only deaf people can see their feet. When a *k'ok'o'* gets "old" (*chämach*), it "opens up the earth" (*kujenkesik a' lu'um*), "sprouts horns" (*kuch'iil ukaachoj*), and "has wings also" (*yan uxik' xan*), some "more heads" (*maas yaab' upol*), and flies to the East" (*tak ti lak'in*) "to the sea" (*ti k'ab' naab'*). The East is the source of "everything" (*tulakal*).

VII. "God" (*dyoos*, i.e., the Spanish God) "knows everything" (*uyojel tu-lakal*), so you must always confess the truth to him. . . . He is every-where, all around [waving hand around] up and down [puts hand under table]. But "our Big Ancestors lived before God" (*ki nukuch ch'ib'al kuxlajoo' taanil ti dyoos*).

Itzaj clearly believe what they say here is true. We, just as clearly, cannot believe what they say here is true. Although we may try to translate what they say in terms that make some factual sense to us, it is unlikely that any factual sense we make out of what they say would make relevant sense to them. For if such statements do represent commonsense facts for the Itzaj, then obviously their ways of deciding what the facts are differ significantly from ours. And if such statements do represent commonsense facts for the Itzaj, then obviously their ways of deciding what the facts are differ signif-icantly from ours. And if such statements do not represent commonsense facts for the Itzaj, then our giving them some factual sense misses the point.

13.2.3 THE MUNDANE CONSEQUENCES OF SUPERNATURAL BELIEFS

From the foregoing we might conclude that we and the Itzaj just live in conceptually different everyday worlds. That people abide such apparently different worlds may, in turn, be taken as support for the flexibility of a human mind; that is, a mind unconstrained by innately determined, content-giving cognitive structures.

Consider, first, the notion that cultural diversity entails lack of innate di-versity. Take any culture, say American English culture, and the set of innate abilities needed to acquire American culture (including the English language). For argument's sake, assume such innate abilities are simple and few. Now, take another culture, say, Itzaj Maya. It is logically the case that the innate abilities required to learn American and Itzaj cultures (including the English *and* Itzaj languages) must be at least as complex and diverse as the innate abilities required to learn just American culture. Certainly they can't be *less* diverse and complex. So, if the diversity and complexity of innate abilities involved in "acculturation" is affected *at all* by the degree of diversity be-tween cultures, then the relationship between innate diversity and cultural diversity *must be positive*: more cultural diversity entails more innate diver-sity for the mind of the individual learner (cf. Sperber, 1987; Chomsky, 1988).[9]

If it were true that we and the Maya, say, live in profoundly different conceptual worlds, then how could the anthropologist ever become aware of this? We can observe, say, goldfish and infer from their behavior that it is not likely motivated by the same conceptual structures that motivate our own behavior. But we cannot as easily infer how *different* goldfish conceptual structures are from our own or even what conceptual structures, if any, they might have. Because we interact with, say, dogs and can predict some of their behavior as a function of our own, we may be inclined to attribute some conceptual belief structure to a dog's "pretending" (e.g., to let you take the ball off the ground before snatching it up at the last possible moment). But we also readily intuit profound differences between a dog's pretending and a child's (if only in the number of embedded levels of propositional attitude).[10]

The notion that people in different cultures live in different conceptual worlds is rooted in two false premises, which are interrelated: (A) people process symbolic beliefs in the same way that they process commonsense beliefs and therefore do not recognize a principled distinction between intuitive and counter-intuitive beliefs; (B) symbolic beliefs pervade thinking about the everyday world, so that there is no clear distinction between natural and supernatural phenomena.

There are two objections to A: First (A1), if symbolic beliefs were processed in the same way as commonsense beliefs, then the former would invariably contradict the latter. Second (A2), magical, mythical, and religious beliefs are as counter-intuitive for people who hold and transmit them as they seem to us.

(A1) If symbolic beliefs were processed just like beliefs of brute fact, then any conclusion would logically follow from any belief. Consequently, any systematic intentional behavior, much less any systematic knowledge, would be unimaginable. Suppose, for example, that Itzaj held stories I to VII above to be true states of affairs in the same way that they hold the following corresponding inferences to represent true states of affairs:

(i) Humans and animals belong to mutually exclusive core domains, whose respective members behave in accordance with distinctive causal schema. For example, only humans usually behave in accordance with embedded beliefs and desires, so that animals cannot intentionally plan a person's sickness or death. Moreover, members of one animal species, like the pig, cannot transform themselves into members of another species.

(ii) Humans and artifacts belong to different core domains. For example, houses do not live and therefore cannot get sick.

(iii) Same as (i).

(iv) Animate beings and inert, non-solid physical phenomena belong to different core domains. For example, stones are not sensate and therefore cannot fear the sound of a radio.

(v) Inert solid objects, animate beings that can fly by themselves, and entities with minds belong to different core domains. For example, inert solid objects cannot defy gravity, remember things, or have beliefs, desires, and knowledge.

(vi) Winged creatures that can fly (*ch'iich'* = bats and birds save chickens) and snakes (*kan*) belong to mutually exclusive folkbiological taxonomies, whose respective members behave in accordance with distinctive causal schema. For example, snakes can only displace themselves over long distances when the full length of their body is in contact with a hard surface. Snakes can kill people, "birds" cannot.

(vii) Non-physical phenomena and entities with minds belong to different core domains. Non-physical phenomena have no independent causal schema attached to them and therefore have no spatial or temporal location or minds with memories, intentions, and knowledge. By contrast, entities with minds cannot remember everything there is to know and must rely on the intentions of other entities with minds in order to apprehend what the others know.

Anyone processing beliefs I to VII and (i) to (vii) in the same register should suspect that someone eating a pork chop might be a cannibal, expect healthy houses to give birth to little houses, believe that animals species can interbreed as indiscriminately as people can mate, turn on the radio to stop the wind from spreading fire, avoid provoking rocks that could fly up and strike you dead, look for flocks of snakes in the air above the Caribbean to the East but not above the Pacific in the West, confess their sins to a toothpick because if God is everywhere then God is there.

During the long months that I lived in an Itzaj village, I never observed anything remotely resembling such behavior, although I must admit that I did not look for it. Still, for such behavior to manifest itself anywhere, it would have to manifest itself everywhere if, indeed, Itzaj behavior were truly irrational, "pre-rational," or "alternatively rational" in this way. If it ever were, survival would not be for long.

Not only is there no evidence that Itzaj behave in accordance with a defective or alternative rationality in going about their daily affairs, but there seems to be a cross-cultural method to the apparent madness of their symbolic beliefs. Thus, Itzaj *waay* have many of the characteristics of sorcerers, witches, and shamans the world over, including a capacity and desire to do evil in an animal guise. Itzaj "ensoul" some of their more important artifacts much as other "traditional" peoples do, like the native folk of West Futuna-Aniwa in Polynesia. Itzaj association of families to animal species is likely a vestige of totemism, which was common among the historical Maya and widespread over all the earth's habitable continents. Itzaj *arux* have many of the same characteristics of Irish elves and Russian wood fairies. The Itzaj *sas'tun*, which is rooted in pre-Columbian tradition, has many of the same features as the Arabic *tilasm* (talisman or crystal ball). The Itzaj story of flying serpents, which is related to the pre-Columbian "feathered-serpent" cults of *quetzal-coatl* (Toltec) and *kukul-kan* (Maya), resembles the flying serpents of *One Thousand and One Arabian Nights* and has many similar or inverted aspects of the ancient Egyptian myth of the phoenix. If we reject the unlikely possibility that these thematic recurrences stem from historical contact and diffusion or are spontaneous instantiations of a Platonistic set of innate religious forms (e.g., Jungian archetypes), then how could such apparent recurrences take place across cultures?

13.2.4 RELIGIOUS RECURRENCE
(A2) As an initial approach to the problem of the recurrence of mythico-religious themes, Pascal Boyer (1994) begins from the premise that "*unnat-*

uralness is an intuitive property.'' It is *because* supernatural phenomena are so outrageous that they are so easily remembered and transmitted among minds in a culture and also why they figure so prominently in anthropological reports across cultures. By violating the core principles of universal, commonsense empirical ontology – and the ordinary causal schemata that apply to our (and everybody else's) everyday world – such phenomena become immediately attention getting. This makes them easily communicable and memorable, hence prime candidates for cultural survival.

Although necessary, however, being strongly counter-intuitive is not sufficient to assure cultural survival. Indeed, if outrageousness was all there was to supernatural beliefs, they could not survive very long. This is because, being apparently contradictory or contrary to our most entrenched factual beliefs, they carry with them no constraints on interpretation. Public expression of supernatural beliefs is strikingly poor in assumptions from which further information can be inferred. Almost nothing is directly derivable from them.

Take Einstein's (1948) omnipotent but impersonal God, who not only neglects to play dice with the universe but neither interferes in human affairs nor natural events. Such a causally all-powerful entity is surely as counter-intuitive as an invisible father figure. But at least with the Old Testament's stern patriarch we can seek solace by readily inferring a rich set of intuitively plausible relationships to the world we know. With Einstein's God, we can intuit almost no place further for the idea to go. Thus, while Einstein's God may, in fact, be the one true God, its chances for cultural fame, devotion, and a recurring spot on CNN is infinitesimal.

What, then, might be the sufficient criterion for making strongly counter-intuitive beliefs cultural survivors? Outrageous beliefs should not be maximally counter-intuitive, only *optimally* so. This means that violations of our basic commonsense ontologies should be limited enough so that the rich intuitive bases of these ontologies remain largely intact and thus readily mobilizable for generating inferences. The intuitive inferences that any optimally counter-intuitive set of assumptions might evoke will then be, by necessity, highly constrained and easily remembered. In other words, by violating intuitive core beliefs, optimally counter-intuitive assumptions canonically activate the rich residue of the non-violated core. As Boyer (1994) aptly puts it:

> to create religious ideas that have some chance of cultural survival . . .
> one must strike a balance between requirements of imagination (attention-demanding potential) and learnability (inferential potential). . . . One
> of the ways of striking a balance is to take all the intuitive ontologies as
> confirmed, except a few assumptions which are then explicitly described
> as violated in the case of the religious entity. . . . Such assumptions are
> more likely than others to be easily acquired, memorized and transmitted than other assumptions . . . they are certainly not universal, but they
> are more frequent than other types of religious ideas.

To support his analysis, Boyer builds on some recent work in experimental psychology (Kelly and Keil, 1985) and cognitive anthropology (Atran and

Sperber, 1991). Analyzing Ovid's *Metamorphoses* and other similar folktales, Kelly and Keil showed that metamorphoses were far more frequent between adjacent categories of universal ontology (e.g., PERSON ↔ ANIMAL ↔ PLANT) than between non-adjacent categories (e.g., PERSON ↔ ARTIFACT ↔ NON-SOLID SUBSTANCE). The further apart the ontological categories are from one another in the "ordinary ontology tree" (Sommers, 1959; Pap, 1960; Keil, 1979), the wider the range of causal expectations suspended by the metamorphosis and the poorer the range of inferences that might be evoked to give some ordinary sense to an extraordinary being. As Atran and Sperber note in relation to animal symbolism: "only to the degree that . . . impossible worlds remain bridged to the everyday world can information about them be stored and evoked in plausible grades."[11]

13.2.5 MYTH

Public expressions of supernatural beliefs rarely, if ever, take the form of generalized or universally quantified statements, such as "God reasons," "all spirits fly" or "every frog turns into a prince." Instead, supernatural phenomena are usually embedded in explicitly contextualized episodes: for example, "the *arux* came as a child to steal my mocassins but disappeared as a gust of wind before I could catch it." Such personalized instances suffice to generate an anticipation in anyone hearing the story that *all* such imaginary entities are, for example, ethereal, elflike tricksters. This expectation, in turn, activates the interlocutor's specific intuitive schemas about wind behavior, child behavior, and cheating behavior as well as more general causal schema associated with basic conceptual domains: solid and non-solid physical substances, non-human living kinds and persons, and social life (contractual obligations for cooperative behavior).

These singular events personalize the phenomena so as to enhance their memorability (Tulving, 1983). In so doing, they also provide specific contextual scripts that other people can alter or embellish, thus enhancing transmissibility (Abelson, 1981). Such episodes, then, balance and optimize the personal and social relevance of the information by flexibly accommodating idiosyncratic requirements of individual understanding to the more general requirements of fable and folklore (Bartlett, 1932).

A good myth, then, must be open to variant readings, which allows speakers and hearers to best fit their personal experiences into the story's episodes (cf. Bruner, 1990, chap. 2). Here, as with religion, core domains invest the cognitive processing of mythic episodes and experiences with canonicality (default conditions). Exceptions to core expectations are not arbitrary but structured so as to make violation of canonical expectations comprehensible.

In pre-literate societies, which do not have the option of storing their accumulated knowledge and history in an indefinitely expandable public repository of information, this cognitive negotiation between the requirements of personal and social relevance is crucial to the cultural survival of "collective memory" in myth. As Claude Lévi-Strauss (1969, 1971) illustrates in his great multi-volume *Mythologiques*, the aboriginal myths of the Americas are structured so as to inter-relate cosmic happenings, local environments, social requirements, and so on to personal memories in ways that are (optimally) cognitively salient for a given population. Because conditions of optimal cognitive salience change from population to population and environment to environment, myths of any one native group undergo more or less profound structural transformations in how information is organized and content selected as the myths are diffused to other groups.

Nevertheless, Lévi-Strauss is able to show that the myths of Alaskan and Amazonian tribes not only share certain recurrent themes, but also predictable patterns of transformation. These predictable patterns follow the lines of differences between indigenous populations and their environments as observed by anthropologists or gleaned from the historical record (following European contact): for example, differences in kin reckoning, residency arrangements, architecture, hunting strategies, species distributions of local fauna and flora, the patterns of seasons, and the night sky at various latitudes, and so on. Although Lévi-Strauss pays little attention to the actual operation of psychological processes, his magnum opus is tantamount to a cognitive history of the pre-historical Americas.

Like most other anthropologists, Lévi-Strauss's own approach is interpretive rather than cognitive, in that it describes generalized meanings or themes in terms of synthetically broad, culturewide categories, such as kinship, religion, myth, politics, and so on. For the cognitive anthropologist, such synthetic categories do reflect important regularities in the distribution of representations, but they tell us little about the material processes whereby minds in their physical environments actually produce these distributions. Interpretive categories help cognitive anthropologists to focus their research by targeting the end products of a complex causal story of information processing, communication, and transformation that is yet to be told. They do not explain, but rather beg explanation.

Unlike Europe's written folktales or fables, which may be the "frozen" vestiges of myths outworn, the public content of a myth changes at each telling through a dynamic process of cognitive negotiation between teller(s) and audience. Such collective memories or cultural representations are never fixed once and for all even within a population but comprise a more or less loosely connected (fuzzy) set of public representations that share and evoke informational content only in a "family resemblance" sort of way. In this sense, myths are more typical of cultural representations generally than the fixed representations that popular conceptions of culture focus upon.

13.2.6 HEALTH CARE AS AN AMERICAN CULTURAL REPRESENTATION

Consider the cultural representation of health care in America today. Many people have very many thoughts about health care, whereas others have few or none. The overwhelming majority of the mental representations produced by the many minds that think about health care never become public. Only a small fraction of what people are actually thinking about health care is ever communicated from one person to another. The overwhelming majority of the public representations, in turn, never become culturally widespread. For example, frequent discussion of the issue among family members rarely gets beyond the dinner table. By contrast, when the president of the United States utters something about health care, a small portion of his public representation (i.e., a portion that can fit into an average eight-second sound bite) is communicated to millions of people on the evening television news.

Television commentators and other media "experts" (doctors, politicians, insurance executives, etc.) give their own rendition of the president's public representation, which almost invariably changes the content of the original representation. These variously altered versions then elicit "comment" and inevitable alteration. Parts of these versions are then mentally represented by television listeners who, in turn, automatically alter the information content in order to make it personally relevant.

These personally relevant versions are, in their turn, uttered, discussed, and transformed as public representations. Some of these do get beyond the dinner table and eventually find their way after innumerable other transformations to the media commentators, experts, and even the president. The president may then internally revise and publicly express yet a different version of health care and so on. Notice that the flow of information is conditioned by certain "ecological" aspects of the culture that constrain interactions between public representations; for example, the dinner table and the sound bite – themselves the complex causal products of social history.[12]

Meanwhile, the communication media intones with the oxymoron that nobody seems to know exactly what health care is "all about," although most everybody seems to think it is "about something" that is socially relevant. This, of course, is how most cultural representations actually manifest themselves. But the media's message is that the time has come for politicians, experts, and "the public" to sum up their cognitive negotiations on the issue of health care and decide on a "policy" written into "law."

Policies and laws are established as parts of cultural *institutions*. Institutions are physically constituted public mechanisms, which are variously composed of selected "ecological" features of the cultural environment, such as police batons, jails, demonstrations, parliamentary buildings, archives, other cultural representations, and so on. Institutions – whether political, religious, or scientific – serve the cognitive function of providing conduits for sequencing the flow and interpretation of information through what may be indefinitely many versions of "a" (or "a set" of) cultural representation(s).

Institutions do this by establishing a hierarchy of representations, with the highest often corresponding to a legal prescription that orients the more fluid and less bounded representations that follow and circulate. The legal prescription not only channels information that directly pertains to its designated representational field, but its institutional status enables it wide-ranging influence over other legal, moral, and ideological representations (e.g., the debate over health care legislation as one over "democracy" and "socialism").

Religious institutions, like those of politics or science, usually embrace *ritual* displays of information. Religious ritual displays serve both to ensure activation of intuitive beliefs and to restrict them to more or less definite contextual frames for imagining the supernatural: the public display of supernatural episodes in ritualized ceremonies. Anthropologists have interpreted the "social function" of such ceremonies as creating a "liminal space" between the natural and supernatural realms (Leach, 1976). Here, select persons (priests, shamans, sorcerers, etc.) are jointly "anointed" by supernatural beings and appointed by the public in order to mediate the flow of information between the two realms. From a cognitive standpoint, the mediator's task is to focus attention on precisely those counter-intuitive assumptions whose liminal, public expression serves as a "conduit metaphor" for activating and constraining the far more wide-ranging subliminal assumptions and inferences that the audience intuitively shares.[13]

13.2.7 MAGIC AND DIVINATION

Now consider B: the view that symbolic beliefs crucially inform thinking about the everyday world, so that there is no clear distinction between natural and supernatural phenomena. In traditional small-scale societies, ceremonial displays are generally required for the practice of magic – the art of controlling events by incantations or ritualized gests that conjure a combined intervention of natural causes and supernatural spirits. Many psychologists and anthropologists still see magic as a special mode of causal thinking that supposedly pervades the whole of the society in which it is practiced and obeys its own set of laws or rules. This, despite the well-known fact that *the very same* magical or divinatory practices can very often be interpreted in seemingly contradictory ways by the very same person.

Positivist views hold that magical causation is pre-rational pre-operational, or pre-scientific (Piaget, 1967; Horton, 1967; Hallpike, 1976). More romantic views treat magical thinking as alternative modes of rationality and causation (Douglas, 1966) or counter-culture (Roszak, 1970). For example, to understand ancient and modern Maya, one must learn "a different rationality just as one learns a new language," that is, an "alternative reality" different from "our worldview – that thing we call science" (Freidel et al., 1993: 11,36,172).

Whether positivist or romantic, all-encompassing views of magic as pervading everyday thought are somewhat surprising given the oft-reported fact that magic in traditional societies is generally associated with explicitly choreographed and quite extraordinary public displays (even if only a dyadic display, such as between a voodoo "doctor" or priestess and her client). Long ago, Margaret Mead (1932) reported that magical thinking and animism were decidedly *less* common among children than adults in traditional societies, such as Manus (New Guinea). Children in Manus, she argued, understood events in straightforward terms of material causality: canoes go adrift because ropes are unfastened and water currents move them. By contrast, Manus adults *who had gone through special rites of initiation* might "explain" events in terms of ghosts, "the evil eye," or animistic forces.

Similarly, Sheila Walker (1992:656) stresses: "the absence of supernatural explanations even in older Yoruba [Nigeria] children suggests that the inclusion of principled supernatural knowledge in the representations of living kinds occurs much later than the shift to more refined biological concepts." The most traditional adult Yoruba assent to transference of "essences" between natural kinds only when "supported by supernatural explanations in the ritual contexts." For Lévi-Strauss (1962), the myths and rites of totemism, that is, the institutionalized relationship between human groups and natural species, explicitly mark the fact that human totemic groups, unlike their natural species namesakes, generally may not inter-breed. In other words, people organize their cultures not by blindly mimicking nature, but by common-sensically carving nature at its joints and then symbolically re-structuring it so as to arrest attention and incite evocation.

In reporting magic, researchers often *presume* but do not show that the practice aims at causal efficacy in curing or producing illness, bringing or stopping rain, and so on. Descriptions are often accompanied by references to "mystical forces," "occult powers," or "invisible hands." Rarely, if ever, are such causal agents mentioned by the practitioners themselves (so far as can be ascertained from the few literal transcriptions available). Rather, as Tambiah (1973) notes, these terms were invoked in the historical development of Western science to underscore the obscure parts of rival theories or to discredit hermeneutical approaches, such as astrology or alchemy (cf. Hesse, 1961). Explanations of magic that employ such notions without further justification thus unwittingly assume what they seek to demonstrate.

Magic, suggests Tambiah (1973), endures as a social phenomenon *not* because of some presumed causal efficacy, but because it creates a social context that allows participants to conceptually integrate an important situation for which they believe no causal explanation exists: "a sacrifice which creates the cosmos persists because it 'creates' the world in a sense that is different from what is known in the laboratory (p. 210)." Magic is usually practiced precisely in situations where no mundane causal sequence of actions and events is known to affect an outcome that is both personally relevant and socially desired. As Evans-Pritchard (1937) observed in regard to Zande (African) magic: curing rites are most mysterious where the diseases they deal with are most acute and chronic.

This attempt to give cultural representation to causally inscrutable situations does not altogether ignore the mundane causal factors in the situation. Such factors are as necessary (but insufficient) for understanding the situation as is the "mysterious," that is counter-intuitive, part of the magic. Moreover, by preserving what causally efficacious information there is in a magical representation, the representation may, in fact, optimize mundane causal efficacy.

Consider, in this respect, magical practice associated with the Itzaj *sas~tun* described in V in section 13.2.2. The purported causal powers of the *sas~tun* are intrinsic to it, in much the same way that causally efficacious intentions are intrinsic to people. One cannot make a stone into a *sas~tun* any more than one can give a person a mind. But what, exactly, are the *sas~tun*'s causal powers beyond those of *restricted* set of human intentions (i.e., *sas~tun* never lie, engage in irony)? The *sas~tun* can "recognize" unknown events of the past (e.g., who stole the pig) and unknown events of the future (e.g., who will die or get well). The *sas͂tun*'s knowledge, however, is only intermittently apparent to the curer/diviner, who the *sas͂tun* has chosen as its medium.

Now, the curer/diviner usually consults the *sas͂tun* upon the request of a client who wishes to know of some past or future event, such as who stole the family pig or whether a sick child will die or get well. The curer/diviner typically asks for all of the information that the client deems relevant to the event, much as a detective or a doctor would. Only *then* does she consult the *sas͂tun*. For someone possessed by a supposedly pre-rational or alternatively rational mentality, this behavior is odd indeed. Why not just consult the *sas͂tun* directly, without bothering with this mundanely rational routine?

A partial answer may be that the curer/diviner uses the client's information in order to build up a "best hypothesis" causal scenario involving only mundane causes. Because not enough information is known (and is unlikely ever to be known) to complete the scenario, it can never be deterministic. The scenario must remain somewhat uncertain, that is, probabilistic. This uncertainty makes it difficult to act. Suppose the wrong person is accused of stealing, or the child who was predicted to live actually dies. Such uncertainty can block action aimed at rationally maximizing benefit, even if the likelihood of a positive outcome exceeds the likelihood of failure (Kahneman and Tversky, 1979).

Arguably, consultation of the *sas͂tun* allows the curer/diviner to take decisive action in somewhat risky cases where it would be most rational to do so; that is, where the benefit of the action taken less the cost of a failed action is greater than the benefit of inaction:

$$B(\text{action}) - C(\text{failed action}) > B(\text{inaction})$$

For example, suppose a child is ill, and the curer/diviner knows from experience that about four out of every five persons with this type of illness dies if not treated; that is, B (inaction) = 20 percent. From experience, she also knows that every other person who is given an herbal potion (whose recipe she jealously guards) survives; that is B(action) = 50 percent. However, she also knows that the potion can sometimes kill people who might otherwise get well without treatment. Suppose, as a worst-case scenario, she imagines that the treatment could kill half the people it is given to. Given that the expectation of the untreated child's survival is only 20 percent, then the worst case would halve this expectation; that is, C (failure) = 50 percent × 20 percent = 10 percent. Thus, even in a worst-case scenario, the decision to give the potion is most likely to produce the happy outcome of seeing the person well:

$$[B \text{ (action)} = 50 \text{ percent} - C(\text{failure}) = 50 \text{ percent} \times 20 \text{ percent} = 10 \text{ percent}] = 40 \text{ percent} > B(\text{inaction}) = 20 \text{ percent}$$

This is not to say that all, or even most, magical acts are designed to encourage and maximize rational decision making. It is only to suggest that there is nothing in magic per se that opposes, blocks, or substitutes for mundane conceptions of rationality and causation – conceptions that are likely the same for humans everywhere. In some cases, magic and divination may even enhance rational decision making and causal analysis. But this usually occurs within the broader context of optimizing the relevance of such practices by symbolically binding personal problems of mind and body to the larger cultural ecology:

> The question [the sas‑tun divinator] asks his clients can be as subtly penetrating as those of a trained and experienced psychiatrist. But most of all, the divination gives clients a chance to focus on their problems, to share them with other people, and to receive advice that often links them back to their community and the greater cosmos. In our world, medicine addresses the body, while divination and healing in the Maya world work with the mind and spirit. (Freidel et al., 1993:231)

Far from indicating an "alternative reality" that has "no rational explanation" (Freidel et al., 1993:230), such experiences partake of panhuman cognitive principles applied to a different ecological context. This different context is one where sustaining a millennial communal tradition is as much a part of the epidemiological environment as combating the pathogens of disease.

In fact, argues Geertz, magic functions precisely in order to make sure that the inevitable failure of common sense to understand everything about the world does not undermine what can be understood commonsensically:

> The cry of witchcraft functions of the Azande as the cry of Insha Allah functions for some Muslims or crossing oneself functions for some Christians, less to lead into more troubling questions – religious, philosophical, scientific, moral – about how the world is put together and what life comes to, than to block such questions from view; to seal up the commonsense view of the world. (Geertz, 1975:12)

The problem with such functional interpretations of magic – as with all interpretations of functional effects – is that they can never account for how the function came into being nor how it acquired the belief structures and ceremonial forms that make its practice so evocative and study so interesting. Why the sas-tun, and why the peculiar properties and practices associated with it? What are its cognitive causes? That is the question.

13.2.8 SUMMARY

The episodic expressions and ritual performances associated with symbolic beliefs are instrumental in activating and focusing the intuitive assumptions and inferences that underlie religion and cosmology. But they do no more than that. The overwhelming bulk of information that is stored and evoked with symbolic beliefs is rarely, if ever, rendered public, explicitly communicated, and culturally transmitted. Nobody, even the most faithful believer or religious functionary, ever articulates more than a fraction of the intuitive beliefs that underpin devotion. Indeed, people are largely oblivious to them unless expressly prodded to become mindful (e.g., in theology class, by a persistent anthropologist). Even the relatively sporadic and loosely articulated public expressions of symbolic belief are parasitically rooted in the deep range of ordinary assumptions and inferences that make counter-intuitive beliefs both remarkable and memorable.

These public representations never amount to some cultural theory, system, worldview, code, grammar, or any such determinate structure. They are distributed phenomena, with probabilistic recurrences. In fact, there are no such unified frameworks that comprise bounded domains of culture any more than culture itself constitutes a bounded domain of meaning or matter. The conceptual foundations of religion, like those of culture itself, are intuitively given by highly specialized, universal cognitive domains that are the evolutionary endowments of every human being. These domains, and they alone, provide the cognitive means that people use, often unaware, to sort out the supernatural from the natural.

13.3 The nature of culture

Cultures are assemblages of people and "prosthetic devices," like Bibles and ballistic missiles. These devices both further constrain and extend the ranges of thoughts and actions that human biological nature, that is, mind and body, evolved to produce (cf. Bruner, 1990). From a cognitive standpoint, each culture is constituted by a more or less loosely connected ecological network of cultural representations, which are themselves only more or less loosely connected ecological networks of their various public and private versions. Representations that are stable over time within a culture, like those that recur across cultures, do so because they are easily remembered and readily communicated (Sperber, 1990). The most memorable and transmissible ideas are those most congenial to people's innate habits of mind, that is, those compatible with naive physics, naive biology, naive psychology, naive sociology, and whatever other "mental modules" the human brain may harbor.

These habits of mind evolved to capture recurrent features of hominid environments relevant to species survival. Once emitted in a cultural environment, such core-compatible ideas will spread "contagiously" through a population of minds. They will be little affected by subsequent changes in a culture's history or institutional ecology. They are learned with or without formal or informal teaching and, once learned, cannot be easily or wholly unlearned. They remain inordinately stable within a culture and are by and large structurally isomorphic across cultures. One example is the categorization and reasoning schema in folkbiological taxonomy.

13.3.1 META REPRESENTATION

Human knowledge and beliefs develop and diversify beyond the common-sense core with elaborated systems of representations, like those in religion or science. Such elaborated representations are not spontaneously triggered and formed by cognitive modules that require minimum exposure to relevant input. These other harder-to-master representations tend to be less limited in their domain of application and less rigidly structured.

They also seem to require particular ecological accommodations in the cultural environment, such as institutions of education or devotion that can sequence and constrain the flow of information in ways that allow the learner to capture and accumulate the relevant input for more elaborate processing. When such sophisticated representations are elaborated as cultural represen- tations, they may require a *cognitive division of labor* in the sense that no one individual possesses the mnemonic or inferential aptitude to process all of the relevant information. In such cases, institutions are indispensable to the cultural survival of such representations.

This elaborate conceptual processing involves cognitive proficiencies dif- ferent from the other core abilities. In particular, it involves the typically human ability of retaining only partly understood information in order to work on it and understand it better. Such processing of half-understood in- formation is characteristic of deliberate efforts to elaborate initially counter- intuitive ideas and is found in both science and mythico-religious symbolism.

Such elaborative processing thus requires a capacity for meta- representation, that is, an ability to embed (potentially many levels of) rep- resentations within representations. To believe that dogs bark or the grass is green requires only an intuitively direct analysis and storage of brute fact. To believe, either scientifically or religiously, that the microcosm of the atom behaves in the same way as the macrocosm of the solar system requires an additional competency, which allows suspension of the processing of intuitive facts and a search for new, initially counter-intuitive facts (science) or counter-factual possibilities (religion). In other words, a human mind, in ad- dition to being able to directly process the (often sensory) input out of which brute facts are formed, must also be able to process as input the different outputs (representations) generated by the various core domains. Without this facility, cross-domain fertilization and integration of information would be literally inconceivable.

Anthropologist Dan Sperber (1994) has recently argued that this capacity is itself a ''core module'' of the human mind, which is perhaps an evolu- tionary extension of naive psychology (i.e., the ability to infer the beliefs of other minds and to embed those beliefs within one's own beliefs). Like the other core domains, it too evolved under selection pressures to adapt to cer- tain recurrent features in ancestral hominid environments. Unlike the other core domains, however, the persistent features of hominid environments that the meta-representational faculty emerged to deal with were primarily inter- nal to the organism rather than external to it. This ''meta-representational module,'' as he calls it, thus embodies an evolutionary design uniquely at- tuned to the representational structure of our internal cognitive environment rather than to the stimulus-structure of the outside world.

13.3.2 SCIENCE AND SYMBOLISM
The ability of the meta-representational module to take as input the output of other conceptual modules allows for wide-ranging conceptual integration and production of new knowledge, but it does so along lines that seem some- what predictable and in a manner that must preserve at least some of the distinctive knowledge produced by more basic conceptual modules.

For example, suppose naive physics constitutes a distinct core domain. Suppose further, as Rochel Gelman (1980) suggests, that number constitutes another core domain that defines the countable relations among sets of discrete, abstract objects, or perhaps, as Chomsky (1988) suggests, numbers and the logic governing them are just restricted products of the language faculty. Suppose now that some enterprising ancient hit upon the idea of meta-representing the output of the naive physics module with the output of the number module. Then Archimedes' statics, Newton's mechanics, and much of ensuing "hard science" would become conceivable.

Obviously the story is more complicated and in a number of important ways. Once (meta-representational) rules of correspondence link object schema to number schema, there is no a priori reason why such mathematized objects could not themselves become inputs to the naive (but now slightly more sophisticated) physics module, *provided they can be readily integrated with prior commonsense notions.* For example, even young children in our society appear to comprehend contemporary Western notions of the earth and other heavenly objects as spherelike objects (Vosniadou and Brewer, 1987), although they are likely to be unaware that such notions were the result of laborious scientific discoveries involving mathematics. Similarly children as well as adults may readily comprehend whales and bats as mammals despite only vague awareness of the anatomical insights that made these identifications possible (Medin, 1989). Thus, even when there are demonstrable and pervasive affects of meta-cognitive (e.g., scientific) reasoning on basic conceptualization, effects are not likely to be uniform nor such as to have commonsense structures wholly replaced by new structures (e.g., theories).

In the case of symbolic cognitions, such as those involved in religion and belief in the supernatural, concepts are studiously structured so as to *disallow* any fixed intuitions to be associated with them and thus to preclude them from supplanting or being fully assimilated to core beliefs. In multiplying senses and metaphors (e.g., God as father, son, and earth mother) symbolism allows endless interpretation and exegesis. In suspending basic factual beliefs (e.g., animate beings without bodily substance, animals that reincarnate people or blood that transmutates into wine, plants that desire revenge symbolism guarantees that no such interpretation will ever be empirically confirmed or disconfirmed. Ever since (Kant 1951, sec. 59), philosophers have long emphasized that any genuinely symbolic concept is at best quasi-schematized and designed to remain open-textured meta-representations of whatever other conceptual interpretations or facts are brought to bear.

Although symbolism and science may both draw on the same initial, open-textured analogies (e.g., the plant as an upturned animal, the correspondence between the macrocosm and the microcosm), what they ultimately do with them is diametrically opposed. The informative analogies of science constitute reference-fixing research programs. They suggest (meta-representational) strategies for future research intended to reveal significant, hitherto unforeseen similarities between domains whose initial resemblance is assumedly but the tip of the iceberg. If such reference-fixing programs were applied to mythico-religious symbolism, the end result would be dead metaphors – platitudes of little evocative or spiritual value. By contrast, science seeks to kill off metaphorical uncertainty by (ideally) assimilating and explaining it in terms of a logically consequent set of beliefs that can be empirically assessed. Even if shown false (which symbolic beliefs never can be), scientifically reduced analogies and metaphors can represent significant advances in learning and knowledge.

For example, the Rutherford–Bohr analogy of the atom with the solar system was an acceptable conceptual frame for research in physics from about 1912 to 1925. Its empirical disconfirmation remains a valuable pedagogic guide to understanding more likely theories. Followers of the Maharishi Mahesh Yogi, too, put out yearly advertisements in the *International Herald Tribune* claiming that the microcosm and macrocosm, the atom and the solar system, and gravity and electromagetism, combine into a unified religious–scientific "field theory." But the maharishi's disciples, unlike those of Einstein and Bohr, seek an eternal "truth" that is sustained by faith in the authority of those charged with continually reinterpreting it and fitting it to new circumstances.

Religious beliefs, however, are not unconnected to commonsense knowledge. They are generally inconsistent with commonsense knowledge but not at random. Rather, by flatly contradicting a limited number of basic commonsense assumptions about physical, biological, psychological, and social phenomena, symbolic beliefs become particularly attention arresting and memorable. As a result, these beliefs are more likely to be retained and transmitted in a human group than random departures from common sense and thus to become part of a group's culture.

The emotional comforts and poetically creative imaginings that religion evokes need not only "encourage stupidity," as Bertrand Russell (1950) declaimed. Religion can help fill the void where clarity fails, truth lies in the abyss, and only suffering unto death remains. To be sure, interpreters of religion, like those of science, may believe that the extraordinary worlds that only they feel privy to extend not only to an imagined cosmos, but to ordinary ways of thinking about our commonsense world as well. This is a category mistake, not an example of cultural relativism.

The commonsense knowledge underscored by basic cognitive dispositions remains somewhat separate from more sophisticated, originally meta-representational conceptions despite the subtle and pervasive interactions between the two kinds of knowledge (Dupré, 1981). Thus, such basic "common sense" may remain valid for everyday understanding of the world but perhaps not for the vastly extended or reduced dimensions of modern science. New, meta-representationally created knowledge can filter back into basic conceptual modules and alter its database but within limits. These innately determined limits may be such as to preserve enough of the "default" ontology and structure of the core domain to make the notion of domain-specific cross-cultural universals meaningful. This leads to a strong expectation that core principles guide learning in much the same way across cultures. The genesis and understanding of cultural variation depend on it.

Conclusion: Relativism and naturalism

Naturalism in cognitive anthropology describes the attempt to causally locate the objects of study – cultures – inside the larger network of scientific knowledge. This approach posits no special phenomena, ontologies, causes, or laws beyond those of material objects and their inter-relationships. It studies the structure and content of representations, both private and public, and their statistically patterned distributions within and between human populations. From this standpoint, the most (diachronically) stable and (synchronically) recurrent patterns – and those that provide the (physical) bases for cultural patterns less steadfast – are generated by specialized causal schemata of the human mind/brain, for example, those responsible for the core domains of folkphysics, folkbiology, folkpsychology, and folksociology.

In addition, another core set of meta-cognitive schemata assure a modicum of integration between basic empirical domains and allows for more elaborate conceptual diversification and inter-connection. All core schemata appear to be naturally selected features of human cognitive architecture, which are designed to spontaneously and effortlessly map those regularities in the natural world that crucially influenced the course of hominid evolution. They plausibly determine the range of possibilities for the existence, content, and organization of any and all cultures.

Ignorance or disregard of our evolutionary heritage and of the basic cognitive domains upon which much in everyday human life and thought depend can lead to speculative philosophies and empirical programs that misconstrue the natural scope and limits of the species-specific core of our common sense. This, in turn, incites misappreciation of the cognitive foundations of culture and cosmology, science and society. The intellectual and moral consequences of this misconstrual have varying significance, both for ourselves and for others, for example, in the ways relativism informs currently popular notions of separate but equal cultural worlds whose peoples are in some sense incommensurably different from ourselves and from one another. Relativism, it appears, aspires directly to mutual tolerance of irreducible differences. Naturalism – the cognitive understanding of our common nature and humanity – aims first to render cultural diversity a comprehensible outcome of what we all share.

Notes

1 No culture in the world, except those exposed to Aristotle, considers humans and non-human living kinds to belong to the same ontological category. Nor do people ordinarily process information about persons in the same way that they process information about non-human living kinds. Thus, "For the Kayapó (Indians of the Amazon) all things are divided into 4 categories: 1) things that move and grow, 2) things that grow but do not move, 3) things that neither move nor grow, and 4) man, a creature that is akin to all animals, yet unique and more powerful than most animals because of his social organization" (Posey, 1981:168).

2 Such groups may be named or not. English speakers ambiguously use the term

animal to refer to at least three distinct classes of living things: non-human animals, animals including humans, and mammals (the prototypical animals). The term *beast* seems to pick out non-human animals in English but is seldom used today. The English term *plant* is also ambiguously used to refer to the plant kingdom or to members of that kingdom that are not trees. Maya languages generally have no name for *plant* as such, although these languages do permit a clear distinction to be made between plants and all other things by other means (e.g., by assigning a particular numeral classifier to all and only plants).

3 Life forms may differ somewhat from culture to culture. For example, cultures such as ancient Hebrew or modern Rangi (Tanzania) include the herpetofauna (reptiles and amphibians) with insects, worms, and other "creeping crawlers" (Kesby, 1979). Other cultures, such as Itza Maya and (until recently) most Western cultures, include the herpetofauna with mammals as quadrupeds. Some cultures, such as Itza Maya, place phenomenally isolated mammals like the bat with birds, just as Rofaifo (New Guinea) place phenomenally isolated birds like the cassowary with mammals (Dwyer, 1976). Whatever the particular constitution of life form groupings, or *taxa*, the life form level, or *rank*, universally partitions the living world into broadly equivalent divisions.

4 Botanists and ethnobotanists prefer to emphasize morphological criteria and to identify this basic folkbiological level with the scientific genus (Bartlett, 1940; Berlin, 1972), whereas zoologists and ethnozoologists tend to emphasize behavioral (especially reproductive) criteria and identify with the species (Diamond, 1966; Bulmer, 1970). For the most salient organisms, including mammals and other large vertebrates as well as most trees and phylogenetically isolated flowering plants (cacti, palms), local genera are usually monospecific; hence, no readily perceptible distinction is possible between genus and species. In fact, there was no principled notion of species (Cesalpino, 1583) and genus (Tournefort, 1694) until post-Renaissance Europe. Invariably, these primary groupings are mutually exclusive. They also represent virtually exhaustive partitionings of the local fauna and flora in the sense that hitherto unknown or unfamiliar organisms are generally assigned to a basic taxon when attention is directed toward them.

5 Folk sub-species are generally polynomial, whereas folk species are usually labeled by a single lexical item. Foreign organisms suddenly introduced into a local environment are often initially assimilated to basic taxa as sub-species. For example, the Lowland Maya originally labeled the Spanish horse "village tapir," just as they termed wheat "Castillian maize." Similarly, the Spanish referred to the indigenous pacas and agoutis as "bastard hares," just as they denoted the Maya breadnut tree "Indian fig."

6 Thus, for Linnaeus (1751, sec. 153), the Natural System was rooted in "a natural instinct [that] teaches us to know first those objects closest to us, and at length the smallest ones: for example, Man, Quadrupeds, Birds, Fish, Insects, Mites, or firstly the large Plants, lastly the smallest mosses."

7 Aristotle first proposed that both living and inert kinds had essential underlying natures. Locke (1689/1848) deemed these unknowable kinds, nature's "real kinds," and claimed that their underlying features could never be completely fathomed by the mind. Mill (1843) referred these kinds to nature's own "limited varieties" and thereby considered them to be the predicates of scientific laws. He dubbed them "natural kinds," including biological species and the fundamental elements of inert substance (e.g., lead, gold). Cross-culturally, it is not clear that inert substances comprise a cognitive domain that is conceived in terms of underlying essences or natures. Nor is it obvious what the basic elements might be across cultures, since

the Greek EARTH, AIR, FIRE, and WATER are not apparently universal. In other words, the conception of natural kind, which supposedly spans all sorts of lawful natural phenomena, may turn out not to be a *psychologically real* predicate of ordinary thinking (i.e., a natural kind of cognitive science). It may be, instead, simply an *epistemic* notion peculiar to Western science and philosophy of science.

8 I wish to thank Lorraine Daston for pointing out the similarity of Davidson's argument to any earlier draft of my own.

9 This assumes no genetic racial bias to learning one culture (or language) rather than another. There surely isn't: full-blooded Maya seem to be able to learn Spanish and systematic biology with at least the ease that Americans learn Spanish and systematic biology; and the children of New Guinea Highlanders who had never seen a white person before the arrival of Margaret Mead in the late 1920s today easily and proficiently engage in parliamentary debate over English Common Law and the social consequences of debt borrowing under the bylaws of the International Monetary Fund. Even if there were marked *individual* differences in language learning or acculturation capacities (and there isn't the slightest notion around of how one would even go about investigating *this*, since next to nothing is known about the genetic basis or biological structure of conceptual cognition), there would still be no racially based cultural difference. This is because genetic variation between two randomly chosen individuals of a cultural community, such as the Swedes, is at least an order of magnitude greater than the variation between the average Swede and the average member of, say, the Amazonian tribe of Jívaro headhunters (cf. Cavalli-Sforza, 1991).

10 For example, a child (pretending to peel the telephone) believes that the mother knows that the child knows (that the telephone is not a banana) because the mother believes that the child believes that the mother remembers (that yesterday the child pretended to talk to a banana) because the child knew that the mother knew that the child knew (that the banana was not a telephone), etc.

11 Thus, Itza sorcerers can best control a person's heart or "soul" (*ol*) via the essence or "heart" (*puksik'al*) of an animal species. Sorcerers can thus invest the heart of an animal species but cannot ensoul an animal or plant because these already have living essences. By contrast, people can endow artifacts with a living soul, although an artifact's soul differs from the essence of a person, animal, or even a plant in that the artifact can only harbor the forces of life but cannot interact with them.

12 For example, dinner tables imply a coordination of biological nutrient cycles, access to nutrients, work schedules that conform to and condition this coordination, etc. The emergence of "sound biting" is a more recent product of two cultural innovations, one economic and the other technological. In the 1970s first local news stations and then national networks began to compete for greater amounts of attention-arresting information with which to capture audience markets (before then, news was considered a non-profit public service). This was greatly facilitated by new techniques of film and video editing (James Wertsch, personal communication).

13 The cognitive devices involved in understanding symbolic utterances are those used in everyday understanding of the natural world. Hence, the relation of symbolic belief to commonsense belief is much like that of metaphorical to literal utterances: "A search for optimal relevance leads the speaker to adopt, on different occasions, a more or less faithful interpretation of her thoughts. The result is in some cases literalness [e.g., if the terms of the subject and predicate are normally related by stored or easily inferable encyclopedic knowledge], in

others metaphor [e.g., "all the world's a stage," where terms do not usually come together]. Metaphor thus requires no special interpretive abilities or procedures: it is the natural outcome of some very general abilities and procedures used in verbal communication" (Sperber and Wilson, 1986:237). The weaker the ency-clopedic relation between terms in a figurative utterance, the more creative its potential to activate a memory search for assumptions to enrich the input. Intuitive assumptions are triggered and constrained by shared background knowledge to produce (non-demonstrative) inferences that interpret contextually pertinent as-pects of the enriched input as if they were true.

References

Abelson, R. (1981) Psychological status of the script concept. *American Psychologist*, *36*, 715–729.
Adanson, M. (1763) *Familles des plantes*, 2 vols. Paris: Vincent.
Astington, J., & Gopnik, A. (1991) Theoretical explanations of children's understand-ing of the mind. *British Journal of Developmental Psychology*, *9*, 7–31.
Atran, S. (1983) Covert fragmenta and the origins of the botanical family. *Man*, *18*, 51–71.
   (1985) Pre-theoretical aspects of Aristotelian definition and classification of ani-mals. *Studies in History and Philosophy of Science*, *16*, 113–163.
   (1987) Constraints on the ordinary semantics of living kinds. *Mind and Language*, *2*, 27–63.
   (1990) *Cognitive foundations of natural history: Towards an anthropology of sci-ence*. Cambridge: Cambridge Univ. Press.
   (1993) Itza Maya tropical agro-forestry. *Current Anthropology*, *34*, 633–700.
   (1994) Core domains versus scientific theories. In L. Hirschfeld & S. Gelman (Eds.), *Mapping the mind: Domain specificity in cognition and culture*. New York: Cambridge Univ. Press.
   (1996) From folk biology to scientific biology. In D. Olson & N. Torrance (Eds.), *Handbook of education and human development: New models of learning, teaching and schooling*. Oxford: Blackwell.
Atran, S., & Sperber, D. (1991) Learning without teaching: Its place in culture. In L. Tolchinsky-Landsmann (Ed.), *Culture, schooling and psychological develop-ment*. Norwood, NJ: Ablex.
Avis, J., & Harris, P. (1991) Belief-desire among Baka children. *Child Development*, *62*, 460–467.
Baillargeon, R. (1986) Representing the existence and location of hidden objects: Object permanence in 6- and 8-month-old infants. *Cognition*, *23*, 21–41.
Bartlett, F. (1932) *Remembering: an experimental and social study*. Cambridge: Cam-bridge Univ. Press.
Bartlett, H. (1940) History of the generic concept in botany. *Bulletin of the Torrey Botanical Club*, *47*, 319–362.
Berlin, B. (1972) Speculations on the growth of ethnobotanical nomenclature. *Lan-guage and Society*, *1*, 63–98.
   (1992) *Ethnobiological classification: Principles of categorization of plants and animals in traditional societies*. Princeton: Princeton Univ. Press.
Berlin, B., Breedlove, D., & Raven, P. (1973) General principles of classification and nomenclature in folk biology. *American Anthropologist*, *74*, 214–242.
   (1974). *Principles of Tzeltal plant classification*. New York: Academic Press.

Boster, J. (1988) Natural sources of internal category structure: Typicality, familiarity, and similarity of birds. *Memory & Cognition, 16*, 258–270.

Boyer, P. (1994) *The naturalness of religious ideas.* Berkeley: Univ. of California Press.

Brown, C. (1984) *Language and living things: Uniformities in folk classification and naming.* New Brunswick: Rutgers Univ. Press.

Brown, D. (1991) *Human universals.* New York: McGraw-Hill.

Bruner, J. (1990) *Acts of meaning.* Cambridge, MA: Harvard Univ. Press.

Bulmer, R. (1970) Which came first, the chicken or the egg-head? In J. Pouillon & P. Maranda (Eds.), *Echanges et communications: Mélanges offerts à Claude Lévi-Strauss.* The Hague: Mouton.

Carey, S. (1985) *Conceptual change in childhood.* Cambridge, MA: MIT Press.

Carey, S., Klatt, L., & Schlaffer, M. (1992) "Infants' representations of objects and nonsolid substances." Unpublished manuscript, MIT, Cambridge, MA.

Cavalli-Sforza, L. (1991) Genes, peoples, languages. *Scientific American, 265,* 104–110.

Cesalpino, A. (1583) *De plantis libri XVI.* Florence: Marescot.

Chomsky, N. (1988) *Language and problems of knowledge.* Cambridge, MA: MIT Press.

Coley, J., Medin, D., & Atran, S. (submitted). Does privilege have its rank? Inductive inferences within folkbiological taxonomies. *Cognition.*

Cosmides, L., & Tooby, J. (1992). Cognitive adaptations for social exchange. In J. Barkow, L. Cosmides, & J. Tooby (Eds.), *The adapted mind: Evolutionary psychology and the generation of culture.* New York: Oxford Univ. Press.

Darwin, C. (1859) *On the origins of species by natural selection.* London: Murray.

Davidson, D. (1984) On the very idea of a conceptual scheme. In *Inquiries into truth and interpretation.* Oxford: Clarendon.

Descartes, R. (1681) *Les principes de la philosophie,* 4th ed. Paris: Theodore Gerard.

Diamond, J. (1966) Zoological classification of a primitive people. *Science, 151,* 1102–1104.

Donnellan, K. (1971) Necessity and criteria. In J. Rosenberg & C. Travis (Eds.), *Readings in the philosophy of language.* Englewood Cliffs, NJ: Prentice-Hall.

Dougherty, J. (1978) Salience and relativity in classification. *American Ethnologist, 5,* 66–80.

——— (1979) Learning names for plants and plants for names. *Anthropological Linguistics, 21,* 298–315.

Douglas, M. (1966) *Purity and danger.* London: Routledge & Kegan Paul.

Dupré, J. (1981) Natural kinds and biological taxa. *The Philosophical Review, 90,* 66–90.

Dwyer, P. (1976) An analysis of Rofaifo mammal taxonomy. *American Ethnologist, 3,* 425–445.

Einstein, A. (1948) Religion and science: Irreconcilable? *The Christian Register,* June 1948.

Evans-Pritchard, E. (1937) *Witchcraft, oracles and magic among the Azande.* Oxford: Clarendon Press.

Freidel, D., Schele, L., & Parker, J. (1993) *Maya cosmos: Three thousand years on the shaman's path.* New York: William Morrow.

Geertz, C. (1975) Common sense as a cultural system. *The Antioch Review, 33,* 5–26.

——— (1983) *Local knowledge.* New York: Basic.

Gelman, R. (1980) What young children know about numbers. *The Educational Psychologist, 15*, 54–68.

Gelman, S., & Coley, J. (1991) Language and categorization: The acquisition of natural kind terms. In S. Gelman & J. Byrnes (Eds.), *Perspectives on language and thought: Interrelations and development.* New York: Cambridge Univ. Press.

Gelman, S., & Wellman, H. (1991) Insides and essences: Early understanding of the non-obvious. *Cognition, 38*, 214–244.

Hallpike, C. (1976) Is there a primitive mentality? *Man, 11*, 253–270.

Hatano, G., & Inagaki, K. (1994) Young children's naive theory of biology. *Cognition, 50*, 171–188.

Hays, T. (1983) Ndumba folk biology. *American Anthropologist, 85*, 592–611.

Henley, N. (1969) A psychological study of the semantics of animal terms. *Journal of Verbal Learning and Verbal Behavior, 8*, 176–184.

Hesse, M. (1961) *Forces and fields: The concept of action at a distance in the history of physics.* London: Nelson.

Hirschfeld, L., & Gelman, S. (Eds.). (1994) *Mapping the mind: Domain-specificity in cognition and culture.* New York: Cambridge Univ. Press.

Horton, R. (1967) African thought and Western science. *Africa, 37*, 50–71, 159–187.

    (1973) Lévy-Bruhl, Durkeim and the scientific revolution. In R. Horton & R. Finnegan (Eds.), *Modes of thought: Essays in thinking in Western and non-Western societies.* London: Faber & Faber.

Horton, R., & Finnegan, R. (Eds.) (1973) *Modes of thought: Essays in thinking in Western and non-Western societies.* London: Faber & Faber.

Hough, W. (1897) The Hopi in relation to their plant environment. *American Anthropologist, 10*, 33–44.

Hunn, E. (1976) Toward a perceptual model of folk biological classification. *American Ethnologist, 3*, 508–524.

    (1977) *Tzeltal folk zoology.* New York: Academic Press.

Jeyifous, S. (1985) Atimodemo: Semantic conceptual development among the Yoruba. Ph.D. dissertation, Cornell University, Ithaca, NY.

Kahneman, D., & Tversky, A. (1979) Prospect theory: An analysis of decision under risk. *Econometrica, 47*, 263–291.

Kant, I. (1790/1951) *Critique of judgement.* New York: Hafner Press.

Keil, F. (1979) *Semantic and conceptual development: An ontological perspective.* Cambridge, MA: Harvard Univ. Press.

    (1989) *Concepts, kinds, and cognitive development.* Cambridge, MA: MIT Press.

    (1994) The birth and nurturance of concepts by domains: The origins of concepts of living things. In L. Hirschfeld & S. Gelman (Eds.), *Mapping the mind: Domain specificity in cognition and culture.* New York: Cambridge Univ. Press.

Kelly, M., & Keil, F. (1985) The more things change: Metamorphoses and conceptual development. *Cognitive Science, 9*, 403–416.

Kesby, J. (1979) The Rangi classification of animals and plants. In R. Reason & D. Ellen (Eds.), *Classification in their social contexts.* New York: Academic Press.

Labandeira, C., & Sepkoski, J. (1993) Insect diversity in the fossil record. *Science, 261*, 310–315.

Lamarck, J. B. (1809) *Philosophie zoologique.* Paris: Dentu.

Leach, E. (1976) *Culture and communication: The logic by which symbols are created.* Cambridge: Cambridge Univ. Press.

Leslie, A. (1990) Understanding other minds: Natural origins. In *Golem: Special Issue for the 12th Cognitive Science Conference, 1990.* Cambridge, MA: MIT Press.

Lévi-Strauss, C. (1962) *Totemism.* Boston: Beacon Press.

(1969) *The raw and the cooked.* New York: Harper.

(1971) *L'Homme nu.* Paris: Plon.

Linnaeus, C. (1751) *Philosophia botanica.* Stockholm: Kiesewetter.

Lloyd, G. (1990) *Demystifying mentalities.* Cambridge: Cambridge Univ. Press.

Locke, J. (1689/1848) *An essay concerning human understanding.* London: Tegg.

López, A., Atran, S., Coley, J., Medin, D., & Smith, E. (forthcoming) The tree of life: Universals of folk taxonomies and inductions.

Marks, I. (1987) *Fears, phobias, and rituals.* New York: Oxford Univ. Press.

Mayr, E. (1969) *Principles of systematic zoology.* New York: McGraw-Hill.

Mead, M. (1932) An investigation of the thought of primitive children with special reference to animism. *Journal of the Royal Anthropological Institute, 62,* 173–190.

Medin, D. (1989) Concepts and conceptual structure. *American Psychologist, 44,* 1469–1481.

Mill, J. (1843) *A system of logic.* London: Longmans, Green.

Munkur, B. (1983) *The cult of the serpent: An interdisciplinary survey of its manifestations and origins.* Albany: State Univ. of New York Press.

Murphy, G., & Medin, D. (1985) The role of theories in conceptual coherence. *Psychological Review, 92,* 289–316.

Needham, R. (1975) Polythetic classification. *Man, 10,* 349–369.

Osherson, D., Smith, E., Wilkie, O., López, A., & Shafir, E. (1990) Category-based induction. *Psychological Review, 97,* 185–200.

Pap, A. (1960) Types and meaninglessness. *Mind, 69,* 41–54.

Piaget, J. (1967) *The child's conception of the world.* Totowa, NJ: Littlefield & Adams.

Posey, D. (1981) Wasps, warriors and fearless men: Ethnoentomology of the Kayapó Indians of Central Brazil. *Journal of Ethnobiology, 1,* 165–174.

Rips, L. (1975) Inductive judgments about natural categories. *Journal of Verbal Learning and Verbal Behavior, 14,* 665–681.

Rips, L., Shoben, E., & Smith, E. (1973) Semantic distance and the verification of semantic relations. *Journal of Verbal Learning and Verbal Behavior, 12,* 1–20.

Rosch, E. (1975) Cognitive representations of semantic categories. *Journal of Experimental Psychology, 104,* 192–233.

Rosch, E., Mervis, C., Gray, W., Johnson, D., & Boyes-Braem, P. (1976) Basic objects in natural categories. *Cognitive Psychology, 8,* 382–439.

Roszak, T. (1970) *The making of counter-culture.* London: Faber.

Russell, B. (1950) *Unpopular essays.* New York: Simon & Schuster.

Seligman, M. (1971) Phobias and preparedness. *Behavior Therapy, 2,* 307–320.

Shweder, R. (1991) *Thinking through cultures.* New York: Harvard Univ. Press.

Simpson, G. (1961) *Principles of animal taxonomy.* New York: Columbia Univ. Press.

Sommers, F. (1959) The ordinary language tree. *Mind, 68,* 160–185.

Spelke, E. (1990) Principle of object perception. *Cognitive Science, 14,* 29–56.

Sperber, D. (1987) *On anthropological knowledge.* Cambridge: Cambridge Univ. Press.

(1990) The epidemiology of beliefs. In C. Fraser & G. Gaskell (Eds.), *The social psychological study of widespread beliefs.* Oxford: Clarendon Press.

(1994) The modularity of thought and the epidemiology of representations. In L. Hirschfeld & S. Gelman (Eds.), *Mapping the mind: Domain specificity in cognition and culture.* New York: Cambridge Univ. Press.

Sperber, D., & Wilson, D. (1986) *Relevance: Communication and cognition*. Oxford: Blackwell.

Stross, B. (1973) Acquisition of botanical terminology by Tzeltal children. In M. Edmonson (Ed.), *Meaning in Mayan languages*. The Hague: Mouton.

Tambiah, S. (1973) Form and meaning of magical acts: A point of view. In R. Horton & R. Finnegan (Eds.), *Modes of thought: Essays in thinking in Western and non-Western societies*. London: Faber & Faber.

Tournefort, J. (1694) *Elémens de botanique*. Paris: Imprimerie Royale.

Tulving, E. (1983) *Elements of episodic memory*. New York: Oxford Univ. Press.

Turiel, E. (1983) *The development of social knowledge: Morality and convention*. New York: Cambridge Univ. Press.

Vosniadou, S., & Brewer, W. (1987) Theories of knowledge restructuring in development. *Review of Educational Research, 57,* 51–67.

Walker, S. (1992) Supernatural beliefs, natural kinds and conceptual structure. *Memory and Cognition, 20,* 655–662.

Wallace, A. (1889) *Darwinism*. London: Macmillan.

Warburton, F. (1967) The purposes of classification. *Systematic Zoology, 16,* 241–245.

Zubin, D., & Köpcke, K.-M. (1986) Gender and folk taxonomy. In C. Craig (Ed.), *Noun classes and categorization*. Amsterdam: John Benjamins.

14
Is good thinking scientific thinking?

Deanna Kuhn

A subtitle of my chapter should perhaps be "Why scientific thinking has gotten a bad name and what to do about it." In addressing this question, I follow Shelley and Thagard (this volume) and Atran (this volume) in examining the relation between scientific and "ordinary" thinking. The prevailing conception of scientific thinking, I claim in this chapter, has been an overly narrow one that compartmentalizes scientific thinking as a technical, rarefied form of thought, accessible and relevant only to specialists trained in its use. A richer and more useful conception is one that brings scientific thinking into the realm of the ordinary.

In pursuing this direction, I follow no less a thinker than Albert Einstein (1954, p. 290), who proclaimed

> The whole of science is nothing more than a refinement of everyday thinking. It is for this reason that the critical thinking of the physicist cannot possibly be restricted to the examination of the concepts of his own specific field. He cannot proceed without considering critically a much more difficult problem, the problem of analyzing the nature of everyday thinking.

My purpose is to try to make explicit some of the connections that Einstein envisioned and, in so doing, to contribute to this difficult problem of analyzing everyday thinking. I begin by proposing, like Einstein, that we should expect connection, not dissociation, between scientific and ordinary thought. We have witnessed rapid change from the positivist view of science as an accumulative body of facts, disembodied from the human thinking that gave rise to them. The thinking of scientists necessarily develops out of the intuitive thinking of children. To begin to understand how this happens, we need ways to characterize both.

Science as argument

The direction I have taken in addressing this objective is to regard scientific thinking as argument, and thereby link it to the argumentive reasoning that occurs in everyday thought (Kuhn, 1991, 1992, 1993a). Science as argument is not difficult to justify in the case of professional science. Science is fundamentally a social activity. The contexts of both discovery and justification (Reichenbach, 1938) have their place, but we have arguably focused overly

on the internal creative thought of the scientist working in isolation and ne-
glected the social exchange in which these ideas are articulated, clarified,
elaborated, questioned, defended, and indeed may even have given rise to in
the first place. Moreover, this social process itself takes an interiorized form.
Scientists are well aware that explicitly justified arguments are needed to
convince the scientific community of which they are a part, and they learn
to think in such terms.

We can look, then, for the roots of scientific thought in children's and
adolescents' verbal exchanges. But, similarly, these have interiorized counterparts, since children's thinking "tends to replicate the procedural logic of
the social communications in which they participate" (Damon, 1990). We
thus need to study everyday argument in its interiorized (or rhetorical) as
well as its social form (Billig, 1987).

In pursuing such work, I focus on the core reasoning form of inductive
inference. I've characterized the reasoning process that leads to inductive
inferences as one of *theory-evidence coordination* (Kuhn, 1989). As I conceive it, it is a general enough process to span scientific and ordinary thinking. It should also be noted that the process of coordinating theory and
evidence takes us to the core of conceptual change by addressing the mechanism that effects it. One of my main claims is that this mechanism is not
constant across different ages and types of subjects.

In our research, we have looked for the scientific in ordinary thinking as
well as asked ordinary people to think in traditionally scientific ways. In one
line of work (Kuhn, 1991, 1992) we examine people's argumentive reasoning
skills with respect to real social issues. We asked subjects from adolescence
through late adulthood for their opinions, or, more formally, their causal
theories, on three topics: (1) What causes prisoners to return to a life of crime
after they're released? (2) What causes children to fail in school? (3) What
causes unemployment? These topics were chosen as ones that ordinary people
have occasion to think and talk about. They are also ones about which people
are able and willing to make causal inferences without a large base of technical knowledge. They nevertheless involve phenomena the true causal structure of which is complex and uncertain.

Following the framework of a dialogic argument, subjects were asked for
evidence to support their theories and then were asked to generate alternative
theories, counterarguments, and rebuttals. A number of questions were also
asked that addressed subjects' epistemological understanding, a topic I return
to later in this chapter. They were asked, for example, whether experts know
or could potentially know for certain the causes of school failure or criminal
recidivism and how sure they were of the correctness of their own theories
compared to experts. Finally, we presented some evidence of our own for
subjects to evaluate.

The 160 subjects who participated in this research were selected to represent average people across the life span, beginning with adolescents (ninth
graders) and including young adults in their 20s, middle adults their 40s, and
older adults in their 60s. Within each age group as well as among males and
females, two different education levels were included, generally those who

had high school versus at least some college education (these differences were prospective among the adolescent group). We also included a group of experts of three different types: experienced parole officers, regarded as having domain expertise in the return to crime topic; experienced teachers, regarded as having domain expertise in the school failure topic; and philosophers, who we regarded as having expertise in reasoning itself.

Overall, people described their causal theories readily and expressed considerable certainty that these theories were correct. Yet they showed surprising variability in the argument skills that would enable them to justify this certainty. In a word, poorly performing subjects did not regard their theories in the framework of alternative possibilities and could not conceive of evidence that would disconfirm them. Instead, these theories regarding why children fail in school or prisoners return to crime when they're released take a decidedly narrative form – "this is the way it happens" – with little conception that it could be otherwise. Theories are not reflected on as objects of cognition – as claims needing to be evaluated in the light of alternatives and evidence. Unsurprisingly, such subjects show limited ability to generate alternative theories or counterarguments.

Moreover, the evidence that we presented, subjects tended to simply assimilate to their own theories. "This pretty much goes along with my own view" was the typical response. We saw this stance as further indication of the difficulties people have in reflecting on their own thought in a way that would allow them to clearly distinguish and coordinate theories and evidence. If new evidence is simply assimilated to a theory, any potential for constructing relations between the two is lost.

Results across subject groups are easily summarized. Reasoning skills did not differ significantly by sex or age group, but consistent and substantial differences appeared by education group at every age level. For example, only 16 to 29 percent of all noncollege subjects (across topics) generated what we defined as genuine evidence to support their theories compared to 53 to 66 percent of college subjects. These findings suggest that it is some very broad kinds of experience associated with education that figure most prominently in the wide variability in observed performance. Another important finding is the significant degree of generality of skills across the three topics that were examined (see Kuhn, 1991, for details). This outcome is critical because it indicates that we have identified forms of thinking that transcend the particular content in terms of which they are expressed. Finally, domain expertise did not improve the quality of argumentive reasoning. Although philosophers reasoned well on all topics, as we expected, parole officers reasonsed no better about the crime topic than they did about the other topics, nor did teachers reason better about the school failure topic.

In an extension of this work (Kuhn, Weinstock, & Flaton, 1994a), we examined the ability of these same subjects to justify their verdict choices after hearing an abbreviated version of an authentic murder trial adapted from the court record. Differences similar to those just described were evident in juror reasoning. Some subjects were satisfied with construction of a single account that they took to be true, omitting discrepant evidence from consideration. Others reflected on the presented evidence in a framework of alternatives, weighing the supportive and discrepant evidence for each of the verdicts. These cognitive differences were related both to the subject's certainty regarding the correctness of his or her verdict choice and to the verdict choice itself, with less adequate reasoners more likely to make extreme verdict choices (first-degree murder or self-defense).

Scientific thinking as the coordination of theory and evidence

In another line of research (Kuhn, Schauble, and Garcia-Mila, 1992; Kuhn, Garcia-Mila, Zohar, and Andersen, 1995), we explicitly asked subjects to behave like scientists. Specifically, we asked them to generate and interpret evidence regarding a set of potential causes that might be implicated in an outcome and to draw the appropriate inductive inferences. The content of the problems we've used spaned physical and social sciences. The content of one problem was again children's school failure (Kuhn et al., 1995). The subject was presented a "file cabinet" of student records, each containing a summary evaluation of a student's school performance in terms of 1 of 4 outcomes (ranging from excellent to poor). Also included is information regarding 5 factors that were the subject of a study being done on factors that might affect school performance. The subject was asked to examine the records to find out which factors do and do not make a difference to the outcome. In a parallel problem, subjects were asked to investigate factors that do and do not make a difference in the popularity of children's TV programs. In corresponding problems in the physical science domain, subjects investigated factors influencing the speed at which model boats travel across a tank of water and the speed at which cars travel along a microcomputer racetrack. Prior to investigating the evidence, subjects' own theories about effects of the factors were assessed, enabling us to examine how these theories affect strategies of investigation and inference.

In a 10-week microgenetic design (Kuhn et al., 1995), preadolescent and adult subjects participated in weekly sessions in both physical and social science domains; after 5 weeks, new content was substituted in both domains to assess the generality of any improvement in reasoning skills. To examine subjects' performance, we need to take a more detailed look at inductive inference strategies.

INDUCTIVE CAUSAL AND NONCAUSAL INFERENCE IN
MULTIVARIABLE CONTEXTS
Causal inference (inclusion). On what evidence might someone base the inference that antecedent a has a causal influence on outcome o? In the framework adopted here, we assume a multivariable context and we assume that the individual is able to select instances to attend to. The question facing the individual is whether a particular factor a makes a difference to the outcome. For simplicity of exposition, we consider the case in which the identified factors – $a,b,c,d,$ and e – are dichotomous (two-level) variables. A further assumption we make is that selection of instances is at least partially theory

motivated. In other words, the individual's prior beliefs about the causal and noncausal status of the identified factors influences the selection of instances to attend to. This selectivity takes a variety of forms that need not be identified in detail here; some examples are the tendency to select instances believed to produce the most positive level of an outcome (a success rather than explanation orientation) and to fail to investigate factors that are believed noncausal.

A minimal (but, as I shall illustrate, frequent) basis for the inference that an antecedent a and an outcome o are causally related – an inference henceforth referred to as the *inclusion* of a – is their co-occurrence within a multivariable context:

$$a_1b_1c_1d_1e_1 \to o_1 \qquad (14.1)$$

We can refer to such an inference as a *co-occurrence* false inclusion inference (since a and o merely co-occur on one occasion). Such inferences are based on only a single instance and are of course invalid since the co-occurrence does not establish that a played a causal role in producing o.

In the case in which an individual selects at least two instances for examination, an informative second instance would be

$$a_2b_1c_1d_1e_1 \to o_2 \qquad (14.2a)$$

Such an instance, with the outcome shown, allows the valid inclusion inference that a is causally implicated in o. This inference, based on two instances, is the product of a *controlled comparison*.

In most natural settings, however, people do not have the opportunity to select for observation exactly those instances that would be most informative, or if they do, they may not exercise it. A more likely second instance, then, might be

$$a_2b_1c_2d_1e_2 \to o_2 \qquad (14.2b)$$

The pair of instances (14.1) and (14.2b) do not of course allow a valid inclusion inference. Nonetheless, people commonly make what we refer to as a *covariation* false inclusion inference: The covariation of a and o over two or more instances is taken as evidence for the causal role of a in producing o despite the presence of additional covariates.

Despite the fact that natural settings typically present multivariable instances with no opportunity for controlled comparison, people frequently make correct causal inferences on the basis of covariation in ways that facilitate adaptive behavior. How do they do so? A likely answer is that they do so on the basis of a larger quantity of instances of the form of (14.1) and (14.2b). Over a larger number of such instances, a person can observe consistent covariation of a and o (i.e., when a_1 is present, o_1 occurs, and when a_2 is present, o_2 occurs) despite the uncontrolled variation of remaining factors. In the more complex (and more common) case in which some or all of the remaining factors (b, c, d, and e) also have effects on the outcome, a greater range of outcomes may be observed (e.g., o_1, o_2, o_3, o_4, with o_1 the most positive and o_4 the least positive). But it will still be the case, if a has a causal effect on o, that over many instances involving uncontrolled variation, those instances containing a_1 will overall be associated with more positive outcomes than those instances containing a_2. The contrast in the outcomes produced by a_1 and those produced by a_2 may be perceived even when instances become available sequentially and are separated in time, precluding any precise computation of its magnitude.

Such inferences we have termed *generalized* inclusion inferences. Their defining feature is that they are not based on comparison of any specific instances and instead refer generally to an entire database of (uncontrolled) instances; one variable is the focus of attention and one of its levels is perceived to be associated with a different outcome or range of outcomes than the other level. For example, after observing a number of uncontrolled instances including both large and small classes, a subject might conclude, "Small classes do better than big ones." The variable of class size is thus inferred to have a causal effect on outcome.

A problem with generalized inclusion inferences is that even though they often are correct, they may not be. Specifically, they can be incorrect in two ways. First, they may be correct for the available database of instances, but this sample may not be representative of the true population of instances. This possibility is a particularly likely one because of the likelihood that selection of instances that comprise the available database is theory motivated. If an individual wishes to generate the most positive outcome or is motivated to produce theory-consistent evidence, the alleged positive levels of all factors believed to be causal will be carried along with those that may already have been established as causal. Assume, for example, that a database consisting of (14.1) and (14.2b) is available, with a a true causal variable and c believed causal but in fact noncausal, leading the subject to make false inclusion covariation inferences for both a and c. In selecting further instances, the subject is likely to continue to select instances in which both a_1 and c_1 are present (a pattern to be illustrated shortly). This selection pattern will produce a larger database in which both a and c covary with o. It sets the stage for an incorrect generalized inclusion inference, the noncausal factor having attained illusory causal power through its deliberate covariation with a true causal factor. Illusory correlation and resulting incorrect generalized inclusion inferences are thus particularly likely to arise when individuals select the evidence on which they base their inferences.

A second kind of incorrect generalized inclusion inference may result from incorrect or biased representation of the database, again most likely for the-ory-motivated reasons. In other words, the covariation between variable and outcome is in fact not present in the available database (e.g., large and small classes produce the same distribution of outcomes in this subsample of the total database), and the subject only asserts that such a covariation exists (a pattern we also observe frequently). In incorrect generalized inclusion inferences, then, bias in the selection and/or the characterization of the database is responsible for faulty inference.

Generalized inclusion inference is thus a potentially powerful but error-prone strategy for inferring causal relations. In natural settings in which controlled comparisons are impossible, it is the only way of processing co-variation information to make inferences of causality (although a number of other well-known cues, such as temporal contiguity, may influence causal inference). For this reason, generalized inclusion takes on particular signifi-cance. It may be used as an effective tool of knowledge acquisition, but theory-motivated instance selection and interpretation are the obstacles that must be overcome if it is to do so.

Noncausal inference (exclusion). Let us proceed now to the contrasting case of *exclusion* inference – the inference that a factor has no causal effect on an outcome. Noncausal inference has received much less attention than causal inference, with noncausal inferences treated in effect as noninferences by both theorists and researchers. Especially in multivariable contexts, however, non-causal inferences are critical, enabling the individual to remove many irrel-evant factors from consideration and thereby focus attention on a more manageable number of factors.

The controlled comparison of (14.1) and (14.2a), we noted, allows a valid inclusion inference. The same controlled comparison, with modification only of the second outcome, yields a valid exclusion inference:

$$a_1b_1c_1d_1e_1 \rightarrow o_1 \tag{14.1}$$

$$a_2b_1c_1d_1e_1 \rightarrow o_1 \tag{14.2c}$$

The variation in *a* produces a constant outcome, and *a* can therefore be excluded as a causal factor in producing *o*.

In the absence of control, however, this inference becomes invalid:

$$a_2b_1c_2d_1e_2 \rightarrow o_1 \tag{14.2d}$$

Comparison of (14.1) and (14.2d) does not allow a valid inference regarding *a* because the varying factors *c* and *e* may exert their own effects on the outcome. These effects could compensate one another, producing a mislead-ing constant outcome and consequent false exclusion inference.

How, then, do exclusion inferences get made in the typical situation in which controlled comparison is not feasible? Generalized exclusion inference, parallel to generalized inclusion inference, is theoretically possible: Over a set of instances, an absence of covariation between *a* and *o* is noted, that is, those instances containing a_1 are overall associated with no more positive outcomes than those instances containing a_2. However, the absence of co-variation would be exceedingly hard to compute over a database of any size in comparison to the much more readily observed presence of covariation. Although generalized exclusion is theoretically possible, our work shows that it is very rare, and even in these rare cases it is dubious whether any proc-essing of the evidence is involved; more likely, the subject's reference to a noncovariation pattern (which may or may not in fact be present in the data) is invoked as justification for a theory-motivated assertion of noncausality.

Asymmetries between inclusion and exclusion. An implication of the preceding analysis is that certain asymmetries exist between inclusion and exclusion. As just noted, generalized inclusion is a feasible strategy. In the case of exclusion, in contrast, the primary means available for excluding a factor as a causal candidate are either the valid strategy of controlled comparison or the invalid strategy of belief-based assumption (typically leading to the factor being ignored in the selection and examination of evidence). Because the required conditions for controlled comparison are infrequently available and may be infrequently used even if they are available, the second strategy is a common one.

A further difference between inclusion and exclusion lies in the relative frequency of opportunity for application, at least in the context that uncontrolled observation offers. Uncontrolled comparisons of two instances are more likely to generate differences in outcome than equivalences, since multiple effects only infrequently exactly compensate one another to produce an outcome of equivalence. Uncontrolled observations are thus more likely to offer opportunity for inclusion than exclusion. Both of these differences help to explain the greater attention in general that people pay to identifying causal, rather than noncausal, factors.

If you overlook its weakness in identifying noncausal factors, the generalized inference strategy can work fairly well with respect to inclusion, as we have noted, enabling people to construct representations of the causal factors operating in multivariable settings with at least some degree of accuracy. The challenge is to select and interpret instances in ways that minimize the bias of prior expectations. Because the method is powerful (in the sense of the amount of cognitive work it can do), it may be resistant to extinction even when the more powerful method of controlled comparison becomes available. Correspondingly, because the controlled comparison method is so seldom available, people are unlikely to recognize its value or power and therefore may be disinclined to make use of it even if they have the competence to do so and the situation allows it. Our data yielded ample evidence that this is the case. We turn next to some illustrative examples.

THE LIMITS OF SCIENTIFIC METHOD IN THE HANDS OF A NOVICE

The multivariable problem format has proven a particularly rich one for observing the theory-evidence coordination process. One reason is that it contains high degrees of freedom with respect to causal attribution. If an outcome appears to conflict with expectations with respect to one variable, these implications can be avoided simply by shifting to other variables to do the explanatory work. The cost of such freedom, however, is in the validity of the inferences that are drawn. The resulting variability in validity is exactly what our data show. People explain events by drawing from a repertory that includes both the valid and invalid inference strategies described in the preceding section. As reasoning skill improves with repeated engagement, as our microgenetic studies show it most often does, the ratios of usage of higher and lower-quality strategies may shift, but strategies of varying quality coexist in the individual's repertory for extended periods of time.

Table 14.1. *Evidence generated by Geoff for the TV problem*

Session 1		
Instance 1	−C2ts	Fair
Instance 2	MC0wf	Excellent
Instance 3	M-1wf	Good
Session 2		
Instance 4	MC0wf	Excellent
Instance 5	M−2wf	Good
Instance 6	−−2ws	Poor
Instance 7	MC2ts	Good
Instance 8	MC2tf	Good
Instance 9	MC2wf	Good

True effects: Music (M or −): Simple causal effect; Commercials (C or −): Interactive causal effect (causal only in absence of music); Length (0, 1, 2): Curvilinear causal effect (0 > 1 = 2); Day (t or w): Noncausal; Humor (f or s): Noncausal.

As an example of the reasoning we observed, we can consider Geoff, a young adult who was one of our community college sample. Geoff for the first 5 weeks worked with the TV content in the social science domain. His task was to make inferences about the effects of 5 factors on the popularity ratings given by a group of children to different TV programs. These factors are whether or not the show has music, whether it has commercials, whether it has humor, whether it is shown on Tuesday or Wednesday, and its length (a half hour, hour, or 2 hours).

After his own theories about the effects of these factors were assessed, Geoff was asked to choose a record from our file cabinet. He said he was going to "pick just any program." The record he chose to see was of a program with commercials but without music or humor, 2 hours long, and on Tuesday. (A summary of the problem structure and the evidence Geoff generated at the first two sessions is shown in Table 14.1.) After making a prediction, he was allowed to examine the record and he learned that the outcome was a rating of fair. He was asked what he had found out, and his interpretation was as follows:

You see, this shows you that the factors I was saying about . . . that you have to be funny to make it good or excellent and the day doesn't really matter, and it's too long.

Geoff's inference is slightly more complex than many because he is interpreting a negative instance – absence of one or more things leads to a poor outcome – yet his is nonetheless a classical false inclusion inference, in which one or more variables are causally implicated in an outcome simply because they co-occur with it.

When asked to choose a second record, Geoff added humor and music and changed the length to a half hour and the day to Wednesday (see Table 14.1). The outcome this time was excellent, which he interpreted as follows:

It has basically what I thought. It does make a difference when you put music and have commercials and the length of time and the humor. Basically the day is the only thing that doesn't really matter.

So, we see, the two initial pieces of evidence Geoff chose to examine provided him the opportunity to confirm all of his initial theories. Three of the factors that covaried with outcome (music, humor, and length) he interpreted as causal. The commercials factor, despite the fact it did not vary, he also included as causal, while day, which did vary, he nonetheless excluded as noncausal. (None of these inferences, of course, is valid.)

Yet before the end of the second session, Geoff generated and intended to interpret a potentially valid comparison (instances 7 and 8). In generating instance 8, he predicted

I know that if we make it funny, it will be even better. (How do you know?) Because we've seen records with funny and it was excellent.

The outcome, however, remained the same (good), providing the opportunity for a valid exclusion strategy, that is, to conclude that humor in fact does not make a difference. But Geoff shied away from this conclusion and instead made this interpretation:

It [the rating] was less than I expected. This brings me back to what I thought . . . it's rated less because it's too long.

We know, furthermore, that Geoff understood and could use the valid exclusion strategy, because the very next instance he generated (instance 9) enabled him to achieve his stated intent of "finding out that the day doesn't make a difference." The outcome was again good, and he concluded

The day doesn't make a difference, because the previous one was a different day and it still was good.

What we are seeing here is the difficulty Geoff had in relinquishing a casual theory (that humor affects outcome). This challenge was the most difficult one for all of our subjects; they had much less difficulty in detecting covariation where they did not anticipate it and constructing a causal theory to explain it. Also well illustrated by Geoff were the limits of scientific method in the hands of a novice. Both valid and invalid strategies were used variably, as needed, in the effort to coordinate theories and evidence.

What was the longer-term outcome of the shifting criteria for strategy application that subjects like Geoff exhibited? The most frequent answer is that such biases were maintained, resulting in a disinclination to apply to certain features the valid strategies that had been practiced and perfected with respect to others. The intent appeared to be one of protecting the theories in which the subject had an investment. We can again consider as an illustration the case of a subject, Carmen, who, like Geoff, was unable to relinquish her theory that humor in the TV problem was causal. In the first instance she examined (MC0wf with excellent outcome; see Table 14.2), Carmen took as evidence that her theory regarding humor was correct. The next two instances (Table 14.2), however, form a controlled comparison that would allow her to disconfirm the theory. In choosing instance 3, she said, "Let's take a chance with serious. I don't think they'll rate it very high." When the outcome contradicted this prediction, Carmen first appeared to relinquish her causal theory regarding humor by means of a valid exclusion strategy:

(What have you found out?) Children are just as interested in watching the serious stuff. They do not necessarily have to watch something with humor.

The interviewer went on, however, to inquire

(So does it make a difference whether there is humor or not?) Yes it does, because in the other one [instance 1] they rated excellent but here they just rated it good, so humor still overpowers the seriousness. I think children would understand comedy better than if it is serious.

Thus, comparing instances 2 and 3, Carmen drew the correct inference, but this conclusion apparently did not sit well with her, and in response to a further probe, she instead compared instance 3 to instance 1, enabling her to draw a different (and valid) inference. Furthermore, she justified this inference with theory-based reasoning – this is a conclusion that makes sense, she suggests. In choosing instance 4, Carmen then turned her attention to a different factor entirely.

At session 2, however, Carmen returned to humor. Here (instance 5) the outcome strongly contradicted her humor theory. She again showed a similar sequence of first valid, then invalid, reasoning, and we can sense her confusion:

I did not think the children would have gone for it. I was thinking that they might . . . if they had rated poor . . . but I see that it does not, this is a good one.

But Carmen then took a different tack:

You see, it's not that serious, because it has music in it. Maybe that's what made a difference.

The outcome of the next instance (6) allowed Carmen to pursue this line of thought. The absence of music, she inferred, played a role, but humor also "helped":

If I had put fun in, I think that children would have rated it a little bit better.

In choosing the next instance (7), Carmen hoped to improve the outcome (and thereby demonstrate the power of the humor factor):

Table 14.2. *Evidence generated by Carmen for the TV problem*

Session 1		
Instance 1	MC0wf	Excellent
Instance 2	M−1wf	Good
Instance 3	M−1ws	Good
Instance 4	MC2tf	Good
Session 2		
Instance 5	MC0ws	Excellent
Instance 6	−−1ts	Poor
Instance 7	−C2tf	Fair
Instance 8	MC0wf	Excellent
Instance 9	MC1ws	Good
Session 3		
Instance 10	MC0tf	Excellent
Instance 11	−−2ts	Poor
Instance 12	−−1tf	Poor
Instance 13	MC2wf	Good
Instance 14	MC0wf	Excellent
Session 4		
Instance 15	MC0wf	Excellent
Instance 16	MC0tf	Excellent
Instance 17	−−2ws	Poor
Instance 18	−−2ts	Poor
Instance 19	−−2tf	Poor
Session 5		
Instance 20	−−2ws	Poor
Instance 21	−−2ts	Poor
Instance 22	−C2ts	Fair
Instance 23	−C0ts	Good
Instance 24	MC2tf	Good

True effects: Music (M or −): Simple causal effect; Commercials (C or −): Interactive causal effect (causal only in absence of music); Length (0, 1, 2): Curvilinear causal effect (0 > 1 = 2); Day (t or w): Noncausal; Humor (f or s): Noncausal.

I hope that humor will play a big part in it.

The outcome was only slightly better, however, and she concluded

Oh, music still plays a big part . . . the fact there was no music made a difference in how they rated it. (Anything else?) Maybe humor helped.

Still holding on to her humor theory and having established to her satisfaction that music also plays a causal role, Carmen then turned to the common strategy of trying to maximize the overall outcome: "I'll do what I think is positive now." This strategy, note, set up the conditions for false inclusion inference: The alleged positive levels of factors believed to be causal were carried along with those a subject may already have validly established as causal. In other words, the ineffective factor attained its illusory causal power through its deliberate covariation with an actual causal factor.

Carmen exploited this strategy with instance 8, implicating both music and humor as well as length as casual. In choosing the final instance (9) at this session, Carmen appeared to turn her attention to length, predicting an outcome of good because the program was longer than instance 8. In interpreting the outcome, however, she initially said nothing about length and instead exploited the opportunity to note the apparent implication regarding humor (which she had also varied):

> They seem not to like it serious. When it had humor, they rated it excellent.

At the third session, we see more of the same. Carmen noted regarding instance 12, "They rated it bad, even though humor was involved." Rather than relinquish the humor theory, however, a reference to instance 10 allowed her to reach this notable conclusion:

> I found out that humor and music together make a difference.

The comparison of instances 13 and 14 produced the first valid inclusion inference for length, and at session 4 the tide seemed to turn, with two successive valid exclusion inferences for day of the week (based on a comparison of instances 15 and 16 and instances 17 and 18). Presumably because it fit well with her theoretical beliefs, Carmen liked to demonstrate the irrelevance of this feature and did so repeatedly. Then, with instances 18 and 19, Carmen set the stage for a similar valid exclusion of humor. But here, where her theoretical involvement was greater, Carmen instead concluded with evident disappointment:

> I thought humor might balance all these, but it did not. They still rated it bad.

In other words, she believed the presence of humor might compensate for the absence of the other features she perceived as positive (music and a short length). Instead of using the data she had generated to make an exclusion inference for humor, however, Carmen drew this conclusion:

> I think humor still makes a difference. (How do you know?) From previous ratings . . . every time the humor was with the music, they rated it excellent. (And what did you learn from this instance here [19]?) They rated it bad. In this particular one, humor did not make a difference.

Carmen's final session with the TV problem showed clearly sophisticated and efficient strategy use. Instances 20 and 21 were used to validly exclude day. Instance 21 was then used again with instance 22 to validly include commercials, and then 22 and 23 were used to validly include length. For humor, however, Carmen did not construct the controlled comparison she by now had shown herself quite capable of doing. Instead, in constructing the final instance (24), she changed three variables rather than only one, thereby not risking putting her humor theory to a serious test. In interpreting instance 24, she concluded that humor was causal, with the justification:

When I chose serious, even with commercials, the rating was bad.

Carmen exhibited two means of saving an incorrect theory that were common to many subjects. The first was to particularize an inference – "In this particular one, humor did not make a difference" – with the implication that the theory was by no means dead and might well apply elsewhere. The second, and more common, strategy was to particularize the theory by linking the factor to another one with perceived causal power – "humor and music together make a difference."

Still another means subjects used to save a theory was to invent data to which an inference strategy can be applied, enabling the subject to maintain compatibility between theory and evidence. During his second session with the TV problem, Juan, for example, justified his claim that day of the week makes no difference with the assertion that "I tried it with both days and got the same outcome." In fact he had generated instances involving both days, but these were uncontrolled with respect to other features and they never yielded the same outcome. Data invention was particularly likely to arise in the case of generalized inferences, given the freedom in characterizing data that they allow.

In the excerpts presented here, investigation is theory driven to a counterproductive extent. A major problem with highly theory-driven investigation is that subjects did not access enough of the database to disconfirm their theories. They were satisfied with the average one-third of the data that they accessed and were convinced that the information they had was sufficient to allow firm conclusions.

Failure to generate sufficient data is by no means the whole problem, however. The excerpts presented from Carmen's protocol suggest that no amount of data would have led her to exclude humor as a factor. More broadly, the limitations in reasoning shown by Geoff and Carmen can be characterized as metastrategic rather than strategic in nature. Strategic competence, that is, ability to execute valid inference strategies, was observed in all of our adult subjects. Where subjects appeared weak, in contrast, is in reflection on both the valid and invalid strategies that they used in a way that might promote their consistent application. In the absence of this metastrategic competence, claims can be justified by identifying even the most minimal piece of evidence that appears to support them. As the excerpts presented here illustrate, subjects may apply a variety of devices to protect these claims from the evidence bearing on them. In cases in which the evidence is acknowledged, these devices include particularizing the inference (as an exception) or particularizing the theory (by limiting its applicability). Alternative devices include simply ignoring the evidence and/or inventing different evidence. Each of these devices succeeds in maintaining alignment between theory and evidence but at a cost we consider further in the next section.

Connecting scientific and everyday thought

Inductive reasoning skills, especially those involving causal inferences in a multivariable framework, are traditionally associated with scientific thinking. Everyday argumentive reasoning about causes of school failure or criminal recidivism, in contrast, are not. I have tried here to establish a deep connection between the two. The challenges that subjects confront as scientists in the inductive reasoning studies are at heart the same ones as those we have identified in our argumentive reasoning research. First, subjects must be able to reflect on their own theories as objects of cognition to an extent sufficient to recognize they could be wrong. Second, they need to recognize evidence that could disconfirm the theory. Less competent subjects do not conceive of the possibility that theorized relations are wrong and avoid evidence capable of disconfirming them. Both scientific and everyday theories must be regarded as representation of possible states of affairs that are subject to confirmation or disconfirmation by evidence.

We were not asking Carmen to discard her own intuitions or theories but only to recognize the implications of evidence bearing on them. Coordination of theories and evidence implies reciprocal adjustment. Not only must evidence serve as the basis for evaluating and possibly revising theories, but theories legitimately influence the direction and form of investigation. The difference between skilled and unskilled reasoning lies in the degree of control that is attained of the coordination process (Kuhn, 1989). Without such control, beliefs come into contact with new evidence in an unstable way. Evidence is either ignored or distorted to protect the belief, or the individual is unduly swayed by it, leaving beliefs at the mercy of transitory, unpredictable external influences. In contrast, those who have achieved control of the interaction of theory and evidence in their own thinking are able to distinguish what comes from their own thought and what comes from external sources. They exercise this control because they are able to think *about* their theories, not merely *with* them.

In sum, in both scientific and everyday reasoning, people must be able to distance themselves from their own beliefs to a sufficient degree to be able to evaluate them, as objects of cognition, in a framework of alternatives that compete with them and evidence that bears on them. Although it is not possible to go into full detail here, we see the development of skill in coordinating theory and evidence as encompassing three broad components: strategic, metastrategic, and metacognitive competence (Kuhn et al., 1995). *Strategic* competence is competence to execute the investigative and inference strategies that yield valid conclusions. Among adult samples, this competence is typically present, at least for elementary strategies that do not involve additive or interactive effects. The presence of competence, however, does not guarantee that a strategy will be used consistently, a fact that highlights the importance of *metastrategic* competence. It is meta strategic understanding, not strategic competence, that dictates the strategies that will actually be applied. Metastrategic competence includes understanding of both the value and the limitations of a strategy – knowing how, when, and why it should be used. Finally, in contrast to metastrategic competence, which has to do with the form of one's knowledge, *metacognitive* competence involves reflection on its content. The inductive inference task we have described entails metacognitive competence since it requires justifying assertions by identifying and retaining knowledge of their sources (i.e., the bases for claiming them to be true) – a capability necessary for differentiation of theory and evidence at a metacognitive level. Without it, representations of theory and evidence are likely to be merged into a single representation of "the way things are," since the sources of this knowledge are not distinguished. When discrepant evidence accumulated, Carmen, we saw, did not recognize it as discrepant with her theory, as the more metacognitively competent subject would have. Instead, she marshaled fragments of this evidence into a role of *supporting* the theory. Rather then compare evidence to theory, she used available evidence to illustrate what she knew to be true. As a consequence, the metacognitive distinction between theory-based and evidence-based justification remained blurred, as it did for many of our subjects. The two merged in the service of a common end, leaving Carmen certain of her causal belief (regarding the humor feature) but not metacognitively aware with regard to its source.

Metacognitive distancing from one's theories is not a routine developmental attainment but an ideal that even professional scientists fall short of (Mahoney, 1976). Throughout their lives, even the most cognitively competent adults remain challenged to be able to justify to themselves and others why they believe what they do and to be aware of the sources of their beliefs. They remain challenged to bring evidence to bear on their beliefs in a way that reflects clear differentiation between the implications of evidence and what they believe to be true. The inclination to draw on available evidence to illustrate what one knows to be true is always present.

An implication of the present analysis is that it is a mistake to equate good or rigorous thinking with scientific thinking. To do so is to view the scientific enterprise and the thinking associated with it much too narrowly. Scientists employ the inferential thinking strategies that they do because they are powerful strategies that well serve the scientist's objectives. It does not follow that such strategies should be confined to or even associated predominantly with science. A method or approach may be fundamental to scientific thinking, without being particular to it. The strategies that serve the scientist well are valuable to the rest of us as well.

In carving the modes-of-thinking pie, then, the first cut, in my view, is not between scientific thinking and another form or forms that might be characterized variously as narrative or associative or creative. Instead, the most significant distinction to be made is between thinking that is more versus less skilled, with skilled thinking defined in its essence as thinking that reflects on itself and is applied under the individual's conscious control. It is this distinction that has the most profound implications with respect to how people use thinking in their own lives to achieve their goals as well as to withstand attempts to be manipulated by the goals of others.

Developing powerful thinking strategies

If we agree that good thinking can be defined in broader terms than scientific thinking, we next want to understand how it develops. A major key appears to be exercise. The majority of our subjects – both preadolescents and adults – in microgenetic studies exhibit progress in reasoning skill with repeated engagement (Kuhn et al., 1992, 1995). The generality of change we observe when subjects work either simultaneously or sequentially in two domains makes it implausible that subjects are simply gaining knowledge of the specific domains in which they are working. The strategic changes we observe have to do with *how* conclusions are drawn, not the particular content of these conclusions. If we examine the development of scientific thinking only as domain-specific conceptual change, we reduce explanatory power by neglecting an important aspect of what is developing during the childhood and adolescent years.

DEVELOPMENTAL ORIGINS OF THINKING SKILLS

The points stressed thus far in this chapter that bear on the development of thinking skills are (1) that sound thinking is very broadly based, rather than narrowly scientific in nature; (2) that its essential dimension is one of thought becoming aware of itself; and (3) that practice of thinking is a critical factor in transforming it into good thinking. To these we can add a fourth point – that this development occurs very gradually rather than at some discrete point. Although it has sometimes been treated this way in the literature, metacognition, like cognition, is not a zero–one, present–absent phenomenon that emerges in full bloom at a particular point in development. The theory-of-mind literature has made clear that young children develop basic metacognitive competencies that serve as underpinnings of more complex forms of reasoning about propositions, most fundamentally the ability to reason about propositions as belief states. The 4-year-old who comes to recognize that an assertion is not necessarily correct – that the candy can be believed (by someone) to be in the cupboard and in truth be elsewhere (Perner, 1991) – has achieved a milestone in cognitive development. The child has made at least a primitive differentiation between what a mind theorizes to be true and information from the external world that bears on this theory. False beliefs, by definition, are subject to disconfirmation by evidence.

Other studies, however, have shown these early metacognitive competencies to be uneven. A series of studies by Flavell, Green, and Flavell (1995) show that preschoolers have considerable difficulty in accurately reporting either their own immediately preceding mental activity or that of another individual. Studies by Gopnik have shown that preschoolers have limited awareness of the source of their beliefs. In very simple situations, 3- and 4-year-olds could not identify where knowledge they had just acquired had come from, for example, whether they had learned the contents of a drawer from seeing them or being told about them (Gopnik and Graf, 1988). Once the knowledge was acquired, the two evidently became fused into a single representation that encompassed only the knowledge itself. By age 5, however, performance was significantly improved. In sum, these studies point to the gradual emergence of a set of crucial metacognitive skills having to do with "knowing how you know" – skills that are critical in managing one's own thinking, as the illustration of Carmen's thinking shows.

A number of other precursors of the skills examined in this chapter have been identified. As long as the situation is very simple and it is not their own beliefs they are asked to reflect on, young school-age children can comprehend the relation between a pattern of evidence and a theory, even when the theory has been explicitly presented as false (Ruffman, Perner, Olson, and Doherty, 1993). Put in different terms, the child can draw appropriate inferences from contrary-to-fact propositions (an ability Piaget tied to the emergence of formal operations). Children of similar age can choose a determinate versus indeterminate test as a means of verifying a proposition (Pieraut-Le Bonniec, 1980; Sodian, Zaitchik, and Carey, 1991), and make inferences of causality from covariation (Ruffman et al., 1993; Shultz and Mendelson, 1975). Elementary school children also have been shown able to choose explanations that do not have these characteristics (Samarapungavan, 1992). (See Kuhn et al., 1995, for fuller discussion of this research.) Again, however, none of these skills is specific to science, even though each may be critical to it. All of them are fundamental skills of inductive inference that serve their users in realms that extend far beyond professional science.

THE EPISTEMOLOGICAL DIMENSION OF COMPETENCE
Until now, we have focused on the development and effective use of broad forms of thinking skills. Yet, the exercise and strengthening of thinking skills isn't everything. Another key factor that our research points to is epistemological understanding of the nature of thinking and knowing. Based on a few questions of an epistemological nature included in our interview in the argumentive reasoning research – questions such as whether experts know for sure the answers to these questions or anyone's answer could be proved right or wrong – we observed the same general progression noted by other researchers who have investigated naive epistemologies. It begins with the most prevalent stance of *absolutism*, in which knowledge is regarded as a "freestanding attribute of the environment" (Chandler, Boyes, and Ball, 1990) that accumulates toward certainty without connection to the human minds that do this knowing and proceeds to an also prevalent stance of *multiplism*, or relativism. Multiplists descend the slippery slope of noting that even experts disagree, going on to conclude that therefore nothing is certain and, from there, that all are merely opinions and are equally valid. Beliefs or opinions are the possessions of their owners, freely chosen according to the owner's tastes and wishes and accordingly not subject to criticism. Hence (in the final step down the slippery slope), because everyone has a right to their opinion, all opinions are equally right. In the words of one of the adolescents

in our sample, "You can't prove an opinion to be wrong because an opinion is something somebody holds for themselves." Only about 15 percent of the adolescents and adults in our sample had progressed to what we called an *evaluative* epistemology, in which knowing is understood as a process that entails judgment, evaluation, and argument. They have reconciled the idea that people have a right to their views with the understanding that some views can nonetheless be more right than others.

This lack of epistemological understanding may be an important factor in the limited argumentive reasoning ability that people display. People must see the point of argument if they are to engage in it. If knowledge is entirely objective, certain, and simply accumulates, as the absolutist believes, or if knowledge is entirely subjective, subject only to the tastes and wishes of the knower, as the multiplist believes, critical thinking and judgment are super-fluous. Empirical findings from the argument research are consistent with an association between skill and epistemological stance (Kuhn, 1991). Those subjects who espoused an evaluative epistemology were more likely to exhibit the key argumentive skills of counterargument and generation of alternative theories. These findings thus point to the importance of epistemological understanding. In sum, they suggest that both skill and disposition are necessary if people are to acquire the critical habit of thinking about their own thought.

Conclusions: Scientific and "ordinary" thinking

Two key points that have been stressed with respect to thinking skill apply as well to epistemological understanding, which is surely intricately connected to the development and application of skill, although it remains to investigate exactly how. First, the development of epistemological understanding is gradual, with origins in the metacognitive achievements of early childhood, for example, the understanding of statements as expressions of someone's belief (Olson and Astington, 1993) and the understanding that genuine differences in belief exist (Flavell, Mumme, Green, and Flavell, 1992; Taylor, Cartwright, and Bowden, 1991).

Second, although a sophisticated epistemological understanding is critical to scientific thinking, it is not particular to it. Carey and Smith (1993) describe students' limited epistemological understanding of the nature of the scientific enterprise, with most junior high school students seeing the process of professional science as an accumulation of factual knowledge derived from unbiased observation and experimentation and unconnected to any body of theory that might play a role in the process. One can readily agree with Carey and Smith that underlying conceptions of science are fundamental in the teaching and learning of science and interact in still poorly understood ways with the development of scientific thinking skills and scientific knowledge. Nonetheless, this epistemological understanding is not confined to the realm of science, as shown by our work on epistemological dimensions of argumentive reasoning (Kuhn, 1991, ch. 7) as well as related work on epistemological understanding in other fields such as history (Kuhn, Weinstock, and Flaton, 1994b; Leadbeater and Kuhn, 1989). Those who have not reached the evaluative level of epistemological understanding conceive of no basis for judging the strength of an argument beyond its power to persuade. There is no need or place for the comparative weighing and evaluation of alternative claims that are the heart of skilled debate. Many of the most fundamental goals of our educational system depend on this understanding. Those who lack it have limited control over their own thought in the respects described earlier and have the capacity for at best limited participation in a democratic society.

I would take exception, then, to some science educators' characterizations of acquainting students with scientific discourse as involving

> young people entering into a different way of thinking about and ex-
> plaining the natural world; becoming socialized to a greater or lesser ex-
> tent into the practices of the scientific community with its particular
> purposes, ways of seeing, and ways of supporting its knowledge claims.
> (Driver, Asoko, Leach, Mortimer, and Scott, 1994, p. 8)

To be sure, nontrivial differences exist between everyday and scientific think-ing (Driver et al., 1994; Reif and Larkin, 1991). Yet, the claim I have tried to support here is that at our present state of knowledge, the connections are more important than the differences. Scientific thinking, I noted at the outset, tends to be viewed narrowly, as relevant and accessible only to those few who pursue science professionally. If science education is to be fruitful, it is essential to counter this view, establishing the place that scientific thinking has in the lives of all students (Kuhn, 1993b). The typical approach to this objective has been to try to connect the *content* of science to phenomena familiar to students in their everyday lives. A more powerful approach may be to connect the *process* of science to thinking processes that figure in ordinary people's lives. If we pursue this approach, scientific thinking may eventually live down its bad name.

References

Billig, M. (1987). *Arguing and thinking: A rhetorical approach to social psychology.* Cambridge: Cambridge Univ. Press.
Carey, S., & Smith, C. (1993). On understanding the nature of scientific knowledge. *Educational Psychologist, 28*(3), 235–251.
Chandler, M., Boyes, M., & Ball, L. (1990). Relativism and stations of epistemic doubt. *Journal of Experimental Child Psychology, 50,* 370–395.
Damon, W. (1990). Social relations and children's thinking skills. In D. Kuhn (Ed.), *Developmental perspectives on teaching and learning thinking skills,* Vol. 21, *Contributions to human development.* Basel: Karger.
Driver, R., Asoko, H., Leach, J., Mortimer, E., & Scott, P. (1994). Constructing scientific knowledge in the classroom. *Educational Researcher, 23*(7), 5–12.
Einstein, A. (1954). *Ideas and opinions.* New York: Crown.
Flavell, J., Mumme, D., Green, F., & Flavell, E. (1992). Young children's understand-ing of different types of beliefs, *Child Development, 63,* 960–977.
Flavell, J., Green, F., & Flavell, E. (1995). Young children's knowledge about think-

ing. *Society for Research in Child Development* Monographs, *60* (1, Serial no. 243).

Gopnik, A., & Graf, P. (1988). Knowing how you know: Young children's ability to identify and remember the sources of their beliefs. *Child Development, 59,* 1366–1371.

Kuhn, D. (1989). Children and adults as intuitive scientists. *Psychological Review, 96,* 674–689.

(1991). *The skills of argument.* New York: Cambridge Univ. Press.

(1992). Thinking as argument. *Harvard Educational Review, 62,* 155–178.

(1993a). Connecting scientific and informal reasoning. *Merrill-Palmer Quarterly* (Special issue: "The Development of Rationality and Critical Thinking"), *39*(1), 74–103.

(1993b). Science as argument: Implications for teaching and learning scientific thinking. *Science Education, 77*(3), 319–337.

Kuhn, D., Garcia-Mila, M., Zohar, A., & Andersen, C. (1995). *Strategies of knowledge acquisition. Society for Research in Child Development Monographs, 60* (4, Serial no. 245).

Kuhn, D., Schauble, L., & Garcia-Mila, M. (1992). Cross-domain development of scientific reasoning. *Cognition and Instruction, 9*(4), 285–327.

Kuhn, D., Weinstock, M., & Flaton, R. (1994a). How well do jurors reason? Competence dimensions of individual variation in a juror reasoning task. *Psychological Science, 5*(5), 289–296.

Kuhn, D., Weinstock, M., & Flaton, R. (1994b). Historical reasoning as theory-evidence coordination. In M. Carretero & J. Voss (Eds.), *Cognitive and instructional processes in history and the social sciences.* Hillsdale, NJ: Erlbaum.

Leadbeater, B., & Kuhn, D. (1989). Interpreting discrepant narratives: Hermeneutics and adult cognition. In J. Sinnott (Ed.), *Everyday problem-solving: Theory and application.* New York: Praeger.

Mahoney, M. (Ed.). (1976). *Scientist as subject: The psychological imperative.* Cambridge, MA: Ballinger.

Olson, D. R., & Astington, J. W. (1993). Thinking about thinking: Learning how to take statements and hold beliefs. *Educational Psychologist, 28*(1), 7–23.

Perner, J. (1991). *Understanding the representational mind.* Cambridge, MA: MIT Press.

Pieraut-Le Bonniec, G. (1980). *The development of modal reasoning.* New York: Academic Press.

Reichenbach, H. (1938). *Experience and prediction.* Chicago: Univ. of Chicago Press.

Reif, F., & Larkin, J. (1991). Cognition in scientific and everyday domains: Comparison and learning implications. *Journal of Research in Science Teaching, 28*(9), 733–760.

Ruffman, T., Perner, J., Olson, D., & Doherty, M. (1993). Reflecting on scientific thinking: Children's understanding of the hypothesis–evidence relation. *Child Development, 64,* 1617–1636.

Samarapungavan, A. (1992). Children's judgments in theory choice tasks: Scientific rationality in childhood. *Cognition, 45,* 1–32.

Shultz, T., & Mendelson, R. (1975). The use of covariation as a principle of causal analysis. *Child Development, 46,* 394–399.

Sodian, B., Zaitchik, D., & Carey, S. (1991). Young children's differentiation of hypothetical beliefs from evidence. *Child Development, 62,* 753–766.

Taylor, M., Cartwright, B., & Bowden, T. (1991). Perspective taking and theory of mind: Do children predict interpretive diversity as a function of differences in observer's knowledge? *Child Development, 62,* 1334–1351.

15
Network, *the verb, and the appeal of collaborative modes of instruction and thought*

Myron Tuman

A dominant metaphor of educational change this century has often been the *bandwagon* – loud and sometimes thoughtless support for a particular ped-agogic practice in an atmosphere that plays off a glorious, irresistible future (once this practice is adopted) against a benighted, reactionary past. The educational bandwagon gathers its seemingly unstoppable momentum by contrasting a future where all problems are solved against a past responsible for creating those problems in the first place. The present thus becomes less a time for thought than for action and change.

During the 1970s and 1980s, for example, teachers of college composition were told that their students wrote so poorly because all their previous teach-ers had emphasized the fixed *product* of writing over the dynamic *process* of composing. Students do not write well because all their previous teachers had followed an outmoded paradigm – one that made them too anxious, too concerned with mechanics, too unwilling to revise. Never mind that *at some crucial point* we all have to wrestle with our inchoate thoughts, struggle to make them follow the highly demanding laws of structure, diction, and syntax that characterize all good writing, that is, that the process of writing has to be forged into a product. (And never mind that George Eliot wrote her first novel, *Adam Bede*, from start to end, revising only a single scene.) Our students would be saved from bad writing – and just as importantly from bad thinking and reactionary forces generally – by valuing ideas and expres-sion more than form and superficial correctness, by getting it out first and worry about dressing it up later – too often, much later.

Perhaps the appropriate metaphor here is not a bandwagon but a floodlight, an intensely bright light that instead of illuminating the landscape does little but attract and then blind all those who are attracted to its brilliance. Yet what is most interesting about the bright light of process pedagogy today is less its triumph, which may well have been complete, than its near total disappearance. In the 1990s, one trend in college composition has been re-placed by another: where we had once been exhorted to revise, we are now urged to collaborate, especially over computer networks. While just a few years ago, we were all enamored of the image of the great writer as someone working alone, hours on end, in a solitary urban garret or distant rural cottage, now we are all instructed on what used to be standing joke: the advantages and the joys of writing by committee. The good writing environment now involves what one advocate calls "a move outward from the writer to others who provide response and input. It is a move away from solipsism" (Handa, 1990, 162). As this writer, Carolyn Handa, makes clear, this new form of writing incorporates, rather than replaces, the good–bad, the process–product dichotomy: "The more authoritative technique of focusing an autonomous student writer on a product now exists alongside one seeking to empower students through process and collaboration" (Handa, 1990, 165).

Good student work, almost by definition, is work done collaboratively with other students: it is, argues Barker and Kemp (1990, 5), "open, inclusive, nonhierarchical, consensus based, and process oriented." Bad student work, likewise, is that which is imposed by the teacher, bad in part, not just because of the outcome – student learning, or the lack of it – but bad because it is enforced, coercive, and based on an outmoded, top-down model of social and economic order. The underlying model of the new writing classroom, like the new office, particularly that of new professional managers of service companies, is that of the computer network:

> The links or lines of contact proceed from every workstation to every other workstation. No link is privileged. There is no master control over them. If the instructor wishes to participate in the discourse, she must choose a workstation and participate at a transactional level equal to that of any other person sitting at any other workstation. (Barker and Kemp, 1990, 16)

Here is networking as the embodiment, not just of revolutionary classroom practice, but of social and, equally importantly, cognitive organization. As one enthusiast writes, computer networks, both in and outside a classroom, "become human networks – electronic circles that support alternative, non-traditional dialogue and dialectic, communities that value revision and re-interpretation of traditional educational structures" (Selfe, 1990, 123). *Networking* – reaching out, making and maintaining human contact (instead of withdrawing), helping others (instead of worrying mainly about oneself), revision, process, and openness (instead of a closed, static conception of the world), a dialogue of equals (instead of being talked by an expert "from above" – as would be the case if this chapter were being read to you by its author at a typical academic conference).

How, we might ask, can we explain this transformation? How has *network* become a verb seemingly overnight and one with such widespread positive connotation? The verb form, for example, is not even mentioned in the 1933 edition of the *Oxford English Dictionary* (with supplement) (OED) and is cited in the all-encompassing *Webster's Third New International Dictionary* from 1966 only in the geographic sense of "networking" a country with canals and so on. And what is the connection between the obviously positive, literal application to computers – having to do (from the 1989 second edition of the OED) "link[ing] (computers) together to make possible . . . the transfer of data, the sharing of processing capability or workloads, and accessibility from many locations" and the even more recent (not in the most recent 1989 edition of the OED), less literal and, at least to some, far less positive definition (from the 1991 edition of *Longman Dictionary*) of "establish[ing] a set of contacts with people in a similar business of situation as oneself, for the informal exchange of information, ideas, and help''? How, in other words, has *network,* the verb, been able to triumph so completely, casting off in the process, its pejorative sense of a kind of smarmy, self-promotion, a path to success based more on personal contacts (the old-boy network) and hype than performance? Why now, at least in educational circles, has networking become so unambiguously a good, denoting the practice of reaching out to others, to connect, with the purpose of achieving some noble, socially beneficial end? And what, if anything, is wrong with this new landscape?

One answer is that impassioned support for networked instruction is part of a larger ideological agenda calling for basic rethinking of all forms of social organization. Traditional classrooms, accordingly, are both a replica and a primary site for the reproduction of the worst aspects of modern culture. ''A traditional, noncollaborative classroom,'' writes Handa (1990, 168), ''run[s] the risk of preventing students from realizing their own power as writers and from challenging the competition, chauvinism, and class structure that have played such a major role in capitalistic societies and academia.'' The collaborative classroom, meanwhile, becomes a replica of the new consumer-driven economy: not just as another aspect of late-capitalist reproduction – another high-tech, postindustrial service industry leading the way to the networked society – but more significantly, as a utopian alternative to the present. The network-based collaborative classroom, perhaps based more on faith than reason, is seen as ''challeng[ing] the assumptions that characterize both capitalistic societies and academia, as well as theories of knowledge reinforced by textbooks built on certain traditions and reactions to those traditions'' (Handa, 1990, 168). The traditional classroom and the teacher who runs it thus get implicated with a full range of past practices (pedagogic and otherwise) involving various aspects of objective science, Western economic expansion, and liberal individualism. Collaborative writing, on the other hand, especially that facilitated by computers, thus becomes a key step on the path to social justice. ''If we can't eliminate the effect of racism, sexism, and classism in our traditional classrooms,'' reason Cooper and Selfe (1990, 867), ''we may be able to set aside smaller electronic spaces in which such problems can find expression and be debated.''

Cooper and Selfe's support of networked instruction, like the support of others in the field, is enlivened by a more encompassing mission – here, a sense of empowerment that is part of grassroots, small-is-better, economic populism. Move the teacher from the center of the classroom and we empower students, just as we empower citizens by limiting the power of the government and large institutions generally, relying instead on grassroots activism: ''Once students became used to setting their own agenda for the conference – determining the topics, the pace, the tone, and the direction of the discussion – they resisted any suggestion the teacher made in class designed to influence the nature of the conference. The students had assumed power within this alternate forum'' (Cooper and Selfe, 1990, 857).

What's wrong here is not the goal – student, or citizen, empowerment, especially that which is available through grassroots organization. Who doesn't want people cooperating locally to work in their own behalf? What's wrong is the lack of critical awareness – the naive, almost Rousseauian confidence in the liberatory effect of computer networks. Just as all educational problems are caused by benighted practice, all the solutions lie in adopting some new method, as it were, climbing on this or that bandwagon – here, computer-facilitated collaboration. Perhaps only in educational circles is it still possible to believe that social justice, like water seeking lower ground, rushes in to fill the vacuum left by the collapse of traditional authority, be it the state or teacher. When the teacher or the state is entirely associated with reactionary practices (again characteristic of bandwagon thinking), then the recipe for progressive change (for schools or society generally) becomes deceptively simple: eliminate the teacher or the state, and what rushes in to take its place will be, ipso facto, better. Here is a psychodrama of immense social import: students overthrowing their teachers and, by implication, workers overthrowing their managers, the citizens overthrowing their rulers – and all of it leading to progress, not just to greater social justice, but to higher levels of knowledge as well.

With regard to social justice, we might ask why should we really expect students to treat other students in a fairer or kinder fashion than teachers have treated them? Or is it just intrinsically better to be bullied by one's cohorts than to be treated fairly by a teacher? And where do students learn the principles and practices of social justice if not from teachers (or parents) and especially from watching these people exercise authority humanely? Or is it just that acts of consensus or majority rule within the classroom are to be deemed just by definition? And what about outside the classroom? What in fact do we really want from worker control of industry – more interesting (more humane?) work, or more efficient production? It's comforting to believe that the two are fully compatible and if they are not, that we can easily absorb less proficient production without seriously affecting living standards. And finally, what about government and society as a whole? Is there always more liberty, greater freedom, more social justice in Rousseau's community, where the people are free to tyrannize each other, than in Hobbes's community where the state is specifically charged with that duty?

All these difficult questions have essentially the same answer, namely, that at some basic level, it really does not matter, that contemporary enthusiasm for the networked classroom is finally inseparable from larger cultural attachment to postindustrial forms of social and economic cooperation. The answer, in other words, is that, given the failures of the past, many have concluded that we have no choice but to put our faith in new forms of social organization and, by extension, new, postmodern modes of thought. The large-scale models of economic and cultural development of the last few hundred years, including the underlying faith in the transformative power of science, appear completely exhausted; problems such as environmental degradation and worldwide underemployment seem largely insoluble in terms of past practices. In fact the environmental degradation and worldwide employment (along with burgeoning population) seem to defy a traditional common resolution. It just does not seem possible for us to grow our way out of this impasse through the recipe of the past hundred years: economic expansion fueled by increased technological efficiency – more goods, more trade, more jobs! We clearly need a new answer, one involving alternate forms of social and economic organization, groups that are smaller and locally based. Why not begin, therefore, with a new form of autonomous, cooperative social organization, including the network-based collaborative classroom?

And the best answer is, we do need to reform classrooms, just as we need to reform society generally, but in neither case, can we expect to effect lasting and substantial change if we ground our efforts on little more than enthusiasm and slogans in support of change. Not all change is progress: the mere removal of central authority – political or academic, either in Eastern Europe or a networked classroom – does not guarantee anyone greater liberty, much less social justice. As the work of two modern social theorists help to explain, real progress must be grounded on a solid understanding of the complex historical relationship between group organization and individual autonomy. As explained in greater detail later, in one important respect the message of both French political theorist Andre Gorz (1982) and American social psychologist G. H. Mead (1934, 1964) is essentially the same: the individual sense of personal autonomy – long seen as the goal of liberatory practice – emerges as part of a complex response to the assertion of public authority and not its collapse. If we alter our cultural understanding of authority, in other words, especially as it is embedded into scientific thinking, then we are likely to alter longstanding and widely valued notions of individualism as well. Such notions may well need changing; what remains at issue, however, is the wisdom in undertaking such changes with such liberatory fervor. There is, in a word, a difference between accepting one's fate and rejoicing in it.

Gorz's work, especially his monograph, *Farewell to the Working Class* (Gorz, 1982), brilliantly portrays both the need to and the difficulties involved in moving from the modern norm of social organization – the regimented, role-based, rule-governed, state-controlled industrialism that on a macroscale mirrors the traditional classroom. In raising the basic question of how best to organize society in a age of increasing awareness of limits in order to benefit citizen-workers, Gorz openly confronts the appeal and danger of post-industrial, alternative social (and, by implication, educational) structures. Here, his main concern is to resist the nostalgia for autarky – the small-scale, self-sufficient community that so commonly served as the basis of preindustrial community. With echoes of Durkheim's notion of the interconnection of job specialization and the modern sense of personal autonomy, Gorz (1982, 102) warns against the "impoverishing effect" of communal autarky: "The more self-sufficient and numerically limited a community is, the smaller the range of activities and choices it can offer to its members. If it has no opening to an area of exogenous activity, knowledge and production, the community becomes a prison."

What is the advantage, Gorz (1982, 107) asks, of "abolishing the sphere of necessity [or the teacher] as a distinct sphere which imposes *external* rules and obligations, in such a way that necessities are assumed and internalized by each community and each individual''? Gorz's answer is that there really is none. Freedom is only possible, he argues, in a social system with well-defined rules, impartially enforced by an impersonal agent – the state or the teacher: ''The objectification of a set of obligations external to each individual yet common to them all is the only means of protecting the members of the community from the personal power of a leader [or teacher], with all its associated emotional blackmail and arbitrary behavior'' (112). The social group without formal restraints, like a commune, Gorz argues, is one prone, alternatively, to excessive suspicion, if not paranoia (in a barter economy, he feels, almost every economic transaction is subject to suspicion) and excessive personal attachment. He specifically warns against the dangers of ''open'' communities where the ''apparent abolition of external constraints is achieved only by transforming them into internal obligations'' (110). In such communities, where ''the realm of necessity is not abolished but sublimated,'' Gorz feels that people no longer have a clear sense of the difference between what they must do and where they are free to act as they please; common rules become internalized as ''ethical duties'' enforced by the fear of ''exclusion, dishonor or the withdrawal of love'': ''Individual goals and collective duties, personal life and group interests are merged into one, so that the love of *each* member of the community for *all* the others (and not the love of *each* other) becomes the prime *duty*. . . . The constraints and sanctions of law are abolished only to give way to the most tyrannical law: the *duty to love*'' (110).

The key for Gorz is to reduce not power and authority per se – either of the state or, for our purpose, the teacher – but domination. And here we have a paradox: with the state (or teacher), the most obvious source of domination being recognized as ''the only agency able to reduce its own power and influence in favor of an enlarged sphere of autonomy'' (115). The state or teacher enlarges autonomy not by abrogating power, withering away and thus becoming, like the homeless Lear, an entity unable to provide for the common good – but through constructive, albeit at times, paradoxical action. In acting effectively, a source of authority (teacher or state) must both protect its own central prerogative while promoting the realm of freedom of individuals: ''As the site at which law is formulated and the material imperatives of the social system are translated into universally applicable objective rules known to everyone, the state serves to free civil society and its individual members from tasks which they could only undertake at the price of impairing both individual and social relations'' (Gorz, 1982, 112).

One key element in this paradoxical play of authority for Gorz turns out to be something quite traditional, albeit one of the elements viewed most suspiciously by educational and social reformers: the notion of science, criticism, and art as autonomous, creative arenas of human expression – areas of cultural life governed by rules determined and enforced *outside* one's immediate social group. ''Only constantly renewed possibilities of discovery, insight, experiment and communication,'' Gorz (1982, 102) argues, what I (Tuman, 1987) have elsewhere defined as *literacy*, ''can prevent communal life from becoming impoverished and eventually suffocating.''

"Discovery, insight, experiment, and communication'' (or literacy) are liberating for Gorz because, by definition, they enable individuals to escape the restraints of their ordinary group; they represent a realm of human experience *not* controlled by the same power relations, regulations, values, epistemological assumptions, as govern everything else. In the language of contemporary educational reform, they are liberating, empowering, precisely because they are *not* socially constructed, at least not in any simple and immediate way, that is, not socially constructed by the same rules and powers that govern one's regular social dealings.

Thus we come full circle inside Gorz's work – from a suspicion of autarky and, by extension, the decentered classroom to a suspicion of the new epistemology of much contemporary social and educational reform: what's regularly trumpeted in the slogan, the social construction of knowledge. The support of the liberatory practice of network instruction, in other words, goes beyond social justice to a new liberatory epistemology, one grounded in the belief that we have all been enslaved in a past and by a past that mistakenly believed in the fixedness, the objectivity of scientific knowledge. "Knowledge conceived as socially constructed or generated,'' writes Anne Gere (1987, 72–3), "validates the 'learning' part of collaborative learning because it assumes that interactions of collaboration can lead to new knowledge or learning. A fixed and hierarchical view of knowledge, in contrast, assumes that learning can occur only when a designated 'knower' imparts wisdom to those less well informed.'' We have for too long seen education largely in terms of mastering some fixed body of knowledge and by so doing have made students and many of their teachers as well overly passive. Truth is out there; we have been taught and in turn have taught our students – the fixed product of a couple hundred or a couple thousands years of human history as developed, organized, and reported largely by (depending on one's point of view) trusted guardians of culture or a host of white men (mostly now dead) interested in protecting the expansive, hence largely invisible, patriarchy of Western cultural dominance. The liberation to be attained both in networks and collaborative learning generally thus comes primarily through an epistemological discovery of Kantian proportion – and one with distinct psychological implications – namely, that knowledge is socially constructed or, as stated by two advocates, that "knowledge is constructed by interactions of individuals within society and that all thought is social in nature'' (McCarthey and McMahon, 1992, 18).

At issue here is not the single assertion of whether or not all thought is (or is not) "social in nature,'' but the need to get beyond such crude reductionist thinking, especially as a warrant for specific changes in instructional practice. We need to avoid dichotomies like the one offered by Gere (1987), where our only choice seems to be between an open, collaborative, democratic world where people work together to determine truth and accepting, in Galileolike fashion, the ex cathedra rulings of distant, authoritarian institutions. McCarthey and McMahon (1992, 33) hardly give us any more choice, asking us to see social construction as entailing the movement "from transmission to transformation of knowledge, from more static roles to dynamic and fluid roles of the knowledgeable other, and from unidirectional to multidirectional types of discourse." Nor are they much more sophisticated in grounding their view of social construction in G. H. Mead's (1934, 17) notion that knowledge is "not based on the objective reality that can be measured and quantified but rather is consensually formed through social interaction."

Yet Mead's views on scientific knowledge are hardly that simplistic. It is true that in the essay "Scientific Method and Individual Thinker," Mead (1964) is intent on dismissing the notion of science as absolute, as something independent of pragmatical, social concerns of real people. In science, he argues, we do not "approach nearer to a self-consistent and universal reality which is independent of our conduct." But that we approach truth at all, he continues, is not the result of consensus, but from the discomfort of individuals, their individual awareness of anomaly, their sense of the mismatch between current norms and their own personal observations: "Science advances," he writes, "by the experiences of individuals, experiences which are different from the world in which they have arisen and which refer to a world which is not yet in existence, so far as scientific experience is concerned" (Mead, 1964, 211). Scientific progress is thus best seen not as something new and scientific replacing something old and personal – Mead is deeply skeptical of the very dichotomy at the center of so much contemporary proponents of social construction – but instead as "a process of logical reconstruction by which out of exceptions the new law arises to replace a structure that has become inadequate" (Mead, 1964, 211).

For Mead there is a paradox at the center of scientific thinking – thinking driven by individuals yet mediated by social norms. In designing and conducting experiments that test hypotheses, "the individual functions in his full particularity, and yet in organic relationship with the society that is responsible for him" (Mead, 1964, 211). Science wants to help us to know how to act next in a changing, emerging world, to make our actions intelligible. As political theorist Yaron Ezrahi (1990, 184) writes, American pragmatism saw in the "republic of science" an exemplary discourse for "the way in which a society of independent inquiring and experimenting individuals can generate disciplined public discourse and action." Thus it is one thing to argue, as does Mead, that all knowledge of the world, including (perhaps his greatest insight) all knowledge of the self, is mediated through our experience of others. It is a very different matter to claim that how one thinks, or perhaps even more importantly, how the world thinks, that is, what is accepted as true, can be reduced to consensus. What Mead was keen on pressing was the insight that our knowledge of the world and of ourselves is inseparable from our pragmatic condition of living in the world and not that this knowledge, of world or self, is ever entirely determined by that condition. For if it were, what would be left to say about one of the central issues in Mead's work: the psychic, cognitive life of the individual, the sense each of us has of our own personal autonomy?

For Mead, the individual is a complex entity, comprised of and torn by dual forces: what he distinguished as "me," or our sense of ourselves as seen through our experience of others, and "I," that presocial, hence un-formed, self full of all our more basic urges, desires, wishes, and dreams. It is the "I," as opposed to the "me," writes Mead (1934, 214) in a key section of *Mind, Self, and Society*, "The Social Creativity of the Emergent Self," whose "values . . . are to be found in the immediate attitude of the artist, the inventor, the scientist in his discovery, in general in the action of the 'I' which cannot be calculated and which involves a reconstruction of the so-ciety, and so of the 'me' which belongs to that society." The two parts of the self are mutually dependent upon each other but hardly at peace: "Just as there could not be individual consciousness except in a social group," "so the individual in a certain sense is not willing to live under certain conditions which would involve a sort of suicide of the self in its process of realization" (214), that is, the creative self, the "I," will not at all times allow itself to be dominated by the "me."

There is something inside us all, Mead believes, that wants to rebel against or, perhaps more accurately, create beyond the widely accepted social norm. We can work profitably in groups, Mead suggests, but never fully at peace. Leaders and "great characters," for Mead (1934, 216), are people who "have enlarged or enriched the community," taken what is given and yet in turn reshaped the group. Artists, meanwhile – and are not student writers artists-in-training – probe far beyond the given, "reveal[ing] contents which rep-resent a wider emotional expression answering to a wider society" (218). Artists, leaders, great characters – yes, but Mead, working in the democratic tradition of American pragmatism, sees the creative power of the "I" as "not peculiar to the artist, the inventor, and the scientific discovered, but belong[ing] to the experience of all selves where there is an 'I' that answers to the 'me' " (214). As he concludes, "to the degree that we make the community in which we live different we all have what is essential to genius, and which becomes genius when the effects are profound" (218).

As those of us who work in education well know, each new movement (trend or fad – and here, networking and collaborative writing in general are no different) attempts to define itself largely by projecting itself as a radical transformation of current practice and thus as a total solution to current prob-lems. There is an intellectual hubris, a historical smugness in such a belief – the idea that most of our predecessors have been blind and that it is only our generation that finally grasps the truth. The implication here is that once everyone agrees with us, can be convinced of the correctness of our position, then in fact our messianic mission will be fulfilled. It is the plea of the evangelist: "The past was riddled with sexism, classism, racism, agism, what-have-you. How do I know? . . . because I was riddled with it too. Now, I've seen the light – what it's like to live openly and freely accepting others, and

once I can convince (or coerce) you to think like me, we will all then live
in the new Jerusalem.''

We seem to be living in an age that promotes educational and social
change as a bandwagon on which only hardened reactionaries refuse to ride.
Where only a few years ago in college composition, for example, we had
"process over product," now we have collaboration and computer networking specifically. Bandwagons come through town with great fanfare and attention and seem to disappear just as quickly, giving hope to traditionalists
that we may yet be able to base educational progress on historically sound
principles. The writings of Mead and Gorz, in particular, force us to look
past impassioned, but empty pleas for radical change. They force us finally
back to the basics, to modes of instruction and social organization that nourish personal autonomy, and thus back to the central lesson of American pragmatism: that the key to attaining social justice – the good – is not to cater
to the collective will, but to help direct it, not to encourage people to do
what they want, but instead to give them the tools (intellectual and otherwise)
that help them gain the wisdom and strength to act in our own collective
best interest, in short, to help the group become a better social entity, in part
by working through its problems in an atmosphere that encourages and rewards creativity, problem solving, and critical thinking.

It is the tradition of American pragmatism and its belief in collective
progress emerging out of diverse individual initiatives that has driven so
many educational bandwagons throughout this century. What remains unclear, however, is the possibility that current interest in collaborative modes
of interaction and thought may represent a radical rethinking of that tradition,
a move away from progressivism and its dual faith in nurturing individual
autonomy and promoting scientific thinking. We do live in an age of fads;
educational programs do seem to follow one another in a tireless procession,
but not just *any* ideas, and, specifically, not likely the ideas of Gorz or Mead.
The current and, one might argue, increasing appeal of networking and, by
extension, collaboration is not happening in a historical vacuum. Where
thinkers like Gorz and Mead are concerned with the preservation of personal
autonomy, and by extension the dynamic relationship between the self and
the group, others today are more concerned with the preservation of social
harmony. Where Gorz and Mead are concerned with the growth of science
and the possibility of cultural innovation and anomaly, others are concerned
with fostering a new spirit of cooperation and adaptation with others and,
even more importantly, with the natural world.

In the terms of sociologist Zygmunt Bauman (1987), we seem to have lost
the self-confidence to act as legislators of the world, people willing to reshape
both the social and natural world in their own (largely Western) image and
thus have, by implication, lost the self-confidence to shape an educational
system designed to produce legislators. We have instead become an age
(again in Bauman's term) of interpreters, people who recognize the legitimacy
of competing ways of living in the world and thus are concerned today with
producing a school system that stresses the teaching and acceptance of difference. We may well have crossed a historical Rubicon, have entered into

an age where we lack the collective self-confidence in our ability (critics might say, the hubris) to direct the world in general and, specifically, to continue altering (these same critics would say, exploiting) nature for our own immediate benefit. We do seem less intent on creating an educational system so completely preoccupied with the nurturing of genius, one that forces all students to compete against each other, in the process breaking down social cohesion, in the hope of producing a few students capable of solving our problems through their own personal insights. And why should we, especially if our problems are fundamentally social in nature – if, for example, we really do believe that the energy crisis will have to be solved by our collective learning to consume less instead of our somehow finding new, more efficient sources of power? After all, perhaps we should educate ourselves differently if we do believe that our destiny lies less with the lone student – the brooding genius – who through some sort of miraculous discovery of room-temperature fusion, or what have you, will revolutionize energy production, and more with our own collective action – all students learning together – engendering new cooperative models of sharing and conservation.

What this suggests is a kind of historical inevitability to the rise of networking and collaborative modes of thought generally, in other words, that beneath the hype and glitter of networking is a new historical imperative, one that mandates that our future existence is tied to our valuing cooperation more and innovation less. Networking is a bandwagon in this scenario, but one signaling a historical change of epic proportions, the end of modern age and its faith in individually initiated social and natural transformation. We urge students and teachers to come together to learn, accordingly, because the knowledge that we want for ourselves and our students is, by definition, social – the goal of education no longer being the discovery of a new technique (perhaps stumbled upon by a solitary student), but the enactment of cooperation, the building of consensus itself.

What Mead and Gorz can help us to see is what we are likely to lose as well as gain in this new bargain, namely, that personal autonomy and scientific thinking, two of the pillars of the modern age, are intricately interrelated, that a new attitude toward science and knowledge generally will have necessary consequences (not all necessarily beneficial) on the mental life and general cognitive processes of individuals. From Mead and Gorz we learn that no change or series of changes in classroom practice (or social organization generally) is going to result in our perfection. We will organize schooling, governing, and thinking differently and often in ways that emphasize heightened collaboration, on this there can be no doubt. But in and of themselves, these changes cannot save us from ourselves. As Gorz (1982, 118) wisely writes, there is "no system able to free us despite ourselves or make us happy or 'moral' behind our backs."

We cannot escape the paradox at the heart of our collective endeavor, what Gorz (1982, 118) calls the dialectic relation between necessity and morality: "the recognition that there are contradictions whose permanent tension has to be lived and which one should never try to resolve." We can only be free in a world of formal obligations, a world that tells us what to do; just as our students, accordingly, can only be autonomous in a classroom where we, their teachers, make demands on them, some explicit. To build a better society as well as to protect the planet we unquestionably do need to do a better job of teaching our students to work together cooperatively. But we should not confuse such instruction with liberation of our students, the planet, or ourselves. Networking can only be a means, not an end. Here we return to Gorz's paradox – that even in a networked classroom or a networked world we cannot escape the interplay of necessity and morality: to set our students free, we must teach them our craft, compel them as it were to master what is not yet theirs, whatever it may be – working collaboratively or not, on a network or off. Paradox or not, for anyone who has ever experienced both the discipline and freedom of education, nay, the discipline and freedom of thinking itself, this is hardly a novel idea!

References

Barker, Thomas T., and Fred O. Kemp (1990). Network Theory: A Postmodern Pedagogy for the Writing Classroom." In *Computers and Community: Teaching Composition in the Twenty-first Century*, C. Handa, Ed., Portsmouth, NH: Boyton/Cook, pp. 1–27.

Bauman, Zygmunt (1987) *Legislators and Interpreters: On Modernity, Postmodernity and Intellectuals*. Cambridge: Polity.

Cooper, Marilyn, and Cynthia Selfe (1990). Computer Conferences and Learning: Authority, Resistance, and Internally Persuasive Discourse. *College English* 52 (December):847–69.

Ezrahi, Yaron (1990). *The Descent of Icarus: Science and the Transformation of Contemporary Democracy*. Cambridge, MA: Harvard Univ. Press.

Gere, Anne Ruggles (1987). *Writing Groups: History, Theory, and Implications*. Carbondale: Southern Illinois Univ. Press.

Gorz, Andre (1982). *Farewell to the Working Class: An Essay on Post-industrial Socialism*. (Trans., Michael Sonenscher.) Boston: South End Press.

Handa, Carolyn (1990). "Politics, Ideology, and the Isolated Composer." In *Computers and Community: Teaching Composition in the Twenty-first Century*, C. Handa, Ed. Portsmouth, NH: Boynton/Cook, pp. 160–84.

Mead, George H. (1934). *Mind, Self and Society: From the Standpoint of a Social Behaviorist*. Chicago: Univ. of Chicago Press.

(1964). "Scientific Method and the Individual Thinker." In *Selected Writings*, Andrew Reck, Ed. Indianapolis: Bobbs-Merrill.

McCarthey, Sarah J., and Susan McMahon (1992). "From Convention to Invention: Three Approaches to Peer Interactions During Writing." In *Interaction in Cooperative Groups: The Theoretical Anatomy of Group Learning*, R. Hertz-Lazarowitz and N. Miller, Eds. Cambridge: Cambridge Univ. Press.

Selfe, Cynthia L. (1990). "Technology in the English Classroom: Computers through the Lens of Feminist Theory." In *Computers and Community: Teaching Composition in the Twenty-first Century*, C. Handa, Ed. Portsmouth, NH: Boyton/Cook, pp. 118–39.

Tuman, Myron (1987). *A Preface to Literacy: An Inquiry into Pedagogy, Practice, and Progress*. Tuscaloosa: Univ. of Alabama Press.

Author index

Subject index